Praise for *Memoirs of a Maverick*

'This book is bursting at the seams with anecdotes. It should be read for that reason alone. Aiyar, in telling these anecdotes, doesn't spare himself.' – **TCA Srinivasa Raghavan**, *The Hindu*

'Anyone who knows Mani as a person, without getting drawn into his vocal political views, will vouch for his irreverence. If that irreverence and ridicule extends to one's own self – a trait very few authors are capable of exhibiting – you have a very readable book.' – **Bibek Debroy**, *The Telegraph*

'A book written by a brilliant mind . . . These are not the memoirs of a maverick but a brilliant ideologue caught in a time capsule.' – **Bhaswati Mukherjee**, *Deccan Chronicle*

'If truthfully recorded, memoirs give the measure of an author, his life and work – both the noble and the petty, and even [the] crass. These never paint a pretty picture. It is to Aiyar's credit that he has tried to be truthful. That makes this memoir a significant contribution to Indian autobiographical literature.' – **Vivek Katju**, *The Tribune*

' . . . a riveting narrative of gripping detail . . . the chapter on his four years in Pakistan as Consul-General in Karachi, reveal a love and understanding of a country the rest of us consider an enemy, which will be literally eye-popping for most of you.' – **Karan Thapar**, *Hindustan Times*

'Mani's frankness, honesty and courage, of which I have been a witness all my life, come across in his memoirs.' – **Khurshid Mahmud Kasuri**, Former Minister of Foreign Affairs, Pakistan, *The Wire*

'The book is highly readable, laced with occasional jibes and often irreverent anecdotes . . . What is striking in the book is that it gives fascinating historical insights into issues and crises experienced by Aiyar that are still active today.' – **John Elliott**

Praise for *The Rajiv I Knew*

'From its opening to its concluding page, Aiyar's narration is about a bond between the author three years and four months older than his subject and who, by the play of an impish fate, was his school-time junior, later his friend, still later his boss and then his hero forever after.' – **Gopalkrishna Gandhi**, *The Hindu*

'The Rajiv that Aiyar knew was not the Rajiv that most people knew. Aiyar was privileged to have worked with Rajiv Gandhi intimately and constructively over a long period. Travelling with the prime minister on all his tours, domestic and foreign, gave him a unique insight into RG's personality and character.' – **Chinmaya R. Gharekhan**, *Hindustan Times*

'The value of this work lies in placing his premiership in its historical perspective and, perhaps even more, in placing the man himself on the pedestal that he so richly deserved as harbinger of a modern India, which for reasons described in the book, has never been fully acknowledged in public discourse.' – **Wajahat Habibullah**, *The New Indian Express*

'Mani Shankar Aiyar has written with integrity, lucidity and fluency. Rich with independent and widely researched information and replete with anecdotes, this fusion of personal reminiscence and national history is a landmark contribution to literature on the political history of India and South Asia.' – **Javed Jabbar**, *Frontline*

'A partisan but spirited and well-documented account of Rajiv Gandhi's time as the prime minister and subsequently, for a brief period, also as the opposition leader.' – **Suhas Palshikar**, *The Indian Express*

'Should be read for bringing back to us an important phase in the passage of modern India with meticulous documentation.' – **Anand K. Sahay**, *Asian Age*

'He is one of the better writers and is always rewarding to read for his turn of phrase, as much as for his content.' – **Aakar Patel**, *The Wire*

A Maverick in Politics

1991–2004

Mani Shankar Aiyar

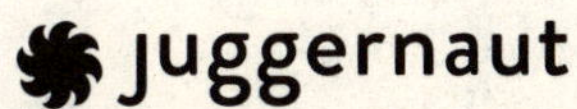

JUGGERNAUT BOOKS
C-I-128, First Floor, Sangam Vihar, Near Holi Chowk,
New Delhi 110080, India

First published by Juggernaut Books 2024

10 9 8 7 6 5 4 3 2 1

P-ISBN: 978-93-5345-767-9
E-ISBN: 978-93-5345-502-6

Typeset in Adobe Caslon Pro by
R. Ajith Kumar, Noida

Printed at Thomson Press India Ltd

To Suneet, who else?
For navigating this craft away from the shoals
for over half a century

AND

my grandchildren
Uma (b.2009)
Kabir (b. 2011)
and
Rukimini (b.2013)
Raghu (b.2015)
and
Ishaan (b. 2013)
Leela (b. 2017)
In the hope that they will read this story of their grandfather
and keep him in mind as they make their own way through life

Contents

Introduction

Readers of my previous two books in this series of three volumes might wonder what happened to *A Half-Life in Politics*. That title was changed to *A Maverick in Politics* to stress the link between my earlier *Memoirs of a Maverick: The First Fifty Years (1941–1991)* and my life in the last thirty-three years (1991–2024) that have seen me stumbling through the ups and downs of half a life in politics.

I tell young people who wonder whether they should come into politics that they must first embark on a well-paid professional career to build up some personal capital, for otherwise they will have no alternative to making a commerce of politics. I also tell them that they must first understand and accept that unlike in almost all other professions and vocations, there is no set trajectory in politics that ensures you are better off tomorrow than you were yesterday. No, there is a volatility in the political curve, which you find only in speculative businesses. There is no guarantee that success will breed success or that failure will lead to more failure.

Hope lies in recognizing that the moment you reach the summit is the moment your descent to the valley floor begins, and the moment you hit the valley floor is the moment your ascent to the summit begins anew. Therefore, the one personality trait that politicians need is persistence in the face of setbacks, in the hope and expectation that today's defeat presages tomorrow's victory, even as tomorrow's victory presages the next reversal of fortune. I tell my young friends that only those who can withstand the amplitudes of changing fortunes are fit for the life political. If you want assured and consistent progress, politics is not for you.

At the present time, when I am at my political journey's end, I realize one factor that I had not quite taken account of earlier – there might come a moment of such total rejection by your own party and political patrons that you are left staring at darkness with no light at the end of any tunnel, 'unwept, unhonoured and unsung'. That is not the fate that overtakes everybody in politics, but only those, like me, who are non-conformists, those who are mavericks, those whose lives are so long as to outlive their usefulness. Writing my memoirs in nearly a thousand printed pages has been my way of reconciling myself to loss and despair. It has been a form of mental and emotional therapy.

What remains are the memories and fantasies of yesteryear. There were high points besides the low. Coping with success was easy, although I needed my wife, to whom this volume is dedicated, to save me from the 'arrogance of power'. Coping with failure was more personal. 'Black ruins of my life rise into view', was one line from Cavafy that reverberated in my mind, and 'No ship exists / To take you from yourself' from the same poem, 'The City', was another. I was also haunted by the concluding lines of John Betjeman's 'Song of the Nightclub Proprietress': 'What on earth was all the fun for I am ill and old and terrified and tight.' I just never thought the Gandhi family that had brought me into politics would bowl me out too.

Do I regret having quit the foreign service midstream to take the plunge into politics? Not for one second. I took my decision consciously, never looking back, knowing that it might end in disaster, not triumph. It turned out that both triumph and disaster were in store for me, and when I suffered a severe setback in 2006, my youngest daughter, Sana, was on hand to comfort me with Rudyard Kipling's lines from his famous poem, 'If':

> If you can meet with Triumph and Disaster
> And treat those two Impostors just the same . . .
> Yours is the Earth and everything that's in it
> And – which is more – you'll be a Man, my son.

No, I regret nothing.

Mani Shankar Aiyar
On board Air India AI 121, Delhi–Frankfurt
27 June 2024

Acknowledgements

I reiterate my deep gratitude to all those mentioned in the earlier volumes of these memoirs, *Memoirs of a Maverick*, 2023, and its companion volume, *The Rajiv I Knew*, 2023, some of whom have helped enormously with this third and final volume, *A Maverick in Politics*, as well.

I also thank with all my heart Swati Chopra who has done a quick, efficient and sympathetic job of editing this volume, as well as Wesley D'Souza who has so ably handled the copy editing of the book. Samarth Menon has been quietly helping in the background. To him too my thanks.

I cannot but single out Chiki Sarkar, the publisher, but for whom this project would never have taken off and whose guiding hand is evident throughout the final version of this volume. I must also mention again N. Venkatraman, my indefatigable aide for more than three decades, whose contribution to this volume, as to the previous two, is, quite literally, immeasurable.

Mani Shankar Aiyar
Bangkok
30 September 2024

1

A Rookie in Parliament

1991–1996

Finding my feet

I returned to Delhi elated and triumphant to find two sets of invitations to dinner from the two rival contestants for the leadership of the Congress party. I decided to attend both to test the waters. Fortunately, before going to either, I first called on my old boss, Dinesh Singh, and got a lesson in shedding my old diplomatic ways.

Dinesh warned me that if I went to Sharad Pawar's party, it would immediately be reported to P.V. Narasimha Rao. And if I went to PV's dinner, Sharad would immediately be notified. If, therefore, I went to both, I would be treated by both as unreliable. This was politics; the parties were not genteel diplomatic receptions. I, therefore, plumped for PV.

The other lesson I learned from Dinesh that evening was that I was now not in a rules-based civil service but an elected member of a political party. Therefore, I had to hang on to whatever I might have saved from the election campaign as no further assistance would be forthcoming from the party for the next five expensive years. The party contribution was not a TA/DA advance to be accounted for and the surplus reimbursed.

Suitably chastened, I went to PV's dinner and found an overwhelming majority of the Congress MPs there. PV was then sworn in as PM and I attended my first Congress Parliamentary Party (CPP) meeting in the Central Hall as a full-fledged and duly anointed member. By sheer coincidence, PV happened to pass by my aisle seat after the meeting was over. One look at his exhausted, sweat-stained face and I wondered whether he would make it alive to the exit. But a high post is an unbeatable tonic, and it soon became evident that he would survive at least as long as he remained in office.

Tribute to Rajiv Gandhi

We convened for the first substantive session of the Lok Sabha. The proceedings were to begin with tributes to the late Prime Minister Rajiv Gandhi before adjourning to honour his memory. I sought out the Speaker, Shivraj Patil, and intimated to him my hope that I would be called to speak. Although condolence tributes are normally allotted only to party leaders, Speaker Patil made an exception in my case as he was aware of my relationship with Rajiv. Thus, I set what is perhaps a world Parliamentary record – of delivering my maiden speech at my first substantive Parliament session.

I spoke extempore, beginning with: 'For all the six years that I knew Rajiv Gandhi, he walked in the shadow of death, and I walked in his shadow. Now, death has taken him away and I am left in the shadows.'

Describing him as a man of exceptional courage, brave and compassionate, I went on to affirm that notwithstanding the omnipresent threat to his life, our former prime minister had 'never allowed the fear of death to stand in the way of taking the decision that he thought was right'. That was my summing up of the actions Rajiv Gandhi had taken to settle the issues of separatism and secession in Punjab, Assam, Mizoram and Darjeeling, apart from sending in the Indian Peace-Keeping Force (IPKF) to stop Sri Lanka from tearing itself apart.

I then turned to the four basic elements of nation-building that Rajiv Gandhi had believed in: strengthening grassroots democracy by amending the Constitution (Panchayati Raj); socialism founded in 'compassion for the common man'; technology 'for the advancement of the humblest and the poorest'; secularism to celebrate the rich diversity of the country and ensure that 'every part of India, however minor it might be' felt it 'belonged' to 'this larger entity' as 'India could not be India' without such a sense of belonging; and non-alignment, whose 'ultimate purpose' was 'to put an end to the Quest for Dominance'.

'If the world is to survive,' I concluded, 'it is necessary that the whole world imbibe the essential values of the Indian civilization', which Rajiv Gandhi had portrayed as 'the capacity to live with diversity', and more as 'the capacity to celebrate diversity'. I went on: 'If we live up to that vision of India, then it is only the body of Shri Rajiv Gandhi that would have died, the soul of Shri Rajiv Gandhi, which is the soul of India, will continue to live.'

My peroration proclaimed that I had 'the privilege of interacting perhaps more closely with him than any other human being at the intellectual level'. Because of the hours we spent discussing his speeches and writings, I came to see

> . . . a human being whose inspiration, particularly his dedication to non-violence, came straight out of the Mahatma's school of thought and whose idiom was that of Jawaharlal Nehru, and whose glory in the spiritual legacy of India came straight out of Swami Vivekananda. That great soul is no more with us; he has gone.[1]

CPP hauls Dr Manmohan Singh over the coals

Soon after, Dr Manmohan Singh presented his first budget. It signalled such a radical departure from the country's economic policy since Independence that there was considerable alarm in the ranks of the CPP. Some sixty Congress MPs participated in the most democratic discussion I had hitherto (or subsequently) experienced in party fora.

Only two of the Congress MPs stood up for the reforms that Doctor Sahib had initiated. One was Nathu Ram Mirdha, the veteran Rajasthan MP who was a respected campaigner for farmers' rights. The other was me. While almost all the speakers had opposed the reforms on account of its reversal of the country's past economic logic, I chose to plead my case in support of the finance minister on quite different grounds, which I imagined would carry the strongest possible political message to the CPP.

Recalling the Congress Working Committee (CWC) meeting in March after I had been briefed by the chief economic adviser on the desperate state of the economy,[2] I recounted how I had found Dr Singh ill in bed and had conveyed the message to him that he should kindly call on Rajiv-ji immediately after he recovered. I, therefore, urged my fellow-Congress MPs to not oppose what was in effect a Rajiv Gandhi-approved budget.

R.K. Dhawan immediately objected to my revealing information involving the former PM imparted to me in strict confidence. I shrugged off the objection. I do not know what impression I made on the audience, but Doctor Sahib has ever since pointed with grace and gratitude to Nathuram Mirdha and me for being the only Congress MPs to openly side with his radical proposals.

Even if the CPP was initially sceptical, the welcome given to Dr Singh's reforms, particularly by the business community and the international community, was so overwhelming that the Narasimha Rao period has come to be recognized for and identified with its reforms of the party's earlier socialist policies.

Later, as the reforms process unfolded, I became increasingly disillusioned and remained an unreconstructed socialist as I saw massive corruption, with governmental acquiescence or unconcern, unfolding in its wake. There was also a disturbing imbalance in the benefits that reforms were giving big business houses and the derisory economic benefits reaching the poor. I also greatly regretted that the Congress party was listening more to business interests and their powerful advocates in the media (particularly the 'pink' newspapers and journals), who were thrilled with being sprung from the shackles of the 'licence-permit raj', than to the poor and deprived who had always been the fundamental constituency of the party.

I would be disturbing the flow of this story if I – as a professed maverick – were to list my reservations about the reforms process here, but plenty follows at the right places in the narrative to explain my reservations. For example, please see my references to the head of the ministry of finance's Directorate of Enforcement Javid Chowdhury's *The Insider's View*[3] (2010) in the context of the Harshad Mehta and Ketan Parekh stock market scams and the casual manner in which Enron's investment in the Dabhol power plant project was approved and which almost bankrupted the state of Maharashtra. Enron collapsed because of legal proceedings against the company in the US, not in India. But more – much more – about all this at the appropriate junctures of this narrative.

Orientation course

The newly minted MPs were invited by the Lok Sabha Secretariat to a briefing session by Jaswant Singh, veteran of many a Lok Sabha. It was a little disconcerting when someone called out to me as we were entering the committee room in the Parliament House annexe, '*Seekhne aaye ho, ya sikhaane?*' (Have you come to learn or to teach?) What most disturbed me at the briefing was Jaswant's insistence that MPs had to decide between being 'constituency' MPs and 'national' MPs. I could not see why we could not be both. So, I set myself to being both, prioritizing my work in the constituency without neglecting my work in Parliament as a 'national' MP (and adding to that my duties as a 'Tamil Nadu' MP).

Let us begin with constituency matters.

2

Life as a 'Constituency' MP

Having determined that my constituency would be my priority, I frequently travelled to Mayiladuturai and somewhat startled my party colleagues there by insisting that they take me to the villages and smaller market towns there, particularly to the village and urban ghettos where the scheduled caste (SC) communities lived, it being axiomatic that the really poor were invariably the SC. (There were no scheduled tribe (ST) communities in the Cauvery delta.)

My constituency comprised an isosceles triangle. Its base was the long stretch of coastline that stretched over 75 km of the shore of the Bay of Bengal on its eastern reaches. I first sought out the fisherfolk who lived near the source of their livelihood, the sea.

And I sought out the minorities who, by and large, lived amicably with the majority community, but isolated in their own villages and towns. However, they were socially well integrated with their Hindu brethren and were to be seen in large numbers at weddings and other festive occasions. Being used to the north, where there was a fair amount of social distancing between the two communities, I asked and was told that the majority community looked upon Muslims as the 'fifth caste'!

On further reflection, I concluded that whereas in the north, Muslims were generally poor, in Tamil Nadu (TN) they constituted a fairly wealthy social group, partly funded by remittances from relatives in the Gulf region. Also, the close association between Hindus and Muslims was reinforced by both communities speaking the Tamil language and sharing the Tamil culture. Indeed, on our rural tours, I was pleasantly surprised to find my team and I would often be entertained to lunch by well-off Muslim landlords who had little difficulty footing the bill to feed my substantial entourage.

The entourage loved the biryani to which they were invariably treated! Economic equality was the bridge across which harmonious social relations were built. That is a lesson still to be learned in much of India (with the exception of Kerala, where too prosperity has eased inter-community relations).

That is also what the Justice Rajinder Sachar Committee concluded decades later – that among the most economically, socially and educationally disadvantaged section of our society are the Muslims, often faring worse than the historically disadvantaged SC/ST communities. This uncomfortable reality is at the bottom of the vicious perception among the more benighted sections of our people that affirmative action in favour of the minority amounts to '*tushtikaran*' (appeasement).

In my constituency, I also made visits to schools and colleges to meet Generation Next.

All this was educative but not too welcome to some local party leaders, who genuinely believed that the poor and disadvantaged were best left to their own devices till elections came round again. They, therefore, became increasingly reluctant to organize and accompany me on these decidedly uncomfortable tours, in weather that varied 'from hot to hotter to hottest'.

The breach was filled by S. Rajakumar, who grew from being the youngest and most marginalized member of my team to becoming my reliable and conscientious right hand. From these tours I would bring back loads of petitions that Nagarajan, an official in the Central government who had grown up in Mayiladuturai, would collate in his spare time and write covering letters to various officials in the district, with copies sent to the petitioners.

After a while, Rajakumar recruited a team in Mayiladuturai to undertake this work, which obviated the need for me to carry the petitions to Delhi. So, my constituents, resigned to politicians rarely visiting them and even more rarely acting on their many woes, began accepting me as one of their own. I too thoroughly enjoyed this prolonged exposure to this tiny corner of the country which had done me the favour of returning me to Parliament.

I spent my first year touring the villages and urban slums of my constituency but had nothing significant to show on the ground. The middle class, however, had been won over by my securing priority allotment of a TV relay station at Chozhachakkaranallur on the outskirts of Mayiladuturai. The fact that I had got the charismatic Madhavrao Scindia to inaugurate it was an additional feather in my cap.

Portrait of a constituency

I poured out my gratitude by 'Falling in love with a constituency', as I titled an article I wrote a few months into my first term.

I wrote that it was a breathtakingly beautiful place, a harmony in all hues of every gorgeous shade of green, the paddy fields with their mischievous standing crops 'gambolling in waves as the wind wafted through their emerald shoots'. I talked of 'gracious coconut palms curving gracefully into the azure sky' and the abundance of 'wide-girthed ancient tamarind trees' and 'wizened old banyans', and the gulmohurs bursting into flames of red and orange. I also exulted in the 'hundreds of naughty rivulets and clever canals darting along the road and diving under its culverts, brimming, for the first time in twenty years, with the waters sent down the Kaveri'.

'And all along the coast, the sea, now blue, now grey, now olive green, stealing into the estuaries, breaking gently on the golden beaches . . . the fisherfolk laugh with delighted pleasure and lead me out to sea. The fishermen clamber on to the prow, pulling me up behind them and sing snatches of song, mostly old hits of MGR playing the fisherman.'

I also travelled inland along the maze of channels, canals, ponds and tanks that constitute the delta's irrigation system, my jeep trailed by an army of public works department (PWD) engineers. We stopped at sluice gates and regulators; inspected bed-dams and revetments; grew knowledgeable about silting and undergrowth, waterlogging and drainage; and argued the intricacies of reaching water to the tail-end farm.

Three major challenges

I had to do something about three major issues in my area to secure my reputation as a 'constituency' MP: first, push a high-profile political intervention on the division of Cauvery waters between upstream Karnataka and the downstream Cauvery delta in Tamil Nadu, where my constituency lay; second, bring new, eye-catching industrial and infrastructure projects to the constituency; third, win the hearts of the fisherfolk of the coast by getting a harbour sanctioned at Poompuhar for fishing vessels. I shall take up in succession my efforts in these three directions.

The Cauvery river waters dispute

My constituency lay entirely within the Cauvery delta, and about 70 per cent of the population lived directly off their farms and the fish in the Bay of Bengal; another 20 per cent lived indirectly off those engaged in agriculture; and only about 10 per cent could be classified as having 'other' occupations. Thus, the issue of the river waters loomed large in the thoughts and apprehensions of virtually everyone in the constituency.

Prospects for an early resolution of the Cauvery waters issue seemed promising. In June 1991, the month I was elected, the Cauvery Waters Tribunal, set up under the Interstate Water Disputes Act, had given an interim award that substantially increased Karnataka's share compared with the earlier 1892 and 1924 agreements that had been entered into between the princely state of Mysore and the Madras Presidency. Yet the award left reasonably assured weekly supplies to the delta areas in Tamil Nadu, when required for cultivation, and made special arrangements for 'distress sharing' in years when the monsoon failed.

But the interim award had been rejected by the Karnataka authorities, leading to attacks on the property and persons of the minority Tamil-speaking population of Bangalore. I intervened in Parliament and wrote columns for *Sunday*, which were translated into Tamil by a leading Tamil daily. But that didn't take matters to a satisfactory resolution. Nor did I (or anyone else, for that matter) foresee that a full thirty years would pass before a minimalist solution acceptable to both states would emerge.

Within a month of the tribunal's award, it had become clear that the Rao government was caught on the horns of a dilemma. The Congress was in office in Karnataka. And Jayalalithaa, a Congress ally, was in office in Tamil Nadu. She had been responsible for shoring up the Rao government by returning twenty-nine out of the twenty-nine Congress candidates from Tamil Nadu, along with ten of her own, thus denying the opposition Dravida Munnetra Kazhagam (DMK) any place in the Lok Sabha. Rao reacted by doing what came easiest to him: nothing. (As Vir Sanghvi perceptively remarked, Rao 'knew 18 languages but could not make up his mind in any of them!')

I, therefore, hit out at the PM and my own government in my very first full month as an MP. On the floor of the House, I charged the Government of India with 'conniving' with the Government of Karnataka by not getting the interim award published in the official Gazette of India (colloquially called 'gazetted').

In my *Sunday* column of 1 August 1991,[1] I accused Rao of the 'Sin of Dhritarashtra', which was 'not a physical inability to see but a moral blindness to right and wrong, a deliberate refusal to distinguish good from evil'. I added, 'By putting Draupadi (Jayalalithaa) and Dushyasan (Bangarappa) in the same dock, the Centre has stung moral sensibility throughout Tamil Nadu.' Mercifully, I was not reprimanded for this act of *lèse-majesté*.

By December, however, the interim award was gazetted, bringing it into operational effect. The Karnataka government countered it by issuing an ordinance rejecting the award and cutting off all water to Tamil Nadu.

The issue came up for debate on 13 December 1991. Dhananjay Kumar of the Bharatiya Janata Party (BJP) (Karnataka) opened it, and there followed a ninety-minute fusillade from Deve Gowda (the future PM), who presented his version of the Cauvery dispute at inordinate length.

I chose to concentrate on Dhananjay's four questions relating to the Central government gazetting the tribunal's interim award: Is the interim award implementable? Is it practical? Is there the political will to solve the incidental problems that might arise out of the implementation? Is this the solution to the burning problem?

I answered all four questions in the affirmative in detail, stressing that there were three times as many Indians living in the delta stretch of the river as the number of Indians living in the upper reaches. Accordingly, I pleaded that this should not be seen as a Tamil Nadu-vs-Karnataka question but as a national issue, and that we had to seek the solution that benefited the greatest number of Indians without damaging the interests of the smaller number.

This the tribunal had achieved by halving Tamil Nadu's share (which the state government had graciously accepted) and greatly increasing the share of the waters to be legitimately retained by Karnataka. I ended my speech by making three suggestions: that the tribunal be urged to expedite its final award (in fact, it took decades); that a Cauvery Delta Rehabilitation Authority be established (never implemented); and that Rajiv Gandhi's initiative to elaborate a National Water Policy be followed up so that river basins are integrally developed as national assets without interstate bickering (not achieved in the last four decades).

I added two further points: the interlinking of peninsular rivers (now a hoary chestnut that no Central or state government has been able to achieve); and, in recognition of the tribunal having conferred on Karnataka the legitimate right to develop their ayacut (command area), to provide the funds needed to irrigate the upper reaches as thoroughly as the delta areas had been irrigated for a thousand years (a suggestion which was not acted on).

Over the next decade, there flowed a torrent of articles by me, two of which were picked up by Jayalalithaa and, without a comma being changed or its authorship acknowledged, put out as the All India Anna Dravida Munnetra Kazhagam's (AIADMK) own press releases! I did not mind, as her gesture confirmed the re-establishment of a personal relationship between her and me, which had been badly damaged by my denunciation of her corruption.

Karnataka's adamant refusal to act on the tribunal's award and numerous clarifications, in the face of TN's wholehearted acceptance of the award, led to the matter being referred to the Supreme Court by both state governments, who impleaded the Central government.

There, at the last moment, just on the eve of the court's judgement being pronounced, the attorney general, on behalf of the Deve Gowda coalition government (1996–97), which included major TN ministers, went along with the Central government in asking for a halt to further court proceedings as the Government of India would be framing a scheme for resolving the issues under section 8(1) of the Interstate Water Disputes Act.

This eventually took the shape of the PM himself presiding over a joint mechanism of the Centre and the chief ministers of the four southern states of TN, Karnataka, Kerala and Pondicherry (Puducherry) meeting regularly to sort out the differences among the states.

The decision to set up the Cauvery River Authority (CRA) was taken but not notified till September 1999, on the eve of the formation in October 1999 of the only stable government the country had under Atal Bihari Vajpayee (his third, which was in power from October 1999 to May 2004). However, in the five years of Vajpayee's reign, the CRA met under the PM's chairmanship only twice.

On 11 August 2000, I was able to vent my anguish in the Lok Sabha in a debate on Cauvery waters through a private member's bill moved by Vaiyapuri Gopalaswamy, 'Vaiko', the acronym by which TN's fiery dissenter was known. Vaiko had split from the DMK to form the Dravidian Progressive Renaissance Party (Dravida Munnetra Marumalarchi Kazhagam, the DMMK).

I argued that although TN had graciously accepted the interim award that had granted it an annual flow of only 205 thousand million cubic feet (tmc), as against 600 tmc under the expired 1924 agreement, this was only because the award specified the minimum weekly flows to be guaranteed for each of the fifty-two weeks of the year, ensuring that supplies were made when water was required for the main *kuruvai* (summer) crop and reduced when not needed.

Moreover, on clarification being sought by Karnataka as to whether any shortfall in a given week would be extinguished if not made up for by the end of the month, the tribunal had issued a clarificatory order (on 19 December 1995), which clearly stated:

> Our Order dated 25th June 1991 (the Interim Award) clearly spelt out that the deficiency in a particular week has to be made good in a subsequent week and not necessarily within the particular month in which the deficit occurs.
>
> . . . We also reject the contention raised on behalf of the State of Karnataka that in fulfilling its obligation to release of water every week, the deficiency, if any, must be limited to a particular month in which such deficiency may occur.

I then cited figures supplied by the ministry of water resources in response to a question by me to show that in July 1999 Tamil Nadu had received only around 37 per cent (3.7 tmc across the four weeks) of the agreed amount of water (9.9 tmc). The figures for July 2000 showed that TN had received only 17.1 tmc instead of the assured 42.6 tmc – again a shortfall of roughly 60 per cent. I intoned, 'This is a scandal. There cannot be any other word for it.'

On the other hand, I said, in October, November and December, when the delta is reeling under floods and 'Tamil Nadu is desperately attempting to cope with too much water, what does Karnataka do? It says this is the right moment to further flood an already flooded state.' In October 1999, the assured supply was to be 30 tmc, but Karnataka released 82 tmc. In November, the release was 40 tmc against the stipulated 16 tmc; and in December, Karnataka flushed out to Tamil Nadu 20 tmc, when supply was to be limited to 10 tmc.

In the face of this, the PM, as chairman of the CRA, had convened a meeting just twice in two years! Instead of implementing the award, the government was taking the whole process back to 'negotiation'.

So, I concluded, if the government could not implement the Cauvery award, it had better convert the Cauvery from a river divided between four states into a river owned by one country. Needless to say, the Centre's initiative came to nothing, but Tamil Nadu lost a golden opportunity to secure a definitive Supreme Court ruling.

Having had my say in the House, I undertook a Cauvery yatra, collecting farmers' signatures on a petition calling for the interim award to be respected and to ensure that flows from the Cauvery to the delta were in accordance with the provision in the award for two-thirds of the guaranteed annual flow to be concentrated in one third of the year to facilitate the main summer (*kuruvai*) crop. It was this provision that had persuaded Tamil Nadu to agree to the tribunal cutting the state's share to one-third of its original demand.

When the Congress president Sonia Gandhi visited the constituency for a rally in February 2001, we presented her with the thousands of signed petitions we had collected asking for resumption of the stalled Supreme Court hearings that had almost reached the stage of pronouncement of judgement. Nothing, however, followed, for the Congress was in the Opposition. So, my attention turned to direct personal action in the Supreme Court.

My eldest daughter, Suranya, then twenty-six, had just returned to India after taking her BA honours in jurisprudence as a Radhakrishnan scholar at Oxford and her LL.M. from New York University. She enthusiastically agreed to prepare, with friends of her age in the profession, a petition that the distinguished senior advocate and my colleague in Parliament, Kapil Sibal, agreed to argue in court.

She and her team worked very hard and conscientiously on the writ petition. We went together to see Kapil. While he was satisfied with the draft, what was bothering Suranya was the question of my 'locus'. She preferred that it be filed in the name of my principal aide, S. Rajakumar, who owned acres of ancestral farmlands in the constituency. Neither Kapil nor I entertained the least doubt that my being a sitting MP would be no impediment to the petition being filed in my name, on the basis of a precedent set in a case relating to the Bhakra Nangal dam.

As it turned out, Suranya was right, and Kapil and I were wrong. When the matter came up for admittance, Justice Barucha, having spotted me in mid-court, did not take even a minute to disallow the petition from being listed. He said (unconsciously echoing my daughter) that as the petitioner was an MP, Parliament was the right forum for him to take his complaint to and seek redress. Sibal tried to make his argument, but the judge cut him off. If only we had met Suranya's concerns, the petition might at least have received a hearing. The grey heads, alas, had not listened to a young voice. That was the fundamental reason for the initiative sputtering out before it was even considered.

Suranya was, of course, disappointed, but has never allowed me to acknowledge that it was my ego that caused the overruling of her wise insistence that the question of 'locus' be given priority.

Later, after the 2004 general elections, when the Congress-led United Progressive Alliance (UPA) scored an upset victory and I was named a cabinet minister, I participated in an internal discussion among the Tamil Nadu UPA MPs with the new PM, at which I was pressed to be the principal spokesman of the TN team. For my pains in doing so, I was reprimanded by the PM and asked to remember that I was 'now a minister'. That effectively silenced both my tongue and my pen.

The dispute has dragged on, and formulae for 'distress sharing' negotiated between the states concerned have in recent years taken the sting out of my crusading ambitions. I am glad, however, that the World Bank-financed Cauvery Modernisation Plan, to which I had drawn attention in my 2000 intervention, is at last taking off, ending a problem that has haunted the delta for the last half-century. But I must add that my earnest endeavours gained me no political capital in my constituency. My constituents were looking for outcomes, not efforts.

Industrial and infrastructure development

This was the second challenge I had to overcome to consolidate my reputation as a 'constituency' MP.

In one of my earliest public appearances in the constituency, I had to sit down when the *azaan* from a nearby mosque interrupted my oration. Spontaneously, and without serious forethought, I said that if elected I would turn Mayiladuturai into an Indian Dubai! I little suspected I would be hoisted with my own petard because the line gained a resonance of its own.

In the light of the Central (Congress) government failing to enforce on Karnataka the interim award of the Cauvery tribunal, the Opposition DMK took to mocking my throwaway line by saying, 'Aiyar will be making a Dubai of Mayiladuturai by turning the delta into a desert and importing a couple of camels.' This line gained as much traction as the original ill-thought-out quip. I had to find a way of fulfilling my pledge.

My first port of call to promote development was the Marine Products Export Development Authority (MPEDA), to explore the possibilities of inland shrimp farming. My second approach was to the Madras (Chennai) branch of the Confederation of Indian Industry (CII) to request them to undertake an in-depth study of the potential for development in the constituency. My third initiative was to interest the private sector in investing in start-ups on the basis of the CII report. My fourth move was to promote a private sector oil refinery through foreign investment, drawing on the crude oil reserves recently discovered in the vicinity of the constituency, as well as from expanding exploration activities in the area.

My fifth was to make a beginning with food processing units based on the constituency's natural resources. The units would produce rice bran cooking oil and process tomatoes and mangoes. Then I suggested initiatives in the handlooms sector and other small and micro-industries; high-class tourism centred on the old Danish fortress of Tharangambadi (Tranquebar); and tapping of the Tamil diaspora in prosperous Singapore.

As for infrastructure, apart from the TV relay station, I concentrated on small harbours for fishing vessels and small bridges for crucial connectivity to the markets for poor fishermen and poorer farmers. Another target was rural telephony.

The objective was noble, but my achievements were nil. My upbeat rhetoric far exceeded progress on the ground. As for the CII exercise, they funded a consultant to focus on my constituency. The report was released in Chennai in the presence of the CII chairman, Dhruv Sawhney. I imagined it provided a solid, objective basis to draw corporate attention to the inherent industrial potential of Mayiladuturai. I called on several well-known industrial houses in Chennai, Mumbai, Kolkata and Delhi, and some miscellaneous others, and fairly widely distributed the CII study. I also acquainted the 'lead bank' for the two districts in which the constituency fell with the report. I then took the major step of asking the finance minister, Dr Manmohan Singh, whether he would kindly visit a remote corner of my remote constituency to launch the programme. He agreed, but only because he wanted to thank me for the support I had extended to his reforms. In his address, he was full of praise for what he described as a 'model' other MPs would be well advised to follow.

As an exercise in 'event management', the PM's visit made a mark. But in terms of rousing corporate 'animal spirits', it was a dismal failure. The representatives of a few recognized business houses who attended the function did not follow up with even exploratory visits, let alone investment decisions. And the few local 'entrepreneurs' there collected unsecured business loans from the lead bank, which had been overawed by the launch, but then most of them reneged on their obligations. At the end of the day, the exercise could only be deemed 'farcical'. The one exception was shrimp farming.

Shrimp farming

It was M. Sakthivel of the MPEDA who remarked that even if I could not turn Mayiladuturai into a Dubai, I could attempt to turn it into a Hawaii!

The response to the prospects of shrimp cultivation was amazing. Some of the most well-known business houses in the country, including DCM, the Goenkas (Sanjeev), the Birlas and others, bought up acres and acres of barren coastal land, and were joined by the Chennai – and Mayiladuturai-based – houses, including S&S and Bismi. The land purchases spread from the northern reaches of the coast, from the island of Kodiyampalayam, to deep into the Karaikal enclave of the Union Territory of Puducherry to the south of the limits of my constituency.

As heavy transport brought heavy earth-moving machinery into the area, the locals forgave the potholes left on the country roads. They were, at first, thrilled to see 'development' coming to their doorstep. They were even more bucked to learn of future diversifications into food processing and packaging factories, which would help this very neglected wilderness to zoom straight into twentieth-century 'modernization'.

A further fillip to expectations was given by the minister of state for commerce, P. Chidambaram, visiting the coastal area to lay the foundation stone for a centre of excellence for aquaculture. The minister of state for shipping and transport, Jagdish Tytler, visited Kodiyampalayam island, and there announced a grant of Rs 1 crore from the Central road cess fund to connect the island by two bridges to the town of Chidambaram, the principal fish market on the mainland. At the same time, I succeeded, in principle, in getting a nod from the concerned Central department for building a harbour for vessels to be safely parked at the legendary seaside site of Poompuhar.

Then the blowback hit me. Two well-known Gandhian social workers from Nagapattinam relentlessly stoked fear among the local farmers that seepage of saline water from the shrimp farms would wreck the fertility of their holdings. The fisherfolk, who for generations had lived with an ever-changing shoreline that required them to shift their huts inland, encroaching on the uncultivated (because they were uncultivable) lands of the local people, found their traditional refuges fenced off by the new owners.

This was compounded by the new corporate owners sending Gorkha guards, who did not know the local language and looked very different from the local populace, to protect their recent acquisitions. Faced with hostility from the displaced farmers and fishermen, the guards brought in fierce-looking Alsatians into a region that had hitherto only known pie-dogs. Rumours soon spread that the Alsatians were 'wolves'! Within months, all the goodwill I had garnered had disappeared. Moreover, all the small shrimp cultivators and most of the larger ones too soon found they did not have the skill to stop disease from ravaging the shrimp.

The last twist of the knife was finding, at the next election, my face on a large poster defaced by someone who had punctured the photograph with a number of dagger holes.

Lands were sold or abandoned, left as graveyards to my failed ambitions. I thus learned the lesson of why most MPs leave 'development' severely alone, as something falling in the ambit of government and not elected representatives. The environmental and displacement issues that follow in the wake of 'development' are impossible for a backbench MP to handle.

Food processing

As for food processing units for the tomatoes and excellent mangoes with which the constituency was blessed, I found a ready investor for a tomato processing plant. Unfortunately, he was more impressed with learning that the factory would be coming up on land leased by a *mutth* (religious endowment) than by the economic prospects *per se*, while the richly saffron-swathed head of the mutth could not get over his suspicion that he was being cheated! Even though I got the union minister of state for food processing, Tarun Gogoi, to visit the constituency to lay the foundation stone for the unit, the initiative was stranded between the Scylla of the entrepreneur's spiritual yearnings and the Charybdis of the swamiji's unassailable suspicion of entrepreneurs from the country's north!

A number of possible processors descended on the constituency with regard to the mangoes. But while they enjoyed the hospitality and attention bestowed on them, we remained an exporter to Bengaluru of raw mangoes and nothing more. The potential for rice bran oil manufacture too remained unexploited because the largest rice mills were state-owned and their managements lacked the imagination and authority to diversify. (I remain convinced that there is a huge potential market for rice bran oil because it is arguably the healthiest of all edible oils, and the residual meal from its manufacture can be used as cattle feed.)

Other project ventures

I undertook two other failed ventures. One involved a relative who seemed to be doing very well with his IT start-up. Playing on the name of the constituency (Mayiladuturai means the bank of the Cauvery on which Siva danced in his incarnation as a peacock), he set up a computer training unit named Peacock Academy in Kumbakonam, holding out to young people the most promising dreams of a prosperous career. But despite some glittering publicity, the project never took off. The locals were unprepared to make the leap from agriculture to the age of information technology.

An oil refinery proposed by a 'son-in-law of the constituency' also met an unpleasant fate. Shankar Ramani, married into a well-known local family, had become a millionaire through oil exploration in Texas and Oklahoma. He was successful enough to own a Boeing-737. I thought I had hit the jackpot when he invited me to his swish Dallas home. He bought a second-hand refinery in Italy and tried to tie up with a Kuwait-based petroleum refining company to shift the refinery bag and baggage from Italy to a site in or near my constituency, to exploit the crude oil strike in the Karaikal enclave abutting the southern end of the constituency.

He even put up a small fortune for an evocative action sculpture of Rajiv Gandhi throwing off his garlands, a well-recognized image from Rajiv's many tours of Tamil Nadu. I invited Sonia Gandhi in September 1995 to unveil the statue. But despite this grand beginning, the refinery project did not get off the ground, leaving Ramani so stressed out that he passed away in Madras leaving huge, unsettled debts as his legacy.

My hopes of converting the seventeenth-century Danish fort at Tranquebar on the coast into a national tourist resort were dashed when a senior Tata representative visited the site in the immediate wake of the worst cyclone in decades to hit the coast. The storm wiped out all the preparatory work put into the project by his junior executive, Camellia Panjabi. The representative declared that the sand beside the sea was 'black'. What did he expect after a cyclone? Silver sands? A modest Neemrana hotel has since come up, but Tranquebar continues to be relatively unknown, and little visited.

A visit to Singapore to attract Tamil diaspora investment also failed. The Indian high commissioner proved a washout. So, I got together with the commercial secretary in the high commission and, within the forty-eight hours available, we gathered a fairly respectable audience. Only one of them, a quite well-heeled businessman of Indian origin, expressed some interest in exploring multiple options in Tamil Nadu, but I found he was far more interested in invoking God's blessings at the numerous famed temples in my constituency than in showing the colour of his money!

I despaired. My wife Suneet then advised me that instead of chasing the will-o'-the-wisp of modernization and development, for which neither my constituents nor investors seemed ready, I should concentrate on meeting the very modest demands of the poorest.

MPLADS

I decided that I would do so. And, to my good fortune, it was during this mounting failure on the industrialization front that the prime minister announced the Member of Parliament Local Area Development Scheme (MPLADS). The district administration was endowed with Rs 1 crore a year, to be spent on my recommendations, subject only to the conditions laid down to ensure that expenditure from the fund would be constructive and oriented towards rural development.

Sceptics derided the concept. The general public seemed to think the Rs 1 crore (now raised Rs 5 crore) was credited to the MP's personal account, from where he could arbitrarily spend what he wanted.

In fact, all an MP could do was to flag where and how the money may be spent, with the administration determining the rates specified, floating a public tender and selecting the contractor (on the basis of self-selection of projects to be funded to the greatest extent practicable). I salami-sliced my tour programmes to cover every block, town panchayat and municipality, thereby earning considerable kudos.

What I learned from this intensive interaction with the poor at their doorstep I condensed into an article for *Sunday* (May 1995) titled 'Rural Priorities: What the Poor Want'. It was later carried by the *Reader's Digest*. Here are some excerpts from it:

> What do the poor want?
>
> As often as I can, but less often than I should, I take myself off to my little bailiwick. Over the last four years of wandering . . . my constituency, I have been compelled to revise much of my received wisdom about what our rural priorities should be.
>
> My own priority is to head straight for the Harijan (*adi dravidar*) colony as Scheduled Caste = Poor is an almost mathematically accurate equation.

What, I ask, can I do for you? The answer used to startle me. Now I can almost anticipate it. Almost always, I am told, 'Build us first a road to the burial ground'! I would have thought the priority would be how to live. This plea for first attending to the grim business of dying is unexpected.

Why, I ask, is a path to the burial ground so important? They explain that if they were to take a short-cut through the heart of the village, it would provoke ugly clashes. So, they pick their way around all human habitation. Therefore, the final resting place has to be reached by delicately negotiating the embankments enclosing the rice paddies. This becomes a major problem when it rains because the pall-bearers slip on embankments, intimating the horror the villagers would experience of seeing the dead body slip on to the wet paddies. Hence, the almost desperate plea for a road. They do not need to have John Donne's lines recited to them: 'Ask not for whom the bell tolls / It tolls for thee'.

One, bolder than the rest, or perhaps only more outspoken, insists, 'A footpath is not enough; you must give us a shelter at the cremation grounds where we can wait while the obsequies are completed.' And the villagers nod in sage agreement.

The next priority is almost always a community hall. Every hut is a one-room tenement. There is nowhere except the village street where the community can foregather – to chat and gossip, celebrate a wedding or a feast, or receive a guest like me. The alternative is a temple. A temple in the Harijan Colony is not merely a place of worship: it is the common gathering ground, the collective drawing room, the village courtyard, the inn with its doors perpetually open to all. Hence the aching need for a community hall.

When one turns from community to family needs, the population explosion makes it imperative for more and more land to be allotted for nuclear families to put up their little huts in tiny fifty, or twenty, or even ten square yard plots. This means *pattas* (title deeds) to government lands. Especially as *pattas* entitle the poor to participate in the lottery to which most state governments have reduced the Indira Awas Yojana (Housing for Harijans). And since *pattas* are hard to come by, most families spend most of their lives with mothers-in-law fighting daughters-in-law; sisters-in-law fighting each other; brothers tearing out each other's hair; intra-family feuds galore.

It is curious, this juxtaposition of collectively sharing in joy and sorrow, and each family which makes up the basic unit of that collectivity, wasting life in internecine bickering because there is not one moment of privacy, not an inch of lebensraum. One room for every nuclear family would do more for human happiness in rural India than any number of fancy development schemes.

Hand pumps: The ultimate argument for drinking water is less thirst, than the avoidance of quarrels. For when the hand pumps don't work, it is not that another hand pump cannot be found within walking distance; it is that when women from one street go to the next to fill their pots, fighting breaks out.

The mindset which believes that capital investment in social assets is the priority has not woken up to the reality that the maintenance of these physical assets and the efficient provision of the services expected of these physical assets is the new priority. Nothing so cruelly mocks village India as electricity in the wires but tube lights which don't switch on; or Mark-II pumps installed at a cost of several thousand rupees but rendered non-functional because a five-rupee rubber washer needs replacement.

We give our Harijans free pucca houses because they cannot build their own; but when I point out deep cracks in the walls even before the building of the unit is completed, the block development officer (BDO) can do little more than shrug his shoulders in helplessness: the returns require him to file the number of units built, not detail the number of cracks that have appeared!

I think it is time we stopped asking the BDO what the people want. Perhaps it is time we asked the people what they want. Or, better still, leave it to the people to ask each other what they want and then decide themselves how they want to spend their resources. The ancient Indian word for this is Panchayati Raj!

And, thus, the constituency came to be dotted with funeral sheds and community halls though the state continued its stranglehold over the huts for the people to live in. I eventually detailed for the readers of my Telegraph column on 18 September 2002 a sample list of the projects I had funded:

> At the start of my sixth year of implementing MPLADS, I find I have built 251 funeral sheds, 132 bus shelters, 95 link roads, 34 bridges and culverts, 61 bathing ghats, 30 revetment walls, 12 TV rooms and 11 public lavatories, besides providing various kinds of facilities to 127 schools, 5 colleges, 4 hospitals, 2 primary health centres and one veterinary centre. Moreover, I have provided 13 drainage works, 8 drinking water facilities, 7 community halls, 4 noonday meal centres, 8 fair price shops, 2 library buildings, a vegetable market and a boating yard. Now, what's wrong with that?

As a result of the funeral sheds, I came to be known as 'Funeral Sheds Aiyar'. It was my proudest moniker!

Other initiatives

MPs in those days of shortages also had access to a large number of telephone and cooking gas connections, which could be handed out as patronage or gratitude. Instead, I held a lottery, and whoever luck favoured got the connections. The story in town was that when the telephone department arrived at the one-room home of the beneficiary, they would be bewildered at the mess and would anxiously inquire where the phone could be installed!

Also, in the interest of prioritizing rural telephony, I persuaded Pandit Sukh Ram, the minister of telecommunications, and his very able private secretary, Ashok Pal Singh, to start a new sub-area dubbed the Cauvery River Delta Authority under the chairmanship of my principal aide in the Thanjavur district portion of my constituency, T.R. Loganathan. It certainly helped expedite solutions to telecommunications problems that were rife till the mobile phone arrived and put an end to all these issues. When Sukh Ram visited my constituency, he paid me a compliment I shall always treasure. Winning an election, he said (adding that he had won nine), 'is easy but gaining the affection of the people is difficult. You have won their affection.'

I also tried to do my best for our fisherfolk. An American businessman introduced to me in New York by the representative of MPEDA, offered to visit the fishing port of Porayar at the northern end of my constituency – a remote corner of my remote constituency – to explore the possibility of developing it into a centre for tuna fishing using fancy geo-tracking systems to spot tuna concentrations. He pithily remarked that it was only in the seas surrounding peninsular India that 'tuna died of old age'!

He came and claimed that Porayar was just what he was looking for. All he needed was an Indian partner. I found one, and the deal he made was that the Indian partner would deposit a large sum of money in an 'escrow' account, which could only be accessed by both partners together. What the Indian did not know was that this American was in cahoots with the US bank concerned and soon siphoned out the money, leaving the Indian partner, the fisherfolk and me high and dry.

As for the fishing harbour at Poompuhar, the authority concerned with building harbours, the Centre for Coastal Engineering, was based in Bengaluru, far from any sight of the sea. The officer concerned had to be cajoled and bullied to actually come and look at the sea. He then said that as the Archaeological Survey of India was undertaking a study to determine whether there were any underwater structures of the legendary Poompuhar, site of the great Tamil epic *Silapadihaaram* (The Golden Anklet), in the sea outside the fishing village, no harbour could be built till their survey ended. So that was that!

While, therefore, my efforts to promote rural development were patchy, the Pollachi Rotary Club honoured me as a 'model MP' and a number of laudatory articles were published. But in my second election in 1996, I was defeated by as wide a margin as I had won by the previous time.

I will explain this election outcome after I have explained my role as a 'national' MP and 'Tamil Nadu' MP.

3

Life as a 'National' MP

My first term in Parliament (1991–96) as a 'national' MP revolved around three issues: first, the demolition of the sixteenth-century Babri Masjid; second, the Harshad Mehta stock market scam; and, third, the Constitution (amendment) bills that ushered in Constitutional status, sanctity and safeguards for local self-government in rural India (Panchayati Raj) and urban agglomerations, first conceived by Rajiv Gandhi but which had failed to pass muster in October 1989.[1]

There was also a fourth issue, Jammu and Kashmir (J&K), on which my interest and involvement had initially been stoked by several visits to J&K with Prime Minister Rajiv Gandhi. It had been further intensified by the crisis that had overtaken the state in the immediate aftermath of V.P. Singh taking over as prime minister and the consequent visit of an all-party delegation to discuss the handling of the crisis by Governor Jagmohan, as well as my controversial review of Jagmohan's exculpation of himself in his book, *My Frozen Turbulence in Kashmir*. There was also the vital link between the state and our relations with Pakistan, a process that saw two lows – the Kargil invasion and Modi breaking off talks for a whole decade (2014–24) with no signs of a revival of dialogue in sight; and two highs – Vajpayee's bus journey to Wagah/Lahore and the Lambah-Tariq back-channel talks on Kashmir (2004–08). As these developments, oscillating between hope and despair, have lasted for three whole decades with no end in sight, I have dealt with them in detail below as an essential part of my life as a 'national' MP and as a concerned Indian.

Babri Masjid

The issue that dominated my first term in Parliament, and which continues to haunt us till today, was the demolition of the Babri Masjid. The controversy stretched into 2019, when the Supreme Court ended the matter with its curious judgement of September 2019 awarding the site to the very organizations that had demolished the mosque on that black Sunday of 6 December 1992. An 'egregious violation of the law', the Supreme Court described it, before awarding the premises to the very same egregious violators the court itself had identified!

I first spoke on the Babri Masjid issue in my first Parliament session, but most of my commentary was outside the House. I spoke loudly and often about the apprehended outrage in the press, and in political discussions on TV. I also spoke on the matter on every platform I could find. And I went with a Parliamentary delegation to the site and got myself a few boxed lines in the morning papers by declining the prasad distributed by the pujari of the makeshift temple of Ram Lalla *virajman* (Baby Ram, present and seated) that had come up, allegedly *swayambhu* (self-created), one night after the state government had ordered locks to be placed on the gates of the masjid to prevent communal clashes. I adamantly held that prasad cannot be distributed in a Muslim place of worship.

Twice in 1992, I was especially vocal in Parliament, clashing, in the first instance, with L.K. Advani in May 1992, in a debate on the setting up of the National Minorities Commission. Advani had claimed that there was no reference to religious minorities in the Constitution. I refuted the contention by underlining that not only did Article 30 explicitly refer to religious (and linguistic) minorities, the Preamble and all the fundamental rights too reflected the apprehension that the rights of the minorities might be and were being questioned in the name of religion. We had to recognize that prejudice and discrimination against the minorities was a 'deep societal problem' requiring 'sympathy and affection' for them. Yet, such compassion was labelled by Advani as 'pseudo-secularism'.

While we accepted Pakistan as a historical reality that had embarked on the road to becoming an Islamic state, we were determined not to become a Hindu state but remain a secular state. I said that was precisely why the Constitution rejected the concept of India as a 'Hindu *rashtra*' (a Hindu nation-state) and opted for a secular India. Till this question was finally resolved, our minorities would be apprehensive about their future in this country. Hence the imperative of setting up a national commission on the minorities.[2]

In July 1992, former prime minister Chandra Shekhar revealed in the House that bricks were being transported in the thousands to the Babri Masjid site for construction of a temple after the mosque was razed to the ground. This belied the apparently innocent intent of the massive '*kar seva*' (voluntary service, a Sikh ritual practice) being projected by the Vishwa Hindu Parishad and its saffron cohort as limited to cleaning the premises.

After this revelation caused an uproar in Parliament, the prime minister, in a doomed effort to reach an accommodation with those pressing for a Ram Mandir at the site of the Babri Masjid, announced a few days later, in mid-July 1992, that the Government of India had reached an 'agreement' with the forces of 'Hindutva'. That gave me another opportunity to deal with the subject. I began by congratulating the government on the 'agreement' but quickly added that I was 'filled with apprehension' because the 'agreement' dealt more with procedure than substance. As the BJP had not changed its view of our past or our future, or their definition of Indian civilization and culture, and given that 'my concept of the mosque, the nationhood of India, was entirely different to theirs', I doubted 'whether the Bharatiya Janata Party can rise above the narrow concerns of the Vishwa Hindu Parishad, the Bajrang Balis (sic) and the Sadhu Samagams'. Adverting to the key question of whether the BJP believed in our Constitution 'or remains an adjunct of sadhus and *sants*, bigots and zealots', I recalled the pledge taken by all those seeking a mandir at the site of the masjid and rhetorically asked whether Advani, as the leader of the Opposition, would confirm that if there were a clash between his oath as an MP to uphold the Constitution and 'any personal oath' he has taken, which would prevail? Advani later clarified that in such an unlikely event, 'he would certainly be true to his oath to the Constitution'. I was not convinced, and so ended my intervention with the words:

'The forces of Hindutva have said that it is the first principle of India's nationhood that the Muslims must not be appeased. I say, it is the first principle of the Congress party that the BJP must not be appeased.'

Alas, that is what Prime Minister Rao proceeded to do – appease the BJP and its associates.

After speaking in the House for a third time on 29 July 1992, I decided it was time for action on the ground. I had heard that the prime minister had rebuffed retired Captain Praveen Davar of the All India Congress Commmittee (AICC) ex-servicemen's cell, who was associated with my Society of Secularism, when Davar had suggested that if the prime minister marched at the head of a procession of secular leaders from the prime minister's office (PMO) in South Block to India Gate along Rajpath, it would make a major impact on the national mood. PVNR had apparently pursed his lips in his standard pout and cuttingly remarked, 'You want me to walk a mile to counter Advani-ji's thousands of kilometres?'

That gave me the idea that I should perhaps make the journey of 'thousands of kilometres'. That journey, I thought, should be along much the same route that, according to the Ramayana, Lord Ram and Sita had undertaken on their journey back to Ayodhya after defeating Ravana. Accordingly, my forty-four-day yatra, starting from Rameswaram at the southern tip of mainland India on Gandhi Jayanti, 2 October 1992, would end at Ayodhya on Jawaharlal Nehru's birth anniversary, 14 November. It would be titled the 'Ram–Rahim Yatra' and seek to spread a message of communal harmony to counter the hatred spread by Advani's rath yatra. I contacted all the Congress MPs and the district Congress committee officials and local friends and sympathizers on the route to make the required arrangements.

We followed a set pattern, leaving early in the morning, visiting religious shrines of all faiths, addressing meetings at those shrines and also stopping at countless wayside villages and small towns to hold impromptu roadside meetings.

We relied on local party workers, MPs, members of legislative assemblies (MLAs), members of my Society for Secularism and many other friends to make the arrangements for us and to spread the word as we travelled.

We were perpetually late because of the endless interactions with the large crowds that gathered along our route. Often we were on the road eighteen to twenty hours a day, or even longer, and I was on my feet throughout. It was exhausting as well as exhilarating.

We lumbered off from Rameswaram and moved through Madurai, Thanjavur, Kumbakonam, Cuddalore, Arani, Kancheepuram and Madras (Chennai), before crossing the Tamil Nadu border into undivided Andhra Pradesh, where our first night halt was Tirupati. Then it was on to the twin cities of Hyderabad/Secunderabad and eastwards to Vijayawada and Rajahmundry. Then we crossed into the first village of Sumki in Orissa (now Odisha) before moving on to Rayagada, Paralakhemundi and Behrampore, when I received an urgent summons from the PM in Delhi.

I cite a few excerpts from my diary to give the reader a flavour of the first phase of the yatra:

> Few outside Tamil Nadu know that Rameshwaram, where the Yatra kicks off, has one of the heaviest concentrations of Muslims in the entire state . . . the opening day takes us to the great Siva temple, where Ram Himself, avatar of Vishnu, worshipped Siva, thus setting himself up as the first patron saint of Indian secularism . . . next day, we visit an exquisite little church in Pattimannur, where I see one of the most beautiful paintings of the Crucifixion I have ever seen . . . at Pattukottai, representatives of the three major religions join us on the platform in a gentle reminder that secularism is not about politics but our survival as a nation . . . At the Velankanni Cathedral, the Lourdes of Asia, the Rev. Father is so enthused he clambers on to our jeep and speaks to a hushed and deeply reverential crowd of Christians about how long-standing are our secular traditions . . . At Thiruppanandal, the Swami who heads the *Aadhinam* (monastery) tells me I am doing the work that religious leaders like him should be doing . . . at Kancheepuram, I find the minaret of the mosque in quiet but firm juxtaposition to the adjacent mutth of Adi Sankara's spiritual successors . . . a huge concourse of railway porters and curious passengers is waiting for me at Madras Central station . . . In Hyderabad, there is a gratifyingly enthusiastic

audience at the Char Minar . . . a visit to the Atheist Centre run by the son of the founder, Gora, one of Gandhiji's companions-at-arms follows . . . the most memorable visual spectacle of the Yatra is watching the Ram–Rahim Rath being transported on a barge across the broad bosom of the river Godavari . . . At Kakinada, I am given a rosary in a church, a rudramala in a temple and a string with amulets as a talisman at a *mazhar*. I wear all three around my neck, feeling strangely blessed, forgiven and protected . . . At the masjid in Srikakulam, a most welcome surprise awaits us. We are actually invited to join and participate in the 'namaz' . . . I make what I think is my most inspired speech at Koraput . . . At Bhavanipatna, we visit the first Gurudwara of our Yatra . . . Deepavali, much to the annoyance of my family, is spent in the palace of a fellow-MP, the Maharaja of Paralakhemundi . . . At Behrampore, I receive the strange summons to proceed immediately to Delhi to meet the Prime Minister. Bidding my companions to continue the Yatra to north and west Odisha, where I will re-join them, I obey the summons from PM.

Meeting with the PM

The PM began by telling me that while he had no objection to my yatra, he didn't agree with my definition of 'secularism'.

Why, I asked, what was wrong with my definition of 'secularism'?

'You don't seem to understand, Mani, that this is a Hindu country!'

I was astonished. 'But, Sir,' I stammered, 'that is exactly what the BJP says.'

The conversation petered out and I went home perplexed.

Weeks later I learnt that the prime minister had been in conversation with assorted Hindu 'holy men' and the BJP's associated outfits. He seemed to have been influenced by them and was keen on arriving at a settlement (on their terms). Someone in the saffron crowd (Advani, I suspect) must have complained to the PM about my yatra, leading to his strange summons. Yet, he did not really reprimand or restrain me. He said just enough to tell anyone who had complained about my speeches that he had tried to guide me on the right path.

Inevitably, the forces of Hindutva took advantage of his vacillation to bring down the Babri Masjid and irrevocably change the facts on the ground – though three decades were to pass before they attained their goal of building a temple.

'I rejoined the yatra at Sambhalpur and moved to Bolangir. I was joined by all four Congress MPs from the region . . . However, my spirits fell at Kharaia Road, on the border with Madhya Pradesh, as I was pulled up by the large Sikh population for not displaying any symbol of Sikhism on my rath. That lapse was quickly rectified . . . We crossed the border into Mahasamund to the good news that the Madhya Pradesh chief minister, Digvijaya Singh, had personally arrived to ensure that all went well with the yatra. The local *Amrit Sandesh* carried no less than eight separate stories on our yatra. At Nagpur, we reached a large gathering of Muslims in the Mominpura locality at 11 p.m., where we were proudly told by a bearded mullah that this heavy concentration of minorities was the very centre of our nation.

'We proceeded through Chhindwara and Seoni to Jabalpur, where Vivek Tankha, the brilliant young lawyer (and future Rajya Sabha MP) had gathered all the numerous factions of the Congress together on a single platform. Our carcade grew to nearly sixty vehicles. The reception we were accorded was described in the local paper as "unprecedented". We crossed the Vindhyachal range into Allahabad, to a somewhat tense meeting of the students' union at the university as the union was and is dominated by the BJP.

'On to Kanpur, the crowning glory of the yatra, where so many top leaders of the party joined us, and the welcoming crowds mobilized by the town president, Abdul Mannan, were so thick that it took us all of seven hours to move the few kilometres from Ranigunj on the outskirts of the city to its heart at the Moolganj–Nai Sarak crossing.

'Driving through the Gandhi family heartland of Rae Bareli and Amethi, we got to Sultanpur, where I was informed that the Uttar Pradesh (UP) government had banned my addressing any meetings in Faizabad and would probably interdict my attempt to reach Ayodhya. I decided to break the unjust law in the best traditions of the freedom movement.

'Next morning, 14 November, which was Jawaharlal Nehru's birthday, I started marching with 300 Congress workers out of the Faizabad Circuit House and towards Ayodhya. My fellow-Congressmen, practised jail-goers all to a man (and, indeed, woman!), and I were herded into waiting police vans. We were driven round and round till the vans eventually slowed down near the gates of a Christian convent. I wondered for a moment whether the Uttar Pradesh chief minister, Kalyan Singh, was going to do the first secular thing in his life – by leading us to a Christian church – when I discovered that the Faizabad Cantonment police station lay opposite the convent.

'We inquired whether there was a portrait of Pandit Nehru on the premises. There wasn't. So, amnesty was sought to send one of our numbers to steal one from the Circuit House. When it came, the flowers from the garlands with which I had been festooned were lovingly taken apart so that all of us could offer our *shraddhanjali* to Pandit Nehru on his 103rd birth anniversary.

'The city magistrate arrived at the detention centre and informed me that I had been arrested under sections 155, 116 and 106 of the Indian Penal Code, but that I now stood released. He apologized for the inconvenience caused and I thanked him for his kindness, adding the hope that he would always stand up for secularism and never compromise with communalism.'

After this homily, I told the waiting press that as I had been prevented from entering Ayodhya to carry my message of communal harmony, it was even more imperative that the same sections of the Penal Code be strictly enforced on the tens, perhaps hundreds of thousands, of 'kar sevaks' to prevent them from entering Ayodhya. Had my advice been heeded, the mosque would have been saved and the most telling blow to our secularism thwarted.

I returned to Delhi as tension gathered over whether the UP government would stick to their pledge to the Supreme Court to restrict the '*kar seva*' to a symbolic show.

At 5 a.m. on 2 December, I was startled out of deep slumber by the insistent ringing of my telephone. A man's voice said that the prime minister wished to speak to me. I asked him to put me through.

P.V. Narasimha Rao came on as if in mid-sentence: 'I've done everything I can, Mani, but they seem to be betraying me . . .'

His voice cracked. He seemed close to tears. So, I asked if he would like me to go over to meet him. He replied, 'Can you?' I said, 'Give me twenty minutes, Sir, and I'll be there.'[3]

For the first and only time in my life, I was taken to the prime minister's residence at Number 3, Race Course Road (I had never been invited inside during Rajiv's term). The prime minister looked composed. He asked me what I would advise him to do. I answered that it was now too late to stop the 'kar seva' as lakhs had already gathered at Ayodhya and the rest were on their way. They could have been stopped earlier but it was now too late.

So, I suggested that he organize a counter demonstration at the Faizabad airfield or Circuit House by non-BJP Parliamentary leaders. They could be flown into the city in convoys through the day to serially address a day-long public meeting. I went on to suggest that the event be televised, with a Doordarshan helicopter showing from the air the contrast between the sectarian frenzy in Ayodhya and the call for secularism by virtually every political leader in the country barring those of the BJP. I ended by proposing that the last to fly in should be the prime minister, to give his definitive message to the nation. The resolve of the nation would thus be pitted against the resolve of the saffron forces.

Prime Minister Rao interrupted to ask if I would be prepared to draft his speech. I, of course, responded in the affirmative, but he insisted the draft be delivered to him by 9 a.m. as he would like to consult others. I baulked at this because I had to send in my weekly column that day. Somehow, I got through both, and the draft was in his hands within his deadline.

I also submitted an 'action plan'. It suggested that the prime minister address Parliament on 4 December as the Vishwa Hindu Parishad was convening its *dharma sansad* (religious parliament) that day. In his address, I suggested he announce that government would be making arrangements for all MPs to proceed to Ayodhya 'to personally witness whether kar seva was being restricted to kirtans and bhajans' and to warn that 'any construction activity will invite the most serious consequences'.

This might be followed by the 'PM considering flying into Faizabad himself and addressing the assembled MPs', an address that should be telecast/broadcast in Hindi and English. I also suggested that the Congress mobilize some 50,000 workers as *sadbhavana senanis* (soldiers for secularism), showing the PM and his *sena* on the Battleground of Sadbhavana. If this resulted in the *kar seva* being limited to kirtans and bhajans, the forces of Hindutva would have been shown for the first time 'to have blinked'. If, on the other hand, the *kar seva* 'results in any damage or desecration to the Masjid', the Uttar Pradesh government should be immediately dismissed for failing its Constitutional obligations.

I further suggested that the prime minister announce in his address to Parliament the formation of a trust to renovate the masjid and build a Ram Mandir that would leave the Babri Masjid in situ, and place the *garbha griha* of the mandir elsewhere, other than in the *mirab* of the masjid. I went on to propose that a single-point reference be made immediately to the Supreme Court under Article 142 of the Constitution (as Rajiv Gandhi had suggested to Chandra Shekhar).

Neither was the 'action plan' acted upon, nor was my draft speech (later found tucked away among the pillows on the prime minister's bed after the disaster) used. Instead, paralysis took over.

I raised the Babri issue in Parliament next day, urging our government to take the matter immediately to the Supreme Court under the relevant article of the Constitution, as urged by the late Rajiv Gandhi. The home minister's reply on 4 December was colourless and anodyne. He only underlined that government could not give answers to hypothetical scenarios. Yet, there were only seventy-two hours to go before the domes of the masjid were toppled. No action was taken to prevent it, notwithstanding the deployment of thousands of paramilitary troops, belying everything that the Kalyan Singh government had promised the highest court.

The sixth of December 1992 proved to be the most shameful day in the history of independent India. As usual, it was Jairam Ramesh who called to convey the bitter news that one of the domes had already fallen and the two others were under assault. He added that the security forces were nowhere to be seen. That Black Sunday, the prime minister removed himself from public view, maintaining such strict silence that I was forced to remark, 'Narasimha Rao has proved that death is not a necessary precondition for *rigor mortis* to set in.'

The road was thus opened to Hindu majoritarianism and to the resultant apprehensions among the Muslim and other minority communities about their place in an India being overtaken by vicious communalism that seemed to be heading towards 'Hindu raj', or, rather, Hindutva raj, for the country.

The Kalyan Singh government (and all other BJP state governments) were dismissed. On 7 December, the prime minister, in a broadcast/telecast to the nation, pledged the Babri Masjid would be rebuilt. The Justice Liberhan Commission was established to identify the culprits responsible for the Ayodhya outrage, and the Lucknow bench of the Allahabad High Court was entrusted with adjudicating the matter.

Over the next quarter of a century, the promised rebuilding was never taken up so that new facts on the ground, particularly the absence of a mosque, came to be established, leading to the curious Supreme Court judgement of September 2019, which held that while the destruction of the mosque was 'barbaric' and the consequence of 'egregious violation of the law', the Ram Janmabhoomi estate would nevertheless be awarded to the very forces that had encouraged and abetted the demolition of the masjid, while a Muslim place of worship could be built on other land to be identified by the state government.

The Lucknow bench held no one guilty for the outrage, terminating all action against L.K. Advani and scores of others indicted by Justice Liberhan. While the present BJP government and the prime minister have very fully and ostentatiously involved themselves in the building and inauguration of the Ram Mandir, with the BJP prime minister himself playing the role of chief Hindu priest (much to the annoyance of the four Shankaracharyas), the mosque complex, to be built 5 km away in the village of Danipur, languishes as a very poor cousin despite there being plans drawn up for a most secular complex where, in addition to a place of worship, they have provided for a 200-bed multi-speciality hospital open to patients from all communities; a school for students from any community; a kitchen and mess to serve delicious Awadhi cuisine in 365 varieties on 365 days, vegetarian and non-vegetarian, at cut prices to all comers; a museum on the region's Awadhi heritage; and a library and a research centre, also accessible to all. I understand that the body which was to build the alternative mosque complex was first denied the required FCRA clearance to raise money abroad and then dissolved altogether, and that perhaps moves are afoot to entrust the building of the mosque to a unit under the minorities' wing of the BJP. Whether the community will accept a mosque built by such tainted hands is a question only the future will answer.

My postscript to this tragic tale that has taken us so close to realization of Muhammad Ali Jinnah's dream of an Islamic State in Pakistan and a Hindu State in India is a passage from Prime Minister Narasimha Rao's address to the CPP in the immediate aftermath of the fall of the Babri Masjid, where he justified his recourse to *sant*s and *sadhu*s, saying that in ancient times kings always consulted wise religious personages, and these religious personages always remained faithful to the king's final decision; but in the instant case, the prime minister had been let down.

Which century did PVNR live in?

Harshad Mehta and the stock market scam

The stockbroker Harshad Mehta had emerged as a middle-class hero by enabling tens of thousands of people with modest incomes to suddenly become modestly rich by playing the stock market in his wake, only to be equally suddenly bankrupted by a stock market crash at the end of April 1992.

It was later found that Harshad Mehta was being illegally bankrolled by several state-owned commercial banks and the government's biggest mutual trust fund, the United Trust of India (UTI), while the finance ministry looked the other way. The finance minister, the legendary Dr Manmohan Singh, had somewhat casually remarked that he could not be bothered losing sleep over volatility in the stock exchanges. The Opposition chose this remark to roast him over the next two years.

Here is a quick summary of the Harshad Mehta scam: Banks – nationalized, private and foreign – are enjoined to maintain strict cash reserve ratios (CRR) and statutory liquidity ratios (SLR), which are percentages of deposits a bank must maintain in cash and liquid instruments, while also being expected to make profits. Caught in the pincer of having to sterilize a substantial part of their assets (estimated at 63.5 per cent) with the Reserve Bank of India (RBI) as CRR and SLR, and also reserve 40 per cent of their lending to 'priority sectors' and at the same time show profits, banks found themselves between a rock and a hard place.

Harshad Mehta and some other brokers showed banks a way to mint money by routing funds to the stock market, bypassing RBI regulations and allowing brokers to fraudulently pick up huge bank funds to play the market. This brought into the brokers' net numerous private and cooperative banks, as also major foreign banks (such as ANZ Grindlays, Standard Chartered, Citibank, among many others), government-run mutual fund trusts (above all, UTI) and a large swathe of private sector corporations.

The regulators and the ministry of finance were speculating about a possible 'foreign hand' when the fraud was primarily domestic. It remained undetected for the best part of a year. The government began worrying only at the beginning of 1992, when a deputy governor of the RBI, R. Janakiraman, was asked to look into the downside of the stupendous market rise.

The flurry of reports he submitted led to an outcry in Parliament, which culminated in the setting up of a Joint Parliamentary Committee (JPC) under the chairmanship of veteran Congress leader Ram Niwas Mirdha, with, among its members, a formidable battery of Opposition leaders ranging from Jaswant Singh to Yashwant Sinha on the right to George Fernandes and Gurudas Dasgupta on the left. Although I was a rookie in comparison, I found myself chosen by the Congress to serve on the JPC.

The Opposition saw this as a golden opportunity to bring down the newly elected minority government of P.V. Narasimha Rao. I realize now that this was even more evident to the prime minister, whose survival depended upon the silent support of the right-wing BJP and elements of the left-oriented Opposition.

This perhaps accounted for my puzzlement at the chair inclining towards the Opposition to establish his credentials as impartial and bipartisan. It also accounted for the ferocity with which S.S. Ahluwalia and some of the other Congress members went for the jugular when it came to the government witnesses summoned to appear before the JPC.

The impression I increasingly gathered was of a conspiracy within our ranks to let Dr Manmohan Singh take the heat, especially after Harshad Mehta claimed in an infamous press conference to have carried a suitcase of currency notes amounting to what was then regarded as an enormous sum of Rs 1 crore to bribe members of the Jharkhand Mukti Morcha to defect from the Opposition in the vote on a no-confidence motion designed to bring the PVNR government to an end. However, the revelation got no one anywhere because the Supreme Court said it had no jurisdiction to determine why a member of the legislature voted the way he did. So, the PVNR government survived.

I had gone to Mayiladuturai and Kumbakonam. My flight back to Delhi was so delayed that I was obliged to rush to Parliament directly from the airport with my suitcase in hand. This was photographed and loudly hailed as a spoof on Harshad Mehta!

The motion was defeated, but it had been a near thing and the government had had a bad fright.

Against this background, I found that among the few who were standing up as best as we could for the besieged finance minister were me and, at a discreet distance, Murli Deora. I, therefore, sought a meeting with the PM. On my way to his residence, I dropped in unannounced on Dr Manmohan Singh. He looked most concerned at the apprehensions I expressed to him and most relieved when I asked if I might drop in on him again after my talk with the PM.

The prime minister received me with great courtesy. I unburdened myself of my concerns that the chair and some Congress members seemed to be conspiring with the Opposition to paint the government's name black in the guise of undertaking an impartial probe into the scam.

He listened with apparent sympathy and nodded his head repeatedly, indicating that he understood what I was driving at – that the JPC report, by now at the edge of the drafting stage, might teeter towards holding the government as a whole responsible for the scam instead of focusing on the fraudsters and regulatory failure.

As I walked out of the room, Bhuvanesh Chaturvedi, Rao's Luca Brasi, who, standing in the wings, had overheard the whole conversation, pulled me aside and warned me to mind my own business. I now realize what I only dimly perceived at the time that Dr Manmohan Singh was being set up as a fall guy so that none of the flak might be directed at the prime minister.

I went directly from 7, Race Course Road to the finance minister's home on Krishna Menon Marg. I was received by Dr Singh in his drawing room where, within seconds of my beginning to speak, he put a finger to his lips and guided me out to his expansive lawns. There, well out of earshot of 'walls that have ears', he said his house was perhaps bugged and he wanted to hear my report without being spied on.

I was taken aback but soldiered on. The gravamen of what I had to say was that while the PM had given me a patient and apparently sympathetic hearing, Bhuvanesh Chaturvedi's unwarranted intervention reinforced my conviction that something dastardly was afoot. Dr Singh contemplated this angle but did not really seem to know how to counter such political machinations. He thanked me for my efforts and hoped I would succeed in keeping anything unfair out of the final report.

I continued fighting my corner word by word in the drafting process, was often overruled and occasionally laughed out of court, but I could not prevail in objecting to the sarcastic observation that while the JPC wished the finance minister sound sleep, they could not countenance his not losing any sleep over a stock market crash that had robbed lakhs of small investors of their life savings.

After the report was tabled in Parliament in December 1993, Murli Deora whispered to me that the finance minister was furious at our not editing out the slighting reference to him, made 'in a lighter vein'. He was holding the likes of Murli and me responsible for this wholly unjustified indictment. Later that evening, I ran into Dr Singh at a CPP dinner. He was normally a man of calm demeanour, but it was obvious that he was seething that day and clearly believed that he had been let down, particularly by Murli and me.

There followed a debate in the Lok Sabha on 28 December 1993, at an especially reconvened post-Christmas session, but despite a powerful speech by Vajpayee at his oratorical best, the government survived, and the finance minister's letter of resignation sent to the prime minister in the immediate wake of the JPC report being tabled in Parliament was not accepted. Dr Singh continued in office, with Destiny biding its time to elevate him to the highest office of the land. Eventually, the JPC proved a mere blink in his long and distinguished career.

Other financial scams: 'The Insider's View'

While there is no end to the paeans of praise (a deluge which continues to this day) heaped on the process of economic reforms that marked P.V. Narasimha Rao's premiership, in Parliament we fought off a number of allegations of dodgy financial issues, apart from the Harshad Mehta business. There were the Jain hawala case, the 'rupee–rouble' Vostro scam, round-tripping of funds via Mauritius, and, later, the Ketan Parekh scam of 2001. These scams seemed to characterize our march away from Nehruvian socialism. Indeed, financial impropriety amounting to criminality seemed to litter the way to increasing private participation in economic development. This was accompanied by the transformation of the public image of big businesses and foreign investors (at least in the pink papers) as being the benevolent drivers of our growth to double-digit figures, and harbingers of a great economic future for our country.

In 2012, Javid Chowdhury, a school friend of mine and a senior Indian Administrative Service (IAS) officer of unimpeachable integrity, published through Penguin/Viking his startling memoirs, *The Insider's View*. In 1992, he had been appointed for a three-year term as head of the Enforcement Directorate, the 'fiscal law enforcement agency', as he describes it, at almost the same time as the launch of the process of economic reforms. He later served as revenue secretary. He thus had a ringside view of how the nexus between liberalization of the economy and criminalization of business panned out. Here are some snatches from the book:

> In the decades leading up to the nineties, we had managed to create a huge mess of economic laws and regulations; this amounted to an open-ended invitation to low-end corruption;
>
> . . . the leaders of the liberalization process adopted the option of encouraging the corporate sector to disregard regulatory provisions [despite] most corporate houses and their principal promoters [having] several cases under investigation at any point in time [p. 109];
>
> [This, in turn, led to] a dim view [being] always [taken of] any efforts to conscientiously enforce economic laws [p. 113];
>
> [Instead of displaying the] patience and expertise to revise or repeal the laws . . . they adopted the arrogant approach of treating the laws and the responsibility for law enforcement as useless and counter-productive [p.113];
>
> Little wonder then that LPG (Liberalization, Privatization, Globalization) spawned a series of scams that persist to this day but did not evoke even a tinge of introspection [p. 111] [among the] fundamentalist liberalizers;
>
> The impression given was that the existence of economic laws was harming the public [p. 113];
>
> If the law enforcers turned a blind eye to corporate infringements . . . they were likely to win a benign nod from the lords of liberalization [p. 115];
>
> [The attitude was that] if laws had been violated, the laws were wrong – because they [the fundamentalist liberalizers] understood economics, and, therefore, what they say should be the law [p. 136].

Javid Chowdhury's conclusion is irresistible:

> . . . it is difficult to ignore the grim reality that there is no law-enforcer, there is no law, and, therefore, by extrapolation, there is also no law-breaker [p. 116].

This casual bypassing of laws came about principally through the lateral induction of middle-aged economic experts into the Indian Economic Service or as specialized consultants to the Planning Commission/ ministry of finance. They were usually ideological warriors drawn from the World Bank, the International Monetary Fund or large foreign corporate houses. They were vocal in condemning the laws in the statute books that emerged from what they scathingly called the 'licence-permit raj' – plagiarizing Rajaji, who had founded the Swatantra Party – as if that was all there was to 'Nehruvian socialism'. However, instead of modifying or nullifying such laws by due democratic procedure, they chose to brush aside legal requirements and become a law unto themselves.

Once economic reforms got under way, they constituted themselves into what Javid Chowdhury labels 'a council of economic tsars' [p. 62]. He writes:

> [They] dismantled [the] apparatus for examination of policy issues [p. 68] [and resorted to] bald and opaque statements . . . with the attitude [of] take it or leave it. [This] specialist class found it useful to create a thick mystique around the issues and was strongly backed by the State establishment. [In consequence], the risk of manipulation of decisions [became] enormous [p.68].
>
> [T]he corporate sector position is often spelt out in sweeping, jargonized language bereft of evidence or nuanced analysis . . . Anything labelled as 'economic reforms' is axiomatically considered a virtuous initiative. If at all there is any claim of broad public interest, it is unabashedly dressed up in cliches of sanctimonious humbug [p. 69].

Chowdhury sees the spectacle of a 'retired Finance Secretary of the Union of India as an upfront lobbyist, his gun ready for hire, a humiliating sight for civil servants, past or present'.[4]

No wonder then that the reforms process has been marked by an exponential rise in the number and, more importantly, scale of business improprieties and crimes, with the connivance, subtle or blatant, of the economic tsars. It has also brought about such a concentration of wealth (and the political heft that comes with it) that, according to one report, the top 1 per cent holds over 40 per cent of the nation's wealth, and that economic inequality in the country is worse than in the pre-Independence era of our notorious princely states.[5]

Thirty years after economic reforms were initiated in India, there is a duopoly of businessmen, among the richest in the world, who dominate an economy in which some 300 million live in absolute poverty (destitution) and about 700 million consider themselves poor. The bulk of the remainder of the population remains 'aspirational', in the sense that they still nurture hopes of improving their lot. The top wealthy businessmen have been co-opted, particularly through the electoral bonds scheme,[6] to provide the money and muscle power that characterize elections in our country, making a commerce of politics. Inequality has grown exponentially, and the India that we dreamt of during the freedom movement and envisioned in the Constitution is a distant, abandoned dream. Crony capitalism has replaced socialism. Growth is cruelly purchased at the expense of equity.

Enron

An egregious example of the link between corruption and exploitation, on the one hand, and the encouragement of the 'animal spirits' of free enterprise, on the other, is the case of Enron and the Dabhol Power Corporation.

In the summer of 1992, about a year into the economic reforms process, finding that apart from McDonald's and KFC, there was little by way of foreign direct investment (FDI) to showcase the results of reforms, a high-level delegation, led by none less than the cabinet secretary, had been dispatched to the West to scour the possibility of fetching significant investments in our problem-ridden power sector. They met, among others, the US-based Enron Corporation, with whom they signed a memorandum of understanding (MoU), which was bruited about as a major achievement of the reforms.

Enron then put together a consortium of themselves, Bechtel and General Electric (GE) to partner the Maharashtra State Electricity Board

(MSEB), which had a token equity stake of 10 per cent in the venture, to build a massive 2,100 MW power plant at Dabhol on the Maharashtra coast. The consortium was called the Dabhol Power Corporation (DPC), and the plant was to be set up in two phases. The thermal plant was to be powered using liquefied natural gas (LNG) and naphtha as fuel.

Within a year or so of the start of the project (phase I), MSEB, hitherto one of the best-performing state electricity boards in the country, found itself sinking in huge losses. The losses amounted to over Rs 1,600 crore annually, owing to Enron having negotiated an exorbitant Rs 8 per unit tariff for power when MSEB was paying less than Re 1 per unit for hydroelectricity and around Rs 2 per unit for coal-based thermal power.

The Dabhol fiasco threatened to consume, in short order, most of Maharashtra's annual development plan outlay of Rs 6,000 crore, in effect bankrupting India's richest state. Meanwhile, a World Bank assessment held that power generated from LNG (imported and re-gasified) would be at a 'much higher cost' than 'low variable-cost coal power' and would 'place a heavy financial burden' on Maharashtra.

Moreover, the gigantic size of the 2,015 MW project was way 'too large' to pay Enron for what are called 'baseload' operations. While Enron's prices might be sustainable for large industry to pay for 'intermediate' and 'peak load demand', this tariff could not be charged by MSEB for general economic activity during most of the day.

So, Sharad Pawar's Congress government (January 1993 to February 1995) slashed the contracted quantity of electricity from 2,015 MW to 695 MW. When, however, the BJP–Shiv Sena alliance won the 1995 assembly elections – partly on the promise that they would 'throw Enron into the Arabian Sea' – Enron's Mumbai representative called on the Shiv Sena leader. It was a one-on-one closed-door meeting. To the astonishment of all, it was learned that far from rationalizing the quantity of power that MSEB would buy from DPC to keep itself afloat, the meeting ended with the quantum allegedly raised beyond 2,015 MW and a firm decision in favour of LNG as the fuel of preference. It was in fact not Enron but the World Bank that was thrown into the Arabian Sea!

To renegotiate the Enron contract, the BJP–Shiv Sena government set up a ‘negotiation group’ to resettle terms. The group was constituted on 8 November 1995 and submitted its report on the renegotiated terms just eleven days later, on 19 November 1995, raising eyebrows over a ‘fixed match’. We will come later to the ‘renegotiated’ terms.

Worse was the role played by Jaswant Singh and Atal Bihari Vajpayee when the BJP came briefly to power for thirteen days after the general elections of 1996. While the initial MoU of 1992 contained the explicit clause that ‘every effort will be made to avoid guarantees from the Government of India for lender’, Enron received the counter-guarantee it had sought from New Delhi on 15 September 1994, subsequently renewed on 28 May 1996, minutes before Prime Minister Vajpayee went into the House to tender his resignation. That perhaps accounts for Enron having spent $20 million on ‘educating’ Indians, as they claimed, on the virtues of the deal!

When, therefore, the Congress won the 1999 state assembly elections and the chief minister of Maharashtra, Vilasrao Deshmukh, decided in February 2001 to appoint an energy review committee under the chairmanship of a distinguished retired IAS officer, Dr Madhav Godbole, it looked as if the truth of Dabhol was about to be unearthed. The Godbole Committee examined the history of negotiations with Enron, focusing on both the first agreement and the renegotiated agreement.

The original agreement had led to the establishment of DPC as a ‘private unlimited liability company, incorporated in India as an Independent Power Producer (IPP)’, to build, own and operate for twenty years ‘a combined cycle gas/naphtha/distillate-fired power plant of 2,184 MW capacity in two phases’. Coal was excluded, despite its lower cost, and in the first phase of 740 MW the plant was to run almost entirely on expensive, imported LNG re-gasified at a facility to be set up at a considerable cost by DPC. Only in the second phase could it resort to the use of ‘liquid fuels like naphtha and distillate’ (section 4.2).

The principal failing here was that although only 45 MW of a total capacity of 740 MW was reserved for ‘intermediate’ and ‘peak’ load, all the power was to be bought from Enron by MSEB at an unbearably high, uniform rate, calculated by including a ‘separate tariff line for recovering the fixed cost' associated with each component of the project. Enron, Bechtel and General Electric Company (GE), as sellers, would be sitting pretty, while MSEB, as the buyer, would drown (sections 4.2 and 4.2.1).

Instead of querying all this, as the World Bank had done, the Central Electricity Authority and the tsars in the finance ministry pushed through the agreement, which had been negotiated by inexperienced, naive and complaisant state civil servants playing to the tune of their political masters. Godbole and his colleagues describe this as 'an inexcusable failure of governance'.

After detailing the shortcomings in the Government of Maharashtra's examination of the initialled agreement, the report turns to the role of the Central government.

The CEA certified the technical aspects of the scheme 'to be generally in order' despite the summary record not establishing that 'issues relating to the technical design of the project' had been 'effectively addressed', says the report.

The minutes of the Foreign Investment Promotion Board's meeting of 5 November 1993 cited the Finance Secretary as saying, 'that the question of the cost of power has been looked into and it has been found that it was more or less in line with other projects being put up in Maharashtra'. This apparently led to the CEA saying that 'the aspects related to import of fuel, foreign exchange rules and deviation from Government of India tariff notification indicating return on equity, have been examined by FIPB and the project has been found acceptable by them'. Hence the CEA wrote to the power ministry on 23 December 1994 that as 'the cost of power has been found reasonable by the Ministry of Finance, CEA feels that since the cost of power is to be derived from the capital cost, the capital cost of Dabhol project may also be considered reasonable'.

This circular argument would have been found unacceptable in any Oxbridge senior combination room. But it then became the ground on which 'techno-economic clearance' was assumed to have been given. The Godbole Committee noted that there was no actual reference to 'techno-economic' clearance in CEA communications. The committee regarded this omission as 'curious', but I think the omission was a clever sleight of hand by an experienced civil servant at the CEA who deliberately avoided describing the FIPB clearance as 'techno-economic clearance'.

The project was, in fact, cleared with a cursory technical examination and no economic examination at all by the Central government. It is because of such negligence that the review committee found the Central government to have failed the test of good governance.

The committee also found that 'the financial institutions showed poor judgement and lack of due diligence in accepting [Maharashtra's] projections without demur'. What they found even more disturbing was that the Union finance ministry had taken decisions 'involving the incurring of liabilities to the extent of over Rs 6,000 crore a year, and rising over 20 years, in so cavalier a fashion' instead of undertaking an 'independent and meticulous appraisal of the project'.

The review committee also examined the renegotiated terms, an exercise completed in just eleven days. That was perhaps because the political authority might have indicated its mind on the broad outlines of the renegotiation to its negotiators in advance of the renegotiations. However that may be, the review committee found that although the group made several recommendations that could have resulted in reducing the cost of the Dabhol power to the consumer, many had not been 'followed through'.

The key elements, such as the design for base load operations, the take-or-pay provisions for LNG, and fixed capacity charge liabilities, remained unchanged. The cost of the project was reduced by $330 million, but the cost of phase I, at $919.8 million, remained 'high'. More importantly, 'given the manner in which DPC's tariff is structured, a reduction in capital cost has *per se* no effect on the tariff and, therefore, affords no benefit to MSEB'. Apart from removing the escalation clause, 'on almost all other parameters, such as limiting the foreign exchange risk, the fuel take-off risk and the allocation of standstill costs, the Group's recommendations proved infructuous'.

The report also noted:

> As is evident today, the Group was mistaken in its conclusion regarding the need for additional baseload energy for MSEB and the LNG supply contract is now another millstone around MSEB's fragile neck. As regards the DPC tariff vis-à-vis the GoI tariff, the entire demonstration of public interest owing to the lower DPC tariff is on extremely shaky ground and, in the opinion of the committee, utterly unsustainable.

Such was the fate of a flagship project of the economic reforms!

When Chairman Godbole submitted the findings of his committee in April 2001, I received an urgent call from my fellow MP in Mumbai, Murli Deora, sounding the alarm, 'Dynamite, yaar, dynamite.' Minutes later, the Congress president Sonia Gandhi's office called to say I should rush over. She inquired whether Murli had informed me of the Godbole report. I said he had called it 'dynamite' (and from her smile I guessed he had used the same expression with her) but I had not seen the report. She said she had a copy and asked me to summarize its main findings. That was the last I heard of the matter.

Neither the Congress state government nor the party at the Centre followed up on the findings or recommendations of the report, although the Enron contract itself was cancelled in mid-2001. I suspected the presence of several skeletons in the reform's cupboard, but interest in the Godbole report's findings petered out when Enron was found guilty of several sins in a US court and one of its top executives in India, Jeff Skilling, was jailed for other wrongs. Although Ratnagiri Gas and Power was established in 2005 to complete and run the Dabhol plant, the truth of the Enron–Dabhol issue still remains buried because the 'clear political mandate' the committee sought in section 1.1 to take the matter to court was never received. It was only the public interest litigations (PILs) that reached the courts.

I was in the cabinet when it was decided to settle matters by getting the Gas Authority of India Limited (GAIL) and the National Thermal Power Corporation (NTPC) to take half the equity of DPC and MSEB the remaining half. The plant is now operational and produces about

1,650 MW. It is a clear example of domestic public sector enterprise succeeding where foreign private enterprise failed and almost drowned the Maharashtra state government in debt.

Panchayati Raj

From the beginning of my first term in Parliament I remained in close touch with the minister of state for rural development, G. Venkataswamy, who was to table the modified Panchayati Raj Constitution amendment bills. He did so in the winter session of 1991, and the bills were immediately referred to two joint select committees, one to deal with the rural self-government institutions (73rd Amendment) and the other with similar institutions in urban India (74th Amendment), under the chairmanship of Nathuram Mirdha and Digvijaya Singh, respectively.

I opted for the Mirdha Committee and found myself with a very knowledgeable and sympathetic chairman and two invaluable companions: Nitish Kumar, an impassioned advocate of Panchayati Raj, kissed by Destiny to be a long-serving chief minister of Bihar; and R. Sankaran, an IAS officer of the Andhra Pradesh cadre who pushed for the inclusion of *gram sabhas*, a crucial omission in the Rajiv draft.

The most helpful and constructive witness was C. Narayanaswamy, former head of the Bangalore rural district panchayat. He had met me in the autumn of 1990 with a delegation of his colleagues to seek an audience with Rajiv Gandhi to protest against the Congress chief minister of Karnataka, S. Bangarappa, calling a special one-day session of the state assembly only to pass legislation to negate the stay order given by the Karnataka High Court on an ordinance the Congress state government had issued. The ordinance had directed the district authorities to dismiss the heads of zilla parishads elected during the previous Ramakrishna Hegde regime.

I arranged for Narayanaswamy and his colleagues to call on Rajiv Gandhi. They presented him with a petition and, after giving them a patient hearing, Rajiv said he would see what could be done about this manifestly mala fide step. Having studied the petition and, presumably, having consulted his senior colleagues, Rajiv Gandhi called me late that night. It was about 3 a.m. when I met him.

Rajiv Gandhi instructed me to immediately ring Bangarappa and convey his orders that the special session should be called off. I succeeded in tracking down Bangarappa and passed on the orders. The special session was called off after most of the MLAs had reached the chamber. This, of course, made Narayanaswamy a staunch ally of mine. He remains one.

With the help of Nitish and Narayanaswamy, and the benevolent guidance of Chairman Nathuram Mirdha, we succeeded, in the joint select committee, in getting all but one point of the new draft on Panchayati Raj settled. That key point was the role of the district planning committee (DPC). I had not succeeded in persuading my colleagues in the joint select committee to incorporate in the amendment bill a section on DPCs. Their argument was that in the Rajiv Gandhi draft (the 64th Amendment) there was no reference to DPCs. I had to confess that that was because we had drafted the amendment for urban local bodies only after presenting the draft 64th amendment in the Lok Sabha. As resistance continued, I reconfirmed from Digvijaya Singh, the chair of our sister committee, that since DPCs were at the heart of the draft amendment dealing with urban local bodies, his committee would be doing so.

He did but, alas, dropped Rajiv's provision that the DPC chairperson would statutorily be the chair of the district panchayat (zilla parishad). Inevitably, this has meant that DPCs have been stultified by local MLAs or, worse still, state government ministers designated as 'district ministers' dominating and subverting the grassroots nature of the model. Still, something was better than nothing.

So, when I was called by chairman Nathu Ram Mirdha while I was in Rio for the Earth Summit to consent to his forwarding to the government the revised draft of the Constitution amendment bill without my draft provision on DPCs, I reluctantly agreed. I could see that Mirdha was under tremendous pressure to see that the work was completed without further delay. Accordingly, the drafts of both Constitution amendment bills were readied for presentation in Parliament at the start of the winter session in 1992.

Despite the destruction of the Babri Masjid on 6 December, the year 1992 ended on an upbeat note in Parliament. The Constitution amendment bills envisaged by Rajiv Gandhi were brought to the Lower House on 21 December. There was a snafu when Somnath Chatterjee of the Communist Party of India (Marxist) [CPI(M)] objected at the very last minute to inclusion of the Darjeeling Hills of West Bengal in the ambit of the amendments. The prime minister looked at me quizzically and the House was adjourned for a short while. I suggested that we regard the Darjeeling Gorkha Hills Council (DGHC) as the 'district panchayat' and hold elections only to the two lower tiers at the intermediate and village levels. This would introduce Panchayati Raj to the Darjeeling Hills while leaving intact the DGHC.

Somnath agreed after Inderjit, the Darjeeling MP hand-picked by Subhash Ghisingh, chairman of the DGHC at the time, had consulted the latter on the phone. We then returned to the House and the reworked amendments were both passed on 22 December, with only the two Tamil Nadu parties in Parliament voting negatively (DMK) or abstaining (AIADMK). The rest unanimously approved. The same voting pattern was repeated in the Upper House the next day. The amendments were through! Rajiv's dream of Panchayati Raj had been realized.

Immediately after the House adjourned, I repaired to 10, Janpath to share the good news with Sonia Gandhi. She beamed and thanked me. As I took my leave, seeing that it was almost Christmas eve, I wished her a cheery 'Merry Christmas'. She responded to say she was not a Christian. I bolted!

Other political issues, domestic and international

To my immense pride, I was selected to lead the defence on a number of issues that shook the House – the foreign policy debate, including the question of Palestine in the context of the Oslo accord; the Verma Commission report on lapses in security arrangements that had led to Rajiv Gandhi's assassination; the sugar scandal; and the Jain hawala scandal.

Foreign policy and Palestine

In January 1992, Yasser Arafat made a state visit to India. There was a banquet in his honour at Rashtrapati Bhavan. The usual practice was for the Indian invitees to be lined up to be introduced to the distinguished guest as he was escorted past them by the Rashtrapati-ji, the chief of protocol mumbling the names as the chief guest smiled his or her way past them. By sheer happenstance, I found myself standing to the right of Atal Bihari Vajpayee as we awaited the chief guest. But Arafat unexpectedly headed straight to the other end of the room, obliging us to re-form into a queue that would go past him.

This meant that I would be ahead of Vajpayee-ji in the line. So, I moved aside and requested the leader of the Opposition to stand ahead of me. Atal-ji took me by the arm and, referring to an article in which I had described the president of the BJP, Murli Manohar Joshi, as a 'Hindu Jinnah', whispered, '*Na, na, na, aakhir mein hoon kya? Bas, hamare Hindu Jinnah ka ek follower!*' (No, no, no, after all who am I? Just a follower of the Hindu Jinnah!) In exuding charm, he was simply unbeatable!

After the banquet ended, the Palestinian ambassador asked me to stay on as Yasser Arafat wanted to meet me in his Rashtrapati Bhavan suite to personally thank me for my championing the Palestinian cause. When I was escorted to his presence, Arafat said a few kind words and presented me with a tray inlaid with mother-of-pearl. I thanked him but added that I had something further to say. Arafat indicated I could proceed. I said our media were hinting at the possibility that India, which from the time of Nehru in 1947 and up to the present (January 1992) had refrained from raising our relationship with Israel to full diplomatic ambassadorial level, was now on the threshold of doing so. I requested him to tell Prime Minister PVNR to desist from doing so. Arafat's reaction was ambiguous to the point of being puzzling. My puzzlement turned to horror when, at the next day's joint press conference, Rao not only confirmed the rumour, but Arafat publicly thanked him for what I considered India's betrayal of Palestine.

All the pieces of the puzzle were to fall in place when the world learned of the Oslo accord, which had been secretly negotiated between Israeli envoys and Arafat's hand-picked representatives in Norway's capital. Perhaps Arafat thought India could play a more effective role in mediating the remaining issues (which were legion) if we had full diplomatic relations with Tel Aviv. If this, indeed, were the case, Arafat was dead wrong, because diplomatic relations over the last three decades have only resulted in New Delhi moving ever closer to Tel Aviv and covering its moving tracks by abstaining on many key votes on the Palestine question in the UN, abandoning the poor Palestinians and becoming complicit in Israel's many human rights crimes and other depredations, the worst being the ongoing genocide in Gaza (2024). The Israelis have also acquired a powerful lobby in India through defence and national security deals such as Pegasus spyware. And, of course, the Israelis betrayed Arafat. They accorded to him no more autonomy or sovereignty than introducing a form of Panchayati Raj in the Gaza Strip. He could lead this unit of local government and was allowed to enter Gaza from Tunisia, where he and his cadres had taken shelter. The Israelis might even have poisoned him when they deemed he was getting above himself on the West Bank. That is at the root of the rise of Hamas.

I asked my wife to put Arafat's mother-of-pearl tray out of human sight.

When the Israeli president visited India, I availed of the opportunity to contribute a stinging article to *The Indian Express*. On reading it, the president called me to say that he was instructing his ambassador to call on me to explain the Israeli side of the argument. When the ambassador arrived, I found him parroting the stale arguments of his principals, and so asked my wife to put away with Arafat's mother-of-pearl tray the bottle of Israeli white wine the ambassador had brought me as a placatory gift. I have seen neither since.

Verma Commission on Rajiv Gandhi's assassination

The Verma Commission report on the security lapses that led to Rajiv Gandhi's assassination was released to the general public in late 1992. The discussion on the report in Parliament was preceded by a curious incident on the evening of 12 May 1993. At about ten minutes to 6 p.m., I received a message from the secretary general asking me to meet him urgently. This was unusual, because Parliamentary officials do not generally speak directly to Members in the House. Anyway, since the secretary general, C.K. Jain, was a good friend, I went up to him. He whispered that I should rush to the 'notice office' before it closed at 6 p.m. and give a notice under Rule 193 for an urgent discussion on the Verma Commission report. He indicated that he was 'making this suggestion' at the instance of the Hon'ble Speaker.

The Verma Commission report had, in fact, been prepared within a year of Rajiv's assassination and submitted to government in June 1992. Along with the 'action taken report' (ATR), it had been tabled in Parliament in December 1992. Six months had elapsed without any discussion. Perhaps Sonia Gandhi's unhappiness at this had reached the Speaker's ear and that was why I had been requested to give notice for the discussion? It was scheduled for the next day. I was given all the time I needed to speak, close to ninety minutes.

I discursively began by describing the many journeys I had taken with Rajiv Gandhi during my five years in the PMO. This, I said, was possible only because of the Special Protection Group (SPG), 'a body specially trained, specially raised'. To supervise the SPG, Rajiv Gandhi had picked a top-notch civil servant, T.N. Seshan, to head the newly created Department of Internal Security. In addition, the former prime minister had placed as the minister of state for internal security's minister he regarded as being of 'exceptional competence, my hon'ble friend, and senior colleague, Shri P. Chidambaram'.

I continued:

> I do say with a lump in my throat but pride in my heart that Rajiv went to Punjab, he did not die; Rajiv went to Mizoram, he did not die; Rajiv went to Darjeeling, he did not die; Rajiv went to Tripura, he did not die; and Rajiv went thirteen times to Tamil Nadu, he came back living . . . All that was possible only because he had this top-notch, highly trained, extraordinarily efficient and totally dedicated set of over 500 people who constituted the core of the SPG and its auxiliary wings.

'I asked whether any of this could have happened if the SPG had been in position.

> . . . the Sriperumbudur incident would never, ever have happened had the SPG been detailed to Rajiv's security on 21 May 1991. Drawing attention to several paragraphs in chapter XI of the report, I pointed out that 'barricading was inadequate; lighting was inadequate; there was a crowd at the rostrum'; and there was 'a total collapse of access control'.

In contrast, all that Rajiv Gandhi had at Sriperumbudur was 'one solitary personal security officer (PSO); even he was without a weapon'. What was worse is that the inspector-general of police Forests had been put in charge, not IGP Security. There was not a single SPG-trained officer deployed at the venue, although there were other SPG-trained police officers in the state who could have been deployed.

In this context, I drew attention to the minister of home affairs having said the V.P. Singh government, in withdrawing SPG cover for Rajiv-ji, had 'a contributory responsibility' for Rajiv-ji's assassination. I stressed that far from shouldering just a contributory responsibility, 'the withdrawal of SPG by the V.P. Singh Government was the root cause' of Rajiv-ji's death, and, therefore, 'responsibility must be fixed on the person who took this decision'.

That person was none other than Prime Minister V.P. Singh. I said I quite agreed that 'the SPG Act did not provide for SPG protections to ex-prime ministers'. But Rajiv-ji received SPG protection for two months after he demitted office. And the high-powered committee under the Cabinet Secretariat came to two important conclusions, recorded in the Verma Commission report in chapter IX:

> The threat to Rajivji remained undiminished 'in spite of his ceasing to be PM'; and 'a fresh threat assessment' needed to be undertaken to determine the level of security required by the former PM.

According to Justice Verma, 'No fresh threat assessment was undertaken by the V.P. Singh government.' Instead, the cabinet secretary was changed, and a new note was put up to the new prime minister by the new cabinet secretary on 13 January 1990 (included in annexure XXIII of the report). The note makes no reference to the previous report and only says the earlier orders were both 'verbal instructions', and since personnel deployed on SPG duty elsewhere could not be spared for Rajiv Gandhi, it was necessary to withdraw the SPG. A further criticism of the previous oral orders had come from some unnamed state government, which had objected to 'the high-profile visibility of the SPG'. Were security decisions to be taken on such grounds?

In chapter XVI of the report, the arguments advanced by the V.P. Singh government are described as 'tenuous' and 'prompted by lack of proper perception' and lacking 'the requisite will'. Justice Verma concludes that the 'stated reasons' advanced for withdrawing SPG cover were 'unjustified . . . Rajiv Gandhi's real security requirements were ignored'. I asked to be informed whether, in the view of the Rao government, there was any Constitutional impediment to the charter of the SPG Act being extended to cover former prime ministers and whether, in fact, there were no adequate personnel available, especially as the Rao government had extended SPG protection to Sonia Gandhi and her family, besides former prime ministers V.P. Singh and Chandra Shekhar and their families.

I then went on to draw attention to letters from Rajiv Gandhi's private office to the secretary (security) in the Cabinet Secretariat, in which it was stated that the prime minister himself had announced that 'no more conversations' would be undertaken with P. Chidambaram, despite the latest intelligence report communicated by the Intelligence Bureau (IB) giving 'an alarming note with regard to the security arrangements for Shri Rajiv Gandhi and his family members' (letter dated 13 February 1991). I then drew attention to the Verma Commission report saying that even on 20 May 1991, the eve of the assassination, the IB 'frantically reiterated' the need for top-class security cover for Rajiv Gandhi, but the Chandra Shekhar government took no action in this matter. I concluded by referring to a sentence in chapter IX of the report:

> The security prescribed and provided for Shri Rajiv Gandhi on the withdrawal of SPG cover was inadequate to meet the threat to him.

Through the Speaker, I asked what action the home minister proposed to take against these two prime ministers, their ministers and their officials, 'for it was their negligence that was the root cause of death of an innocent man'.

None of this was done. But attention shifted to the other commission of inquiry established under the former chief justice of the Rajasthan High Court, Justice Milap Chand Jain, to investigate the conspiracy behind the assassination. He took all of sixty-six months to prepare his report, partly because a little-known lawyer succeeded in obtaining an injunction against the proceedings of the Jain Commission, which took quite a while to be removed.

Meanwhile, the World Tamil Congress was held with great fanfare by Chief Minister Jayalalithaa in Thanjavur. Although, at the instance of G.K. Moopanar, the Rashtrapati had decided at the last moment not to inaugurate the conference, Prime Minister Rao accepted Jayalalithaa's invitation to deliver the valedictory address. As my constituency literally abutted the edges of Thanjavur town, I drove to the helipad to receive the prime minister. I was intrigued to find that no other Congressman was present. It then turned out that Moopanar and his dissident team had received the prime minister at Trichy airport but had declined to proceed to Thanjavur with him as a protest against our continuing alliance with Jayalalithaa. Only two Tamil MPs, Thangkabalu and Akbar Pasha, accompanied Rao in the helicopter.

After the event was over, I went in the helicopter with the prime minister to Tiruchirappalli and got into his aircraft with him for the journey back to Delhi. Before the aircraft had even taken off, the PM invited me into his cabin, and we stayed alone for the entire three-hour flight. This was to discuss his deteriorating relationship with Sonia Gandhi. He pleaded that he had done his best to maintain equable relations with her but had failed to stem her disappointment in, and disapproval of, him.

I replied that her only concern was to ascertain the truth behind the brutal assassination of her husband. She had been shocked to learn from Prime Minister Chandrika Bandaranaike Kumaratunga that the Government of India had not even made a request for extradition of the key Liberation Tigers of Tamil Eelam (LTTE) militants involved in the assassination, and was deeply disturbed at the tardy discussion in Parliament on the Verma Commission report and the patent failure of the Rao government to enable the Jain Commission to get on with its work.

Narasimha Rao asked me whether I had a solution in mind to help him repair his bridges with Mrs Gandhi. Without hesitation, I presented my solution, which was to appoint someone that both she and he trusted as a minister wholly in charge of the follow-up to the Verma Commission and to facilitate expeditious commencement and conclusion of the Jain Commission's work. He shrewdly looked at me and said, 'Do you mean yourself?' I immediately denied that I had suggested this in my personal interest, because the minister I proposed had to be an expert in jurisprudence and I knew nothing of the law. No, I said, the man I had in mind was a former minister whose 'letter of resignation had been as unwarranted as its acceptance has been unjustified'. The prime minister looked astonished and, his eyes widening, asked: 'You mean Chidambaram?'

'That,' I replied, 'is exactly whom I mean. He has needlessly been put out to grass. Mrs Gandhi implicitly trusts him, and you had picked him as your minister of state for commerce.' I concluded that in the circumstances, P. Chidambaram would be the ideal choice. Rao did not immediately react. But about two months later, PC, as we called him, got the job!

However, PC failed to get the injunction vacated, and so the proceedings of the Jain Commission remained stalled till the middle of 1996.

By the time the Jain Commission resumed its hearings, Moopanar had carved out the Tamil Maanila Congress (TMC, Tamil State Congress) from the parent Indian National Congress and, in collaboration with the DMK, had helped form the Deve Gowda government, where PC earned himself a worldwide reputation as the Indian finance minister who 'takes on the world', as my brother's coverage of PC's first budget was heralded in the famed *Economic Times* headline.

But when the Jain Commission report was tabled on 20 November 1997, a full sixty-six months after it was constituted, PC was severely chastised for opportunistically changing his line between 25 February 1991, when he had been fielded as the Congress spokesman to defend the dismissal of the DMK government, and his testimony before the Jain Commission in the winter of 1996 while serving as finance minister in the Deve Gowda government.

Justice Jain did not give much credence to PC's plea that he had spoken in the Lok Sabha in 1991 only on the brief given by the Congress party and that his testimony before the Jain Commission was his own opinion. I was asked by Sonia Gandhi to attend the hearings of the Jain Commission, and my testimony, which was not favourable to PC, stretched to over 100 pages.

The Jain Commission's interim report, tabled in November 1998, revealed that Justice Jain held the then chief minister of Tamil Nadu responsible for 'abetting RG murderers' and scored Prime Ministers V.P. Singh and Chandra Shekhar for 'laxity' in assessing Rajiv Gandhi's security requirements. He also pointed to 'the support of the Tamil Nadu government' and the connivance of the law enforcement authorities in 'LTTE activities of arms smuggling, abduction of Indian citizens and officials, and intimidation of law enforcement authorities', as well as in being 'directly involved in getting many LTTE cadres released from police custody'.

A consequence of the Jain Commission report was the Congress party's withdrawal of support to the I.K. Gujral government. The rest is history.

Sugar scandal

Another issue which agitated the public mind in 1994 was the steep rise in the price of sugar that occurred in May, and the barely disguised charges of corruption raised against Kalpnath Rai, the minister of state for food, and A.K. Antony, minister for civil supplies. Jaswant Singh asserted in the House that the prime minister must 'please accept responsibility and please resign. The responsibility for this is of the entire cabinet. The responsibility for this is not of one single minister'.

I was asked to answer the charges. Although I knew nothing of the issue, I boned up on the information, literally between breakfast and lunch, then made a long intervention in the Lok Sabha on the afternoon of 20 December 1994.

I first delved into the background of the crisis. In the month of May 1994, the price of refined sugar in the open market shot up from less than Rs 10 per kilo to Rs 15–17 per kilo. Although prices dropped back to almost normal the following month, to appease the Opposition a former comptroller and auditor general, Shri Gyan Prakash, had been asked to inquire into the 'administrative derelictions' that had led to the temporary, dizzy rise of prices. His findings led to fingers being pointed at the government, including the prime minister.

On 15 December 1994, the minister of state in the prime minister's office, Bhuvanesh Chaturvedi, issued a statement exonerating the prime minister of personal responsibility in the case. But this did, in a sense, indict both the minister of state for food, Kalpnath Rai, and the minister for civil supplies (in charge of the public distribution system – PDS), A.K. Antony. To clear the implicit slur on his high reputation, Antony submitted his resignation the same day. This, of course, led to a major debate in Parliament on 20 December 1994, with Jaswant Singh taking the lead from the Opposition benches. Principally because this was a hot potato, I was asked to lead the defence from the Treasury benches, with the Hon'ble Speaker giving me close to ninety minutes to make a rather technical case.

The prime minister had earlier stated that he would make up his mind 'within a week' on what further action to take in respect of Kalpnath Rai, whom Gyan Prakash had pronounced as having been 'entirely responsible' for the sugar 'crisis'. I said Jaswant Singh had placed his case cogently before the House; I would attempt to do the same.

I began my argument by stressing that Gyan Prakash had been asked 'to specifically concentrate on the issue of administrative dereliction'. He had done so. 'Therefore, on the basis of his report alone, we would not be in a position to claim mala fides had been established. 'All that a report dealing with administrative dereliction can do is to provide prima facie grounds. It cannot be said to establish mala fides.'

Gyan Prakash had pointed to nine acts of administrative dereliction, and these needed to be examined in the light of what the report itself said, instead of drawing conclusions from a casual reading of the report.

The first and second of these 'derelictions' related to the methodology adopted by the ministry of agriculture for estimating sugarcane output. I argued that the methodology itself had been the same for at least twenty years and could not have been challenged by a junior minister of food.

The Indian Sugar Mills Association (ISMA) had also been making various estimates of refined sugar production, ranging from a high estimate of 112 lakh tonnes on 7 January 1994 to a low estimate of 98 lakh tonnes in March 1994.

I stressed that between January and March, the single most important change (which Gyan Prakash noted but glossed over) consisted of the changes made by the Uttar Pradesh government (the state growing the largest amount of sugarcane) in the regulations governing the share of cane production that had to be sold by the farmer at a subsidized price to mills for refining sugar (levy sugar) and the share that could be earmarked for the cottage and village industries. This amendment drastically reduced the share of cane sold to the mills and led to a fall in the estimates and output of refined sugar.

Rai, on 9 March 1994, raised his objection to imports, which he had opposed in December 1993 too. It had to also be noted that making larger quantities of cane available for unrefined sweeteners benefited both poor producers and poor consumers. A balance had to be struck between the competing interests of sugarcane farmers, the mills producing refined sugar, the small industry producing unrefined sweeteners, and the relatively better-off consumers of refined sugar and the poor consumers of unrefined sweeteners. 'There is no dogma; there is no doctrine; there is no consensus,' I stressed. If Rai had not been punished for not striking the optimal balance, then it should be borne in mind that 'none of his predecessors had been punished for the same fault'.

In March 1994, the Cabinet Committee on Prices (CCP) did not take a decision. It was only two months later that the decision to make marginal imports on open general licence (OGL) was taken. My key point was that 'the situation changed only after (UP Chief Minister) Shri Mulayam Singh Yadav moved the goal posts'. It was only after that that Rai had recommended imports, but related decisions on what to import, how much to import and who would import could only be discussed 'when all the three members of CCP' were present.

When eventually the finance minister fell in with the decision to import a few lakh tonnes of sugar through the State Trading Corporation (STC) and the Minerals and Metals Trading Corporation (MMTC), there was no clarity as to whether these government-owned entities would or would not be given additional subsidies for the imports, given the inexorable and foreseeable commercial losses. MMTC pressed ahead, but STC awaited clarification. There was, estimated Gyan Prakash, 'a loss to STC and MMTC . . . of the order of Rs 42 crore', and the total loss incurred by consumers 'of the order of Rs 150 crore'.

While the Gyan Prakash report attributed responsibility for the loss 'entirely to Minister', I said that the 'responsibility is diffused' among different ministries and departments of the Central government and is 'inherent in our system of Centre–state relations, where a state government by one decision, taken without consulting anybody else, can totally alter the sugar market. If Shri Mulayam Singh Yadav had not been, the crisis would not have been.'

While the Opposition had attributed the rise in sugar prices entirely to lack of confidentiality in taking the decision to import, I drew attention to the Gyan Prakash Committee describing India as not only 'the biggest producer of sugar but also the world's largest consumer of sugar . . . When the world's largest consumer goes into the (international) sugar market, how can prices not rise?'

Kalpnath Rai had also been faulted for recommending a cut of 2.25 lakh tonnes in sugar releases. I pointed out that 2.25 lakh tonnes amounted only to 0.025 per cent of the total annual consumption of 120 lakh tonnes.

I concluded my speech by leaving it to the prime minister to decide whether Rai should be punished, since I trusted the prime minister and believed him to be 'an extremely experienced and wise and honest man

. . . who is capable of taking the right decision on the democratic basis of discussions'.

In the event, Kalpnath Rai was (in my view, unfairly) dropped from the council of ministers. Mukul Wasnik, the young minister of state for parliamentary affairs, referring to Rai from the front row repeatedly craning his neck round to look at me, laughingly remarked that Rai himself could not believe that 'he was as innocent of any wrongdoing', as I had argued.

Tours abroad as MP

European Parliament at Strasbourg

Early in 1991, during my first session as a newly elected MP, I was flattered at being selected in my very first year to participate as a Parliamentarian in two events abroad. The first was to represent our Parliament at a seminar on democracy in Strasbourg, seat of the European Parliament, familiar to me from my posting in the Indian mission to the European Economic Community (EEC).[7] My senior companion was none other than L.K. Advani.

We flew together to Paris by Air India first class. I retreated to a rear seat to see a Hindi film, and in my absence, Advani-ji most courteously moved into the vacant seat next to my wife, Suneet. When I returned to my seat, she reprimanded me saying, 'He is such a nice man, and you write such awful things about him.' So, I decided to be as friendly with him as I could be. And I must say he reciprocated with warmth.

I knew Advani-ji was a strict vegetarian and unfamiliar with French cuisine. So, I accompanied him to most meals and ensured his stringent dietary requirements were met by the somewhat bewildered Alsatian waitresses who could not quite comprehend why mayonnaise was a non-starter until I dolefully informed her that mayonnaise was made with eggs. She had never thought of eggs as non-vegetarian!

Over the many hours we spent together, I checked my watch and found that eight minutes was the maximum that would lapse before 'Muslims' would re-enter our conversation! Still, when he was asked to chair the session at which I was scheduled to speak, he was most appreciative of my remarks, which emphasized secularism and 'affirmative action' for our historically disadvantaged SC/ST and religious minorities as the basis of our democracy.

UN General Assembly

Within a few days of returning to India from Europe, I found myself for the second time in as many months sent abroad, this time in the Parliamentary delegation to the UN General Assembly. I was assigned to the Third Committee, dealing with human rights, with First Secretary Sujata Mehta as my minder.

There was considerable concern in the office of the permanent representative, Ambassador C.R. Gharekhan, at my insistence on drafting my own speech. My insistence was for fear that it would otherwise be an anodyne repetition of past positions, where I felt, on the basis of my experience of having lived in Pakistan for three years as India's consul-general, that we should at least hint at new beginnings. This was unacceptable to the establishment. Sujata was, therefore, under instructions to ensure the draft was shown to our permanent representative. He proceeded to censor large portions of the text I had prepared, mostly those that reflected my reservations over US policy.

I had wanted initially to make some friendly remarks about Pakistan, but in line with government policy, refrained from explicitly mentioning that country. But as the distinguished representative of Pakistan devoted his intervention almost entirely to pouring invective on India, particularly our actions in Kashmir, I was left with no alternative but to reply. At this the Pakistan delegate insisted on exercising his right of reply, which, as expected, was full to the brim with vitriol. So, in exercise of my second right of reply (which Ambassador Gharekhan decided was politic to leave to me to draft as I wished), after rebutting the specifics of Pakistan's allegations, I said:

> My country is confident that our brothers and sisters in Pakistan will, by their own efforts and endeavour, eventually secure the unimpeded enjoyment of their human rights and the exercise in full of their

> fundamental freedoms. That is why my country has consistently refrained from interfering in the internal affairs of Pakistan ... That is also why my delegation has consistently refrained from dragging into this Committee the human rights situation in Pakistan and Pakistan-occupied Kashmir. We believe that good relations between India and Pakistan will make a key contribution to the greater enjoyment of human rights in the subcontinent as a whole.

There! I had slipped in what I wanted to say about my faith in the will of the Pakistani people to work their way back to democracy and a proper human rights regime.

So, I felt justified in concluding by saying:

> In any case, Mr Chairman, the caravan of democracy, fundamental freedoms, human rights and the rule of law in India, including the Indian State of Jammu & Kashmir, moves forward. As the Persian saying has it, 'Let the dogs bark, the caravan moves on'.

At which the Pakistan representative muttered as I exited the chamber, '*Toh ab aap hamein kutte keh rahe ho.*' (So, now you are calling us dogs.) I did not answer, but felt I had failed in creating an atmosphere in which we might move towards better relations between India and Pakistan.

Earth Summit, Rio de Janeiro

In June 1992, at the start of my second year in Parliament, I found myself in Rio de Janeiro for the first Earth Summit. It was my third Parliamentary mission. I nursed a strong suspicion that this had less to do with the prime minister finding any special talent in me than because of his uncertain relationship with Sonia Gandhi and his entirely mistaken impression that I was her confidant.

I flew to London and on to Rio with Kamal Nath, the minister of state for environment. I had requested my friend, Talmiz Ahmad, serving at the high commission as counsellor, whether, during our stopover in London, he could arrange calls for me on the Chancellor of the Exchequer

(Norman Lamont), the Secretary of State for education (Ken Clarke), the Secretary of State for the environment (Michael Howard) and the shadow minister for environment of the Labour party (Bryan Gould).

Talmiz inquired how long my layover would be. About six hours, I replied. Talmiz was taken aback. 'But, sir, it will take at least six days to get all these appointments.' I answered, 'Try. They may be cabinet ministers for you. But they are Cambridge union mates for me, except for the shadow Labour minister who was my counterpart Third Secretary in Brussels.' Sure enough, I got to see them all!

On the onward journey to Rio, Kamal Nath asked whether I would draft his speech at the summit. I had been given to understand that the speech had long been prepared by his senior officials, who had even printed the text and carried with them copies for distribution to delegates. Kamal said he had intended to live with the dull and officialese-ridden version he had been served up, but would I please spice it up and put some life into it? Of course I agreed, but without realizing that jet lag would catch up as we travelled to virtually the other end of the globe. So, I had the steno sit by my bedside as I alternately slept a bit and woke to dictate the next few lines. The draft I delivered to Kamal was, in consequence, not particularly sparkling, but something of an improvement on what his officials had prepared. Of course, I incurred the wrath of the bureaucracy for this act of *lèse-majesté*.

The other memorable moment from the trip was the request registered with our SPG that Prime Minister Rao be asked to walk a little slower because the Brazilian security detail was finding it tough going to keep up with him! Remember what I had told you about the rejuvenating properties of high office?

On the eve of my departure for Rio, I had overheard my middle daughter Yamini talking to her sisters, enviously I thought, about the Reebok running shoes a classmate of hers had acquired.

Those were still the early days of the Manmohan reforms, and luxury imported goods were yet to become standard household items. So, I thought the best present I could bring her from Brazil would be a pair of Reebok running shoes. On the very morning of our arrival, I went to a mall near my hotel, and there in a shop window I saw a pair discounted to 125 cruzeiros. I did some calculations and found out that were I to be invited to three dinners during the course of my week at the Earth Summit, I would be able to save enough from my per diem allowance to buy the shoes.

Thrilled at this prospect, I waited the week out and, as I walked towards the mall once more, an awful thought struck me: what if the shoes I had seen on display had been bought up in the interim? You can imagine my relief on fetching up at the store to see the same pair still on display. Clutching my 125 cruzeiros in my sweaty palms, I went inside and succeeded in conveying in sign language that I wanted the Reeboks displayed in the shop window at the discounted price. They were happy to fetch me a brand-new pair, charged no more than the discounted price and enabled me to proudly walk out with the shoes.

On my arrival in India, I unpacked the box and with considerable self-satisfaction presented the shoes to Yamini at the dinner table. She opened the box, threw a cursory look at the pair and put them aside. I waited for my wife to take the children up to bed, then asked her why Yamini did not seem at all excited to have the shoes. 'You idiot,' my wife replied. 'You've bought her male Reeboks!' How was I to know that shoes too had gender?

The happy fallout was that the women in the family – my wife and three daughters; only the dog shared my sex – unanimously ordered me never to buy them anything but just hand over the foreign exchange I had saved when I returned from abroad, and they would buy their gifts themselves! That really saved me a lot of bother. I hate shopping.

Commonwealth Parliamentary Union meeting in Ottawa

In the autumn of 1993, during my third year in Parliament, I was included in the Parliamentary delegation to Ottawa for a routine meeting of the Commonwealth Parliamentary Union. I thought it would be a good idea to take along my wife Suneet and my eldest daughter Suranya. While the Indian Parliament gave me the right to travel first class, my purse stretched only to the economy class for my wife and daughter. On the way out, we went to Cambridge to try to get Trinity Hall to accept my daughter for a degree in law. The Master welcomed us most courteously and called in the admissions tutor. Thinking the 'old boy's tie' angle would work, I tried to stress that I was a Hall man and that Suranya was my daughter. The tutor cut my boast short, remarking, 'We took your potential into account in admitting you. We can consider your daughter only after evaluating her potential!'

While I have no doubt that she would have secured admission to the Hall, her heart was set on St John's, which we visited, and so she placed Trinity Hall as her second preference. And that effectively ditched her prospects, especially as John's (Dr Manmohan Singh's college) did not take her.

On our return from Ottawa, my wife persuaded me to sit with her in economy and let Suranya have the first-class seat. That turned out to be a stroke of genius, for Suranya found herself seated next to Justice Bhagwati, who found that she was reading mathematics at St Stephen's but intended to change her subject to jurisprudence at Oxbridge. He remarked that while he had taken his LLB in Mumbai, he had gone on to read mathematics at Cambridge and had, in fact, been a Wrangler (the title awarded to mathematicians who achieved a first-class degree).

So, when Suranya appeared for the interview for the Dr S. Radhakrishnan Scholarship to Oxford and the first question thrown at her was whether she knew the name of the famed Indian jurist who, like her, had studied both law and mathematics, she was promptly able to answer, 'Yes, of course, Justice Bhagwati!' She did so well with the other questions that she won the scholarship and went up to St Anne's, Oxford, to get a first degree in jurisprudence before going on to New York to collect her LLM.

As for the Commonwealth Parliamentary Union, I remember only the dreadful accent in which the governor-general of bilingual Canada, opening the conference, read out his obligatory paragraph in French!

A West African interlude

By the mid-nineties we were facing global concerns, particularly among the Western democracies and the Islamic countries, over our stiff response to what was increasingly labelled in India as Pakistan's 'proxy war' in the

Kashmir Valley. While it was essentially Pakistan's coveting of Kashmir that was responsible for the 'proxy war', it was Jagmohan's ham-handed management of Kashmir affairs and the destruction of the Babri Masjid that aggravated the situation and placed international attention on the issue, with the chosen field of battle being the United Nations High Commissioner for Refugees.

A number of Indian Parliamentary delegations were dispatched to different parts of the world to canvass our case. In view of my knowledge of French, I was asked to visit the Francophone countries of West Africa to explain Kashmir, and we decided on landlocked Burkina Faso (earlier known as Upper Volta), Togo and Senegal.

My companion on the mission was a veteran Congress leader from Uttar Pradesh, the ebullient and jovial Ammar Rizvi, who had an abundant treasury of well-recounted off-colour jokes. I chose Ouagadougou, the capital of Burkina Faso, as the starting point, largely because of the very strong friendship I had struck with Hamar Diallou of Burkina Faso on my first visit to the United Nations in 1971, where both of us served on the Second Committee (which deals with economic questions). Hamar later became foreign minister in one of the country's short-lived governments, went to prison and was released to become Burkina Faso's envoy in Beijing, with concurrent accreditation to many Asian countries, including India. Also, the spelling of Ouagdougou made it a suitably exotic location.

In Burkina Faso, the all-powerful president gave us a patient hearing and more or less assured us of his country's support.

However, the ethos of the mission was less over the grave political issue that had brought us to this country's doorstep than the sheer *joie de vivre* of the journey.

Thus, our ambassador to Burkina Faso, concurrently accredited to Togo, the quite incredible Diljit Singh Pannu, was not of the foreign service but was trained for a career in diplomacy during his decade as managing director of the Punjab Backward Classes Land and Finance Development Corporation! I can't think of a better training ground. He was on 'Excellence' (Ex-say-launce) terms with everyone (about the only French word he knew), from the chauffeur to the president. And he knew everybody. We could hardly get a word in edgeways about the purpose for which we had come visiting as the president and all his men were so enthusiastic about singing our ambassador's praises. As for the Ghana Air Force plane the ambassador had arranged to fly us to Accra, the Burkinabe president said, 'No need at all. We shall have an entire Air Burkina plane placed at your disposal.' We were left in no doubt that if Pannu so decreed, we could even take the plane to Amritsar!

In keeping with my Panchayati Raj preoccupations, I asked to be taken into the countryside. We visited a tiny village. Each hut had a quasi-circular protective wall. Only women and children lived in the huts. The husband came visiting occasionally and was entitled to choose each evening to spend between as many huts as he was able to maintain wives. So, with my usual levity, I asked whether someone else could not slip in to say hello to the lonely one when the husband was off squiring another wife. Not on your 1ife, said the guide, for female fidelity was so strong a code that any couple caught *in flagrante delicto* would immediately be trussed around the waist and slowly strangulated. As we took our leave, Ammar pointed to a troika of monkeys tethered to a tree. 'Look at their waists,' he whispered. They were all three trussed around the waist. Now, what do you think the monkeys were up to?

From there we visited the crocodile farm at Sabou, where we were introduced to a crocodile lounging in the sun on the edges off the marsh. Dead, I thought, until an accompanying young man swayed a chicken on a lasso in its direction. Its enormous jaws opened, and in a flash it was goodbye chicken. We were then invited to ride the back of the crocodile. Ammar, the more courageous of us two, took the ride first. Pannu, the more courteous of us two, insisted *aap pehle* (You first). I teetered on the back of the crocodile! I have never done a braver thing in my life.

An entire Air Burkina plane meant for 150 passengers flew the three of us to Lome. We ate Chinese food while Pannu negotiated our encounter with the Togo president with a dozen of the president's closest aides, all in demotic Frenjabi, which Pannu was rapidly making the lingua franca of Francophone West Africa.

The task was made even easier in Lome, the capital of Togo, where I had been tipped off by Ambassador Daljit Singh Pannu that the principal opponent of the president had, in exile, married (or was living with) a lady of Pakistani origin. The president was initially surprised to learn that Pakistan was formed by its secession from India on religious grounds. I hinted at similar trends being in evidence in the northern part of his country, where Muslims were predominant compared with the rest of the country, which was largely Christian. The president seized on this to say that being the case Togo would, of course, support the Indian position. I came away with a feeling of 'Mission Accomplished'!

We headed out to Dakar. The Senegalese must be the most beautiful people in the world. The Semetic and Negro races meet here on the southern fringe of the Sahara. It makes for an irresistible combination. The men and women both are a joy to behold. Tall. Shoulders thrown back. The pride of excellence in their eyes, their smiles a dazzling white. I spent the afternoon at a fish market on the beachfront; the fish was hauled in by the men and sold, in a perfect example of perfect competition, by the women.

We went out to Gorée island. On the way out I saw a group of young and very attractive Senegalese girls literally gheraoing poor Ammar Rizvi. He was enjoying the attention of the *belles du jour* but was not able to decipher a word of their French. He appealed to me to help him out. I asked the girls what they were trying to say to him. Relieved that there was someone French speaking in the party, they clamoured, 'Amitabh Bachchan, Amitabh Bachchan.' All of them turned out to be fans of Hindi films. I asked them why. Because, they replied, our heroes respected women. And their men? I asked in return. They spat out their contempt!

The first white man to set foot on Gorée island was a Portuguese in 1444. The first slave auction was held on the island in 1536. The island was the closest landfall point on the African Atlantic coast to the newly discovered Americas. So, for 312 years thereafter, till the abolition of slavery in the French colonies in 1848, first the Portuguese, then the Dutch, then the British four times, and the French five times over, used the isle as the staging post for the vilest trade known to human history. All of Africa was raided for its human treasure. At least 20 million – some estimates put the figure at nearer 40 million – of the most able-bodied men and women were trapped like animals and brought in chains to Gorée, to be shipped out to the Americas. Six million of them – the same figure as the number that perished in Hitler's gas chambers – died in the ships' holds, of hunger, asphyxiation, disease or just cruelty. I think of all the foolish, chattering characters at the Roosevelt House cocktail parties – the garment exporters and contractors who 'ooh!' and 'aah!' over the American miracle but have never heard of Gorée

We were escorted around the House of Slaves by Jo Ndiaye, the conservator, who put his soul into a straightforward, if spine-chilling, narration of what men have done to men. We were shown the weighing room where the captured were put on the scales. Those falling below 60 kg were moved to a special room and fattened – 'like geese', said Jo Ndiaye bitterly. We were shown the hall in which hundreds of pre-adolescent children, yanked from their mothers, were chained to each other and thrown on the ground to sleep or die. We were shown the chambers for pubescent girls who were told that if they gave birth to 'mulatto' children they might be freed. 'The way to liberty lay through their wombs,' remarked Jo. We were then led to the Gateway of No Return, the tiny door through which the slaves were pushed aboard the slave ships – to Brazil, if the slave master were Portuguese; to Cuba, if he were a Spaniard; to one of the Guyanas, if he were Dutch or French; and to the United States of America, if he were British. No one could flee the island as it was surrounded by the heaving sea. And the sea was full of sharks. Why sharks? Because the slave masters ensured that a regular supply of the dead and the dying were cast to the waves as they were an economic burden too offensive for the market to bear. Unbelievably, but true, the slave masters lived just one floor above, a mere fifteen steps up (I counted) this boundless human misery. A farewell sign hangs on the conservator's wall – 'Lord, give my people who have suffered so much the strength to rise above their suffering.' I think the Lord has listened, for some descendants of those African slaves have acquired some dignity, some position in contemporary America.

Worse was the condition of the Native Americans who welcomed the Pilgrim Fathers with turkey (hence the turkey feast after the Thanksgiving service) and suffered themselves to be murdered by the million in the worst genocide known in human history. Was it better to be shipped out a slave or slaughtered at the other end without being enslaved?

Our main mission in Senegal, a leading member of the Organization of Islamic Countries, was to neutralize a negative vote on Jammu and Kashmir, or at least secure an abstention. The going was a little more difficult in Dakar than in Ouagadougou and Lome, but in the end, we apparently succeeded, as we were able to counter many of the misconceptions of the Senegalese foreign office.

I returned a quarter way round the world by Ethiopian Airways. It was so much more adventurous to fly over Bamako, Timbuctoo, Niamey and Ndjamena to reach Addis Ababa en route Bombay than to fly via Europe. Ethiopian Airlines turned out to be a dream experience. I was coddled like a baby on a birthday outing, leaving me unsure about the Senegalese being the most beautiful people in the world. Perhaps it is the Ethiopians who win by a whisker.

Union of South Africa

About a year after my visit to Burkina Faso, I found myself in South Africa, newly liberated from the horrors of Apartheid. I had been sent by the Hon'ble Speaker in response to an invitation from the South African Parliamentary Committee, which was looking into possible provisions for foreign affairs to be drafted into their upcoming Constitution. I was accompanied by an MP each from Tanzania and Chile. Our meeting took place in Stellenbosch, under the aegis of the University of West Cape. The irony of the choice of venue was that Stellenbosch University and the Dutch Reformed Church pastors there were the leading ideologues of Apartheid.

I said our Constitution made no specific provision for the conduct of foreign policy and, therefore, they were perhaps wrong in asking for an Indian view on what to include on foreign policy in their Constitution. As to their deliberations on personnel changes in their foreign office, I said that while I realized that under the Apartheid regime Africans were deliberately excluded from the diplomatic service, the Indian example of what to do with Indians who had served the British colonial regime might hold some lessons for them. Nehru had let the colonial era civil servants, including the Indian Civil Service work for independent India – despite having earlier labelled the ICS as neither Indian nor civil nor a service! Experience had vindicated that decision. South Africa might wish to do the same while rectifying the balance between white and black South Africans in their foreign office and diplomatic missions abroad. This, indeed, is what Nelson Mandela did – but I doubt that my remarks had any influence on Madiba's resolve!

RGF Conclave on Nuclear Disarmament

Based on Rajiv Gandhi's 1988 Action Plan presented to the United Nations, the Rajiv Gandhi Foundation (RGF) convened a national and international conclave on universal nuclear disarmament in May 1993. I was tasked by the chairperson, Sonia Gandhi, to contact the distinguished international personalities, who were to be invited both by written communication and personal visits to Sri Lanka and Pakistan. In consequence, the conclave was attended by prominent international personalities, including President Jayawardene of Sri Lanka, General Obasanjo, former and future president of Nigeria, the foreign minister of Vietnam and the future foreign minister of Iraq, Adnan Pachachi, then in exile in Abu Dhabi. Benazir Bhutto also accepted the invitation, which I personally carried to her, but was obliged by domestic political developments in Pakistan to drop out at the last minute. There were also leading academics such as Professor Richard Falk of Princeton University who agreed to attend. As the convenor of the conclave, it fell to me to draft and read out the declaration adopted at the end of the meeting. My handling of the consensus was, gratifyingly for me, much praised.

The groundwork was thus laid for an update of the Action Plan, which I undertook with the help of two bright academics at Jawaharlal Nehru University (JNU), Kanti Bajpai and Amitabh Mattoo. But after the Vajpayee government exploded our nuclear weapon, the hawks held that our stand on the issue had to be moderated to take into account our being the new member of the cosy club of nuclear weapons powers. I held that whether we were or not members of the club of evil, the global threat from the use, or threat of use, of nuclear weapons remained as perceived and eloquently argued by Rajiv Gandhi at the UN in 1988. All we needed to do was to update Rajiv Gandhi's Action Plan to take note of the developments since that time. That task was devolved to the two JNU experts and me. I was much relieved when Sonia Gandhi carried the updated Action Plan to the UN Secretary General. I was further relieved that key elements of the updated Action Plan were incorporated in a Working Paper that Foreign Minister Pranab Mukherjee presented at the UN General Assembly in 2006.

While the immediate impact of the Rajiv initiative and the subsequent steps taken by Sonia Gandhi and Pranab Mukherjee were derisory, we have had the satisfaction of seeing the UN General Assembly adopting the Treaty on the Prohibition of Nuclear Weapons (TPNW), which in some respects parallels the perceptions of the original 1988 Rajiv Gandhi Action Plan.[8] Tragically, India after the Bomb is no longer championing universal nuclear disarmament.

I also became a member and then co-president of an international NGO called Parliamentarians for Nuclear Non-Proliferation and Disarmament (PNND). Every time I have attended PNND meetings, as I have for the past twenty years, I reinvoke what I regard as the most important initiative ever to be taken by a head of state or government to save humankind from self-destructing – the Rajiv Gandhi Action Plan. In the UN's nearly seventy-five years of existence, the only practical detailed UN plan for ridding the planet of these dreadful weapons has been Rajiv Gandhi's Action Plan for a Nuclear-Weapons-Free and Nonviolent World Order. I regard my failure to effectively carry forward those ideas even within our own government (2004–14) as one of the most disturbing shortcomings of my political life.

My concerns have grown since the threat of nuclear war has been sounded in the ongoing Russo-Ukraine war. The doomsday clock moves inexorably to M-minute. But nuclear powers (including our own) cling to their nuclear weapons as the ultimate guarantee of their security, ignoring what people from Mahatma Gandhi to Rajiv Gandhi have said about nuclear weapons being the ultimate instrument that will ensure the wiping out of every trace of humankind and life itself from Planet Earth.

Seminars to mark Rajiv Gandhi's 50th birth anniversary

In 1994, the year of Rajiv Gandhi's fiftieth birth anniversary, I organized a series of seminars at the Rajiv Gandhi Foundation (RGF) on his premiership. The proceedings were then published in 1997 by United Booksellers, Publishers and Distributors (UBSPD) in three volumes (relating to politics, economics, foreign policy), and supplemented by a fourth and last volume that looked at the future of the former PM's legacy.

The four volumes were generically titled *Rajiv Gandhi's India.* They comprised the oral and written contributions at the seminars by a star-spangled cast of almost every political personality and civil servant who had been associated with the late prime minister. Their oral contributions were all recorded and carefully transcribed. Ashok Chopra, the very capable editor who handled the publication, and I spent hours over several days and months going through the transcripts and readying them for publication. The four volumes, for which I was the 'General Editor', represent, in my view, the fullest, most detailed account by participants and eyewitnesses of those seven years from 1984 to 1991, from Rajiv's being sworn in as the prime minister on the very evening of his mother's assassination to his own assassination at the hands of a human bomb at Sriperumbudur. I have extensively quoted from the seminar proceedings in the companion volume to my memoirs, *The Rajiv I Knew – and Why He was India's Most Misunderstood Prime Minister* (Juggernaut, 2023).

There were, of course, other matters that preoccupied politics the next three years till the general elections of 1996. In the next few paragraphs, I deal briefly with the more significant of these.

Rajiv Gandhi Foundation

Outside Parliament, I was a participant in a discussion chaired by Sonia Gandhi to consider an appropriate memorial to Rajiv. The obvious choice was Jawahar Bhavan, conceived in Indira Gandhi's time and brought to fruition when Rajiv Gandhi moved to the Opposition. It was decided to rename the tentatively named 'Jawaharlal Nehru Foundation' as the 'Rajiv Gandhi Foundation', and it was further decided to house the foundation itself in Jawahar Bhavan.

There was some objection to my parallel suggestion that the proposed but as-yet-not-functional 'Jawaharlal Nehru Institute of Contemporary Studies' be renamed 'Rajiv Gandhi Institute of Contemporary Studies' (RGICS). Rajiv had desired that the institute work as the Congress party's think tank, patterned on the UK think tanks attached to Transport House (Labour) and the Bow Group (Conservative), but more pertinently the German Stiftungs, such as the Friedrich Ebert Stiftung, attached to the major German political parties.

Eventually, I prevailed as far as the name was concerned, but as I was not included in the foundation's executive committee (although I was named a trustee), I could not further ensure that the work of the RGICS followed the pattern intended by Rajiv. The RGICS has, in the last thirty years, functioned as something of a hybrid – part party think tank, part general discussion forum. My assessment is that the RGICS has not made the national or international impact that one had hoped for.

The Congress splits

Following the disaster at Ayodhya, tension within the Congress reached breaking point in early 1993. Several party stalwarts, led by Narain Dutt Tewari, Arjun Singh, Sheila Dikshit and K. Natwar Singh, split to form the Congress (Tiwari). This was so evidently designed to weaken the party by splitting it than to strengthen it by opposing PVNR that I took to lashing out at the new party in my *Sunday* column and media interviews.

I wrote that Natwar was a 'purloiner of advance copies of books for unauthorized scoop reviews'. The background was that Anand Bazaar Patrika (ABP), the parent company of *Sunday* magazine, had paid a large amount to Penguin India to publish the first extracts of Sonia Gandhi's book on her late husband. However, Natwar had allegedly obtained an advance copy of the book and had published a review of it in the *Hindustan Times*. ABP threatened to sue Natwar. But after a personal talk between the ABP chairman Aveek Sarkar and Natwar, ABP decided not to pursue the legal case. Nevertheless, *Sunday* received not one but two legal notices from Natwar. The entire controversy had been reflected in the media.

I threw in a final jab: 'Throw in with the two K.N. Singhs a gangster's moll in the shape of Sheila Dikshit and Bollywood can truly claim to have come to the Congress at Surajkund (where the split had been finalized).'

This slighting sarcasm and the reference – albeit in humour – to Sheila Dikshit led not only to the matter being referred to the Press Council but also to the Congress party initiating disciplinary action against me. While Sonia Gandhi intervened from distant Almaty to have the 'show cause' notice served on me withdrawn, the case filed with the Press Council was pressed to conclusion. I sought the help of Kapil Sibal, and he did a very good job of legally preparing my defence. This turned out to be exceptionally useful, as Kapil Sibal was held up at the Supreme Court on the day that he was to appear for me at the Press Council. I was most distressed to find that he had sent in his stead a junior, who turned out to be ex-Governor Jagmohan's son. He was also inadequately briefed. So, I took over my own defence. Eventually, *Sunday* and I were 'censured' by the Press Council – the mildest punishment we could have received.

Months later, at a dance performance at the Kamani auditorium, which both of us were attending, Natwar smiled and greeted me. Thus, our friendship was reinstated. As for Sheila Dikshit, I called on her, explained the context of my remarks and recalled my long association with her and her late husband dating back to our days together at Delhi University. Subsequently, normalcy was restored between us too.

Connaught Place as Rajiv Chowk

On 20 August 1995, on the eve of Rajiv Gandhi's fifty-first birth anniversary, the home minister, at my instance, announced that Connaught Circus and Connaught Place were being renamed as Indira Chowk and Rajiv Chowk.

The row that followed almost choked me. In Parliament, an affronted Opposition walked out on two successive days and the Connaught Place traders decided to 'close shop' on 25 August to protest the renaming. The home minister took it all in his stride, quite unfazed.

There was huge criticism of the renaming across media. *India Today* headed their story, 'Pushing the Limits of Sycophancy' (15 September 1995), *Sunday* weighed in saying, 'In Rajiv's Name: Delhiites resent renaming of Connaught Place' (10–16 September 1995). What I took the most seriously was Vir Sanghvi, the editor of *Sunday*, devoting his entire column, 'Counterpoint', to bemoaning, 'Mani Goes Wrong'.

Vir argued that if he were to conduct a poll among *Sunday* readers, he suspected that a vast majority would say that 'it was a terrible mistake to rename the Delhi shopping plaza'. He went on: 'We need to examine why *everybody* reacted so violently to the renaming.' Conceding that my case for renaming the area after Indira and Rajiv Gandhi was 'fairly strong', he said, however, that 'the point is that nobody has bought it', essentially because after fifty years of independence, 'we no longer need to erase traces of our colonial past'.

I must admit Vir's reasoning was substantially right. Three decades later, Connaught Place remains Connaught Place in most people's vocabulary. But with the Rajiv Chowk metro station becoming one of the most important metro hubs in New Delhi, 'Rajiv Chowk' is now on the tongue of lakhs of daily commuters. Perhaps in the end I prevailed!

4

Life as a 'Tamil Nadu' MP

My last year in my first Parliament was rapidly coming to an end. One of my few achievements in trying to bring economic progress to my constituency had been the securing of a liquefied petroleum gas (LPG) bottling plant at Kshetribalapuram, outside Mayiladuturai. I invited Minister Salman Khurshid to inaugurate the plant. As I had made a public speech in which I had criticized 'landlordism', which the Moopanar faction (correctly) assessed as an indirect attack on their leader, they attempted to petition Salman against coming. And when he failed to listen to them, they decided to hold a demonstration. The police warned me that the demonstration may become violent and claimed that the demonstrators might throw eggs injected with acid.

I brought this threat to Salman's attention when his helicopter landed. He signalled that we should go ahead. As we neared Kshetribalapuram, both the police presence and the hostile crowd substantially increased. Our way to the venue was blocked by the surging mass. I got out of the car to clear a path for us and a police officer caught my arm to try to persuade me to return to the safety of the vehicle. I pressed forward but was greatly hampered by the police officer's restraining lock on my arm. To shake him off, I bit his hand. Doubtless this was a criminal offence, but the only way I could ensure the inauguration. Salman's car followed and we were soon at the venue where the foundation stone was unveiled, the orchestra sang with 'full-throated ease' and speeches followed.

When Salman's helicopter landed at Chennai airport, he told Moopanar, who was taking the same flight to Delhi, of the morning's events. Moopanar feigned ignorance of it!

Corruption charges against Jayalalithaa

Credible and widely believed charges about Jayalalithaa's corruption, nepotism and authoritarianism were making the rounds soon after she assumed office. These rumours had reached such a pitch by 1993 that I felt obliged to clarify in my *Sunday* column (25 April) that a 'seat adjustment' did not tantamount to an 'alliance'. Now, there appeared to be 'a dying relationship between the Congress and the AIADMK in Tamil Nadu', I wrote. I stressed that '(t)he understanding (between us) . . . was that the Congress would not share power with the AIADMK at the Centre, just as the AIADMK will not share power with the Congress in Fort St. George'.

In September 1993, the papers reported that Jayalalithaa was inviting L.K. Advani to lunch at her residence at Poes Gardens even as a BJP procession clashed with another procession to mark Milad-un-Nabi (the Prophet's birthday), because the police had not ensured separate routes for them. I wrote a witheringly sarcastic piece citing what Periyar, the atheist founder of the Dravidian movement, had to say about Lord Ram. I suggested that Jayalalithaa quote these passages to keep her lunchtime conversation with Advani flowing. She took great offence at this, stressing that Advani had not in fact had lunch with her.

There were other pinpricks too in our troubled mutual relationship, and these led to Jayalalithaa filing a defamation suit against me. Meanwhile, it was becoming abundantly clear that her popular support was plunging, but few of us guessed the full extent of her alienation from the public that later led to her losing her own constituency in the assembly elections of 1996.

Elections 1996

The AIADMK's alienation from the people led to a Congress dilemma in 1996. Do we fight the election allied to Jayalalithaa's sinking fortunes? Or do we switch sides to the DMK? Or should we go it alone?

I was all in favour of going it alone (with superstar Rajinikanth's outside support, if available) so as to not be stained with Jayalalithaa's terrible reputation, made worse by the ridiculously ostentatious wedding she had arranged for her 'adopted son'.

I was dead against going with the DMK as it was the sins of omission and commission of the DMK government which had set the stage for Rajiv Gandhi's assassination. The politics of principle must surely take precedence over the politics of expediency.

Meanwhile, the Moopanar faction broke with Narasimha Rao and threatened to join hands with the DMK if the PM insisted on renewing the Congress's previous seat adjustments with Jayalalithaa. Rao refused to concede to their demands, and as a result the TMC came into being amid riotous scenes at Sathyamurthy Bhawan, Chennai, (the Tamil Nadu Congress Committee's HQ), with not only vulgar slogans denouncing the prime minister but his effigy being burnt and some of the demonstrators urinating on his posters. I had asked Moopanar's most trusted lieutenant whether Sonia Gandhi had been consulted. He shrugged off the question, saying 'she could be informed later'. I was appalled.

My proposal that we go it alone found no traction in the party. That left us with little choice but to resort again to a 'seat adjustment' with the AIADMK. Nevertheless, I entered the contest with high levels of confidence. A pollster friend of mine had undertaken for me a gratis poll in my constituency. That poll gave me an 80 per cent approval rating. With that I could overcome the disadvantage of being allied with Jayalalithaa, I thought. At the start of the campaign, when Jayalalithaa sent her principal man in the constituency to tell me that in view of my repeated criticism of her in public, her cadres had been instructed not to actively work for me, my relief was immense. I would not have to carry the burden of her sins.

On my fifty-fifth birthday, which fell in the middle of the campaign, my pollster friend sent me his latest finding: my poll rating was only marginally above my TMC rival's. It continued to fall – and fall precipitately. When the vote was counted, I had lost by almost the same margin – 1,50,000 votes – as I had won by the previous election. Every

AIADMK and Congress candidate in all of TN had been worsted. Jayalalithaa herself had been defeated in her assembly segment, such was the public disgust at her.

Reflections on my defeat

I took my time ruminating over this setback. I concluded that I should have known I would lose as early as last January. My wife was seated next to the future PM, I.K. Gujral, at a diplomatic dinner and spoke to him of my plans to spend forty continuous days touring my constituency. Gujral told Suneet, 'Ask him not to waste his time. I've never known of an MP getting re-elected because of his work for the constituency!'

I realized I had lost principally because my voters had a far clearer understanding of the political process than I had. They recognized that this was not a municipal election. Therefore, the issue was which party they wanted to see in office in Madras and Delhi, not who their individual MP was. So, while they gave me a high vote of confidence, their vote at the polls was reserved for the party they wanted to see elected.

No one denied that I had spent an enormous amount of time and energy getting things done for the constituency. None denied either that I could be described as sincere and honest; nor that I had kept myself quite free of any caste considerations, above communal prejudices and beyond party politics.

That was not the issue, though. The point was that a vote for me was a vote for Jayalalithaa. And that the people were not willing to stomach . . . The electorate regarded both me and my opponent, P.V. Rajendran of the TMC, as nominal stand-ins for Jayalalithaa vs Karunanidhi and for Rao vs all comers. The electorate in effect had said, 'Since the issue is not you but her, sorry.'

Experienced MPs know what a callow newcomer like me did not: constituency work pays few electoral dividends. It is not constituency work but political winds that determine the outcome of an election.

If the contest is closely fought, then a candidate's personal record might give him an edge. Otherwise, it is forces far beyond the ambit of the individual candidate that determine victory and defeat for him or her.

It is what Yogendra Yadav of the Centre for the Study of Developing Societies scathingly dismisses as 'the middle-class mindset' that led me to think I could win. I thought an MP's work is about culverts and drains; the electorate said it is about the quality of government, over which the elected individual has virtually no control. Thank you, they had said, for the public lavatories, and thank you for the cremation sheds too, but we can't have you if the package deal means having Jayalalithaa too. And who can quarrel with that?

As the campaign drew to a close, I was infuriated by an interview in which Moopanar was asked whether he had informed Sonia Gandhi before breaking away from the Congress. He replied, 'Why should I? Is she in politics?'

When, therefore, I went to see Sonia Gandhi upon returning defeated to Delhi and indignantly recounted this to her, I was stunned when she replied, 'He's right. I am not in politics.' I felt as if I had stepped on a garden rake, and it had sprung up to hit me in the face!

Life after my electoral defeat

I was only fifty-five and could not just languish in defeat at what seemed the end of a Parliamentary career that had lasted only five years. While I would perhaps have to wait another five years before I got an opportunity to return to active politics, I had, in the meanwhile, to get on with life. I could not give myself the luxury of despairing, much as I found myself in the throes of a kind of panic over where to seek succour. I could not give up. Persistence alone could restore meaning to my existence, which seemed to have reached its bleakest moment. I was out of both the Foreign Service and Parliament. I had to deploy what talents I had in other directions. It was one of the most challenging times of my life.

My great worry was about how to earn a living. Sonia Gandhi very considerately offered me a fellowship at the RGF at Rs 12,000 a month. I grabbed this lifesaver with both hands.

My other great worry was about accommodation. We had already taxed my mother-in-law to the limit by moving in with her when I quit the Indian Foreign Service. Suneet and I were determined to find an alternative. While we were examining the possibilities of buying or renting a home, Kirat Singh, Suneet's cousin, came to our rescue by very generously offering to put us up – and gratis at that! He gave us a spare floor he had in his swish Greater Kailash-I house. We stayed there a year, then moved into accommodation rented from a friend of Kirat's in the more modest Jangpura Extension housing colony while Suneet set herself to building a house of our own in Sainik Farms on a 1,200 square yard plot her mother had bought her. She did an excellent job of it, creating an aesthetic delight at an affordable cost. We moved into a house of our own in 1999.

The RGF fellowship remuneration was modest, and it was only for two years. I had to augment my meagre earnings by exponentially increasing the volume of my writing. I even accepted an invitation to become – mercifully for a brief while – a food critic for one of the leading Delhi newspapers. Not only did I get a good meal for free but also earned handsome remuneration for exercising my taste buds.

I checked out with a businessman friend if he would take me on for government liaison but baulked at the thought of having to receive and see him off at the airport. He laughed uproariously at my apprehension, but I decided that my pen (or, rather, my finger on the laptop) was a more congenial source of income.

So, I gratefully accepted an invitation, very sportingly extended to me by Swapan Dasgupta, politically my ideological opposite, to write a weekly column for *The Indian Express* in addition to my weekly column for *Sunday*. I also continued, thanks to editor Vir Sanghvi and publisher Aveek Sarkar, to syndicate my column for *Sunday* to various regional-language publications. This, combined with a rash of book reviews, kept me fully occupied, even while propelling me to the ranks of India's most well-paid columnists.

I was particularly richly rewarded for the articles I wrote for *India Today* on the national assembly elections in 1997 in Pakistan after a long visit there that took me to many of my favourite haunts. The former Jama'at-e-Islami mayor of Karachi reprimanded me for standing in a losing election in India. He assured me that no politician in Pakistan would have had the '*himmat*' (courage/gall) to oppose me if I had stood for election in Karachi!

Aveek Sarkar also sponsored a very remunerative and nostalgic visit to Bangladesh for me in December 1996 for the celebrations marking the silver jubilee of that country's liberation. He also handsomely rewarded me for a series of daily snippets from the AICC meetings in Kolkata. When, therefore, Swapan Dasgupta, who had moved to *India Today*, called to offer me a weekly column in that most widely read magazine, I was most tempted to accept it. But Prabhu Chawla, with whom I had always had a prickly relationship, insisted that I had to write exclusively for them.

I hesitated, pointing out that two of my daughters were studying abroad and the third was getting ready to go. So, I could not afford to give up my income from the various media outlets publishing me. At this point, Prabhu Chawla challenged me to compute my earnings from all sources so that *India Today* could match the figure. When I mentioned the annual figure, he divided it by twelve to give me a monthly remuneration based on four weeks a month. I had to patiently point out that the calendar comprised fifty-two weeks and not forty-eight. He conceded the point, and in that instant, I became the highest-paid columnist in India, but a 'caged parrot' in a gilded cage with manoeuvrable space of no more than 900 words a week. I took the final offer but felt boxed in and ended the experiment twelve months later.

On returning to *Sunday*, my first column was headed 'Always on a Sunday' and tore into my year at *India Today*. It drew the inevitable response from Swapan Dasgupta. Fair enough.

Private television had through the nineties grown from strength to strength. They also paid their guests quite handsomely. I became a favourite, invited several times a week for confrontations with my ideological opposites. Apart from helping me retain a public presence without being in Parliament, it added to my income. In the end, I found myself far better off than I had ever been as a government officer or Parliamentarian – an entirely unexpected and unanticipated outcome during what I had feared might be a low point for me and my family.

RGF Panchayati Raj task force

The foundation had also set up a Panchayati Raj task force under the chairmanship of Debu Bandyopadhyay, retired secretary (rural development) when Rajiv-ji had been the prime minister, and kick-started the Panchayati Raj work. It was a very high-powered task force of knowledgeable and dedicated experts on the subject. I was involved with the task force from the start, but my involvement had been sporadic when I was in the Lok Sabha. It became much more intense after I joined the foundation as a fellow in mid-1996.

The task force evolved the famous 'Three Fs' – Functions, Finances, Functionaries – to set up a pattern for effective devolution of power to the panchayats. Unfortunately, no state has fully followed the formula. One major lacuna in the Constitutional amendment lay in leaving the concept of 'devolution' undefined. In the thirty years or so that followed the amendment, our states have variously interpreted 'devolution' and 'empowerment' to render the key Article – 243G – either inoperative or distorted in operation. While every state has made palpable progress in implementing the mandatory provisions of the 73rd amendment (now inscribed as Part IX of the Constitution), the performance on the recommendatory provisions has been very uneven, ranging from worst-performing Uttar Pradesh to best-performing Kerala and Karnataka.

Apart from this fundamental thrust on the methodology of devolution, the task force made a really thorough study of implementation and gave a number of suggestions, which prepared me for my future (but then unseen) role as India's first union minister of the Panchayati Raj.

There was a rather amusing interlude in this connection. After H.D. Deve Gowda had been appointed prime minister in the summer of 1996, the RGF task force called on him at the PMO to present our major recommendations. There were about a dozen of us. We assigned one recommendation to each member of our delegation. When the prime minister joined us, we found he would close his eyes and drop off to sleep even as a recommendation was being explained. When the person making the recommendation stopped speaking, Deve Gowda's eyes would open but close again as soon as the interlocutor resumed speaking. What we encountered was the standard experience of anyone attempting to explain anything to the new PM. Asked why he always dropped off to sleep during any briefing, Deve Gowda famously replied that when he closed his eyes he would be thinking of the poor! Thus, the rise and fall of the nation's GDP was rendered dependent on his sleep cycle!

I drew up a charter for Panchayati Raj to fulfil its basic goal of effective devolution through empowerment of the elected local bodies to function as 'institutions of self-government' (Article 243G). After securing approval for the draft charter, with some key amendments, from the task force, I carried the charter to over forty meetings in every state and Union Territory (barring the Sixth Schedule tribal-majority states, largely in the hill areas of the Northeast, and exempted areas such as Jammu and Kashmir and the Darjeeling Gorkha Hills Council [DGHC]). This exercise, spread over several years, earned high praise from the Congress president, who congratulated me in a much-cherished letter. She wrote:

> Dear Mani,
>
> I have gone through your report of 5.8.2003 on the Panchayati Raj Conventions which you gave to me some time back. First, I would like to congratulate you for the successful outcome of the series of conventions. I am aware of the hard work you have put in and it is truly remarkable that you have personally attended all the 40 conventions in different parts of the country This reflects your genuine dedication to the cause of panchayats. The fact that these conventions have made an impact despite the various logistical and coordination difficulties you have faced is an indication of your deep study of the subject and the sustained determination you have displayed to achieve your objectives.
>
> I feel that the logical conclusion of these state-level conventions would be a National Convention of the AICC where a Charter on Panchayats could be adopted by the Party. This could be held in the next 2–3 months. I am asking Shri Ahmed Patel to work with you on this. In the meantime, I will consider placing the Action Plan before the Congress Working Committee in one of its forthcoming meetings.

With good wishes,
Yours sincerely,
Sonia Gandhi

All this led in due course to the All-India Congress Committee (AICC) adopting the charter through an annexe to its political resolution in 2004, the establishment of the AICC Rajiv Gandhi Panchayati Raj Sangathan (RGPRS) and my own elevation to the cabinet as India's first-ever union minister of Panchayati Raj (2004–09).

I am afraid the decision to annex the charter to another resolution failed to give Rajiv Gandhi's principal initiative the profile it deserved. More significantly, the failure to give the RGPRS the status of a 'frontal organization' fatally undermined the entire endeavour. Thirty years on, Rajiv's historic achievement has slipped precipitously in the party's priorities. We have more elected women in India alone (over 14 lakh or 1.4 million) than in the rest of the world put together, but by downgrading the Rajiv initiative, the party has utterly failed to reap the political dividend that would have been gained from it. The loss is as much that of the poorest and hitherto most-discriminated-against segments of our people as it is of a party floundering at the nadir of its fortunes.

I am convinced that if the priority of Panchayati Raj is restored to the heights to which Rajiv Gandhi took it, a revival of our party's fortunes is assured. The reason is not far to seek. The panchayat movement has reached as many as 2.5 lakh village agglomerations in every nook of the country (except in the exempted states/Union Territories, mostly in the Northeast and J&K, where, to a large extent, we have elected traditional bodies constituting local self-government). To these panchayat bodies at the village, intermediate and district levels, and their urban counterparts, have been elected some 32 lakh individuals, including lakhs of other backward caste, SC and ST candidates and an estimated 14–15 lakh women, a hundred thousand of whom have become sarpanches or up-sarpanches. Even at present, in our dog days, the Congress has about a fifth of the total vote. That would indicate, on a rough calculation, that 6–7 lakh panchayat members who have demonstrated that they are electable can be mobilized for the Congress cause at election time. Moreover, if past members and aspirants who ran second in elections are also tapped, the army of grassroots workers for the Congress would swell to at least 10 lakh. This far exceeds the number of 'primary' members (many of them bogus) shown on the rolls of the party.

The RGPRS could perform this task, provided the chairperson is designated as general secretary of the AICC or as a chairperson of a new frontal organization like the Youth Congress or the Mahila Congress. My plea for this has fallen on deaf ears for three long decades. If it is acted on, we can have a strong network at the grassroots. However, in the absence of any real status within the party structure for the RGPRS, this is not possible. Of course, the designation of a general secretary at its headquarters, exclusively for panchayats, would require parallel appointments of general secretaries for Panchayati Raj in the state and Union territory Pradesh Congress Committee (PCC). For fear that this might lead to major extra expenditure and possible resistance from other general secretaries, the suggestion has proved a dead letter.

To act on the suggestion requires bold party leadership that whips the organization into accepting panchayat representatives in an additional but privileged role supplementing the 'active members' and the party hierarchy in the states and Union territories. While Congress party leaders are more than willing to pay lip service to Panchayati Raj, especially because it is seen as a Rajiv Gandhi legacy, they are not willing to make panchayat members part and parcel of the party structure for fear that it might displace some at least of those who have risen through the party ranks rather than through the panchayat system. Attempts I have made to have a full deliberation on this issue within the party have not gained traction in the three decades since Panchayati Raj became an integral element of the Constitution. Had Rajiv Gandhi lived to the present day, I am certain this would have proved feasible. It has not. This is the party's biggest loss on account of his assassination.

Congress post-defeat, 1996

In September 1996, a small group of Bim Bissel's friends had been invited to her country residence on the banks of the Ganga in the vicinity of

Rishikesh. The party included Vir Sanghvi, my editor at *Sunday* magazine. On our return journey, at Haridwar railway station, Vir bought an evening newspaper in Hindi, and saying, 'I think this might interest you', thrust it into my hands.

The headline proclaimed that P.V. Narasimha Rao had been unceremoniously ousted from the post of Congress president and that the treasurer, Sitaram Kesri, had taken over. This had not only important political and personal consequences for me but also introduced the practice of Congressmen and women bending to touch the feet of the new Congress president as a gesture of traditional courtesy.

I adapted myself to these changes as best as I could but never really succeeded in gaining Kesri's confidence – although, I must quickly add, I was never denied access to him either. I also greatly appreciated his decision to organize an AICC convention in Calcutta, at which the Tirupati experiment of holding elections to the CWC was reactivated. I extensively toured the country to garner votes for myself in the elections to the CWC. I was in Shillong when the North East Congress Coordination Committee (NECCC) was meeting. They invited me to place my claim before them, and I much appreciated their decision to vote for me e*n bloc*. This was much more than I had achieved with the other Pradesh Congress Committees, including the Tamil Nadu unit, which, despite the splitting away of the TMC, was still riven with factions in the remaining rump.

Suneet joined me in Calcutta for the last leg of the campaign. In the event, I did not make the grade but scored an impressive result, getting three times more votes than at Tirupati, despite Kesri's right-hand man, Jitendra Prasada, having warned me to withdraw my nomination as a candidate or face the dire political consequence of contesting without the Congress president's approval. So, when Rajesh Pilot in particular started protesting that the elections had been rigged, I thought I too had perhaps been robbed of votes.

Jain Commission on Rajiv Gandhi's assassination

My main preoccupation through the last quarter of 1996 had been the Justice Jain Commission. I had been summoned back from Mayiladuturai by V. George at Sonia Gandhi's instance to sit in on the evidence tendered by V.P. Singh. That resulted in my attending virtually every session of the commission, assisting the Congress counsel, R.N. Mittal. Every now and then, Justice Jain would refer to my articles in *Sunday* magazine titled 'Southern Perfidy', which he had clearly studied carefully. I even took the witness stand, and my testimony, running to a hundred pages, is included in the annexes to the interim report. This somewhat alarmed Sonia Gandhi, but by then my testimony was over. Justice Jain had sarcastic remarks to make about Congressmen and ex-Congressmen fighting over personal issues in the presence of the commission, but I have no quarrel with the conclusions he reached.

In November 1997, the Jain Commission's interim report was formally tabled in Parliament, but its main indictments had long been leaked. In advance of the tabling, I sent two very detailed confidential notes to Sonia-ji, describing what I knew or understood about the report and the politicians and public personalities, including former minister P. Chidambaram, who came in for adverse comments from the commission.

I was not made privy to any reaction to my two notes. They were never acknowledged. Sonia Gandhi never called me to discuss them. Nor was I included in any formal or informal discussions within the party organs on the matter. I doubt the notes were shared with the Congress leadership. I am not even sure my notes were read, or whether they constituted the basis of such action as followed the official tabling of the interim report in November 1997.

But the Congress followed its toppling of the Deve Gowda government the previous April by threatening the fall of the I.K. Gujral government if the DMK ministers were not dropped from the council of ministers. The prime minister preferred to abort his short term of nine months rather than cave in to the Congress. Thus, elections become imminent.

5

Round-Tripping: 1998 Elections

Congress to Trinamool to Independent and Back

One miserably cold and overcast day in December 1997, I wandered into the Central Hall and seated myself next to Mamata Banerjee, who was sipping her tea in the far corner of the hall. Mamata asked me whether I planned to contest the coming elections and, if so, from where. Tamil Nadu, I replied, but the prospects were most uncertain because of him, I said, pointing to Moopanar, who was standing diagonally opposite us in the far corner of the vast Central Hall.

She startled me by abruptly asking whether I would join her in contesting from West Bengal. She said she would be given her quota of seats by the Congress, and I would make a most suitable candidate from the constituency of Barrackpore. 'But,' I protested, 'nobody in West Bengal knows me, and, in any case, I don't speak a word of Bengali.' She answered in her striking Bengali accent, 'Everybody knows you as Rajiv Gandhi's shadow. And as for your not knowing Bengali, I have chosen Barrackpore for you as it is largely Hindi-speaking since most of the workers in the jute mills are from Bihar.'

I thanked her for her suggestion and said I would consider it.

In the eighteen months that had lapsed since my electoral defeat in mid-1996, Jayalalithaa (as she now spelt her name, on astrological advice) had taken the initiative to repair bridges with me largely because I had fed her with much useful information on the Cauvery dispute, which had become a key plank of her electoral platform. Moreover, she appreciated the high praise I had heaped on her for distancing herself from the embrace of the BJP.

When Sitaram Kesri deputed the former Andhra chief minister, Vijay Bhaskar Reddy, to Chennai to negotiate the terms of an alliance with Jayalalithaa, Reddy called me to say that she was ready for an alliance provided the Congress president flew in to Chennai by the following morning to sign the document. With this information in hand, I rushed to see Kesri and was astonished to hear his response that he would prefer to tie up alliances in north India before he moved to the distant south. I was frankly appalled at such regionalism coming from the mouth of a Congress president. I walked out of Kesri's presence, infuriated.

Burning inside, I called on Sonia Gandhi at her residence. I was ushered into her presence where I unburdened myself of my indignation. I said we could not possibly allow the narrow-minded Kesri to continue as Congress president. It was imperative she take over. She gave me a most patient hearing, but at this suggestion shook her head and insisted that she was not in politics and had no desire to be. She added that while she acknowledged the errors that I was pointing out to her, she was not prepared to retreat from her resolve not to play a role in politics. As for my scathing reference to the 'Kesri Congress', she said she believed there was only one Congress, and it could not be sliced into different personality-based factions. Finding I had failed in my mission, I took my leave of her, and at the door turned around to say, 'Madam, this is the last time you are going to see me as a Congressman. I am resigning from the party tomorrow.' She did not reply.

Overnight, I thought a great deal about the next step and decided to first call on Aadhar, the brother-in-law of my Congress companion Archana Dalmia, to seek membership of the Samajwadi (Socialist) Party (SP), being an unredeemed socialist myself. He was the treasurer of the SP. When I fetched up at his house on Hanuman Road and put my request to him, Aadhar replied, 'Why do you want to be killed?' I could not understand what connection there could be between my joining the party and getting killed.

The treasurer patiently explained that he knew how independent my opinions were and how freely I expressed them, even when they ran contrary to the party line. I had emerged unscathed from all these transgressions because I was in the Congress, which took a liberal and tolerant attitude towards dissent. But the SP was different. Mulayam Singh Yadav would not countenance any deviation from his line. Of course, what he said was highly exaggerated, but it prevented me from taking a false step.

As I was determined to resign in protest from what I continued to regard as the 'Kesri Congress', I went to my office at the RGF and started calling up the news channels. They came in their hordes to interview me, and the story became the 'breaking news' of the day. V. George had to call me to plead that I should not be giving such interviews in a non-political locale like the RGF. My leaving turned out to be the proverbial falling pebble that heralds a landslide. An avalanche of exits from the Kesri Congress soon followed. Mamata Banerjee was among those who left the party.

I had a long-pending invitation to visit Kathmandu and Jeddah in quick succession to attend meetings connected with the fiftieth anniversary celebrations of India's independence. It was in Kathmandu that I learnt of Mamata Banerjee having formed the All-India Trinamool Congress (AITC, or Trinamool for short), and spent much of the night calling her from my Kathmandu hotel room.

She told me that Barrackpore was available to me for the asking and she would be happy to welcome me. I begged for a little time to think over her proposal as there was a rumour that Vazhapadi Ramamurthy, the president of the rump Congress in Tamil Nadu, was setting up his own breakaway 'Rajiv Congress'. If he would accept me, that might be a more realistic option. She, nevertheless, insisted on my attending the major rally being held to launch her party in Kolkata on 30 December. In the few days between my visit to Kathmandu and my reaching Kolkata, I visited Jeddah and Chennai to try to meet Ramamurthy and Jayalalithaa, as well as my Congress colleagues from Mayiladuturai.

On my last day in Jeddah, I had a curiously ambiguous call from Vincent George. He hinted against my doing anything precipitate but would not disclose the reason. My mind was in any case made up: no

Kesri Congress; it would be either the Rajiv Congress or the Trinamool Congress. On my arrival in Madras, I spoke to Vazhapadi. He was clear that Jayalalithaa was willing to spare him only one seat, and therefore it would be best for me to try my luck elsewhere.

So, I flew to Kolkata and called Mamata to say I was making a quick turnaround trip to Darjeeling, to see whether Subhash Ghisingh would be ready to field me from the Darjeeling Hills constituency – on the Trinamool symbol, if possible. She encouraged me to go. I took the overnight train from Sealdah to Jalpaiguri, where I was met by an old friend, Shankar Malakar, who, despite being a District Congress Committee (DCC) president, was at the railway station to meet me, guaranteeing that his unit of the Congress would certainly support me were Ghisingh to agree to my candidature.

As I had been involved with Prime Minister Rajiv Gandhi in making several trips to Darjeeling in connection with pacifying Ghisingh and reconciling him to a large measure of autonomy for the DGHC (including its name), I hoped he would look on me with favour. Although his secretary Siddharth, a very competent IAS officer of the West Bengal cadre, was courteous and understanding, Ghisingh was vague and discursive, refusing to commit himself, talking vaguely of the 1835 treaty with Nepal and the ridiculous expectation that the International Court of Justice at The Hague would give him the independence he sought. Otherwise, he kept warning me, 'There would be fire in the hills' (a phrase I pinched for my column). But it became clear he had other plans, for when his Parliamentary candidate was announced, he had picked the former home minister Buta Singh.

I returned empty-handed to Kolkata, carrying in my memory and on my camera the magnificent spectacle of dawn breaking over the Kanchenjunga range.

In and out of the Trinamool

In Kolkata, I was asked to join the contesting Trinamool MP candidates at the residence of Ajit Panja. I was a little startled to find that I had been included in the list of contesting Trinamool MPs, with my constituency being indicated as Barrackpore. I went along with this arrangement because by then I knew I had burnt all my bridges.

On the platform, I found myself unusually honoured by being designated as the last speaker before Mamata herself took the mike. This seemed to indicate that I was Number 2 in the Trinamool hierarchy. When my turn came after all other Trinamool candidates had spoken, mine was the lone voice in Hindi. I then felt the first twinge of loneliness and isolation in a regional party of provincial Bengali aspirations.

Immediately after completing my speech and taking my seat, I found the NDTV reporter frantically signalling to me. As I had already given them an interview while climbing on to the dais, I shook my head in refusal. I then found a handwritten note snaking up to me. When the note eventually reached me, I opened it and was astonished to learn that Sonia Gandhi had joined the Congress as a primary member!

The note queried whether I would comment on this breaking news. I averted my eyes and looked firmly in Mamata's direction. When she sat down a long while later, I whispered to ask whether she had heard the news about Sonia Gandhi's sudden decision to join the party. Maintaining a stoic mien, she whispered back that I should get into the jeep with her.

In the jeep, while merrily greeting the enthusiastic, milling crowds that pressed upon her vehicle, she told me of her resolve to persist with her initiative, and I replied that notwithstanding Sonia Gandhi's unexpected move, I would remain with her. That evening, I gave a telephone interview to *The Indian Express*, in which I regrettably used the word 'half-cocked' to describe Sonia's decision to join the Kesri Congress instead of replacing Kesri and restoring, as Congress president, the dignity and good name of the Indian National Congress.

After the rally, I returned to Delhi to celebrate the silver jubilee of Suneet's and my wedding on 14 January 1998, pledging to be back in Kolkata by 15 January to kick-start my electoral campaign.

In the meanwhile, there was an important task to be accomplished in Delhi – meeting Dr Manmohan Singh on behalf of Mamata Banerjee. She had confirmed Aveek Sarkar's assessment that the safest seat in all of

India for a non-communist candidate was Calcutta Northwest, where the bhadralok had their munificent nineteenth-century mansions and were dead set against Jyoti Basu's Marxists.

Mamata enthusiastically endorsed my proposal that I meet Doctor Sahib in Delhi to make to him the offer of the seat on behalf of the Trinamool Congress. I had broached this suggestion with Mamata because Dr Manmohan Singh had earlier that same month shared with me his huge dissatisfaction with the way the Congress was being run. I also had her authority to offer him the prime ministership if, as I anticipated, confusion were to overtake the country again.

My expectation was that he would probably say 'no', but there was an off chance that he might say 'yes'. But nothing prepared me for the answer I actually received. After listening to me patiently, he shook his head and almost mournfully replied, 'This country will never accept a Sikh as prime minister.' It was a reflection of the long-lasting trauma inflicted on the Sikh community by the country's armed action in the sacred premises of the Golden Temple and the Sikh pogrom in Delhi and elsewhere during the first few days of Rajiv's premiership.[1] Of course, the people of India did, only a few years later, hail Dr Manmohan Singh's premiership, which lasted through two terms for all of a decade. His being a Sikh was neither here nor there!

Nevertheless, what reverberates with me is the extent to which the pogrom of 1984 had shaken the community's belief in India and their confidence in securing a fair deal from the country, despite the many acts of recompense since taken. How much more insecure must Muslims feel then.

While in Delhi, I joined Mamata and her senior colleagues in visiting the Election Commission of India (ECI) to get the Trinamool's party symbol registered. As I emerged from the ECI, V. George rang to ask me why I had not called on Sonia Gandhi. I replied that I had not thought she would want to meet me, but if that was her desire I would certainly do so. George regretted that that was not possible. I had to first ask to meet her. Wearily, I said I was asking to meet her, and he promptly replied that she would meet me. I asked, 'When?' He said, 'Now,' and within fifteen minutes I found myself being ushered into her presence.

After saying that the expression I had used in my comments to *The Indian Express* was likely to be misunderstood, she said that now that she was in the party, would I not return?

I protested that she had joined the Kesri Congress instead of taking over the presidency and leading the Congress party back to its commitments. She reiterated her earlier remark that there was no 'Kesri Congress', only one Congress. I asked her whether Kesri believed in inner party democracy, the principal plank of Rajiv-ji's plan for reviving and rejuvenating the party. I went on to ask what Kesri knew of Panchayati Raj, the principal plank of Rajiv-ji's domestic political platform. And what did he know about universal, time-bound nuclear disarmament, the principal plank of Rajiv-ji's foreign policy?

She conceded that these were not high on Kesri's priorities but insisted that there was only one Congress, which, with great reluctance and considerable cogitation, she had decided to join as a primary member. But she quickly added that she had no political ambitions and was not aspiring to the presidency. I replied that in that case I had no option but to go along the 'road less travelled'.

Over the week or so following the rally, Mamata seemed to have grown uncomfortably close to the BJP and there was talk of seat adjustments. Even as I wrestled with my ideological concerns, my wife warned me that I would regret abandoning the convictions of a lifetime only to promote my personal political prospects. Despite my being in a confused state of mind, we had a splendid celebration of our silver jubilee, which was attended by Prime Minister I.K. Gujral, who had long known Suneet as a TV producer. Both of us greatly appreciated his gracious gesture.

I returned to Kolkata the day after to what was for me the joyous news of a rift between the BJP and Trinamool. The BJP had announced the seats they would be contesting without consulting Mamata. I, therefore, enthusiastically responded to her invitation to take the floor at the press conference that afternoon. In my press statement, I lashed out unreservedly at the BJP.

However, over the next several days I was alarmed by the BJP making up with Mamata and a seat 'adjustment', if not a full-fledged 'alliance', shaping up between her and the saffron party. What alarmed me the most were rumours of Mamata being offered the bait of a cabinet ministership in a BJP-dominated National Democratic Alliance (NDA) government in the next Parliament. I thought I had best settle this before venturing out to Barrackpore. I intercepted Mamata on the highway near Dum Dum airport and put the question straight to her. After a momentary hesitation, she confirmed that she would not be taking the Trinamool into any government which had the BJP at its head.

Although her momentary hesitation had struck me like a thunderbolt, I decided to convey her oral assurance to Sonia Gandhi, who was visiting Bhubaneswar the next day. At the Bhubaneswar Raj Bhavan, I waited for ages in George's temporary office to meet Sonia Gandhi. When, after hours, I was escorted into the drawing room of her suite, I felt as if I was in the North Pole, the coldness of my reception overcoming the heat and humidity of the drawing room.

She did not invite me to sit but stood in frozen silence as I delivered myself of my message that Mamata had asked me to assure her she would not be taking her party into any government headed by the BJP. Without a flicker of expression on her face or a single word, she signalled that I might depart. I exited knowing that there was now no exit for me from the Trinamool.

An 'independent' election

On returning to Calcutta, I found my phone ringing constantly. They were calls from my principal aide in Mayiladuturai, S. Rajakumar, and the numerous friends he had corralled, to press me to return to Mayiladuturai and contest as an independent.

Finding myself increasingly suffocated in my new party, largely because I did not know or understand the lingua franca and could not tune my mind to what I perceived as their rather narrow provincial preoccupations, I allowed myself, against my better judgement, to quit the Trinamool (within three weeks of my having joined it) to save myself the ignominy of being in the same boat as the BJP and take the risk of contesting as an independent from Mayiladuturai. Of course, Mamata had asked me to assure Sonia that she would not be having any truck with the BJP, but her momentary hesitation in giving me that answer had left a suspicion in my mind that were the BJP to offer her a ladder into government, she would clamber aboard. As matters turned out, she did ally the Trinamool with the BJP after the election and secured for herself a seat in the cabinet. By quitting the Trinamool and going back to Mayiladuturai, I had saved myself from a considerable moral dilemma.

To smoothen my re-entry to Mayiladuturai, I decided on a bit of drama. One of my more obscure Congress workers had called to say his relative had died in Saudi Arabia and the family were anxious to receive the body. According to them, the embassy in Riyadh was needlessly delaying matters. I asked the man for the number of the public call office (PCO) from which he and Rajakumar were calling and asked them both to wait there. I then dialled my old friend and ambassador in Riyadh, M. Hamid Ansari (the future Vice President of India), asked him about the dead body, which was apparently just going to be dispatched to India, and asked of him a political favour. I requested him to kindly call the PCO at which my Congress colleagues were waiting to personally give them the good news of the dispatch of the coffin. Hamid sportingly agreed to do so. I returned to my rural backwater to general amazement that I had had the ambassador, no less, personally call a humble Congress worker at a PCO!

The election campaign, which stretched from the last few days of January into the first week of March 1997, was S. Rajakumar's *tour de force*. Fielding me as an independent was his idea; organizing my high-voltage election campaign was his achievement; communicating to me his conviction that I would win was the fuel that ran the campaign.

The campaign was climaxed by a procession down the main street of Mayiladuturai with an enthusiastic, applauding crowd lining the street. I thought I had won, especially when the first round from the Mayiladuturai assembly segment showed me at the top of the heap. Then the underlying political dynamics took over.

The competition was essentially between the DMK and AIADMK, with their alliance partner trailing in their tow. Moopanar's candidate, backed by the DMK, won. I was relegated to third place, with a derisory vote count of just under 73,000. Rajakumar's experiment had failed, but it was a spectacular failure that ultimately led to my political revival. That, however, was in the future.

I returned downcast to Delhi, really worried about what the future held for me and my family. Then, totally to my surprise, I received a call from a friend in Madras to say the CWC was convening in New Delhi to discuss Kesri's ouster. The Ides of March had struck. I rushed to the AICC headquarters and was among the first to greet Sonia Gandhi as she emerged from being elected the Congress president.

I told her, 'Here I am,' fulfilling my promise to return when she took over the Congress presidency. She beamed and I left with a feeling of warmth at my homecoming (notwithstanding the glare bestowed on me by an alarmed Jairam Ramesh, who perceived me as the principal roadblock on his path to prominence). Today, however, I can say that Jairam has won: point, game, set and match, as a leading and most trusted aide of Rahul Gandhi, while I have been cast out of any meaningful role in the Congress.

There were, however, complications to my re-admission, which the new Congress president gamely took on. The first of these was that Congress rules required my expulsion since I had contested against a Congress candidate in Mayiladuturai (the man ended with 15,000 votes against my independent score of five times that figure!). There was then the question of my restoration to active membership. And, finally, the need to overcome the hurdle of the several years prescribed in the rules to secure, after reinduction, a responsible post and future selection as a Parliamentary candidate.

Sonia-ji brushed aside these objections and asked me to rewrite Jairam's first draft for her acceptance speech at the AICC in early April. She delivered my version, almost unchanged.

6

Life as a Congress Functionary

My duties as an aide to the new Congress president turned out to be rather like what they had been when I was special assistant to Rajiv Gandhi. I was delighted to resume the role, but over the next few weeks it became clear, both to the Congress president and to me, that since her style of functioning was quite different from that of her husband, there was perhaps no need for a *de facto* special assistant. One, she was a woman and there might be unnecessary cackling if I were to travel as incessantly with her as I had done with her husband. So, Ambika Soni took my place. Second, she was in those early times very nervous of the media; so the kind of preparations I had to make for Rajiv's remarks to the media were no longer required. Third, the same held for her statements from public platforms. Fourth, while there had to be a huge amount of follow-up on the petitions Rajiv received on his travels as PM, the same would no longer be so with the leader of a party in the Opposition. Fifth, unlike Rajiv, Sonia would be travelling with her personal staff. Circumstances had changed. There would be no photocopying practices from Rajiv's day. I had to be found, or find for myself, a different role and different duties.

Two incidents contributed, I think, to my being eased out of her personal office and into the organizational structure of the AICC. One was her first press conference as Congress president in the town of Bidar in north-east Karnataka.

I persuaded her, despite her great reluctance, to meet the press, arguing that this was not the national press but the local one and she could perhaps test her communication skills on the mofussil media. She agreed. When I went to see her off at the helipad, I brightly remarked that I thought her performance had been quite good. She turned at the head of the ramp and snapped, 'It wasn't – and you know it!'

Then came an invitation from the BBC to participate at Lord Curzon's stately home outside London in a discussion after the screening of Andrew Roberts' film on India after fifty years of independence. I had intended to inform the Congress president about my imminent departure for London, but after a tour of West Bengal on the eve of my departure, Sonia Gandhi suddenly fell ill at Patna airport and had to be resuscitated by a medical team. She was groggy and out of sorts on our flight back to Delhi and I did not have the opportunity to inform her of my quick trip to London and back. She was so annoyed at my sudden departure that she cancelled her appearance at the Panchayati Raj rally scheduled for Gandhi Jayanti day. I knew then that my brief stint with her as an ersatz special assistant was over.

Next month, I was made a secretary in the AICC and put in charge of the smaller Union territories, the emphasis being on the Andaman & Nicobar archipelago in the Bay of Bengal and Lakshadweep in the Arabian Sea. The press corps giggled, saying Aiyar had been made 'secretary, Kalapani'. But I found the assignment fascinating and made many friends in the distant isles as well as in the former Portuguese colonies of Daman, Diu and Nagar Haveli.

I was also made a member of the screening committee for the Delhi elections. While that brought aspiring hordes to my tiny AICC half-office, the screening committee never met except to pass a resolution at R.K. Dhawan's instance leaving it to the Congress president (that is, Dhawan and his coterie) to determine the candidates.

Fortunately, most of the candidates were drawn from Sheila Dikshit's list. The Delhi elections were won handsomely, and Sheila began her fifteen-year career as the very best chief minister the National Capital Region had ever had. Her transformation of the capital remains a standing monument to her achievements.

Soon after the Delhi elections, there were rumblings within the second, thirteen-month government of Atal Bihari Vajpayee, caused largely by Jayalalithaa first threatening to, and then withdrawing, her support to it. I rushed back from Sri Lanka where I had been on a lecture tour.

I arrived to witness on television the Opposition winning the no-confidence motion by a single vote, cast by Giridhar Gomango, who had not yet resigned his Parliament seat despite having departed months earlier for Bhubaneswar as chief minister of Orissa (now Odisha). That one decisive vote made all the difference.

After the fall of the second Vajpayee government on 17 April 1999 (thirteen months after it was preceded by thirteen days of Vaipayee-I), the president requested Vajpayee to continue as caretaker prime minister till alternative arrangements were made. Arjun Singh had been in contact with non-BJP Opposition leaders like Mulayam Singh Yadav and secured signs of their support for a possible alternative Congress-led government.

Unfortunately, the Congress staked its claim before tying up all the loose ends. Thus, on 21 April 1999, four days after the government fell, Sonia Gandhi met the President, K.R. Narayanan, and on emerging told the press, 'The Congress party is willing to form a government – on our own,' adding that she had called on the President only 'to explore the possibility of our forming the government'.

Distressingly, Arjun Singh's autobiography, *A Grain of Sand in the Hourglass of Time*, sheds little light on this incident, which almost wrecked Sonia Gandhi's political career virtually at its start. 'The Congress could not form the government because Mulayam Singh Yadav . . . backed out at the last minute,' is all he is prepared to reveal.

The press conference signalled Sonia Gandhi's emergence from behind the screen and marked a defining moment in her political life. At one level, she seemed to have mistimed her arrival, because within twenty-four hours of it Mulayam Singh Yadav withdrew his pledge and there was no rush of smaller parties to support the Congress bid for government. Indeed, within days, three prominent Congressmen – Sharad Pawar, Purno Sangma and Tariq Anwar – challenged her leadership. I hold myself responsible in some small measure for Sangma taking the position he did.

As the confusing results of the 1996 election came in, I called on him and idly suggested that he might find himself prime minister because no one else was as obvious a consensus candidate as he was. Of course, Sonia being made Congress president a few days later would have dashed whatever hopes my remarks might have kindled in him.

However that might be, on finding the party rallying behind her rather than them, the three walked out to found a rival party, the Nationalist Congress Party. This spurred Sonia Gandhi into debuting into open political warfare. She found she could not be shy and retiring as a political leader. Hesitantly at first, and then determinedly, she overcame her inhibitions, and by the time elections were declared for September–October 1999, she was in full bloom, a bloom that has never since left her, notwithstanding the stinging abuse hurled at her for her birth in another land – shameful racism, to my mind.

Blatant racism

I was personally sickened by the racism that permeated the Opposition. Having spent a large part of my life abroad, apprehending but never facing discrimination, I was aware of nothing more irrational than holding anyone's race, colour or religion against them, whether they are black, brown – or white. If we sought equality for the Indian diaspora – whether in Africa, Oceania, Southeast Asia, the US, the UK or, indeed, nearer home in Nepal, Sri Lanka and Burma – by what right could anyone object to Sonia Gandhi leading a party, and possibly becoming prime minister, on the grounds solely of her place of birth or the colour of her skin or the religion she was born into?

The worst offender I found was Amar Singh, then making his name as a principal political aide to a very gullible Mulayam Singh Yadav. Amar Singh frequently battled me in public, even claiming to have kicked me for calling him a 'racist' for his attacks on Sonia, again and again asking whether Italy or any other 'white' country in Europe or America would dream of having an Indian at its head. One of the reasons I regret Amar Singh's passing away in 2020 is that I am unable to rub his nose into the perfectly smooth transition of a person of Indian origin to the prime ministership of the UK, of a Pakistani as first minister of Scotland, of a black as first minister of Wales, a Pakistani as the mayor of London and an Indian as his deputy, not to mention a long-serving Indian as prime minister of Ireland, and another in Portugal, besides, of course, an Indo-West Indian woman as vice president of the United States. (As I write this, she stands a very good chance of becoming the first woman to be elected President of the United States, whatever her Indian-Jamaican genes and whatever her skin colour.)

While to me this was all clearly in the offing at the turn of the century, for those cast in the narrow-minded world of the Sangh Parivar (like Sushma Swaraj), the only answer they could think of to a naturalized Indian citizen becoming the prime minister was to threaten to shave the hair off their heads – comical, if it were not so disgusting.

Of course, Sonia declined to become the prime minister, but it would appear from K. Natwar Singh's eyewitness account of that unfortunate episode[1] that it was for reasons of her son's objections to her taking office, which he feared might lead to yet another assassination in the family, than any of the racist slurs being hurled at her by the defeated Opposition. She then decided to get Manmohan Singh sworn in the place she had earned at the behest of the Indian voter and the goodwill of the large number of allies she had generated.

The Congress party reacted by firmly anchoring itself to Sonia, thus legitimizing the March 1998 CWC coup that brought her in. The basic reason is that the Congress is a cosmopolitan party and has always been so. It was founded by a British civil servant, Allan Octavian Hume, and counted William Wedderburn among its early presidents. It had had two women presidents born outside the shores of the country: Annie Besant of Irish origin and Nellie Sengupta of US origin. Gandhi-ji had set the tone by declaring that while he was against English rule, he was not against any individual Englishman or woman. Indeed, he went further and expressed the hope that after India had won its independence, its British friends would stay on to participate in nation-building.

The BJP in particular (Amar Singh of the SP fell in the same category) did all it could to paint Sonia as a foreigner and therefore unfit to hold high political office in an independent India. But these racial slurs had few takers. The millennia-old Indian tradition of regarding the wife, whatever her provenance, as one of the family, prevailed, and now, a quarter of a century later, no one resorts to such remarks about a lady who has voluntarily become Indian and regards herself as a patriotic daughter of this land. Moreover, the emergence of persons of Indian origin as political leaders across the world has rather taken the sting out of the tail of Indian racial prejudice. I personally continue to hold that had Sonia taken office as PM in 2004, the Congress might have still been in office – in 2024 – and the nation spared the spectacle of Hindutva sectarianism and authoritarianism.

War in Kargil

In May 1999, the country learned that Pakistani irregulars and regular forces, with the backing of the Pakistan army under General Pervez Musharraf, had attempted to occupy the heights in Kargil with a view to cutting off the Srinagar–Leh highway.

Thus, the Vajpayee peace initiative with Pakistan of February 1999 came a cropper. His much-heralded decision to travel by the inaugural bus from Amritsar to Lahore, and his much-appreciated gesture of paying homage at the Minar-e-Pakistan, site of the 1940 'Pakistan' resolution, to demonstrate his and his party's renunciation of 'Akhand Bharat' and acceptance of Pakistan as a geographical and political reality, was broken on the mountain ridges.

It showed that I was right in holding that sudden grand gestures by heads of government may give them momentary glory but do not constitute the building blocks of a successful diplomatic initiative. In my view, Vajpayee-ji should have first sent in the sherpas before ascending the summit. They would have prepared the ground, and perhaps our advance team would have picked up signals of the extent to which the Pakistan civil and army establishments were divided on the question of the reception to be accorded to the visiting Indian PM.

Vajpayee's visit is often described as the inaugural run of the bus from Amritsar to Lahore. In actual fact, the bus only got its nose past the Pakistan border at Wagah. Vajpayee was the only Indian to step on Pakistani soil from the bus. The others got off on No Man's Land. None of the armed forces chiefs accompanied the Pakistani prime minister Nawaz Sharif to receive the Indian PM. All made the excuse that they were busy with a Chinese military delegation in Islamabad. And Musharraf was busy funding and arming mujahideen irregulars to attack India from the Kargil heights as soon as the winter thaw gave way to spring. As for the political parties, while there were muted grumblings in most of them, the Jama'at-e-Islami was loud in its protestations.

I happened to be in Islamabad with a combined delegation of the media and MPs a couple of weeks before the visit when the Indian high commissioner informed MPs in our delegation at a luncheon in their honour (to which I was not invited as I was at the time an ex-MP) that Vajpayee's bus would not be going to Lahore owing to security threats and would instead be received at the nearby border. Meanwhile, army commanders in Kashmir were receiving intelligence inputs, mainly from shepherds and other grazers, of unusual happenings at the heights (later confirmed by the K. Subrahmanyam inquiry.) Curiously, the Congress in the Opposition never demanded a debate on the report; such is the awe in which the army is held in public opinion at large. The euphoria in the Indian camp was so high that little attention was paid to these dissident noises. The visit went ahead and was a great success, until the balloon was punctured by the Kargil war that followed in May-June 1999.

Between Vajpayee's visit to Lahore and the Kargil war, his government fell. The government was asked to continue as an interim measure until the elections scheduled for the autumn. While this, of course, meant the Lok Sabha was dissolved, the Rajya Sabha, which is never dissolved, continued in existence. In connection with researching an article on whether the Rajya Sabha could be summoned to discuss Kargil, I happened to come across a small news item in the *Hindustan Times* of 27 October 1962, saying a four-member delegation of all the Jana Sangh MPs, led by thirty-six-year-old Atal Bihari Vajpayee, had called on the prime minister,

Jawaharlal Nehru, to demand a discussion in Parliament on the ongoing Chinese invasion. Nehru, democrat that he was, immediately conceded the demand and reconvened Parliament from recess, doubtless aware that in both the world wars the UK Houses of Parliament had functioned. Taking up these precedents, my article asked that the Rajya Sabha be summoned. The article had dredged up a little nugget from the past relevant to the present and involved Vajpayee himself, so when Vajpayee refused to convene the Rajya Sabha the Congress president rang me to congratulate me on having pushed the government into a corner.

7

Back to Parliament

Elections 1999

When elections were announced for September–October 1999, I returned to Mayiladuturai in August and remained there till polling in September. It was a tough fight, for although the DMK was facing the consequences of aligning with the BJP at the Centre, there was insufficient evidence of the AIADMK bouncing back. I put myself through an exhausting campaign schedule, which started at the break of dawn and ended at 10 p.m., under the new rules promulgated by the Central Election Commissioner, T.N. Seshan, that all campaigning must cease between 10 p.m. and early morning. Were it not for this, the campaigning would have continued till well past midnight!

When the campaign started, my biggest difficulty was the impossible financial demands placed on me by the AIADMK district secretary and his colleagues. The demands for money arose because the alliance party and its local leaders had to motivate their cadres to work for a candidate who was not a member of their party. In consequence, my first task as a candidate had always been to block the excessive financial demands of the local alliance leaders but keep the enthusiasm of the alliance partners going.

Therefore, I went to Chidambaram town, across the river Kollidam from my constituency, to receive Jayalalithaa, with whom, by then, I had built up an excellent rapport.

I frankly complained to her about the misbehaviour and non-cooperation of her political lieutenants in the constituency. She said that as she was setting out to campaign, I should meet her at Thiruvarur the following afternoon. Although my candidature was still to be officially announced, she asked me to stand in the candidates' jeep following her SUV, and at every campaign stop she would say, referring to me, that she could not take my name as the Congress had not formally announced it, but as they all knew who the Congress candidate would be, they should vote for me.

Next day, when I went to her hotel in Thiruvarur, she told me she had sorted out my problems with the local AIADMK. She was going to herself fund her cadres in the constituency. I need have no further concerns. But she wondered why I continued to look so anxious instead of looking relieved. I replied, 'Madam, this is an election, so naturally I am concerned.' She replied that every other candidate was starting at zero whereas I was kicking off from 72,411, the exact number of votes I had got as an independent candidate in the previous 1998 general election. That alone, she assured me, would guarantee my victory.

Earlier, she had told the Congress observer that she would be releasing to the Congress all the seats the Congress could win. 'Who do you think are these winnable candidates?' the observer had asked, to which she replied, 'Mani Shankar Aiyar.' So, the observer asked, 'And?' She riposted, 'You tell me!'

My morale thus raised and the cooperation of the AIADMK assured, Rajakumar and I returned to the battlefield bristling with self-confidence, despite my opponent being a prominent leader of the DMK-allied Pattali Makkal Katchi (PMK), a party that sought to speak in the name of the Vanniyar belt, which was alleged to stretch into my constituency. I did not believe the voters of Mayiladuturai made their choice by caste affiliations and so ended the campaign with a feeling of optimism.

On counting day, I was discouraged from going to the counting booths and spent the day in a fever of anxiety on the telephone. After the usual ups and downs, my count took the lead, and by about 4 p.m. it was clear that I was going to win. I called Suneet in Delhi, and she decided to join me for the formal ceremony where my victory would be announced and certified. Although my margin was small – a mere 45,000 votes – it was the highest for any Congress candidate in Tamil Nadu. After a three-year hiatus, I was back in Parliament.

The following day I learned that I was one of only two Congress candidates who had won from Tamil Nadu. My joy compounded at learning that Sudarsana Natchiappan had edged out the powerful TMC candidate, P. Chidambaram, in Sivaganga by a margin that was about half of mine. Nevertheless, for the leadership of the Tamil Nadu unit of the CPP, I proposed, seconded and cast the only vote for Sudarsana Natchiappan to occupy the post! For, although my margin of victory was double his, his achievement, I sincerely believed, far outshone mine.

My return to Parliament coincided almost to the day with the tenth anniversary of my voluntary retirement from the foreign service. To celebrate both events, Suneet and I threw a huge party at our new Sainik Farms home. Our home was an outstanding aesthetic achievement, largely because of Suneet. That, however, was overshadowed by my mother-in-law, for whom I had great respect and affection, slipping in the bathroom and suffering a head injury and drifting into dementia, from which she never recovered.

In my first term, I had been something of a loner, often at cross-purposes with my own government. Now, at the start of my second term, I was co-opted into the executive committee of the CPP, which convened every morning about an hour before the commencement of Parliament to discuss the issues likely to come up. That converted me from an outsider into something of an insider and gave me almost daily exposure to my senior colleagues.

The Savarkar portrait

While driving to the CPP meeting in Parliament House one memorable day, I opened an envelope I had received from the Parliament secretariat. To my horror, I found it to be an invitation to the unveiling of a portrait of V.D. Savarkar. This portrait was to be hung in the Central Hall immediately opposite the portrait of Mahatma Gandhi. Savarkar had been freed at the trial of Nathuram Godse but had been later indicted by the Kapoor Commission as a co-conspirator in the Mahatma's assassination.

I entered the conference room in a flurry of concern. I was there accosted by Natwar Singh who, waving the same invitation card in my face, asked me what I thought of it. I said there could be no question of the Congress president attending the unveiling. Natwar asked me to raise the issue as soon as the meeting convened and offered to back me up. When the moment arrived, I raised my hand and delivered myself of a short but sharp statement. Natwar backed me as promised, and then came the embarrassment of Dr Manmohan Singh and Pranab Mukherjee saying they had raised no objection when the proposal came before the relevant Parliament committee of which they were members.

Fortunately, the Congress president was firm in endorsing the view expressed by Natwar and me that there could be no question of the Congress participating in a ceremony to honour the memory of a man responsible for the martyrdom of the Mahatma. In the end, the Congress boycotted the ceremony.

Disruptions and debates

At the instance of the chief whip Priya Ranjan Dasmunsi, the CPP increasingly instructed Congress MPs to walk into the Well of the House, boycott the proceedings and demonstrate at the Gandhi statue in front of Parliament about matters on which we disagreed with the government. In my view, this disruptive behaviour was not a constructive way of voicing opposition, as it amounted to the self-goal of denying ourselves the opportunity to explain our stand.

More than once, I found myself at odds with the chief whip in the CPP executive. Unfortunately, most of my colleagues backed Priya. I fear the chickens came to roost when we took over the Treasury benches in 2004 and there followed the worst decade (until now!) in Parliamentary decorum, decency and dignity as the BJP-led Opposition outdid us in disrupting proceedings. Today, disrespect for the dignity of Parliament has become the norm rather than the exception.

Parliamentary Debates

In 2000, I sought the Congress president's permission to lead the debate on the budget. To this end, I had made assiduous preparations, including carrying the budget papers and the Economic Survey, 2000, to Hanoi, where I had been invited by the UN to present a paper on the Palestine issue on the eve of the budget session. After the presentation, I purchased a ticket to travel by train from Hanoi to Saigon (Ho Chi Minh Ville), a journey I could not even have dreamt of when I was posted in Hanoi during the war.

The journey took a little over two days, largely because I made a stopover at Hue to visit the Citadel which, in February 1968, had been the headquarters of the heroic Tet Offensive. The communists lost but shook America's youth into protesting the draft. But much of my time on that remarkable journey was taken in poring over the very dull, statistics-ridden budget papers.

Imagine my disappointment, therefore, to find on returning to Delhi that Madhavrao Scindia, in his capacity as deputy leader of the CPP, had opted to initiate the debate. However, the Congress president allowed me to lead for the Opposition in the motion-of-thanks debate that followed. I was later given even more opportunity to represent the Congress in Lok Sabha debates than in my first term.

Madhavrao Scindia and I

I also built a warm personal relationship with Madhav. One day, in a whimsical vein, he asked me what portfolio he should ask for should the Congress come to power. 'Anything,' I replied, 'except defence.' Startled, he asked why. 'Because,' I smoothly replied, 'we could not possibly entrust the nation's defences to the descendant of the family that lost the Third Battle of Panipat.' He laughed uproariously.

In 2001, he was invited to a Congress rally in Kanpur and the organizers asked me to attend. I had to decline because my second daughter, Yamini, was leaving the same evening for London. The organizers got back to say

Madhav was flying to and from Kanpur in his private jet and so I could get back to Delhi in time to see my daughter off. I rang him, found he was out of town and left a message to ask if I could fly with him to Kanpur and back. But his flight was already full with Sheila Dikshit and some mediapersons. So, Madhav sent me a message to say he regretted he did not have place to accommodate me. Sheila dropped out at the last minute, but Madhav forgot to invite me to take her place. And thus, I fortuitously escaped when the plane crashed in central UP near Farrukhabad in bad weather, killing everyone on board.

Strangely, at around the time the plane crashed, Suneet wandered into my study and extinguished a smouldering short circuit that might have set the house on fire. Saved by the bell, twice over! I was most distressed over the untimely passing away of a wonderful human being who, had he survived, might well have made it to the post of prime minister.

Truly, as I had discovered with Siddharth and the blowing up of the Kanishka aircraft in 1985, Yama calls only when he wants to, not when he is not ready to take one. I am reminded of a favourite story from Uzbekistan.[1] A feudal lord in Bukhara orders his slave to go to the bazaar to fetch him something. The slave returns quaking with fright. 'Master,' he explains, 'I went to the bazaar and saw Death beckoning me. I ran back. Please loan me your fastest horse and I will flee to Samarkand.' After seeing the slave ride off, the master goes himself to the bazaar, and seeing Death reprimands him, 'How dare you frighten my servant!', and Death, surprised, responds, 'I was not frightening your servant. I was only wondering why he was here when I have an appointment with him this evening in Samarkand!'

Ketan Parekh scam

In 2002, yet another major stock market scam surfaced, one Ketan Parekh being the main player. Given the precedent of the 1992 Harshad Mehta stock market scam, when Parliament had responded by setting up a JPC, one was set up again and I was nominated to it.

This time the boot was on the other foot. Many of the prominent Opposition members at the time of the Harshad Mehta JPC were now prominent members of the Vajpayee cabinet. In particular, Yashwant Sinha and Jaswant Singh were finance ministers in succession and then switched roles as foreign minister during the period of the JPC. S.S. Ahluwalia, then in the Congress but a vociferous critic of Manmohan, had switched sides and now represented the BJP. Kirit Somaiyya, as before, remained a knowledgeable and loquacious, if somewhat difficult-to-follow, expert member. Other holdovers from 1992 included me.

I went to the task with a vengeance – literally, for I was bent on avenging the fair name of Dr Manmohan Singh, so unfairly stained by the political misuse of the Harshad Mehta JPC.

So, I was not only more conscientious about attending sessions, but I also took to spending hours in the Secretariat servicing the JPC with the affable young Ashutosh Dikshit of the Indian Revenue Service, who had been recruited by the chairman, General Prakash Mani Tripathi, to head the Secretariat. I pored over the written version of the proceedings and looked through the vast documentation. Ashutosh ensured a delicious (if vegetarian) lunch was served.

This assiduous study – deliberately biased towards indicting those who had attacked Dr Manmohan Singh a decade earlier – enabled me to ready myself for the tedious and time-consuming process of drafting the JPC report. In the face of enormous resistance from the chairman and the BJP members, I succeeded in inserting most of the adverse findings I had chanced upon. But it was the chairman, acting at his own discretion, who would determine which passages in the report would be highlighted in bold black print, and not the JPC as a whole by consensus. This was a sad fact. Tripathi ensured that almost none of the damning references to government negligence or governance failure were highlighted. Since the media did not have the time, energy or interest to go through the report with a fine-tooth comb, the chairman was able to get away with feeding them the bits he had chosen to highlight.

My own party was surprisingly reluctant to press aggressively for a debate. While Sonia Gandhi had asked me to draft a speech of no longer than fifteen minutes to open the expected debate on the Action Taken Report (ATR) traditionally submitted along with the tabling of the main report, I learned, to my astonishment, that the Opposition led by the Congress would not, in fact, be pressing for a debate.

Bewildered, I tried to find out why we were flinching. The new deputy leader of the CPP, Shivraj Patil, who was usually the personification of grace and unfailing courtesy, suddenly started taking offence at my repeatedly asking him why the matter was not being discussed. I then ventured to raise the issue in the morning executive committee meeting of the CPP. All I succeeded in evoking was a sneer from Dr Manmohan Singh asking what the JPC had discovered that was not already public knowledge. I tried to respond by saying that the report had indicted many of his tormentors, but that fell on sceptical ears. In consequence, the debate on the report/ATR took place a ridiculous 368 days after the tabling of the report. On reflection, but without proof, I concluded that this unexpected volte face was on account of Dr Manmohan Singh not wanting to see his wounds of 1992 reopened. That is my speculative and unproven conclusion, but I can think of no other reason.

In December 2003, a full year after the tabling of the JPC report, I was afforded the opportunity to speak. In the intervening year, I wrote a number of articles underlining the JPC's very damaging findings, but my speech in the Lok Sabha summarizes all that I had to say.

As Finance Minister Jaswant Singh, was on an official visit to Moscow, his place on the Treasury benches was taken by Yashwant Sinha, who had presided over the ministry of finance for the duration of the scam and the proceedings of the JPC but had been switched to the foreign ministry while the ATR was being prepared. Both Sonia Gandhi, as leader of the Opposition, and Prime Minister Atal Bihari Vajpayee took the time out to hear my speech.

Although the time allotted to me was only twenty minutes, taking into account the further allocation of time to other speakers from my party, and conceding that what I was saying was relevant and, therefore, required a grace period, the Hon'ble Speaker eventually allowed me a full fifty-five minutes.

I began by saying the JPC report had raised three issues of high importance: 'Constitutional jurisprudence, Parliamentary propriety and public morality' – the very same issues raised in 1993 by Prime Minister Atal Bihari Vajpayee, then leader of the Opposition, in respect of the previous JPC on the Harshad Mehta scam. Citing his very words in Hindi, I asked him to remember he had then held that there prevailed a 'culture of shirking responsibility', reflected, according to him, in Finance Minister Manmohan Singh not being ready 'to confess that his assessment was wrong . . . and seek forgiveness'. Vajpayee-ji had ended his oration by demanding that 'the finance minister must take the responsibility' for the failures of his ministry and the regulators supervised by his ministry. I saw Vajpayee transfixed to hear his own words of a decade ago quoted back at him!

I then went on to point out that Finance Minister Manmohan Singh had responded to Vajpayee by gracefully accepting 'full constitutional responsibility' and offering to 'gladly accept whatever punishment this House chooses for me'.

I then asked the prime minister what moral responsibility he would now ask his minister of finance to take? I also inquired what responsibility he himself would take as the Central Bureau of Investigation (CBI) and the Department of Company Affairs, both of which had been indicted in the JPC report, fell under the PMO. I went on to contrast the reaction of the BJP's finance minister with Dr Manmohan Singh's. Instead of expressing any regret, the BJP minister had shamelessly retorted: 'Why should I resign? It is the job of the Opposition to demand my resignation. I am not going to accept.'

Referring to the relevant paragraph in the JPC report, I pointed out that the scam had started in October 1999, the very month the BJP government had assumed charge. I then went on to describe the 'nature of the scam' as involving 'a bewildering number of banks, brokers and corporates . . . exploiting every available loophole left gaping open by government regulators'; 'rampant irregularities in all major exchanges'; 'persistent irregularities in several banks' notwithstanding adverse RBI inspection reports; and the failure of the RBI 'to take follow-up action on its own reports'. Most importantly, although Ketan Parekh's name was in every financial newspaper, this government 'did nothing except allow him to continue, without examination (and) and without investigation of what he was doing'.

I went on to highlight the section of the report which said that at 'the heart of the scam are swindles that took place in two urban cooperative banks', the Madhavpura Mercantile Cooperative Bank, Ahmedabad, located in the Hon'ble Deputy Prime Minister's home state of Gujarat next to his own constituency of Gandhinagar, and the City Cooperative Bank, located in the PM's constituency of Lucknow. Thus, 'the epicentres of this scam' were in the constituencies of the PM and deputy PM of India. What then, I asked, is the prime minister's 'moral responsibility' for this scam?

I then pointed to the 'huge mismatch' between 'stagnation in the primary stock market and the boom in the secondary market', which had caused the scam, and the government's failure to take 'effective pre-emptive and corrective action to forestall or moderate the scam by the early detection of wrong-doing'. I particularly drew attention to the JPC's unanimous conclusion of 'dissonance in the approach to issues of regulation and good governance', marked by stoking the 'feel good' factor when stock markets were rising and 'sudden concern' when the markets went into a steep fall. Yet, the ATR had said the government 'cannot find any systemic weakness' and attributed the whole problem to 'basically a violation of RBI norms' and 'transactions of a fraudulent nature by a few private banks'. The JPC, on the other hand, had itemized 'the numbers of systemic weakness that should have been addressed'.

I reminded the House that on the recommendation of the previous JPC, a High-Level Coordination Committee for Capital Markets, 'normally called HLCC', had been established under the chairmanship of the governor, Reserve Bank of India, but when it came to the Ketan Parekh scam, the current JPC had found that the HLCC 'has not carried out its mandate to regularly review the position regarding financial/capital markets'. Indeed, the report went on to say, 'The Ministry of Finance, on its part, has not referred such crucial issues to the HLCC.' I concluded this point by emphasizing that the 'HLCC did not once, through the entire period of the scam from October to March 2001, hold a single meeting'. What, I asked, were these people put together for? 'Is it to eat pakoras and munch sandwiches and to drink tea? Or is it to review financial/capital markets?' I then quoted a sentence from the report: 'Had these issues been taken up by the HLCC periodically, it would have definitely helped in minimizing, if not averting altogether, the irregularities which have surfaced in the present scam.'

Turning to the external dimension of the scam, I drew attention to the finance minister of Mauritius having written to our finance minister in March 2000 offering to discuss with India 'any recent concern'. The Indian FM did not take up this offer despite everybody knowing that out of the Rs 45,000 crore of foreign institutional investment (FII) that had poured into the market, nearly one-third had come from Mauritius. That was why the JPC report had said, 'The Committee are particularly disturbed to note that notwithstanding the offer made to the FM by the Mauritius FM in March 2000 to address Indian concerns of recent origin, little or nothing was done by the Ministry or the Minister to raise these issues with Mauritius', even though the 'misuse of this route appears to have been signally responsible for market manipulation for the boom of 1999–2000, which led to the bust of 2001.' Also, owing to the failure of the ministry of finance to put in place a regulatory framework for inward flows from foreign countries, the governor of the RBI was able to claim before the JPC that in the absence of a regulatory framework the RBI could not regulate the inflows!

The next issue I raised was regarding the UTI, a big loser in the scam, involving major financial losses to a whole host of small investors who had helplessly seen their life savings vanish into thin air. I said that notwithstanding the finance minister's assertion in the Rajya Sabha that he had been 'repeatedly assured' by the UTI chairman that 'all was hunky-dory', the file submitted to the JPC showed that even the file on the subject was not started at the time of the scam but only after the JPC was constituted. All it contained was a solitary communication from the UTI chairman saying starkly that they would be able to 'maintain their dividend' on unit no US-

64 only if the Sensex went up to 4300 by June (!) and sustained the rise to an impossible 20–25 per cent higher. Instead, the entire evidence showed that the minister of finance could not have been 'repeatedly assured' by the chairman of UTI that all was well because the ministry of finance had not, as revealed, 'repeatedly asked' the UTI for an update. Therefore, as the JPC had noted, 'Even if Chairman, UTI, did, indeed, keep everybody in the dark, as FM told in the Rajya Sabha, the Committee finds that the Ministry did little to bring itself out of the darkness.'

Indeed, with regard to the crisis on the Calcutta Stock Exchange (CSE), the JPC had found that 'the Securities and Exchange Board of India (SEBI) in consultation with Ministry of Finance had permitted resumption of *badla* (short-term loans, often of no more than a day's duration, of masses of money) without arranging for curbing or regulating rampant off-market internal *badla*'. Despite the FM having claimed in Parliament that the delay in investigating and correcting this was of only 'one day', the JPC had found that 'the delay was on account of the unravelling of a conspiracy between crooked brokers colluding with dodgy bankers, dodgy promoters, dodgy broker-directors on the CSE, and a criminally culpable public sector mutual fund, UTI, which quite illegitimately, purchased Rs 25,000 crores worth of dud DSQ shares in order to bail out a defaulting broker on the CSE'. I pointedly added that 'the Minister was directly responsible to Parliament' for the actions of UTI, especially the collapse of Unit Trust number US-64.

What we wanted, I said, concluding my speech, was '*prayaschit*' – the word Vajpayee-ji had used in the House in the debate on the Harshad Mehta scam – and, as in 1994, the submission of a revised ATR.

At this point, I was obliged by the chair to terminate my speech even though I had to leave a great deal unsaid. I thought I had laid the groundwork for the CPP to carry things further forward, as the BJP had done in the Harshad Mehta scam a decade earlier. Instead, it was decided by the Congress to not push the matter further. I suspect this decision was taken to not arouse again the allegations hurled against the Congress finance minister a decade earlier. I have always regretted the party's failure to capitalize on this issue in the manner the BJP had the Harshad Mehta scam.

Time for introspection

My blooding in internal Congress party politics began when I was named by the Congress president to the committee she had constituted under A.K. Antony to examine the reasons for our setbacks in the 1999 elections. Just before we set out, she called me to say Arjun Singh had asked to join the committee.

I replied that as most of the party held him responsible for letting down the party and her personally by wrongly advising her to claim she had 272 seats and should, therefore, be invited to form the government, I felt it would be injudicious to add his name to the list. She agreed.

We travelled all over the country – to Lucknow, Calcutta, Imphal, Hyderabad and Mumbai – meeting and interviewing representatives of all the PCCs. I served as the principal draftsman, with Prithviraj Chavan helping out. We produced what I described as the 'Encyclopaedia Congressica', because it comprehensively covered the state of the Congress in every state and Union territory.

To the enthusiastic approval of the chairman A.K. Antony, like me an unredeemed socialist of the Nehru–Indira day, I added a short section arguing that it was phrasing our economic policy in the language of '*garibi hatao*' that had served us well in the past half-century, and that if we were to continue being the voice of the people, that idiom should be revived in this age of liberalization, globalization and privatization. The report argued that failure to maintain that idiom was the fundamental disconnect that had lost us three elections in a row.

It was this section that set the cat among the pigeons. After holding back for several weeks on taking our recommendations to the CWC, the Congress president asked me to summarize the report into a shorter version. I did as I was told, but as the section on the idiom and articulation of economic policy was no longer than a page or two, I retained it in toto in the summary that was circulated.

Summarizing the summary

The summary argued that 'the party is somewhat confused over where it stands in relation to the traditional preoccupations and priorities of the party. Ever since Mahatma Gandhi . . . the Congress has been the Party of the Poor. We are still a poor country, amongst the poorest in the world. While it is recognized that reforms are required to take and sustain the economy at a higher rate of growth, the stark political fact is that the programme of economic reforms has its highest appeal among the urban bourgeoisie. It has not proved a vote-catcher in the ranks of the poor.' Meanwhile, the apparent discontinuity between the 'socialistic pattern of society', which for half a century had been the hallmark of the Congress, and the post-reforms priorities of the party had confused most Congress men and women about the ideological purity of the Congress they knew and had grown up with.

The committee, the report continued, 'is convinced the Congress must remain a left-of-centre party' with a 'distinct demarcation between the Congress Party's left-wing approach to economic reforms and the BJP's right-wing approach to economic reforms'.

Hence, the summary concluded, the need to present the reforms in the idiom of focusing on the key goal of removing poverty. (Please note that the report did not argue that reforms should be abandoned but only that they needed to be presented as a continuity with the '*garibi hatao*' approach that had served us electorally so well.)

The punchline was that 'secularism alone without socialism will not be enough to combat the communalism and narrow nationalism of the BJP and its sangh parivar'. A quarter of a century later, and in the wake of ten years of Modi rule, which has seen inequality of income and wealth in India grow worse than in the hey-day of monarchy and feudalism in the 16th and 17th centuries, principally owing to the astronomic rise of government-blessed oligopolists like Ambani and Adani, I think it would be safe to claim that the first Antony-led introspection report was prophetic.

When, at long last, the CWC was convened to discuss our recommendations, my first intimation of the storm to come was the look of fury that the normally calm and collected Dr Manmohan Singh directed at me as we walked into the meeting.

Arjun Singh, doubtless relieved that he had not been indicted, opened the innings with a blistering attack on our having departed from past economic policy as the root cause of our successive defeats, adding that 'trickle-down' economics did not work.

An increasingly infuriated Manmohan Singh hit back, saying he did not believe in the 'trickle-down' theory. The Congress president, apprehensive that things were getting out of hand, temporarily terminated the discussion on economic and other policy questions and turned instead to the less controversial issues of organizational reforms.

In the chastened atmosphere, most of the organizational recommendations were accepted without amendment, including our proposal that candidates for assembly elections should be selected at least six weeks in advance and Parliamentary candidates at least six months in advance of elections. This smooth passage of our proposals was doubtless because no one had the least intention of implementing them. Two decades on, the Congress continues its damaging practice of announcing its candidates at the last minute.

We broke for lunch. The Congress president whispered her thanks for my contribution and said my presence would not be needed after lunch. Thus ended my first and only opportunity to participate in high-level discussions in party fora. I was never asked again.

As for what happened to our take on economic policy, I was told years later by Meira Kumar that Dr Manmohan Singh had disappeared soon after lunch and she was sent by Sonia Gandhi to find him. She claimed she found him wiping his tears. I cannot and do not vouch for this story as he was perhaps only wiping his face after washing it. But when I was accidentally shown the minutes years later, the record stated the CWC had reiterated the stand it had taken on economic policy at Pachmarhi the previous year. I have remained in a bit of a fog as to what this reiteration was, but it was cloaked in language that started with reiterating continuity and consistency with the basic principles of prioritizing the poor and ensuring equity for all, particularly the poor, and went on to say that when circumstances change, policy must also change, and hence lauded the reforms process. A bit of something for everyone!

I was, of course, disappointed at being excluded from further participation in the proceedings (even though I did not realize that my exclusion was to continue for decades after and persists to this day) but I was also distressed that Dr Manmohan Singh took the recommendation that we revert to the idiom of '*garibi hatao*' as a personal attack on him. Antony and I both felt that whatever the virtues of the reforms, they had much greater appeal for a small section of the better-off and had not yet persuaded the vast majority of the poor that they were ultimately for their benefit too – which was why they had not voted for the Congress.

I was not given the opportunity to explain our observations, and Antony was wise in keeping his opinions to himself while Arjun Singh thought he was scoring inner party political brownie points in targeting Manmohan. I was the fall guy. I should have realized then – but did not – that without any political base of my own, and wholly dependent as I was on the goodwill of the Gandhis, husband and wife, I could never make the grade on my own. Hence, whatever my other uses, I was politically dispensable.

I must add that after this one episode, Dr Manmohan Singh never held the matter against me, gently brushing off the issue by saying we had 'ideological differences' and actually pitching for me to have a 'heavy economic portfolio' if and when the Congress came to power.

Cancellation of CWC elections

Of the twenty CWC seats, ten were to be chosen by the Congress president and the other ten through elections in the AICC. I was extremely distressed, in fact felt betrayed, when suddenly the elections to the ten seats reserved for the AICC by elections were cancelled and all twenty seats were left to the Congress president Sonia Gandhi to decide.

This was to take the party in precisely the opposite direction to the one indicated in the Uma Shankar Dikshit report and the resolutions passed by the extended CWC in April 1990 and the AICC in July 1990 under the explicit directions of Rajiv Gandhi. The Tamil Nadu Congress was informed of this decision by the general secretary in charge of the state, Ghulam Nabi Azad. I was outraged and continued campaigning until the futility of doing so was borne in on me. This further compounded my frustration at not having been made a general secretary in the reshuffle of party posts that followed Sonia Gandhi's re-election as party president, with her winning 9,400 votes against Jitendra Prasad's pathetic 94. I rang Sonia from Goa, where we were on a family holiday, to register my feelings of having been let down.

Perhaps to compensate me for any disappointment or resentment I might harbour at these developments, I found myself elevated to the status of special invitee to the CWC. That I was never 'specially invited' to any meeting of the CWC is another matter! But it meant I could be made the Congress observer (equal in rank to a general secretary) of the hill states of the Northeast, four of which – Manipur, Meghalaya, Nagaland and Tripura – were going to the polls the following February.

After initially touring the states allotted to me, it seemed to me that Manipur and Meghalaya would easily fall to the Congress, but we had a fight on our hands in Nagaland and Tripura. I, therefore, took time out for the two states where we were challenged and entirely put off Arunachal Pradesh and Mizoram to a further day, since both these states, I assessed, had stable Congress governments and were not going to the polls.

In Nagaland, S.C. Jamir had been for decades the unchallenged Congress chief, but of late he was being taken on by a young rival, Neiphiu Rio, a talented politician-statesman with much going for him. Jamir rightly assessed that if Rio were not removed, his own continuance at the head of the party was in danger. I, on the other hand, felt that if Rio were not appeased he might defect and set himself up on his own. Jamir sought to persuade me to sack Rio, and when he found me hesitant to recommend this to the Congress president, decided to approach her directly. I was then instructed to dismiss Rio from the Congress for violating party discipline. Rio not only went on to form his own party but so thoroughly defeated Jamir at the polls that the Congress has never since recovered its erstwhile bastion. Rio remains the longest-serving chief minister of Nagaland, now allied with the BJP. We scored an own goal.

In Tripura, we were presented with an opportunity to repeat our solitary 1988 victory against the CPI(M) – which had been ruling continuously since the 1950s – provided we could negotiate an appropriate seat-sharing agreement with the tribal party, the Indigenous Nationalist Party of Twipra (INPT), whose spokesman, Bijoy Kumar Hrangkhawl, was an old friend of mine, initially having been introduced to me by Rajiv Gandhi when Hrangkhawl had lent support to the Congress in 1988 after emerging from a decade in the maquis fighting the Indian security forces. I found him articulate and reasonable, and I thought I had pulled it off. But when he reached Delhi with his titular leader, Rabindra Debbarma, the agreement I had worked out tentatively with Hrangkhawl was rudely repudiated by Debbarma, thoroughly embarrassing Sonia Gandhi when I led them to her presence. In the absence of an agreement with the INPT and given the intense factionalism that characterized the Congress in Tripura, we lost the election to Manik Sarkar and his CPI(M) and have never recovered since. Now that the CPI(M) has lost its mojo in the state, it has not been replaced by the Congress but by the BJP! I cannot think of a worse outcome.

In Manipur, Okram Ibobi Singh smoothly coasted to victory. Stupidly, I antagonized him rather than going along with his whimsical ways. He was very gracious about that, and we made up, especially after I became the union minister for the development of the North Eastern Region (DoNER) some years later. But I suspect my troubled relations with Ibobi persuaded Sonia to regard me as unfit for handling Congress leaders in the states.

Similarly, my attending a Naga Students Union meeting in Ukhrul instead of rushing before the counting to Shillong invited Sonia Gandhi's disapproval, and so our victory in Meghalaya was chalked up as having happened not because of me but in spite of me.

My territorial responsibilities in the party ended with our winning Manipur and Meghalaya but losing Nagaland and Tripura. Happily, that did not come in the way of my being appointed minister for the the

DoNER in 2006, a very fruitful and satisfactory assignment that lasted three fulfilling years.

Gujarat pogrom 2002

A major issue arose when I was in Imphal for the election. My wife telephoned to inform me of the ghastly happenings in Godhra on 27 February 2002 and the subsequent pogrom against Muslims in Ahmedabad and other cities of Gujarat. This was a turning point in our nation's history. The mood in the country was deeply emotional, and even in Parliament tempers had flared to such an extent that two speeches I had attempted to deliver in the Lok Sabha, one directed at *raksha mantri* George Fernandes in March and the other at PM Vajpayee in May 2002, were so badly interrupted by the Treasury benches that I was compelled to publish them as articles in my column for the *Telegraph.*[2]

In early 2001, before the Godhra outrage, I had been to Vadodara for a training camp as the head of the Congress party's political training department. There I met a middle-aged lady, Bismillah Begum, and her daughter Shenaz, who ended up becoming my principal guides to the tragedy of Gujarat.

Bismillah Begum was and remains a dedicated Congress worker. She lives in a modest home in a slum in the heart of Maninagar, Modi's assembly constituency in Ahmedabad. It had not been burned down only because the rioters ran out of fuel after setting on fire most of the houses on the periphery of hers.

A few weeks after the pogrom, I had an unexpected call from Shenaz from the Shah Alam camp where the internally displaced Muslims had taken refuge and among whom she and her mother were diligently working. She gave me an earful of complaints about the shortage of food and how the local Congress were doing precious little about it. I got through to Ahmed Patel, and within hours the required supplies reached the mosque. That sealed my friendship with the family.

Modi, having fooled Vajpayee into giving him a good chit, took the pulse of the people and found that far from being disapproving of the bloody pogrom that followed Godhra, they were applauding him for having taught 'the Muslims a lesson'. He, therefore, called early elections in December 2002. I put my name down for the campaign, seeking specifically to visit Godhra on the tenth anniversary of the destruction of the Babri Masjid on 6 December 1992. The Gujarat unit of the Congress requested me not to go to Godhra but confine myself to Ahmedabad.

On arrival at Ahmedabad, I was a bit surprised at the lack of the usual *bandobast* (welcome arrangements). Only a ragged collection of minor Congress workers dragooned with fading marigold garlands in their hands came to the airport to receive me. The one office assistant sent to meet me taciturnly indicated that his instructions were to take me to the hotel in which I had been booked and that Raju Parmar, a middle-ranking Congressman, would later meet me.

I took this stoically but was disappointed to learn from Raju Parmar that Godhra was not on the menu and that, in fact, it had been decided that no 'outsider' would be campaigning in the last stages of this election. (Later, I was to learn that Ghulam Nabi Azad had been turned back five times on his way to the airport for fear that a Muslim Congressman might set back the chances of the Congress edging its way past Modi in the state.)

I accepted that if the PCC thought it would be counterproductive for me to voice my strongly secular views, they were within their rights to stop me in my tracks, but as I had already reached Ahmedabad, would Raju please arrange for me to accompany any one Congress candidate on his walking election campaign?

Raju reluctantly agreed. In the meanwhile, Shenaz arrived to confirm that I was expected at lunch by her mother, Bismillah Begum, as it was the festival of Eid. When she learned that I was about to embark on a campaign tour, she asked if she might accompany me. I was happy to take her along, and off we went.

At the site, I saw the slogan-shouting Congress procession coming up to where we had stopped and got out of the car to join it. We wandered around a couple of streets before returning to where the car was parked, and I was surprised to see Shenaz looking sullen but not joining the procession. We continued the round and stopped about an hour later.

As I waited for my car, a breathless young man whispered that I should not take it amiss that 'Madam' was angry. When the car arrived with Shenaz in it, she certainly looked upset, and I asked her why she had not joined the procession. She explained, as we drove off, that she had indeed stepped out of the car by the other door as soon as I had got off, but the Congressman standing at the door had spotted that she was not wearing a 'bindi' on her forehead and had asked her if she was a Muslim. Indignantly, she had replied that she was. At that point, she was told to hold back because if the public saw a Muslim it would hurt the candidate's prospects.

Worse was to come. I learnt that a public meeting had been scheduled that evening and insisted on being taken there. At the foot of the platform, I ran into Milind Ranade of the Lal Nishan party, an old friend and activist for the scavengers' cause. I hauled him on to the platform and introduced him as a 'thoroughly secular comrade'. I was shushed and sternly ordered never to use the word 'secular' anywhere in Gujarat.

That was the beginning of our losing Gujarat without a fight, and now (April 2024, in the middle of a general election, losing almost all our sitting MLAs to the BJP). Of course, it had been put about that Rahul would be winning the 2017 election, but the results showed that that was no more than whistling in the dark and that attempting to place a 'Hindu' halo on a Congress leader's head would only backfire. We could either be secular and remain relevant to the national debate or fade away as a pale version of the saffron mob.

Meanwhile, at the delicious Eid lunch thrown for me by Begum Bismillah's family, I mentioned that I had been invited to breakfast next morning by Yatin Oza, the Congress candidate who was pitted against Modi in Maninagar. I was begged by Bismillah Begum to take her along as she had never met her candidate although she had been trudging to every house in the neighbourhood distributing pamphlets and canvassing votes for Oza.

When I fetched up next morning, her two daughters insisted on hopping into the car. On arrival, I was delighted to find that Congress candidate Oza was very pleased to welcome Bismillah Begum for he had felt the shortage of Congress workers in Maninagar and promised her the extra supplies of his pamphlets she needed to help her continue her campaign in the depths of her place of residence where Oza was taking on the Modi challenge. To me, Oza explained that if every Muslim who could vote was persuaded to come out and vote for him, then, with the help of a few secular-minded Hindus, he might be able to tip the balance in his favour.

But, breakfast over, he asked me to please arrange for the ladies to go home. When I protested that they had come to join his campaign, he replied that if ladies without bindis were seen in his entourage that would be the end of his campaign. The Congress could not be seen in the company of the Muslim minority. That, for me, was the final straw. The Congress in Gujarat had so aligned itself with Modi's view of a 'Hindu India' that given a choice between the real Hindutva and the Congress's ersatz Hindutva, the electorate would obviously vote for the real thing.[3]

This was in sharp contrast to the extraordinarily warm welcome accorded to me by the Muslims whom Shenaz took me to meet in the Muslim ghettos of the city. In a later election, the Congress PCC president of Gujarat was to reprimand me for 'taking Modi's name' in an election meeting in his home constituency of Porbandar. (The PCC president concerned, Arjun Modhwadia, has defected to the BJP even as these lines are being written.) I despair of ever getting the Gujarat Pradesh Congress back to Mahatma Gandhi's path – unless the exit of Modhwadia and his cohort signals an ideological rejuvenation.

I firmly believe that we will never replace the BJP by adopting a 'soft saffron approach' to appease the Hindu majority. We will either triumph as a secular party appealing to the patriotism of all sections of society, majority and minority, or perish along with the nation. For, as Rajiv Gandhi had said in the Lok Sabha on 3 May 1989, 'A secular India alone can survive. Perhaps, an India that is not secular does not deserve to survive.'[4]

Moopanar passes away

In August 2001, G.K. Moopanar suddenly passed away. I am glad I made up with him before this happened. After the 1999 election, at which

Moopanar's TMC was wiped out, I called on Jayalalithaa to congratulate her on her victory and to thank her for the AIADMK's contribution to mine.

She remarked that Moopanar had been to see her and had told her it had been a mistake on his part to have opposed her. I felt then that I should meet Moopanar to seek his blessings. He was somewhat wary of my calling on him and it took a while to persuade him that I had not come to gloat over his defeat.

His resistance slowly melted and disappeared when I bent to touch his feet and ask for his goodwill. It was only then that he moved to his cupboard, pulled out the traditional Tamil shawl and put it over my shoulders as a sign of welcome. I had made my peace with him.

When he died, his party died with him. Sonia Gandhi picked up the overtures from his young son, G.K. Vasan, and a ceremony was held at Madurai to merge the breakaway faction with the parent party. Alarmed at this development, Jayalalithaa hit back by holding a press conference in Delhi, at which she denounced Sonia as a 'foreigner' and said she would protest the outrage of an Italian aspiring to the premiership of India.

I turn on Jayalalithaa

That, of course, broke the AIADMK–Congress alliance. I hit back at Jayalalithaa by opening my next column in the *Telegraph* with the line:

> When Jayalalithaa became chief minister of Tamil Nadu, she presented a baby elephant to the Guruvayur temple. When I become CM of TN, I will present Jayalalithaa to the Guruvayur temple.

I am still to meet a woman who finds the line funny. My wife was, and remains, particularly disapproving of it. But I thought nothing more about it. Few Tamils know English and fewer still read the Kolkata *Telegraph*. But Jayalalithaa did, as I was soon to find out.

On 13 October 2003, Jayalalithaa was scheduled to visit Nagapattinam (the district in which Mayiladuturai then lay) to announce various development projects she had included in her recently announced budget. I thought this an opportunity to go along and present her a petition with respect to that portion of my constituency that fell in the district, particularly on the need to desilt a large waterbody that had the potential of irrigating hundreds of hectares of rich, fertile land.

I made the mistake of stopping, on my way to the meeting, at a specialty restaurant that served French cuisine in Karaikal, an enclave of the Union Territory of Pondicherry (now Puducherry) that had been under French colonial authority for centuries. So, I arrived after the function had started.

No sooner had I had taken my place on the stage, somewhat apologetically, in view of my late arrival, than one of her aides approached me and asked if I wished to speak before the chief minister. I was taken by surprise. However, I said I would be happy to do so but would limit myself to five minutes. I raised the issue of the water body and said my other requests were written in the petition, which I then presented to her.

The next speaker was the CM herself. She began by referring to my *Telegraph* article before thundering on about what a rotter I was. Furious at this onslaught, I walked up to her and said in English, 'I thought this was a development function, not a political rally. You're such a cheapskate.' And I walked out. A stunned silence followed as I descended the ramp.

Rajakumar, much more *au fait* with the politics of what he had seen, dragged me to the car and pressed the driver to move off, ignoring the media that were beginning to crowd around the car. I was wondering what the urgency was as the car drove at breakneck speed out of Nagapattinam city, then through the narrow, congested streets of the Muslim pilgrimage town of Nagore Sharif, and finally across the bridge over the creek that the CM had just inaugurated.

It marked the border with Karaikal, ruled by the Congress. Karaikal was instantly identifiable because alcohol was cheap and plentifully available in the Union Territory of Pondicherry, and there were scores of AIADMK workers in their distinctive *veshti*s lying sprawled on the ground in consequence of excessively celebrating their 'Amma's' arrival!

Here, the first of a caravan of vehicles full of incensed AIADMK goons caught up with us and parked itself diagonally across the road. Out came an irate 'rowdy', as they are labelled in Tamil, armed, luckily, with nothing more lethal than his rubber chappals. Within seconds our car was surrounded by a mob and its windows smashed to smithereens. I put up my glass, but not before the chappal-wielding goon had caught hold of my sleeve and torn a gaping hole in it.

I heard Rajakumar urging the driver to drive at full throttle, and we were soon able to put some distance between us and our assailants. Rajakumar realized that the mob would catch up with us before we reached the Tamil Nadu border, about 30 km further up, and indeed that the TN border guards might have been alerted to not let our vehicle through.

As Rajakumar had had some of his schooling in Karaikal, he was familiar with the layout of the town and so got us through the gates of the (Congress) government complex before any AIADMK man caught up with us. The complex included a guest house, which provided us refuge. The AIADMK carcade, not knowing we had diverted to the government complex, sped past us and must have been utterly bewildered to learn at the border that I had not gone through.

It was rumoured that Jayalalithaa was at the helipad, waiting to get news of her assailants having caught up with me before taking off. Had they done so in Tamil Nadu, we could not have shaken them off in the narrow lanes of Nagore Sharif; and if they had caught up with us on the bridge, it would have taken little effort to push me into the creek.

Rajakumar went up to his room and isolated himself for the next twenty-four hours calling everyone he knew, particularly the local DMK men. I, stirred but not shaken, retired to mine and called the Congress president, who was more amused than angered, and reprimanded me for being so foolish as to attend an AIADMK meeting.

Suddenly, a TV team from Sun TV, the DMK's own, burst into my room. I faithfully recounted the truth of what had happened and remarked that I had not been injured beyond the sleeve of my shirt having been torn. I was then seated before the TV cameras and, before the cameras started rolling, one of the TV team tore my sleeve even further open so that the audience could better savour my pitiful plight.

It worked because the very moderate words I used to describe what had happened were blanked out, and instead a pseudo voice-over described in the most lurid terms the 'assault' on my person. Overnight, I became a darling of Sun TV viewers!

My next visitor was the local DMK MLA, accompanied by a doctor. They too seemed disappointed that I did not have more visible injuries. So, one of my fingers – although uninjured – was dressed in Elastoplast. The MLA assured me that the DMK would escort me safely to Mayiladuturai. I suddenly found myself transformed into a favourite of the very party I had excoriated for over a decade!

The DMK certainly knew how to catch an opportunity by the forelock. They came out to welcome me, so outraged were they, or, more probably, because they were under party orders to do so. The top DMK leader of Mayiladuturai constituency, Ko. Si. Mani, no admirer of mine, was yanked out of the train at Kumbakonam station on his leader's orders and made to join me at a welcome meeting in my Mayiladuturai office (much against his will, I need hardly add).

The DMK cadres mobilized for my welcome far outnumbered the number of sympathetic Congress workers present. Next day, I found as I drove around the constituency, women coming out of their huts to greet me – so shocked were they by Sun TV's (somewhat exaggerated) version of what had happened the previous day. (Later, it struck me that this would have been par for the course in West Bengal, but inter party violence in TN is so rare that Jayalalithaa deploying her goons to inflict physical injury on me was just not acceptable.)

On arrival in Madras en route to Delhi, I found that Rajakumar had arranged for me to speak to the DMK leader, Dr Karunanidhi, generally referred to by his honorific, 'Kalaignar' (Great Artiste), who invited me to meet him at his Gopalpuram residence.

I had great difficulty following his Tamil, largely because my grasp of the language was as weak as his was strong, and partly because of his guttural voice. Rajakumar later told me the thrust of his remarks was that the Congress had thoroughly misread him; that far from having been instrumental in the assassination of Rajiv Gandhi, he had deeply regretted it; and that he remained a great admirer of Jawaharlal Nehru and Indira Gandhi, which is what had led him to coin his famous slogan,

'*Nehruvin magal varuga / Nilayana aatchi tharuga*' (Welcome to Nehru's daughter / who will give us a stable government) – far more effective as a slogan in Tamil than in English translation. We then exchanged shawls and I took my leave, little realizing that the seeds had been sown for a Congress–DMK alliance that has lasted two decades and seems set to carry on forever.

To my surprise, Kalaignar seemed to look on me as a kind of symbol of his renewed relationship with the Congress. It worked to my immense advantage, because Mayiladuturai was announced as the very first constituency to be allotted to the Congress. When asked the standard question by the Congress observer as to how many seats he would allocate to the Congress, Kalaignar gave an answer eerily similar to the one given by Jayalalithaa five years earlier, 'All the ones you can win.'

'Which are those?'

Kalaignar replied, 'Mani Shankar Aiyar.'

'And?' said the hapless observer.

'You tell me,' was the answer.

I attribute this to two basic reasons. One, my personal popularity among the people of Mayiladuturai despite my speaking only pidgin Tamil and overcoming the handicap of my Brahmin origins. Two, my unprecedented score of 72,411 votes when I stood as an independent.

The Lok Sabha was terminated by Prime Minister Vajpayee on 5 February 2004, several months before it was due to end, as he was under the hopelessly wrong impression that he was riding a wave of successes against a weak Opposition helmed by a lady of foreign origin whose public acceptance was in some doubt.

As the elections got under way, Kalaignar instructed the local leadership to ensure, on their (political) life, that I won. His son, 'Dalapati' Mu. Ka. Stalin, was present at my nomination and visited the constituency twice during the campaign. Kalaignar himself visited the constituency for a roadshow that lasted several hours, during the course of which he showered eloquent praise on me. Unsurprisingly, the margin of my victory was nearly 2,00,000.

Kalaignar

I had first very briefly met Kalaignar Karunanidhi when I was in the PMO. He had called on Prime Minister Rajiv Gandhi. One of the TN cadre officers accompanying him had put his head through the door to my office and asked if I would please come out to greet his chief minister. I was surprised but readily agreed. We met for a minute or two in the corridor. He seemed intrigued that a Tamilian should be seen so often on TV screens accompanying the PM. He was not, however, surprised to find me stumbling in my pidgin Tamil. He was familiar with Tambrahms, deracinated because the Dravidian movement, having simply migrated to brighter horizons in the north, east and west of the country, and even abroad, on finding themselves discriminated against in their homeland.[5] Extraordinarily, he had principally relied on Brahmin IAS officers, like S. Guhan and S. Narayan,[6] to dismantle the institutional framework which the Brahmin community had historically used to keep themselves in dominating (and domineering) positions in virtually every walk of life – politics, the civil service, the judiciary, the bar, engineering, medicine, other professions, academia and journalism, the fine arts and literature, corporate management and chartered accountancy; even banking and business (and in landholdings too, although it was the dominant Other Backward Castes (OBCs) like the Pillais, the Thevars and the Mukkalathoor who led the Brahmins in this sector of the colonial economy). All this, of course, in addition to soaring over all other castes in places of worship and spiritual discourse.

Having satisfied his curiosity, Karunanidhi moved on. Rajiv lit into him on the thirteen pre-election and election tours of Tamil Nadu he undertook, me in tow, mostly driving himself, in the run-up to the state assembly polls of January 1989. Notwithstanding this whirlwind campaign, the DMK thrashed the Congress, reducing it to a mere twenty-six seats in a house of nearly ten times that number. Rajiv continued his fusillade against the DMK and its leader, accusing them of blatantly supporting the LTTE and letting them have a free run of the state for sanctuary, supplies and even arms. The peak of LTTE depredations was the massacre of thirteen of their rival Sri Lankan Tamil militant cadres hiding out in Chennai and the state government's alleged role in letting the assassins escape to Jaffna in Sri Lanka.

When the Chandra Shekhar government secretly airlifted paramilitary forces into TN in December 1990 to put a stop to these excesses, it was said the state government authorities tipped off the Tigers, who simply vanished by the time the paramilitary landed. At Rajiv Gandhi's insistence, the Chandra Shekhar government moved to get President Venkataraman to dismiss the DMK government and declare President's rule in the state by the end of January 1991. Therefore, my speeches in my first electoral campaign a few months later targeted the DMK and their leader. Further, I had targeted Karunanidhi in my many articles, the most blistering of which was my four-part series in *Sunday* magazine (June 1996) titled 'Southern Perfidy'. I continued the tirade after the Jain Commission's interim report indicting the DMK was tabled in Parliament.

All this, one would have thought, would have led to Kalaignar thoroughly approving my roughing up and perhaps even murder at the hands of Jayalalithaa's 'rowdies' in October 2003. To my astonishment, Kalaignar instructed his cadres and his local leaders to demonstrate their solidarity with me – and that too at the Congress office in Mayiladuturai. Indeed, he got his top local leader, Ko.Si. Mani, to disembark from the train to Chennai, which he had already boarded, to head the welcome party when I reached Mayiladuturai. When Kalaignar received me at his Chennai home, then and later, there was no hint of any resentment or reprimand, only a dead keenness on my getting the message across to Sonia Gandhi and the Congress leadership that he was an unrelenting admirer of Pandit Nehru and Indira Gandhi. Moreover, he said, he continued to have the highest respect for the Nehru–Gandhi family. I was surprised as the Congress had made dire allegations against him, and undermined the Gujral government because of the PM refusing to dismiss DMK Central ministers after the tabling of the Jain Commission's interim report (later redacted from the final report),

I, of course, was ready to accept his protestations at face value. On further reflection, I came to the conclusion that Kalaignar found in the assault on me an opening to lay the foundation of what has turned out to be a quarter of a century's alliance with the Congress that looks all set to be permanent. Nevertheless, even after learning from his nephew, Member of Parliament Dayanidhi Maran, that I counted for nothing politically in the Congress or personally with Sonia Gandhi, he continued to be kind and gracious to me. I will remain ever grateful to him for his unfailing courtesy. I will also never forget his repeated assertion whenever he saw me that he had the highest regard for both Pandit Nehru and Indira Gandhi.

He was most intrigued when he learned I had authored a book titled *Confessions of a Secular Fundamentalist* (Penguin, 2004). A Brahmin and an atheist! He said he would release it himself if I got it translated into Tamil. Somehow, I was never able to accomplish that. He was also intrigued to find me invited as a principal speaker at a ceremony to launch a biography of A. Sattanathan, a revered figure of the DMK movement, who had headed the state's first OBC commission. He was delighted to learn of my close family ties with Sattanathan, who had formed a friendship with my mother based on their common love of Tamil literature and had, indeed, loaned her the money to embark on her aborted journey to London.

M.K. Stalin

With Kalaignar's son, 'Dalapati' (commander) Mu. Ka. Stalin, it has been more of a roller-coaster ride. Although in my early days as the union minister of Panchayati Raj, I had succeeded in securing his approval in principle for a joint tour by us to some panchayats in the state, as he was the Tamil Nadu minister of local government, I did not adequately have regard to the DMK having consistently voted against the Rajiv Gandhi-sponsored Constitutional amendments on the ground that not only was Panchayati Raj a state subject under the Constitution, but Tamil Nadu had also been amongst the first states to enact legislation and put in place a very effective system of local self-government. They saw no reason to be held accountable by an interfering Central minister. Even when P. Chidambaram warned me that the DMK state government thought I was overstepping the mark, I failed to recognize this objection in principle to associating themselves with any initiative the Central government might take. So, when there was no follow-up and no response to my letters asking for a suitable date and itinerary, I started using opportunities like weddings in my constituency, where I was seated next to Stalin, to whisper reminders of the pending tours. Although there was never a hint in person to his minding this repeated request from me, I learned from the comments he vouchsafed my principal aide that he was very annoyed at my asking him the same question again and again. I immediately refrained from making that request again, but the damage had been done. His not campaigning for me personally in the 2009 election, after having done so several times at his father's instance in 2004, was one of the principal contributory factors for my election defeat in 2009. His workers had got the underlying message that it did not much matter to the DMK whether I won or lost.

Nevertheless, I must acknowledge that he has put all that behind him, to the extent that he let it be known that he would back my candidacy from the Mayiladuturai constituency in the 2024 election and that if I felt I was too old to campaign he would back my daughter. I was denied a ticket by Rahul Gandhi, who insisted that the candidate should be anyone but me. Yet, in such grim circumstances, I was chuffed by Dalapati's ringing endorsement that had shades of his father's generosity and largeness of heart, but even more by the irony of a Brahmin – or even his daughter – being backed to create a constituency dynasty on the very banks of the Cauvery from which my father had departed nearly a century ago in despair at not being treated fairly by the very forces now led by 'Dalapati' Stalin!

The Congress returns to office

I revert to the 2004 election that I won handsomely. I had watched the counting in the room of the returning officer, less to see my votes coming in and more to look at television to watch the Congress and its allies galloping to victory. Although I had sneered at the Treasury benches on my last day in the previous Parliament, saying that we would soon be exchanging places, I just did not believe we would be able to defeat the formidable Atal Bihari Vajpayee.

But defeat him we did. I think a major reason was that the Vajpayee-led BJP had grown overconfident. That overconfidence was reflected in their 'India Shining' campaign. The fact is that India was not shining, and the electorate was looking for parties to say what they would do for them, not by resorting to self-congratulation about what a wonderful lot they were but by laying down an attractive road map for the future. The BJP failed to do so. Perhaps the Congress manifesto, in which I had a hand, scored over the BJP's.

A second factor could be that Vajpayee was more influenced by Nehru than by Savarkar. He clearly did not subscribe to the extreme religious fundamentalism of Hindutva, such as denying the nation's composite civilizational heritage. He not only did not subscribe to oppression as the only narrative of Muslim rule in India but also refused to translate the excesses of some Muslim rulers in the distant past into prejudice against Indian Muslims in the present. Moreover, he did not hold Partition against Pakistan but openly proclaimed his firm intention to cultivate good relations with our neighbour. Indeed, it was over his signature as external affairs minister in the Morarji Desai government that I was sent to Karachi as India's first-ever consul-general in December 1978. He famously said one can choose one's friends but not one's neighbours and persisted in his efforts to find a *via media* with Pakistan, notwithstanding Kargil in May 1999, notwithstanding the December 2001 attack on Parliament and notwithstanding the last-minute breakdown of talks at the Agra summit (July 2003). He achieved a major breakthrough on the sidelines of the South Asian Association for Regional Cooperation (SAARC) summit in Islamabad (January 2004) in resuming the dialogue. It was on the Islamabad declaration that Dr Manmohan Singh was to build his initiative on this front.

Vajpayee combined his outreach to Pakistan with an outreach to Kashmiris, in stabilizing New Delhi's relationship with Srinagar through dialogue with all shades of Kashmiri opinion, including the Hurriyat, as the necessary corollary to opening the dialogue with Pakistan. Indeed, he even approved of the Pakistanis bringing the Hurriyat into the loop, even allowing the visit of a Hurriyat delegation to Pakistan. He immortally said the solution to the problems in Jammu and Kashmir lay in '*insaniyat* (humanity), *Kashmiriyat* (Kashmiri traditions of mutual tolerance) and *jamhooriyat* (democracy)'. The Rashtriya Swayamsevak Sangh (RSS) wanted none of this, with one of its most articulate voices, Govindacharya, dismissing Vajpayee as a *mukhauta* (mask). My guess is that the RSS did not back Vajpayee in the 2004 election and the BJP did not have adequate cadre strength to make up for that.

I also think the BJP underestimated the drawing power of Sonia Gandhi, the president of the Indian National Congress. Where they emphasized Sonia's birth in Italy, the people of India, in keeping with ancient Indian traditions, looked on her as a daughter-in-law of our motherland and therefore entitled to be held in high regard. They scoffed at Sushma Swaraj threatening to tonsure her head of its abundant hair in protest if Sonia was to become the PM of India. Further, I believe there was widespread public approbation at Sonia demonstrating that she regarded India as her homeland by not quitting the country when her husband was cruelly assassinated. In hard political terms, by 2004 Sonia Gandhi had established her credentials as an Indian political leader, one who could not only take on the formidable Vajpayee but also succeed him. Even Amar Singh of the SP, whose racist remarks pre-election against Sonia were legion, came knocking at the doors of 10, Janpath (Sonia Gandhi's residence), only to be firmly turned away. The communists, who had ideological objections to joining hands with a bourgeois party, were charmed by Sonia, working through Comrade Harkishan Singh Surjeet, to, at a minimum, extend 'outside support' to the coalition government, if only to keep the BJP at arm's length from the government.

That charisma enabled her to win over 140 seats for the Congress. But she needed coalition partners to stake her claim to form the government. Karunanidhi was the first to enter the coalition, followed by a stream of other parties. The communists initially refused to join in, but later declared their 'outside support' to a Sonia-led government. When she declined the PM's chair there was such an uproar in the coalition ranks that she relented, but only for a day, finally nominating Dr Manmohan Singh as the PM while herself remaining the head of the coalition. This too appealed to the general public as an act of renunciation, of sacrifice. I would conclude that she made it into the people's hearts on her own, not as a 'dynast' but as the magnet in our politics that attracted the iron shavings of several parties to give the anti-BJP coalition a comfortable majority. This was reinforced in the next election, when the Congress score went up to 206.

Towards ministership

The UPA led by Congress won 145 seats and was joined by the Left, the DMK, Lalu Prasad Yadav's Rashtriya Janata Dal (RJD) and several other parties to form the government. This was my golden opportunity to become part of the ruling establishment. Suneet said I would forever regret it if I did not stretch myself to grab the opportunity. So, when we returned to Delhi, Suneet took charge of the luggage and the children and sent me out to canvass a place in the council of ministers as a minister of state, if possible, with independent charge, my hopes not extending to the cabinet.

I first called on Arjun Singh. He regretted he did not have the influence to help me. My next port of call was Natwar. He countered my request to be made a minister of state by asking, 'Why not the cabinet?' I confessed I did not have the chutzpah to ask for it. 'Nonsense,' was his reply, 'ask for the cabinet, that is the least you deserve.'

With my confidence boosted, I called on the Congress president. She confirmed that I was being considered for the new portfolio of Panchayati Raj. 'As minister of state under someone else, or as minister of state with independent charge, or as cabinet minister?' I inquired, and then, emboldened by Natwar, said that as the Constitution had relegated local self-government to the state list, I would have to interact with chief ministers to nudge them in the right direction. This was possible only if I held cabinet rank. She appeared convinced. But before anything specific could be done, she dropped a bombshell.

While all of us newly elected Congress MPs were waiting for her to address us on her lawns, rumour spread that she had decided to decline the prime minister's post. When she finally arrived to speak, a sigh of relief went around as she did not confirm the rumour. Apparently, her partners in the coalition that she had brought together (after shutting out Amar Singh on behalf of Mulayam Singh) had unanimously pressed her not to move down that road of self-denial.

But by next day's CPP meeting, it was confirmed that she preferred Dr Manmohan Singh to herself as the head of government. A detailed account of the behind-the-scenes events responsible for this wholly unexpected (and, in my view, wholly unwarranted) denouement may be seen in K. Natwar Singh's autobiography, *One Life Is Not Enough*. According to him, Rahul Gandhi had vehemently put his foot down, refusing to allow his mother to endanger her life as his father and grandmother had done theirs.[7]

At the CPP meeting, I persuaded Priya Ranjan Dasmunsi, the chief whip, to allow me to initiate the discussion. He did. I began by thundering, 'Madam prime minister,' before continuing in Hindi to plead that as all of us had been elected on the promise of bringing her in as PM, how could we face our constituencies to explain the situation? Others spoke in the same vein. The argument was fine as an exercise in polemics, but her mind was made up. Dr Manmohan Singh became the prime minister.

Next day, the new cabinet was sworn in. Pillai from Sonia Gandhi's office had tipped me off that my name was on the list of cabinet ministers but no portfolio was indicated. That was confirmed by a call from the Cabinet Secretariat. I rang Suneet with the news – she and the three girls were thrilled. We agreed to meet at my Tilak Lane MP's office, and they said they would bring me a freshly ironed white bush shirt and a spotless *veshti* to wear to the swearing-in, adding that we must go to the Ganesh temple my father had built before proceeding to Rashtrapati Bhavan. I fell in with their wishes.

In the afternoon, I went to my favourite 'dhaba' (street food shack) outside the RGF and had my favourite meal of rice and chhole for what I assumed to be the last time. I made a chance acquaintance with a fellow lunch companion, who did not recognize me but introduced himself. In returning the courtesy, I couldn't help remarking that this was my last lunch at the dhaba as I was to be sworn in as a cabinet minister that evening. He looked at me as if I were stark, raving mad.

At the Presidential palace, I was separated from the family but assured that they would be ushered into the Durbar Hall. I kept looking for them through the ceremony but could not spot them. I found myself twelfth in the ranking and mentally contemplated the possibility of rising higher (little realizing I had reached my political plateau). I took my oath in a loud, stentorian voice, as became the occasion. When it was over, Natwar insisted on the three of us – Meira Kumar, himself and me – getting a photograph of us taken together as former members of the Indian Foreign Service (I never managed to get a copy).

The following day, a Sunday, I attended my first cabinet meeting. It was a routine affair to suggest a date to the President for his opening address to both Houses of Parliament. I then went into the prime minister's South Block office to learn which portfolio I had been allotted.

Dr Singh said he had wanted to invest me with a 'heavy economic portfolio', like petroleum, but the Congress president had told him that my heart was set on Panchayati Raj. He felt that would not 'stretch' me adequately and had added a few more charges. Rummaging among his papers, he announced culture and tribal affairs as additional portfolios. As these were precisely my areas of specialization under Rajiv Gandhi, I walked out of his room as if on air.

No sooner had I come home than the Congress president's political secretary, Ahmed Patel, rang to say that my other portfolio (temporary) was petroleum and natural gas, that I should keep this confidential, and that I should meet him before going to office the next morning.

8

My Ministerial Assignments: Ministry of Petroleum and Natural Gas (2004–2006)

Next morning, I found Ahmed Patel had left his home before I got to him. So, I went to Shastri Bhavan on my own, driving myself, and stood in the queue at the reception for a pass to get into my office. On learning that I had come to meet myself, reception rang the ministry and were told that I had entered the building by the wrong entrance and should be advised to go to the rear of the building, where I would be formally received.

I found the correct gate with some difficulty and saw the startled look on the faces of the assembled welcome party as I struggled to find a place to park. When I got out, I was solemnly introduced to the 'oil honchos' one by one, each of whom was staggering under the weight of the huge garlands and bouquets they had brought with them to greet me.

Riding up to my floor in the lift, I entered my office to find it overcrowded with the media, falling over themselves to get the first 'byte'. Above the din could be heard a voice shouting, 'What is your priority?' I signalled that I would answer if the shouting stopped. It did, and I answered, 'My priority is to get all of you out of this room so that I might get myself briefed by my officers.' There was at least one correspondent who took offence. The rest took it sportingly and filed out. Thus began my first day as minister of petroleum and natural gas.

I soon discovered the reason for this unexpected honour. The price of crude oil had shot up to the unprecedented level of $32 a barrel in the past few weeks. It had been reigning at $10 a barrel for most of the past decade. In consequence, domestic prices of petroleum products had to be raised. So, this ministry was a crown of thorns. Whatever decision we took, I would be blamed for raising the price of petroleum products – a dire necessity of everyday life for everyone, from the wealthiest to the most destitute.

All these products were subsidized and cross-subsidized consumer items of high sensitivity that called for a complex balancing of sensitive economic and political factors without being distracted by market fundamentalists, who demanded the complete freeing of petroleum prices in a highly volatile market. It also called for the minister to fully understand the issues before shooting off his mouth. Beginning with the acronyms – MS (motor spirit, 'petrol'), HSD (high speed diesel, 'diesel'), SKO (superior kerosene oil, 'kerosene') and LPG (liquefied petroleum gas, 'cooking gas') – I needed time to learn. But my guys had fixed a press conference that afternoon, which I had to address.

I decided to give the press another bone to chew on. Among my earliest visitors was the Saudi ambassador, a genial character. He delightedly accepted my invitation to join me at what had been touted by our PR guys as the new minister's inaugural press conference. And, happily, the Saudi ambassador gave the press the headline they sought by assuring them that Saudi Arabia wanted to see crude oil international prices capped at $27 a barrel; for if they went higher, the developed countries would use their economic and technological clout to divert world attention to other energy sources, such as shale oil and gas (which is exactly what happened when crude oil prices surged towards and beyond $100 a barrel).

This was prescient, but our press correspondents did not explore this interesting observation any further. I was, however, spared the embarrassment of having to explain what our government's approach was to the coming crunch on domestic prices. I simply did not know – and neither did the government – because the spike had occurred even as we were fighting the elections.

My petroleum secretary, B.K. Chaturvedi, was away in Amsterdam attending a meeting of the International Energy Forum (IEF). He was being sounded out on India hosting the next meeting. I asked him to unreservedly agree and not to return to India till matters had been settled. I found him to be an exceptionally competent and knowledgeable officer with both intelligence and imagination. The immediate problem was to address the rise in the administered prices of petroleum products.

Chaturvedi was ably assisted in this task by Additional Secretary M.S. Srinivasan and his alert joint secretary, Prabh Das. But I found my comfort level most with a young director, Anil Kumar Jain, whom I persuaded (with some difficulty) to take on the job of heading my personal office in addition to his other duties. He reluctantly agreed, but on a strictly 'temporary' basis and only till his imminent promotion came through. Between all of us, and in consultation with the finance ministry, we succeeded in working out a formula, to which I gave the name 'equitable burden sharing'. This name reflected the instrument devised to deal with the problem, which was to equitably share the rise in prices by all stakeholders taking what they called a 'hit', the cash-rich ONGC taking the biggest hit and then the other stakeholders in descending order so that the burden was the least on the consumer.

There were seven principal stakeholders in the petroleum sector:

- the Union government, which derived a large portion of its revenues from taxes and cesses on the import and domestic sale of petroleum products
- the state governments, dependent for their financial survival on state levies on petroleum products
- the upstream petroleum exploration companies, led by the Oil and Natural Gas Corporation (ONGC) and Oil India Limited (OIL) who were entitled to international prices for their domestic output but subject to giving a commercial discount to downstream state refineries
- the downstream refining and retail distribution companies in the oil sector, led by the Indian Oil Corporation (IOC) and the nationalized companies, Bharat Petroleum Corporation Limited (BPCL) and Hindustan Petroleum Corporation Limited (HPCL), who would

not be permitted to pass on the totality of their higher input costs to consumers

- the nascent petroleum refining entities in the private sector, overwhelmingly the chief of which was Reliance under Mukesh Ambani
- the emerging state corporations in the petroleum sector, principally the Gujarat State Petroleum Corporation (GSPC)
- the consumer, who was by far the biggest stakeholder

Instead of placing the entire burden of higher prices on the consumer, as market forces left on their own would have done, we had always structured prices in such a manner as to put the least strain on kerosene, consumed by the poorest of the poor; then, rising in ascending order through LPG, used increasingly in cooking by all classes; then diesel, used in commercial transportation; and petrol, principally for private transport for the better-off. For years, international oil prices had stabilized at around $10 per barrel until the spike on the eve of my taking charge, when prices had suddenly gone up three times to over $30 per barrel, thus upsetting the price balance that had held for a decade past.

We met with Finance Minister P. Chidambaram, who pointedly addressed his answers to my additional secretary, thus underlining that I was a novice in such matters, and he had no time to educate me. The finance minister agreed to take what he described as a 'hit' on his excise revenues by lowering excise duties, compensated to some extent by marginally raising import duties on around 70 per cent of our crude consumption that we obtained from abroad.

There was nothing we could do about state government duties on petroleum products other than leave it to them to cut rates, which, understandably, they were most reluctant to do. It was easier to lay down the law to our own oil companies. Our upstream oil companies had always been permitted to sell whatever domestic oil they were able to find at international prices, but at a discount to the domestic state-owned refining companies. So, upstream companies were asked to compensate for the 'unearned' bonus profits they were receiving on account of the rise in international oil prices by giving deeper discounts to domestic refiners. At the same time, domestic refiners in the public sector were asked to hold back from passing on the full impact of higher market prices. Given the tiny share of private sector refiners and retailers at that time, they had no alternative but to follow public sector retailing prices to retain their toe hold in the market.

Government subsidies on petroleum products were readjusted to the advantage of the poorer consumer. Thus, the increased burden on the consumer was lowered as far as possible. Otherwise, had market forces been allowed to take complete control, there would have been a hyper-increase that would have hit consumers hard.

Although the doctrine of 'equitable burden sharing' displeased the market fundamentalists in the Planning Commission, the academics, the experts and the right-wing financial press, its logic was largely accepted by our general public. This had the effect of launching me as a competent minister in the public eye, handling a sector of which, I frankly confessed, I had no previous experience or expertise.

Indeed, knowing that this was a temporary assignment till the higher authorities found a permanent replacement for me, I frequently described myself as a temporary minister until the Cabinet Secretariat called to say that there was no provision in the Constitution for a 'temporary minister'; I was either a minister or not.

Unfortunately for me, Chaturvedi was picked up by the prime minister to serve in the top civil service position of Cabinet Secretary. He was replaced by the very pleasant and hard-working S.K. Tripathi who, however, lacked Chaturvedi's panache and domain expertise. Tripathi stood rock solid with me, but at critical points (still in the future) his lack of domain expertise in the petroleum sector left me swimming (and sometimes drowning) on my own. Both swimming and drowning were to be part of my first ministerial assignment and constitute the bulk of this chapter. So, here goes.

The experience of my first three weeks in office imparted to me a confidence, which grew considerably over the next year and a half. I was fascinated with the multiple facets of the ministry. The public image of it was that of a den of favouritism, where the minister's only work was to hand out petrol pumps and gas stations to his favourites or, at the instance of his party bosses, to those to whom political favours were owed or who needed to be thus bought over.

I was fortunate that the Supreme Court had come down heavily on my predecessor, who had indeed spent a disproportionate part of his time on the arbitrary allotment of petrol pumps and LPG retail outlets. The Supreme Court had cancelled 300 to 400 allotments made by him on a discretionary basis and had laid down firm guidelines on the procedure to be followed for what, till then, had been a principal function of the minister.

This enabled me to withstand pressures to do special favours. All this gave me an exaggerated image as an 'honest' minister but did not dissuade some from continuing subtly, and less subtly, to hold out temptations and blandishments. Falling back on the Supreme Court orders passed before my time, I found the judgement to be a useful shield in deflecting these overtures.

However, very early in my term as a minister, there occurred an event that blotted my copybook in the eyes of my party leadership. After I took my oath as an MP and went up to the Hon'ble pro tempore Speaker to receive his felicitations, I followed the usual practice of going round to greet the leader of the Opposition and other Opposition leaders.

I found Vajpayee sitting at the far end of the first row, looking miserable. Notwithstanding my numerous clashes with him in Parliament and our many differences of opinion, I felt very sorry for him and did admire him for combating the worst elements of the RSS. So, instinctively, I bent to touch his feet, seeking his blessings for the new phase of my life upon which I was embarking.

When I straightened up, I saw the look of strong disapproval that passed like a shadow over the Congress president's face. Still, I was taken aback when Rahul Gandhi dropped in on me at my office immediately after the session and, perhaps jocularly, inquired whether I had joined the BJP. It was then that I really learned that the Marquess of Queensbury's rules don't apply in our home-grown politics.

That should have alerted me to what followed. I received a letter from Rahul inquiring about the progress in establishing the Rajiv Gandhi Institute of Petroleum Technology in his constituency of Amethi. I sent for the file and found that soon after then Petroleum and Natural Gas minister, Captain Satish Sharma, had announced the project, the P.V. Narasimha Rao government, of which he was a prominent member, had fallen. At this, BPCL, which had been entrusted with the project, had commissioned a feasibility study that reported negatively on it. I sent a summary of the feasibility report to the new MP for Amethi. I was promptly rapped on the knuckles and ordered to get on with the project. I learned my second lesson: that ministers initiate ideas in as facile a manner as their successors dismantle them. So, instead of sitting at an Olympian height trying to be objective in an inherently partisan political world, the minister is best advised to suspend judgement and get cracking! The institute was inaugurated in 2007 and seems to be faring very well. But there was no doubt that I had indeed blotted my party copybook a second time.

The two incidents were minor, but I was new to the game of being a minister and, therefore, fumbled when it came to the politics of the post. I put the incidents behind me and turned to trying to understand our major strategic issues in this sector.

Setting the sights: Strategic objectives

The public image of the ministry of petroleum and natural gas was that of a house of patronage and a cash cow of political funding. I had no desire to preside over such a ministry. My primary task had to be to make the ministry the focus of a larger national interest.

At the end of my first briefing, I thought I had found the answer: energy security as a key component of Prime Minister Dr Manmohan Singh's relentless drive to get the country on to a higher growth path aimed at sustained annual double-digit economic development. As this would require higher and higher availability of fuel, at reasonable or affordable prices, my job as minister must be to focus the ministry (and public perception of the ministry) as a key partner in the acceleration of economic growth by making available much higher levels of fuel at reasonable prices, while also ensuring that the poorer sections of society continued to access their fuel requirements at affordable rates.

My strategic vision did not come to me in a flash in my opening briefing at a ministry I knew nothing about. It evolved slowly as I set myself to widely consulting others who knew much more about the subject than I did. And I spread my net as wide as I could. I was learning on the job. My first source of information were the senior officers in the ministry. My second were my personal staff, especially Anil Kumar Jain and Basudev Mohanty. My third and invaluable source was my foreign service friend and colleague Talmiz Ahmad, who I succeeded with some difficulty in bringing into the ministry as additional secretary. Then came the technical experts, above all then director general of hydrocarbons, V.K. Sibal, and his very knowledgeable predecessor, Avinash Chandra. Along with them were the heads of the state oil corporations, particularly Subir Raha of ONGC, R.S. Butalia, Managing Director (MD) of ONGC Videsh Limited (OVL), M.S. Ramachandran of IOC, S. Behuria of Bharat Petroleum, Proshanto Banerjee of the Gas Authority of India Ltd (GAIL), and others. Mukesh Ambani made a presentation which was succinct and to the point. I congratulated him but did not agree with him when he next came to see me to protest the rise in import duties on crude. He never visited me again.

I also spent long hours with well-informed media mavens and academics, and knowledgeable Indian experts like Vijay Kelkar, Vikram Mehta (Shell, who were putting up a re-gasification plant at Hazira), and Hari S. Bhartia, who headed the petroleum wing of the CII, as also with big businessmen like Lakshmi Mittal. I was much impressed with the insights of foreign private sector executives like Bill Gammell and Mike Watts of Cairn. Another major source of learning were my foreign counterparts, above all the Saudi, Iranian and Kazakh oil ministers. I also acquired a shelf full of books on the subject, the most significant of which was Dan Yergin's *The Prize*. I met Yergin in Istanbul and got on with him very well indeed.

It took over a year of intense and wide-ranging interaction with Indian and foreign experts and authorities, and extensive travel within and outside the country, to identify and seek solutions to the key parameters of our petroleum paradigm and slowly evolve a framework for petroleum and natural gas to make a signal contribution to energy security in the country. It was like studying while running, and I am grateful to all those who trained and mentored me.

I would first like to mention the head of Cairn Energy, Bill Gammell and his exploration wizard, Mike Watts. On the eve of my taking over as minister, Cairn had made a potentially significant onshore discovery of oil in the vicinity of Barmer, Rajasthan.

They met me within days of my becoming minister to say that while their practice overseas was to name the oil and gas fields they discovered after Greek gods and goddesses, in India they had decided to name them after Hindu gods and goddesses. They wanted to name the field they had discovered in Rajasthan after my '*ishta devata*' (favourite god). I replied that I was a non-believer and, therefore, did not have an *ishta devata*, but that I did have a suggestion: could they name the discovered oilfield after my mother, Bhagyam, whose name meant 'good fortune'.

The suggestion was accepted, and Bhagyam is today among the biggest on-land oilfields in India! When I went, along with the state chief minister, to inaugurate the Barmer refinery, I found that Bhagyam and its two other sister fields were due to run dry by 2040, and hence the refinery had been designed to run only till that date. So, in my inaugural speech, I pleaded that the life of the refinery be extended by a year to 2041 so that I could attend its closing in my centenary year!

Little did I know that the finance ministry would drive Cairn out of India by backdating a tax demand for thousands of crores of rupees. Cairn has just won an award from the International Arbitration Tribunal for an enormous compensation running to over a billion dollars, but my biggest regret is that we lost the services of that oil exploration genius, Mike Watts.

We all know about the water diviners of yore. Well, Mike was an oil diviner! He had looked very closely at the Terai region – in fact, the ONGC headquarters were established at Dehradun in 1956 as the Terai appeared to hold the highest potential for oil. Watts concluded that because the international border between Nepal and India lay in the Terai, the geological integrity of the Terai's potential oilfields had been split between India and Nepal.

That was the main reason for ONGC having made no discoveries of oil in the Terai over fifty years, despite its relentless efforts at exploration. If only the integrity of the Terai in geological terms could be restored by promoting cooperative regional oil exploration, both nations could be transformed from oil deprived to oil rich. Watts's vision caught my imagination, and I did all I could to ensure it was acted on. But Cairn and I were soon out, and, to the best of my knowledge, the prospect has not been followed up since.

I have already described what I learnt from others. Energy security, I had found, had two equally important dimensions: the domestic and the external, and the two were interrelated.

Domestic: Emphasis on exploration

The domestic scenario was most discouraging. During colonial times, the oil exploration companies, mostly British and American, had written off the British Indian subcontinent as incorrigibly hydrocarbons short, except for Burma and the north-eastern part of Assam, around Digboi, which the British, after defeating Burma in 1826, had attached to their Indian empire. Oil struck at Digboi in the third quarter of the nineteenth century was the second biggest oil strike after Pennsylvania. Thereafter, there were no other finds until independent India, under the dynamic leadership of a predecessor of mine, Keshav Dev Malviya (known usually by his initials, KD), bucked the conventional view and discovered petroleum reserves around Ankleshwar in Gujarat in the mid-fifties.

Subsequently, under Indira Gandhi's government, substantial oil reserves had been discovered in the deep waters offshore at Bombay High. This, and imaginative long-term oil purchase deals with the Soviet Union/Iraq, had enabled us to secure the fuel required to sustain the modest rates of economic growth in the seventies and into the eighties to overcome the 'shokku' of the Organization of the Petroleum Exporting Countries

(OPEC) jacking up crude oil prices to unprecedented levels after the Yom Kippur war of 1973. Fortunately for us, international oil prices had moderated and stabilized in the nineties at about the same time that our economic reforms were taking off.

As I took office, international prices had nearly tripled, and it was vital that renewed attention be paid to our securing or innovating the complex and sophisticated technology required to access our own hitherto hidden reserves of oil and gas, particularly onshore in the 'Deccan Trap', where oil was expected to be found under heavy and hitherto impregnable layers of volcanic rock and lava. The only comparable problem of drilling to great depths below hard rock had been in Colorado, but on a much smaller scale than required in the Deccan Trap.

The Deccan Trap was laid, I learned, nearly 60 million years ago when Gondwana broke from the Antarctic and started drifting north towards Eurasia. Unfortunately for us, it had stalled near Madagascar just as the volcanic explosions that killed the dinosaurs were blowing up, spewing huge quantities of hard rock and lava on what was to become the Deccan when Gondwana crashed into Eurasia. Hence the Deccan Trap, below which geologists believed were trapped vast reserves of oil and gas. Could we find the technology to bore through the barrier?

Then there were encouraging signs of discoveries in the very deep seas that surrounded India on three sides. Reliance and Gujarat State Petroleum Corporation (GSPC) were letting it be known that huge reserves had been discovered by them offshore in the Bay of Bengal (albeit 'yet to be certified' by the Directorate–General of Hydrocarbons, and later shown to be largely illusory). The ONGC was also making interesting soundings in the Krishna–Godavari basin, offshore Andhra Pradesh, and the Mahanadi basin, offshore Orissa, besides offshore the Sundarbans in West Bengal. We also needed to further explore the coast of Kerala–Konkan and the Palk Straits that narrowly separated Sri Lanka (Jaffna peninsula) from southern India. There was, further, the exciting prospect of commercial exploitation of the gas hydrates available in abundance in the Andaman Sea. The problem was how to invent the technology required to drill deep enough into the Arabian Sea to reach the estimated depth of 10,000 metres and in the somewhat shallower depths of the Bay of Bengal.

To get some idea of that, I asked experts about it in Norway, which was drilling in the North Sea. When they said they averaged 150 metres, I said that in India we would call such shallow waters the 'North Lake'! However, I took heart from the factoid I picked up that Philip Conaco wanted to give up when they did not find any North Sea oil after searching for it in thirty-two wells. It was only when the Norwegians persuaded them to drill the last contracted well – and triumphed – that the North Sea bonanza was achieved. It has driven Norway from being among the lowest per-capita-income countries in western Europe to the highest. Could we achieve that in India? One little quotation persuaded me we could. The aphorism was from a US oil billionaire, who said that successful exploration begins in the mind: it is only the will to find it that leads to success. I tried to instil that spirit in our exploration and production (E&P) parastatals, but I doubt that I succeeded!

The major hurdle was that oil majors with the technology and R&D back-up and financial resources to make the risky investments in finding our domestic sources of oil and gas had not been forthcoming, although we had been seeking to harness their interest in the New Exploration Licensing Policy that had been in operation under the previous government. The New Exploration Licensing Policy had not really had any notable impact. So, investment (domestic and foreign) in our oil and gas fields, onshore and offshore, as well as securing or innovating high-tech cutting-edge technology to augment domestic discoveries, had to be a high ministerial priority on the domestic front.

External: Asian suppliers, Asian consumers

On the external front, there were separate problems relating, first, to the 'Asian premium' charged on West Asian crude sold to Asian buyers; and second, to the non-availability of Asian oil from all Asian sources in the Indian Ocean area. The 'Asian premium', which raised the prices we paid above the rates charged to non-Asian buyers, was 'unfair' because it used Western price indices for deriving the Asian price. Moreover, it was grossly outdated, because Asian consumers now accounted for two-thirds of Asian oil supplies, displacing the hitherto dominant Western buyers. This necessitated an Asian oil price marker to reflect the evolving ground realities.

The second key step, I reckoned, was to supplement West Asian and Iranian oil supplies with Central Asian oil supplies in the Indian Ocean area so that a 'cocktail' of oil supplies would set the prices instead of a West Asian cartel overcharging Asian buyers while favouring Western buyers. This, in my view, required a forum to bring Asian suppliers and Asian buyers together on a common platform. There was an augury of great expectations from a recent decision to establish an all-encompassing International Energy Forum (IEF) secretariat in Riyadh that would include both buyers and sellers and be open to member-states worldwide, developed or developing, net exporters or net importers (in contrast to OPEC, where membership was limited to petroleum exporting countries, and the Paris-based International Energy Agency (IEA), with membership limited to the 'major buyers', i.e., developed countries). How then to leverage IEF Riyadh to serve our interest in a harmonious and cooperative manner between the Asian net exporters and the Asian net importers? And how to build a cooperative relationship with our principal competitor, the People's Republic of China?

Finally, and, in my view, most importantly, as natural gas, the fuel of the twenty-first century, was in very short supply from domestic sources, we needed to access by pipeline the natural gas available in our immediate and proximate neighbourhood. Going by concentric circles radiating out from India, the regions where natural gas was available were: West Asia to Iran; then Central Asia, the countries grouped around the Caspian Sea; Central to North Asia, stretching from the Russian Urals to Sakhalin; and perhaps even the Kamchatka Peninsula, and from there an arc of countries from Myanmar, Malaysia, Indonesia and Papua New Guinea in Southeast Asia to Australia. They were all brimming with gas. Did the answer lie in a network of Asian gas pipelines, beginning with an Iran–Pakistan–India pipeline? Could we urge an Asian gas grid to ensure Asian gas for Asian consumers?

Where progress was already being made, particularly by ONGC Videsh Limited (OVL), it seemed to me that ministerial-level intervention to supplement the commercial efforts by our parastatals might significantly enhance our success rate. My own background in diplomacy was perhaps responsible for this emphasis. Although I had apprehended the charge of ministerial interference in the work of the autonomous, if state-owned 'navaratnas', our 'oil honchos' seemed to welcome the interest I was evincing in their work.

What follows in this chapter is the story of the evolution of these thoughts in my mind and the steps I took to realize these ambitious goals. I was given only twenty months to do so, and inevitably many of my initiatives withered on the vine. But while the sun shone on me, I received high recognition. *India Today* selected me at the end of the first year in office of our government as the best minister; the *Hindustan Times* followed, finding me, somewhat to their startled surprise, the most popular minister in Dr Manmohan Singh's government in a straw poll they conducted in our larger metros; the Hong Kong-based *Businessweek* (of the *Newsweek* group) picked me and a Korean minister among the twenty-five most innovative 'Stars of Asia', whom they described as 'Leaders at the Forefront of Change'; the Indian Institute of Mines, Dhanbad, our leading petroleum institute of learning, conferred on me the title of Honorary Doctor of Science; and the Hon'ble Speaker, in consultation with the Indian Parliamentary Group, named me the 'Outstanding Parliamentarian' for 2006 (more, I suspect, for my work on Panchayati Raj, but I am sure my work on petroleum too contributed) at a glittering ceremony in Parliament's Central Hall. The President of India, Pratibha Patil, presented me the award in the presence of the Vice President M. Hamid Ansari, Prime Minister Dr Manmohan Singh and the Hon'ble Speaker Somnath Chatterjee.

I now invite the reader to accompany me on this dizzying twenty-month odyssey.

Fora to elaborate my thoughts: OPEC

Fortunately, India had already been invited to make a major presentation at the annual meeting in Vienna in September 2004 of the OPEC. That was a golden opportunity to place our concerns over the 'Asian premium' before the most influential members of the global petroleum community.

I worked hard on my speech to OPEC, taking inputs from the ministry officials, the state-owned oil and gas companies, the Directorate General of Hydrocarbons, and miscellaneous retired and outside experts. I also tested out my ideas on them. So, although I drafted my own speech, it was really the composite result of inputs from several sources.

Speaking on the theme of 'Petroleum and Sustainable Development', I focused on the 'Asian premium', emphasizing that outdated market practices were imposing on Asian importers, amounting to a presumptive loss to Asian countries of some $5–10 billion a year, according to an eminent Japanese professor at the Institute of Energy Economics, Tokyo. Pointing to the fall in output in several key petroleum exporting countries and the surge in Asian demand, especially from China, Japan, Korea and India, I argued that instead of deriving prices for the Asian market from what had hitherto been the primary markets and markers in the West, it was necessary to create a new Asian marker that would be 'a genuine and representative marker' for the official selling price of crude in Asia, supplemented by more intensive spot trading of Middle Eastern crude in Asia and increased liquidity in the Asian market. In short, my plea was to reconceive the determination of international marker prices of crude in the light of Asian countries now constituting two-thirds of the global customers for Asian oil, to 'encourage sustainable development and discourage uneconomic consumption'.[1]

The speech paved the way for what was described as 'India's diplomatic blitzkrieg' in Vienna, where within forty-eight hours I met a total of fifteen of my counterparts, six from Asia (Iran, Saudi Arabia, Malaysia, Indonesia, Syria and Qatar), six from Africa (Angola, Sudan, Nigeria, Egypt, Libya and Algeria), two from Europe (Norway and Austria) and one from Latin America (Venezuela). With each of them, discussions were pointed and related to specific projects in India and in their countries where India had a vital stake. I concentrated on personally inviting the Asian ministers to the meeting of Asian oil ministers I was convening in New Delhi under the aegis of the IEF in January 2005.

I also gave a major interview to Reuters,[2] in which I elaborated that US output reflected in the Western Texas Index had fallen by 74 per cent in the last twenty years, Brent by 59 per cent in the last ten years, and Dubai's output was now lower than Bombay High's. What the world needed to recognize was that 'while two-thirds of West Asian oil used to go to America a few decades ago, two-thirds of that oil is now going to Asia'. This, I explained, was the logic of my plea for an 'Asian marker'.

As we needed to progressively use more gas and less oil, I said we needed to recognize that India was 'a kind of island sitting in a lake of gas'. And to secure that gas, I said, India's 'conversation without commitment' (a phrase I had picked up from my Iranian counterpart) in sets of three partners: the first set comprising Iran, Pakistan and India; the second comprising Myanmar, Bangladesh and India; the third comprising Turkmenistan, Afghanistan, Pakistan and India.

The highlight of the visit was a grand banquet for our delegation organized in the bewitching Schwarzenburg Palace by Ali bin Ibrahim al-Naimi, the Saudi oil minister, with the august participation of the Crown Prince of Saudi Arabia, Abdul Aziz bin Salman, and the president of Aramco, Abdullah S. Jum'ah. It was an occasion the Saudis would have never forgotten because the entire Indian delegation was vegetarian[3] and the host decreed the Saudis would also eat vegetarian. For one evening at least, the dietary habits of the desert were overturned and the delegation graciously kept company with their Indian guests.

More substantively, we talked of how we might leverage the IEF, and then establish its headquarters in Riyadh, for more equitable access to Asian buyers of Asian oil. Al-Naimi enthusiastically agreed to attend the meeting I was convening in New Delhi of Asian ministers of oil in January the following year under the aegis of the IEF, and I accepted al-Naimi's pressing invitation to visit Saudi Arabia, on condition, I insisted, that I be taken to the Rab al-Khali, the fabled Empty Quarter of the Arabian Desert, with which I had long been fascinated and where much of Saudi oil lay. He not only readily agreed to this but also inquired whether I would be available to deliver the inaugural address at the formal launch of the IEF in Riyadh. What an honour! Of course, I readily accepted.

Two pivotal meetings

India had been requested to convene the next meeting of the IEF to give a voice to non-OPEC countries. The former Norwegian ambassador to New Delhi, Arne Walther, had been named secretary general of the Riyadh-based IEF. He was an old friend and more than ready to cooperate with us on the novel proposals I had for convening meetings of petroleum exporting and importing countries under the aegis of the IEF in New Delhi in January and November 2005. Unlike OPEC, which was only open for membership to oil-exporting countries, and the Paris-based IEA which was exclusive for membership to economically developed countries, the IEF was open to both petroleum-exporting and petroleum-importing nations, as well as developing and developed countries, without prejudice or privilege – all were equal.

A key plank of the platform I had in mind for ensuring our energy security to keep pace with the momentum being imparted to our GDP growth was to raise consciousness about the role that Asian oil and gas could play in meeting Asian energy requirements.

A major opportunity to pursue this line came with our convening in New Delhi in January 2005 the first-ever conclave of oil ministers of West and Southeast Asia. It was a spectacular affair, perhaps the first time Asian importers and exporters had come together on a common platform to jointly address each other's concerns. Among the exporters, we had the oil ministers of Saudi Arabia, Iran, Kuwait, Oman and the UAE from West Asia, and Malaysia and Indonesia from Southeast Asia. Among Asia's net importers, China, Korea and Japan were represented, in addition to India in the chair. The theme was summed up in the title 'Stability, Security, Sustainability through Mutual Interdependence'.

In my opening remarks I described this first-ever gathering of Asian oil ministers as 'historic', particularly if we were to persevere on the path of such dialogue to discover our 'common destiny . . . as we traverse the twenty-first century – the Asian century'. Attributing the recent volatility in oil prices to 'speculation and apprehensions' in the Western metal exchanges rather than any fundamental disequilibria in demand

and supply, I urged 'a sophisticated Asian market for petroleum and petroleum products' as Asia was no longer a 'residual' but a 'principal consumer of Asian oil production'. With such an Asian market, we could ensure 'stability' through longer contracts, transparent price discovery, spot purchases and the establishment and use of Asian petroleum exchanges.

For 'security', I urged 'mutual interdependence', pointing to an estimate of 1,580 billion dollar investment needed over the next twenty-five years in Asian upstream, midstream and downstream oil and gas development. Could not Asia itself provide the bulk of this investment? As for 'sustainability', I held up Japan as the exemplar of 'both conservation and technology for conservation'.

I ended my address by saying: 'We would be more than happy to share what we know with fellow Asians – and even more to learn from others, above all from our fellow Asians.'

After the others had spoken and given their suggestions, I hammered out the major conclusions on my laptop at the conference table. The most important of these was to institutionalize the dialogue by holding biannual meetings that would be co-hosted by one exporter and one importer. Saudi Arabia (net exporter) and Japan (net importer) agreed to co-host the next round table in 2007; Japan and Kuwait offered to co-host the following meeting in 2009; and thus other net importers and exporters offered to host meetings, all the way to 2013!

A second major conclusion was that 'Asian consumers' should be encouraged to 'increase their purchases of Asian produce' and that 'criss-cross investments in oil and gas' value chains should be a 'priority'. It was particularly highlighted that 'strategic storage and stockpiling' would contribute to stability. It was agreed by consensus that an 'Asian Bank for Energy Development', as proposed by Iran, 'merits deeper consideration'. For 'sustainability', the conference concluded that 'cooperation among Asian research and development centres' should be regarded as a 'key' instrumentality.

I was relieved of the ministry a little over a year later and am, therefore, not aware of subsequent developments, but the schedule set out seems to be humming along, albeit in a somewhat routine manner.

In November of the same year, north and central Asian ministers convened in New Delhi for a multilateral dialogue similar to the earlier round. Compared with the earlier January round table, it was far less glamorous and far less substantive. The principal reason for this was that the Russian minister, V. Kristenko, was far less enthused with the idea than al-Naimi, the Saudi minister, had been about our January meeting. Indeed, the only reason Kristenko came at all was that the Russian ambassador to New Delhi, who was deeply impressed with the direction in which I was steering the ministry, had leveraged his clout as Putin's former boss in the KGB to get Kristenko's higher authorities to order him to New Delhi. He came, but after cursorily reading out his speech, departed from the conference hall and did not return even for the concluding session.

I think Kristenko saw his country as a European power with a global market, which he did not want to see segmented into different continental markets. Most of all, he did not subscribe to the concept of a distinct Asian market. He was not persuaded by my argument that oil west of the Urals was running out and Russia's largest reserves lay in the vast Asian region to the east of the Urals, stretching all the way to Sakhalin in the Far East, where a joint Indo–Japanese–US–Russian consortium had just struck gas and was poised to also strike oil. The round table, therefore, lacked the sparkle that had characterized our January conclave. I must hasten to add that there was no such reluctance on the part of other participants, such as Turkmenistan, Uzbekistan, Kazakhstan and Azerbaijan from Central Asia; or the major consuming countries, such as Japan, the Republic of Korea, China and Turkey, straddling Asia and Europe. I represented India and acted as chairman.

My inaugural address began with a rehash of the points I had made at OPEC and the first round-table of the need for an Asian identity in the global hydrocarbons markets as Asia's role as the world's largest oil and gas producer was also being complemented by its emerging as the biggest consumer of global oil and gas. I pointed to the pipeline being laid across vast stretches of the Asian continent, from Kazakhstan to China and from Siberia to the Pacific coast. I also underlined the significance for Asian cooperation that characterized the Baku–Tblisi–Ceyhan oil pipeline, which, once the Samsung–Ceyhan sector was completed, would bring Caspian oil not only to the east Mediterranean (its primary destination) but also potentially to the Indian Ocean area. Invoking our proposals to promote gas pipelines on the Myanmar-Bangladesh-India and the Iran–Pakistan–India routes, I drew attention to our interest in extending the proposed Turkmenistan–Afghanistan–Pakistan pipeline by adding India to the project (turning TAP into TAPI). I also suggested bringing in other Caspian basin producers – Uzbekistan, Kazakhstan, Russia and Azerbaijan – to expand TAPI into ARUKUTAPI. All these initiatives, I held, pointed the way to an Asian gas grid. We could achieve all our goals of 'stability, security and sustainability' by anchoring our cooperation on 'mutual interdependence' through criss-cross investments along the entire hydrocarbons chain.

The Russian minister, for all his reservations about attending, had presented his ideas in great detail. Acknowledging the Asia-Pacific region as 'the new centre of gravity for the world economy', he stressed that 'the stability, security and sustainability' of the hydrocarbons economy of Asia was 'not feasible without solving the problem of global energy security'. He proposed to take up questions relating to global security at the forthcoming G8 summit that Russia was scheduled to chair. But global energy security, he conceded, 'would be impossible without . . . the basic hydrocarbon exporter and consumer countries, including in Asia'. That gave me the opening to working out a consensus, especially as the Russian agenda of ideas and action for global security appeared to comprise many of the thoughts and actions at the Asian level that we had aired at our January meeting.

I was, therefore, able to hammer out a consensus that 'regional cooperation in the Asian oil and gas economy must be pursued within the framework of global cooperation'. But, that said, we needed to undertake a series of studies on 'promoting and developing gas and oil connections through LPG (liquefied petroleum gas transported in liquid form by special tankers and re-gasified at the importing end) and trans-national pipelines within the Asian region' (which was my particular emphasis, as piped natural gas [PNG] was much more economical than LNG). It was also agreed that 'mutual cross-investment' needed to be encouraged as it would be the 'optimal means' of securing our goals of 'stability, security and sustainability'. Besides joint ventures, we needed to 'take practical steps . . . for networking the knowledge base of participating countries' (a key national interest for India). It was also agreed that further study be undertaken of the Japanese proposal for a 'Sustainable and Flexible Energy System' (SAFE).[4]

Finally, this round table of northern and Central Asian oil ministers with their counterparts from the major Asian consuming countries was institutionalized in the same way as the ministers at the January round-table had agreed, with Azerbaijan, as a net exporter, and Turkey, as a net importer, offering to co-host the next round table.

All this was slightly short of what had been agreed on in January, but nevertheless constituted major progress in defining Asia, and India within Asia, as major players who could no longer be sidelined on the global hydrocarbons stage.

But before I could follow up on all this, I was out on my ear within the next three months. I do not know what happened thereafter.

I leave the subject with this tribute to me from Arne Walther, the first and long-serving chief of the IEF, Riyadh (now resident in Oslo):

> Clearly, there was an 'Asian Energy Identity' that lacked an international forum. Thanks to you, India could spearhead the move with the Asian Ministerial Energy Round Tables, as they are now called, growing stronger.

Listening, learning, informing

I used every forum I could find – and invitations to do so ceaselessly flowed in – to listen, learn and inform India and the regional/global petroleum world about possible solutions to our apparently insolvable problems of energy security. Major opportunities to do all this arose out of intensive travels to oil exploration sites in India and to places of exploration interest abroad, as also participation in all fora available in India – the annual

Petrotech conference and exhibition organized by ONGC and the Asian Gas conference organized by GAIL – among numerous other seminars and conclaves organized by the CII and organizations. At these places, I could pick up hints that could be woven into hypotheses with the help of experts, Indian and foreign.

I was all over India, from Duliajan in the Northeast to Barmer at the edge of the Rajasthan desert; from the ONGC oil rigs off the Sundarbans to the ONGC headquarters in Dehradun; from oil exploration vans and helium-producing units in my Tamil Nadu constituency to the Andaman Islands. I also went abroad a lot to canvas support for our oil and gas exploration efforts and participate in international conferences: Moscow; Astana and Almaty in Kazakhstan; Tokyo and Sakhalin; Tehran and Islamabad; Azerbaijan, Turkey and Romania; Yangon and Dhaka in our immediate vicinity; Saudi Arabia and Doha; Stavenger, Oslo and Reykjavik – and deployed, as best as I could, the innovative ideas I gleaned at all these locales and the detailed, sometimes, highly technical discussions I had with my ministerial counterparts, academic experts and oilmen with long experience. I was particularly taken with Daniel Yergin of the Cambridge Energy Research Association, whom I met in Istanbul. He is the author of the Pulitzer-winning *The Prize*, which tells the tangled and murky tale of global oil exploration since the mid-nineteenth century. I invited him to India to clear the fuzz over whether we were in fact a hydrocarbons-deprived country.

In consequence of this frenetic activity, I was requested by the Iranian minister to address a conference he convened in Tehran; by the Saudi oil minister to deliver the inaugural address at the launch of the IEF secretariat in Riyadh; and by the Qatar oil minister to give the keynote address at a petroleum conference in Doha.

Roadshows for India's New Exploration Policy (NEP)

A major opportunity to put all this ideas-gathering into practice arose when I was tasked to undertake 'roadshows' in London, Moscow, Houston, Amsterdam and Calgary to promote the fifth round of India's New Exploration Licensing Policy (NELP-V). These roadshows had been held on an annual basis since the turn of the millennium. My first round took me to London; the second to Houston and Calgary; the third to Moscow and Amsterdam.

To audiences which averaged 200 of some of the best and biggest names in the global hydrocarbons industry – Exxon Mobil, Chevron Texaco, Shell – and a host of small- and medium-sized companies, I laid out our goals in expanding exploration, setting up international pipelines and trying to create a public sector undertaking (PSU) oil major which could be thirty-fourth on the Fortune 500 list, largely based on attracting foreign exploration expertise and capital in a sector that till the economic reforms of the 1990s had been tightly preserved within India's public sector. I also stressed the importance of aggressively acquiring oil and gas assets abroad and leveraging diplomacy to these ends.

Describing the Bay of Bengal as Asia's North Sea, I tried, through PowerPoint presentations garnished with quotations from Shakespeare to T.S. Eliot and bits of world history and geological insights, to interest investors not only in the Krishna–Godavari basin where Reliance and Niko had made the world's biggest gas discovery in 2002, but in the existing and potential hotspots for oil and gas all the way from the Palk Straits that separated the southern tip of India from Sri Lanka to the coast of Myanmar. Moving on to the west coast of India, I sought to catch investors' attention by calling the Arabian Sea the Gulf of Mexico in its potential for petroleum reserves. The audiences seemed entertained but sceptical. I persisted because I saw they were taking notes, which would doubtless be discussed in their boardrooms.

I then talked about India's onshore potential, outlining the geological history of the Deccan Trap, explaining that if only we could find the right technology in collaboration with our foreign friends, enough oil could be found below the hard volcanic rocks and lava to perhaps make the Deccan in the twenty-first century as productive as the Arabian Empty Quarter.

Then came my final call: Indian black gold, I affirmed, was akin to Californian yellow gold in 1848: 'Come join the oil rush to the country.' For those who found such rhetoric unfathomable, I threw in some figures, which I reckoned would be elaborated on by the knowledgeable technical experts in the follow-up talks after the inauguration.

India, I said, has total prognosticated hydrocarbon reserves of 30 billion tonnes, spread across twenty-six sedimentary basins. Only 18 per cent of this estimated bounty had been explored so far. The remaining 82 per cent was up for grabs for those willing to bring the financial and technological resources to explore and produce along with us or on their own. In either case, they would be granted international prices to haul in the returns on their investment.

When I went on to Houston and Calgary, I changed my literary references to John Steinbeck's *Grapes of Wrath* to suit North American listeners, and my historical references to Dr Livingstone's exploration of Africa.[5]

Whatever the potential investors took away from my spiel, the high point of my visit to Houston was my visit to the R&D facilities at Exxon. It was a revelation. Here lay the key to deep-sea drilling in the Arabian Sea and the Bay of Bengal, as drilling at similar depths was taking place next door in the Gulf of Mexico. Here too lay potentially the answer to drilling through the hard rock and lava that kept our onshore oil locked up in the Deccan Trap, as well, perhaps, as the hydrocarbon secrets of the Terai, divided as it was politically between sovereign Nepal and India.

Beginning with Exxon, Houston, could not some deft footwork by P&NG, DGH and our oil and gas parastatals network R&D centres around the world in seeking technological breakthroughs that would ramp up our domestic output instead of deepening our import dependence from 30 per cent before the oil 'shokku' of 1973 to 70 per cent at the start of the millennium (and now, in 2024, tottering on the edge of 85 per cent)? The Exxon executives welcomed the idea, and I set DGH to exploring the prospect of our own world hydrocarbons web. But this initiative too withered on the vine after I was dropped from my post.

In Calgary, I learned about oil exploration chiefly from my very smartly dressed Sikh chauffeur. After getting to know him a little, I asked how he had come to Canada. He said he had arrived in the sixties with $20 in his pocket, eight of which had been taken from him at entry to pay for his health insurance. Not knowing any English, nor anyone in Calgary, nor how to earn his keep, he met up at the airport with an earlier Sikh immigrant who said he had met many idiots like my chauffeur and the only way they could pull through was by going into the Arctic wilderness of north Alberta to work for an oil exploration company. He would be housed and fed for free and – if he survived – he would return to find three years' salary credited to his account.

My chauffeur took up the deal. On finding himself flush with funds after the ordeal, he wondered where to invest them. He found that land around the airport was cheap because Canadians did not like to be disturbed by aircraft noise. He bought acres. Then oil was struck in Alberta and Calgary airport had to be expanded. They could not expand the airport without compensating him for his land, which they needed to acquire. The bonanza had made him a millionaire, so he brought across his wife and sons. Bewildered, I asked him why, being a millionaire, he was driving a taxi. Because, he replied, his sons had grown up and taken over the running of his multiple businesses, including the taxi service he owned. So, with nothing to do but watch Hindi films on TV, he decided that when Indian VIPs came, he would himself drive them around. How else would he get to meet them?

It was that spirit of adventure and risk-taking that I found our distinguished parastatal heads short of. They had fallen into a mindset of despair about finding any more oil or gas in the country. They needed to be shaken out of their lack of initiative and enterprise. A saying by an oil billionaire I had come across summed it up – successful exploration, his aphorism held, begins in the mind; without conviction and persistence, oil can't be found. I passed this on to our 'honchos'. They were not amused.

With India holding less than 1 per cent of the world's proven hydrocarbon reserves, the two obvious ways to increase oil and gas supplies are to (a) explore more; and (b) acquire more abroad. Our parastatals pushed back on both fronts. They insisted they were doing all the exploration possible and scooping more oil out of drying wells, and that ONGC Videsh Ltd (OVL) and Petronet LPG (GAIL's external arm) were already acquiring all the field assets and LPG they could, battling China's much deeper pockets all the way.

If this was not working – or, at any rate, not working significantly – the way forward was to bring in more global oil majors and ramp up our R&D. The 2005 roadshows made a difference. There were as many as fifty-five bids for NELP–V certified blocks, the largest number ever. Most of the oil majors were among the fifty-five. But before the winning bids were awarded, my term as minister was terminated.

As far as I know, foreign interest in the NELP has ebbed, Reliance has not succeeded (to anywhere the extent claimed) in the Krishna–Godavari (KG) basin, GSPC has gone bankrupt and the Modi government have compelled ONGC to take over GSPC's massive debts, and, for their part, the upstream state oil companies, principally ONGC, OVL, OIL and GAIL, are chugging along delinking oil diplomacy from oil and gas assets abroad and pipeline transmission to India. Domestic output of oil and gas has increased by only a trickle. It is only large gains in our foreign exchange reserves that have kept our economy afloat, despite the slogan of '*atmanirbharta*' (self-reliance).

Iran–Pakistan–India gas pipeline

I was anxious to get on with my long-cherished idea of a pipeline carrying natural gas overland from the western oilfields of Iran through Iran and Pakistan to the state of Rajasthan in western India. Rajasthan was not only short of gas but almost the entire breadth of India away from our coal deposits, which lay largely in the east. I dubbed my idea 'the pipeline of peace', hoping it would build lasting bridges between us and Pakistan. (Perhaps, instead, I burnt my bridges with the Ministry of External Affairs (MEA), who regarded war and peace as their business!)

The background to my championing IPI perhaps needs some detailing. My immediate inspiration had been the Lovraj Memorial Lecture in 1996 by Vijay Kelkar, generally counted among India's most knowledgeable experts in the petroleum sector. He argued that even as the centuries before the eighteenth were the Age of Wood and Water (for energy), the nineteenth the Age of Steam, and the twentieth the Age of Petroleum, the coming twenty-first century would be known as the Age of Natural Gas.

He foresaw natural gas replacing petroleum in several fields, including transportation.

At about the same time, a leading member of the South Asian diaspora in the United States, Ambassador Shirin Tahir-Kheli (of Pakistani and Hyderabadi origin), who had served in the US Permanent Mission to the United Nations as the only Ambassador till then of South Asian origin, inspired by a similar assessment of the role of natural gas in the future energy scenario, began to explore the idea of an IPI gas pipeline project.

Shirin secured funding from the UN Economic and Social Commission for Asia and the Pacific (ESCAP, earlier known as ECAFE). She then put together a group of Indian and Pakistani politicians representing the spectrum of political opinion in their respective countries.

Of the two Pakistani backbenchers she chose, one, Shahid Khaqan Abbasi, went on to become prime minister (2017–18), and the second, Shah Mehmood Qureshi, has had two spells as foreign minister (2008–11, and 2018–23).

On the Indian side, Shirin picked Jaswant Singh – a future foreign minister – and me – a future petroleum minister. As Jaswant was from the BJP and I from the Congress, this meant our approach to the issue was bipartisan. So also on the Pakistan side, the approach was bipartisan because Shahid Khaqan Abbasi was then with the Pakistan Muslim League of Nawaz Sharif and Shah Mehmood Qureshi was a promising young leader of Benazir's Pakistan People's Party. In addition to the politicians, there were also technical experts from Pakistan.

We had three meetings in successive years: 1995 (Bangkok), 1996 (Stockholm), and a third wrap-up meeting in 1997 in Udaipur because both sides agreed it was absurd to keep meeting outside the subcontinent. Our work was sufficiently advanced, both in political and in technical terms, for the future Pakistan PM, Shahid Khaqan Abbasi, and me to finalize and sign the document in Udaipur.

Jaswant was hesitant about meeting the minister of external affairs for us to present the document to the Indian government but agreed to a meeting with Foreign Secretary Salman Haidar in the MEA committee room to place our report on record. In Pakistan, there was a far warmer official reception to our conclusions, but there were voices linking IPI to Kashmir.

Having been given the opportunity of translating this Track II initiative on to Track I, one of my earliest acts as minister of petroleum and natural gas was to drop in on my former ambassador in Pakistan and our new foreign minister, K. Natwar Singh, to seek his blessings. He was most encouraging and asked me to have the details of my proposal set forth in a formal cabinet note.

I found that some technical work on this hypothetical pipeline had earlier been undertaken by the ministry in consultation with GAIL and Indian Oil Corporation (IOC), with some inputs from ONGC.

Based on the initial work already done, the joint secretary, Avinash Kumar Srivastav, with the enthusiastic participation of then GAIL chairman and managing director (CMD), Proshanto Banerjee, and I started getting the cabinet paper ready. (My main contribution was to get punctuation, syntax and idiom right!) It took us about six months.

When the paper was ready and had been circulated among ministers by the Cabinet Secretariat, I had a most intriguing call from Natwar. He asked me what I thought he should say when the subject came up the next day in the cabinet. I replied that it would be best if he said absolutely nothing. I explained that he was the only minister who was likely to have anything to say on the subject and that the prime minister was sufficiently well disposed towards improving relations with Pakistan for us to get the in-principle clearance we needed to initiate our dialogue. If the external affairs minister (EAM) said nothing, other ministers too would not intervene, thus leaving the prime minister free to carry forward his own decision without others dissenting.

So, when the subject came up in the cabinet on 9 February 2005 and the PM invited comments, there were none, as I had anticipated. The PM then asked the EAM to speak. Natwar said he would follow the PM's decision. At this, the PM said I could begin the process by separately sounding out Pakistan and Iran but not trilaterally, and the talks should be of an exploratory nature without making any definitive commitments. That was fine with me. I had got what I wanted.

Later, I found that the foreign secretary was frothing with objections and waiting in the anteroom to be called in to present them. His objections, I guess (for they were never spelled out to me), were, first, to a major initiative relating to a sensitive foreign country being taken by a ministry other than the MEA. Fair enough, except that my initiative was in the full knowledge of, indeed at the instance of, his boss, the minister of external affairs. Indeed, it was the minister who had asked me to draft a cabinet paper to seek in-principle approval for further exploring the technical and political aspects of the proposal, with crucial inputs from our proposed partners, Pakistan and Iran.

The second major objection might have been to any initiative other than the conventionally negative one being taken with a country with whom suspicion and hostility, not constructive cooperation, was the foreign office norm.

I did not want a bureaucratic entanglement with the MEA at a level lower than the ministerial because the cabinet paper would then be awash with negativity. Of course, once in-principle clearance was given by the cabinet, the MEA would be fully involved both at headquarters and through our high commission in Islamabad and our embassy in Tehran.

Unlike the ministry of petroleum and natural gas which had initiated some work on the hypothetical IPI pipeline when this had initially been mooted in the second half of the nineties, the foreign office had chosen not to follow up this proposal despite the outcome of the 1995–97 Track–II talks having been formally communicated in writing by Jaswant Singh and me to Salman Haidar, the Indian foreign secretary at the time. Although the sectoral ministry concerned, P&NG, had drafted a technical paper on the subject, the MEA had not shown any interest in even exploring the idea further. And this despite the Indian foreign secretary's negotiations with his Pakistani interlocutor, Abdus Sattar, having kicked off the 'composite dialogue' that very year.

Also, it was not as if the MEA was kept in the dark. That the foreign office, unlike the sectoral economic ministry concerned, had chosen to not follow up was a different matter.

Non-Congress governments were in office in the intervening eight years (1996–2004) and the incoming Congress government was certainly entitled to take a fresh look at the proposal, especially as the new PM, Dr Manmohan Singh, had made clear his intention to build on the opening created by his predecessor Atal Bihari Vajpayee's visit to Islamabad in January 2004. There, on the sidelines of the SAARC summit, he and President Parvez Musharraf had proclaimed the Islamabad Declaration, thus paving the way to the resumption of talks between the two countries.

Preliminary soundings had convinced me that in addition to Natwar, the new PM was clear in his mind that we needed to add new dimensions to the relationship with our neighbour. If there were political objections, or objections in principle to this, I preferred that the objections be voiced at the political level in cabinet rather than getting into an endless inter-ministerial argument at the bureaucratic level. Foreign service bureaucrats are trained to be cautious, conservative and go by precedent, especially when it comes to a difficult and high-profile neighbour, more so in a matter of great public sensitivity where the outcome would remain uncertain. Energy security was not an issue in which, at the time, the MEA had much interest in or any institutional knowledge of. (That has now changed, with a foreign service joint secretary permanently posted to P&NG and a high-level officer in the MEA itself to handle energy security issues. I pride myself at having majorly contributed to these welcome developments by raising awareness of the energy security dimension of foreign and petroleum policy.)

Then there were technical issues to resolve. Did the three countries have the technology and experience to lay the sophisticated pipelines over thousands of kilometres of, possibly, difficult terrain? If technical help were needed, who would we turn to and on what terms? Could the three countries themselves finance the project, and, if so, in what shares? If additional resources were required, where and who should we attempt to find it? How would we ensure the security of supplies should the Pakistanis decide to turn off the tap? There were precedents, notably the Baku–Tblisi–Ceyhan pipeline (BTC), which was being laid amid serious internal and international terrorist threats. Could we have a station in a neutral location, such as Dubai, where every millimetre of the IPI pipeline could be monitored 24x7? How had other countries, including US majors like Halliburton, overcome the problem of the US legislature having passed the Iran Libya Sanctions Act (ILSA) under which the executive was authorized to impose sanctions on any country taking any step to strengthen economic cooperation with Iran? A Halliburton representative called on me to say he was from Halliburton Dubai, not Halliburton USA, and would have no difficulty in collaborating with us on the IPI. Also, US Ambassador David Mulford visited me to underline that while ILSA was on the US statute book, ILSA had never actually been invoked. The US Ambassador to Islamabad had made a similar statement in public. Natwar and I agreed that instead of being fazed at the outset by the US threat, we would tackle the threat when it came. That would, of course, involve the MEA and a whole range of other ministries, including finance, commerce and law. We agreed that it was premature to look into these hypothetical questions when what was needed was a joint technical assessment by the oil ministries of the three countries of the feasibility of the IPI to meet the imperatives of their pressing energy requirements.

Much of my diplomatic career had been spent reporting to ministries other than the MEA, principally the commerce ministry. In my first posting to Brussels as a probationer, my substantive work involved the Department of Culture (with Kapila Vatsyayan) rather than the political side. My very brief assignment in Hanoi had involved me with the MEA, but my acerbic boss kept the political side firmly out of my reporting tasks. At headquarters, my posting to the newly constituted Economic Division, at a time when no senior foreign service officer had the least notion of trade or other economic issues, meant that I was reporting largely to the commerce secretary, my old Brussels guru, K.B. Lall, and occasionally to sectoral ministries like finance and agriculture and to the Planning Commission. My interim posting for about half a year (September 1970 to March 1971) as private secretary to the minister of industrial development and internal trade kept me firmly out of the MEA's ken.

On returning to India in December 1971, after three months at the Economic Committee of the UN General Assembly, I found the nation plunged into the Bangladesh liberation war. My appointment as secretary of the high-powered committee set up to rush urgent relief supplies to Bangladesh and initiate economic relations with our newly liberated eastern neighbour meant that I was liaising with most of the economic ministries and parastatals but hardly at all with my own ministry (much to their relief, I might add).

My second posting to Brussels, this time to our mission to the European Economic Community (predecessor to today's European Union), involved me with the entire gamut of our economic ministries but hardly at all with the MEA. In Baghdad, as commercial counsellor, a commerce ministry post, my connection to the MEA was no more than token. From Karachi, I found that the MEA Pakistan desk barely understood, and had no particular interest in, my long, detailed paper, 'Towards a Revival of the Pakistan Economy'. This personal background in economic diplomacy made me profoundly aware that on most non-political issues, the sectoral ministry concerned functioned autonomously, with the MEA on the fringes. Therefore, I was inclined to keep the cards on the IPI pipeline in my hands rather than see them placed in the MEA's recalcitrant hands, especially as I had the EAM and the PM on my side.

Perhaps the most important point here was that the PM had himself bypassed the MEA and its plodding bureaucracy when it came to taking an imaginative leap over our relations with Pakistan. He appointed Sati Lambah (IFS retd) as his special envoy for the back-channel talks but kept him firmly in the PMO, reporting directly only to the PM himself.[6] Sati's principal advisers were also PMO men, albeit from the IFS but not at the time serving in the MEA: Vikram Doraiswamy, Jawed Ashraf, Jaideep Sarkar and Vikram Misri.[7] Musharraf did the same, naming a Pakistani Revenue Service officer, Tariq Aziz, who was a personal friend of the president and not a serving or retired Pakistan Foreign Service officer, as Lambah's counterpart special envoy. Of course, both leaders kept their respective foreign ministers in the loop, who were Natwar succeeded by Pranab Mukherjee on the Indian side, and Khurshid Kasuri, on the Pakistan side, but reporting was directly to the heads of government/state, and instructions emanated from that level. In Pakistan's case, the intelligence chief and army chief and a number of other army generals were kept fully informed.[8] (In India, this was not necessary.)

Finally, my apprehensions about dealing with an obdurate MEA on the IPI at less than the level of EAM and PM were proved right when in November 2004 the foreign secretary called on me on discovering, to his consternation, that I had sought and obtained an appointment to meet the visiting Pakistani prime minister, Shaukat Aziz. He insisted that I should stress to the Pakistani prime minister that unless he opened up the trade route between Afghanistan and India through Pakistan, and agreed to various other conditionalities relating to India's trade and economic relations with Pakistan, there could be no question of routing Iranian gas to India through Pakistan. Although I could not for the life of me quite grasp the foreign office's equivalence of pomegranates from Afghanistan, delicious as they are, with the nation's energy security requirements, I humbly did as I was told.

After a cordial but essentially unconstructive meeting with the Pakistani PM in accordance with the foreign secretary's briefing, I told the media that we needed to look at the IPI 'as part of a wider economic and trade cooperation between New Delhi and Islamabad . . . The project cannot be looked at in isolation'. I added that we first needed 'most favoured nation' treatment in the Pakistan market. The pipeline 'is only one of the issues'.

The Pakistani PM hit back immediately. Addressing the media as soon as I had finished, he underlined that Pakistan envisaged the IPI as 'a standalone project of great significance' and 'a huge and successful confidence-building measure' (CBM). As such, it should not be 'linked to other issues'. I silently noted that quite unlike his predecessors, the Pakistan PM was not linking the IPI to a settlement on Kashmir – which was possibly a first for any Pakistani PM. He stressed that 'we can offer India an energy corridor, *if it wants*' (emphasis added). If not, 'Pakistan would go ahead with the construction of a gas pipeline from Iran even if India were not interested in it'.[9]

It was clear that notwithstanding Pakistan delinking the IPI from other sensitive political issues, such as Kashmir, MEA officials only regarded the project as a debating point and were not concerned with the significance the project had for our energy security nor as a 'peace line', as the Pakistani PM later described it in Davos on 27 January 2005.[10]

On that date, 27 January 2005, we were on the edge of the crucial cabinet meeting that would decide whether India would move forward with discussions on the proposed project. As I saw it, hope for realizing the IPI lay only at the level of the EAM and PM.

Therefore, when Natwar chose to say nothing in the cabinet beyond the words 'I will abide by your direction, Sir' to the prime minister, there was no occasion for the foreign secretary to be called. The PM decided that exploratory talks might be held by me separately with the authorities concerned in Pakistan and Iran, then I could return to the cabinet with specific proposals.

The acceptance in principle of my cabinet note led to banner headlines next morning. I suddenly found myself catapulted into the realm of 'breaking news'.

In June 2005, I visited Islamabad and Tehran in succession. Such a large press contingent followed that I decided we would not fly but take the train to Amritsar and then go by road to the Attari–Wagah land crossing. The Pakistanis made quite a thing over our arrival, a motorbike escort taking us into Lahore with sirens screaming.

At a personal level, there was a touching private welcome ceremony arranged by the Residents Welfare Association of Lakshmi Mansions, my first home as an infant. The current occupant of our flat no. 44, Dr Mahmood Ali Malik, asked me for a blow-up of a photograph of my parents as they were when they lived in Lakshmi Mansions. The best I could do was provide a large portrait of the two of them taken in Delhi soon after Partition. We added a few more family photographs. The residents and the media were invited in to view the exhibition. The city supplement of the Lahore edition of *The News* carried a detailed account of the exhibition and the reunion. I was requested to carry a petition to President Musharraf urging that the residential complex be preserved as a heritage property as investors were planning to demolish it to make way for a shopping mall. (That, in fact, is what has now happened, although, as of the date of writing, no. 44 is in the last wing left standing.)

I went on to Islamabad. My counterpart was Amanullah Khan Jadoon, who I found early in our conversation had been elected from Abbottabad. A strong personal bond was established when I told him that Field Marshal Ayub Khan, Abbottabad's most famous resident, had been the best of friends with my late father-in-law, Major Vir Singh, when they served together in the same British Indian regiment. Jadoon promptly invited me and my wife to Abbottabad as his personal guests.

My credentials thus established, we turned to the more serious issues at hand.

I said I first needed to be informed of the dimensions of energy demand in Pakistan. Jadoon offered to set up that very afternoon a detailed technical presentation for me and my delegation, adding that he would himself acquaint me with the overall scenario of Pakistan's energy needs. He began by underlining that notwithstanding some recent coal finds near Badin in Sind, Pakistan at birth found itself entirely without coal. When, therefore, gas was struck at the Sui gas fields in Balochistan in the mid-fifties, all domestic and most industrial units were switched to Sui gas. Cooking, especially in the urban areas, was on gas (with wood or hay or other bio-waste being used as a primary or supplementary fuel in rural Pakistan). Given the cold weather that overtook much of west Pakistan in the winter, domestic heating was by gas, again especially in urban areas. But Sui gas was running out and it was essential to look for gas elsewhere – and where better than by pipeline from Iran? He added that if Pakistan were the sole buyer of Iranian gas, its price would shoot up, but if India and Pakistan were joint buyers, prices would moderate.

This backgrounder was confirmed with detailed facts and figures in the PowerPoint presentation made to us. The estimate given was that by 2025, Pakistan's requirements of natural gas would shoot up to 300 billion cubic metres a day as against an Indian requirement of 200 billion cubic metres a day, that is, a third higher, despite Pakistan's much smaller population and geographic area. This assessment confirmed for me my view that if the Pakistanis were to arbitrarily cut off supplies or inordinately delay repairing the pipeline for political reasons, it would amount to cutting off their nose to spite their own face, provided we worked that into the contract documents. Moreover, at no point did Jadoon or his colleagues or the Pakistani media mention a settlement of the Kashmir issue or any other issue as a precondition to progressing with the pipeline.

That seemed as good a basis as any for a joint approach to Iran. It also seemed to forestall any deliberate sabotage of the IPI, especially if we made it a condition in the deal that Iranian supplies to Pakistan by the pipeline would be halted if there were any unconscionable delays in repairing the sabotage.

My Cambridge friend, Foreign Minister Khurshid Kasuri, arranged for me to pay a call on President Musharraf, who had just returned from Oman, where he had discussed the prospects for a possible underwater gas pipeline between Oman and Gwadar in Pakistan. I, therefore, opened with a question about his Oman visit. The president airily dismissed my question, saying an underwater pipeline was a pipe dream, not technically feasible. Much more important were the overground gas pipelines from Iran and Turkmenistan, he said, adding that so long as Afghanistan remained disturbed, the only immediately feasible option was an overland pipeline from Iran to Pakistan, extendable to India, if India wanted.

What I thought would be a courtesy call of ten to fifteen minutes extended to over an hour as the president asked further questions about our assessment of the actual reserves in the Daulatabad gas field in Turkmenistan, which the Asian Development Bank (and the US oil giant, Bechtel) had identified as the principal source of gas supplies. I replied that our experts too were sceptical of Daulatabad's potential, but if we were to extend Turkmenistan–Afghanistan–Pakistan–India (TAPI) to Uzbekistan, landlocked and Russia-locked with abundant reserves, making TAPI into UTAPI, the issue of supplies could be resolved. Indeed, I went on, why not also include Kazakhstan, which had struck quantities of hydrocarbons in the Caspian basin to extend UTAPI to KUTAPI, then on to Astrakhan on the Caspian Sea in the Russian Federation to convert KUTAPI into RUKUTAPI. I triumphantly ended my oration by saying that we should also rope in Azerbaijan, thus ending with ARUKUTAPI! Musharraf smiled and said he thought that might be feasible as 'the vowels and the consonants have fallen into place'! He then asked Kasuri to get this studied. I came away feeling rewarded, as my ministry might yet be a major beneficiary of the growing détente between Pakistan and India, symbolized by the back-channel talks on Kashmir the two leaders had initiated through trusted personal envoys.

With the Iranian oil minister scheduled to be in Islamabad in the next few weeks to discuss the IPI, and the Pakistan minister Jadoon having been sounded on an early visit to New Delhi, possibly just a month later, and President Musharraf having given his 'full backing' to the project, working groups had been formed to tackle the technical and security aspects of the proposal. This, I said, showed 'there has been positive forward movement' and 'milestones put in place'.

I thus felt I had good reason to be upbeat at the press conference I addressed in Islamabad at the conclusion of my visit. I said, 'We have signposted the way forward. We can smile with confidence.' I affirmed my long-held belief that what was needed was for the two countries 'to have a stake in each other's economies'. I said Pakistan and India were of the view that the IPI was 'technologically and economically' more viable than other options, so other options (such as TAPI) should be regarded as 'additional' to IPI, not alternatives. On the question of security, I said, 'We have now moved from the stage of asking questions about security to addressing security concerns in a serious and sincere manner.' As for US objections, I stuck to my line that 'we are sensitive to their concerns, and we trust they are aware of our requirements'.[11]

With that perspective in mind, I went on to Tehran. The meeting opened with the Iranian oil minister, Bijan Namdar Zangeneh, saying he had heard that I had been 'plotting' with Pakistan against Iranian interests. I hastened to assure him that the rumour could not possibly be true but, yes, as Pakistan and India were buyers, it was necessary for us to coordinate our offer on prices. Zanganeh seemed reassured. At any rate, the meeting went forward in a harmonious and constructive manner. The note of caution I heard from our ambassador, K.C. Singh, was not to rely on word of mouth with Iranian elections in the offing. For my part, I felt satisfied at having carried out my mandate from the cabinet.

Meanwhile, and almost at the same time that I was in Pakistan and Iran, the prime minister and the External Affairs Minister Natwar Singh were in Washington, DC, visiting with US President George W. Bush and Secretary of State Condoleezza Rice. From what I have been able to gather, the US leaders dangled the prospect of a civil nuclear deal, provided India called off negotiations on the IPI.[12]

In early July, I was in Turkey, nominally to attend a large gathering of petroleum experts, but my main objective was to visit Ceyhan, the terminal point of the Baku–Tblisi–Ceyhan (BTC) oil pipeline, whose point of commencement, Baku, I had already visited. I needed to get a fix on how BTC had ensured the security of its long oil pipeline that lay close to the highly disputed flashpoint of Nagorno-Karabakh and the sensitive border points of Nakhchivian and Gegharkunik, which witnessed repeated armed clashes amounting to war between Azerbaijan and Armenia. The pipeline also lay close to terrorist and armed uprisings in Abkhazia and South Ossetia, troubled southern provinces of the Russian Federation. Its entire route through eastern Turkey to the port of Ceyhan lay in Turkey's insurgency-ridden Kurdish areas. How had the BTC been immunized against terrorist disruption of oil supplies? That, it seemed to me, was a key question to be answered as we went forward with the IPI. Fortunately, I had found an Indian, Shashi Mukundan, working for BP, perhaps the most important of the BTC partners, whom I had first consulted in Baku and now found in Ceyhan. His answer was simplicity itself. He said they had worked on the legal safeguards for six times longer than it had taken to lay the pipeline. That was when safeguards had been written into the highly detailed agreements before work on the pipeline began.

I was surprised to receive in Istanbul a call from the prime minister's principal secretary asking me to report to the PM the minute I got back to Delhi. I was in for the coldest shower I have ever taken. The PM asked me to go slow on the IPI, saying he thought the technological problems were overwhelming and he did not know where we were going to find the required finances. I protested that the three countries between them had plenty of experience in laying pipelines and, in any case, I had been approached by Rosneft and another Russian private party, and even

Halliburton Dubai, offering to provide technical assistance, even take up the project, if needed. As for finances, the estimated amount was in the region of $3–4 billion and could be found in the treasuries of the three countries and the internal resources and creditworthiness of the participating commercial entities, state-owned and private. The PM mentioned neither the US nor ILSA, but it would have taken a child to spot that the stumbling block was US objections.

I had to sit it out, but working group meetings went on while I was minister under the joint chairmanship of Petroleum Secretary S.K. Tripathi and Dr M.H. Nejad Hosseinian, the Iranian deputy minister of the new Iranian government (which had ushered out my friend Zanganeh). The India–Iran special joint working group, set up in my predecessor's time, met on 28–29 December 2005. And took a number of far-reaching decisions, including those relating to the 'project structure', the 'framework agreement' and the 'gas price structure'. It was further agreed that there would be a tripartite meeting (which would need cabinet approval) in February 2006 and an itemized roadmap for further meetings in the quarter January–March 2006. But I was out of the ministry at the end of January and never learned whether the talks had gone forward. In any case, the IPI now stands shelved. Twenty years later, we are where we were.

When in February, a Sui gas delegation from Pakistan arrived after I had been dropped from the ministry, I had them over for a very cordial, amiable, informal dinner at my home.

Thus ended the IPI, with a whimper rather than a bang.

India–US civil nuclear deal

The civil nuclear deal with the US was concluded and cleared with the International Atomic Energy Agency (IAEA), the Nuclear Suppliers Group being strong-armed to consent by the US. Foreign Secretary Shivshankar Menon described to me in personal conversation the US diplomatic arm-twisting at Vienna as 'awesome' – 'aa-sum', in an American accent! But seventeen years later we are still to obtain a single unit of electricity because of the nuclear deal. In any case, nuclear energy could never have met more than 5–6 per cent of our energy needs. Of course, the deal signalled India coming on board the American ship (and all the good things that followed), but holding the IPI hostage to the civil nuclear deal has proved a heavy price to pay. I was so distressed that when it came to the vote in Parliament approving the India–US civil nuclear deal, subconsciously and for the only time in my twenty-one years in Parliament, I pressed the 'NO' button, and then, totally alarmed at my own impudence, quickly changed my vote to 'AYE' using the correction slips distributed routinely by the tellers.

While UPA-I lasted (2004–09), IPI continued to breathe, as affirmed by Natwar's successor Pranab Mukherjee in Tehran on 2 November 2008, nearly three years after I had been dropped from the ministry: 'Nuclear power is one source of energy. The other important source is the IPI gas pipeline. One is not exclusive of the other.' Earlier, delivering a lecture at a seminar, he had said, 'The basic imperative of the India–US civil nuclear agreement is the same that binds us to the Iran–Pakistan-India gas pipeline. Our energy needs are too large to be met from a single source.'[13]

To go by press reports of the current minister of P&NG taking office again after the 2024 general elections, no pipelines, and certainly not IPI, are on the agenda. Meanwhile, our import dependence on crude oil has shot up from around 70 per cent in my time as minister to 85 per cent now. How's that for *atmanirbharata* (self-reliance), a key slogan, along with 'Make in India', of the Modi establishment?

Myanmar-Bangladesh-India (MBI) gas pipeline

There was also a clash with the MEA over my attempting to route natural gas from Myanmar to India through Bangladesh. In January 2005 came the very welcome news that GAIL, partnering a South Korean hydrocarbons exploration company, had found gas in substantial quantity off Myanmar at a rig known as A–3 outside Sittwe in the Bay of Bengal (the port had attained fame in the Second World War when it was called Akyab).

This gas, I thought, would facilitate our proposed petrochemical complex in Haldia, West Bengal. The CPI(M) chief minister of West Bengal, Buddhadeb Bhattacharya, specially called on me at my hotel when my other ministerial responsibility, Panchayati Raj, took me to Kolkata, to discuss with me his concerns about adequate gas for the Haldia petrochemical complex. As GAIL's imaginative suggestion for an LPG ship to ply between Akyab and Haldia had not found any takers, as the cost of liquefying the gas at Akyab and re-gasifying it at Haldia was too high, I thought a pipeline from Akyab to Haldia via Cox's Bazar in Bangladesh might be the answer.

As far as Myanmar was concerned, their fear was that Chinese domination over their economy and polity would only be strengthened if India were to let China be the principal beneficiary of the A–3 discovery.

As for Bangladesh, our high commissioner in Dhaka had shared with me in a secret telegram the intelligence that had reached her of the Bangladesh PM's office having laid down three conditions before their minister could agree to our suggestion that Myanmar gas be pumped out through Bangladesh to India: one, that a share be sold to Bangladesh for their industrial complex in Jessore on the border of West Bengal; two, that hydroelectricity from Bhutan be routed directly to Bangladesh instead of through India; and, three, that there be tangible improvement in the balance of trade between the two countries, which was heavily weighted in favour of India.

Armed with this information, straight from the horse's mouth as it were, I sought a bilateral meeting with the Bangladesh minister, A.K.M. Mosharraf Hossain, before our trilateral with the Myanmar minister, Brigadier Lun Thi, to confirm that I was sure GAIL could be persuaded to sell some of the gas at Jessore through which the pipeline had to pass; second, that Bangladesh must secure Bhutan's agreement to buying hydroelectricity directly from them (which, I assured the MEA, India could block secretly with Bhutan, if deemed essential); and, third, while it was impossible to ensure rectification of the balance of trade between the two countries, payment of transit fees for the proposed pipeline would tilt the capital account so much in favour of Bangladesh that the balance of payment (as different from the balance of trade) could be presented to the people of Bangladesh as a major victory.

He nodded his agreement, and almost leaped up when I pointed out that Bangladesh, through a branch line linked to the Myanmar–Bangladesh–India (MBI) transit line, could carry the hitherto unused gas discovered at Bangladesh near Brahmanbari in the north-east of Bangladesh to their industrial complex at Jessore in the south-west.

Once we were of one mind, we went along to the Myanmar minister and presented our bilateral accord to him. On the principle of *'Mianbiwi razi / Toh kya karega qazi'* (If husband and wife are agreed, what role is left for the arbitrator?), Myanmar promptly agreed. At this, I jocularly remarked to the Myanmar minister, Brigadier Lun Thi, that this was a 'win-win' proposition and not a Ne Win proposition. He merely looked grim to save himself from a Myanmar army assassination squad!

Thus, we succeeded in a single round over a couple of days' discussion in Yangon (Rangoon) in carrying both the Myanmar and the Bangladesh ministers with us. It was also decided that officials and technical experts from the three countries would meet to iron out the remaining issues in three successive meetings in the three countries. However, my very capable joint secretary, Avinash K. Srivastav, succeeded in the first round itself in wrapping up all the technical issues.

I had reckoned without the MEA's objection in principle to giving a boost to Begum Khaleda Zia, then prime minister of Bangladesh. This was an objective which our high commissioner to Bangladesh was diligently pursuing. The irony is that had the MEA not proved such a dog in the manger, the pipeline would have been inaugurated by Sheikh Hasina, and the pro-India Awami League could have earned all the political credit!

As an alternative to the MBI, and only to not allow Khaleda to get any political advantage, the MEA offered the ridiculous suggestion that I route the gas through a pipeline that would follow the Kaladan river marking the border between southern Mizoram and Myanmar, which we were developing as a sea outlet for landlocked Mizoram. Throwing protocol to the winds, and in my capacity as a former IFS colleague, armed with a map of the region I went to see the joint secretary in her office at the MEA's Bangladesh desk to explain that the Kaladan river, after flowing past Mizoram, returned to near its source in Myanmar. The MEA was, therefore proposing that the pipeline should go from Myanmar to Myanmar through India! She failed to see the humour in my observation. She did not have a map that showed the river's course. I gave her a number of arguments as to why her proposal was totally impracticable, but she remained adamant and utterly unmoved. Thus, a great opportunity for laying the foundations of regional economic cooperation in the Bay of Bengal area was missed. It would have also made it possible to leverage the pipeline to quietly intervene diplomatically to mitigate the genocide that befell the Rohingya much later in the Myanmar state of Rakhine, whose capital is Sittwe.

While I was profusely congratulating my team on their MBI success, the foreign secretary called in the petroleum secretary and thundered over whether the P&NG ministry was taking over foreign policy from the MEA. Quailing at being taken into realms with which he was not familiar, my IAS petroleum secretary, who had no experience of foreign policy and no foreign postings, merely cowed down and rushed back to say it was for me at my level to handle the MEA.

Anger among the high officials at the MEA was at such a pitch that Natwar felt obliged to ask me to slow down on the MBI. While I was allowed to visit Dhaka in September that year, where I met Khaleda and succeeded in getting her key ministers to actually sign with me over dinner an agreement on transit of a pipeline through Cox's Bazar, our government continued to drag its feet. Before departing Dhaka the same evening, I requested our high commissioner to get the handwritten and heavily amended agreement typed and sent to me in Delhi. She added the word 'DRAFT' to what was, in fact, a signed agreement. That too did not help.

Meanwhile, Brigadier Lun Thi, the Myanmar oil minister, was getting alarmed at our delay in confirming our interest in buying for our own use the gas we had ourselves discovered. He arrived in New Delhi while the MEA was adamantly holding out. I was unable to give him the confirmation he needed. The Chinese, spotting Indian hesitancy, ramped up their pressure on Myanmar to route the gas to Kunmin. Against Myanmar's own interests, Myanmar had to let the Chinese have the gas India had discovered in Myanmar. Who gained, and who lost?

Advisory committee on 'Synergy in Energy'

Rhetoric and high-sounding words apart, it was necessary for our petroleum sector to show the world that its pockets were as deep as those of the Chinese, who were beating us in an unconscionably large number of international auctions for oil and gas fields. I started scouting around to see how this might be achieved, when I learned that our most cash-rich public sector enterprise in the petroleum sector, the giant Indian IOC, was listed at around position 130 in the Fortune 500 list.

It had been mentioned to me in passing that if we were to merge all our many oil public sector enterprises (PSEs), we could perhaps wind up at position thirty-four on the Fortune list. I grabbed the figure as the only way in which we could stop losing to the Chinese in so many international bids. Were our oil sector to be pitched at position thirty-four, we could borrow massively in the international markets to give the Chinese a real run for their money.

There was also my conviction that our oil sector needed to be integrated into a single corporation to effectively establish partnerships with petroleum technology entities the world over to undertake the R&D necessary to acquire or develop the technology needed to drill through the Deccan Trap; to exploit the elusive on-land resources of the Terai; to reach down the required 10,000 feet to locate the potential resources in the Konkan-Kerala Exclusive Economic Zone (EEZ); and to secure the commercialization of our enormous deposits of gas hydrates in the Bay of Bengal, particularly in the Andaman Sea. Technology unique to our geological conditions was, I believed, the key to unlocking our indigenous resources.

A third major consideration was that instead of remaining segregated in their designated upstream and downstream roles, the PSUs were integrating across the value chain. ONGC had already become a major stakeholder in Mangalore Refinery, while IOC, BPCL and HPCL were attempting inroads into upstream exploration both in India and abroad. Indeed, while GAIL had been set up expressly for natural gas alone, it was attempting to enter the oil sector upstream and downstream while the oil sector companies were bidding for gas fields in Iran and elsewhere.

This being so, why not a massive public sector conglomerate – a kind of public sector chaebol on the South Korean pattern – extending from upstream to downstream with impressive R&D capacity? I, therefore, started envisaging a single conglomerate covering both petroleum and natural gas.

To this end, I sought out an old friend, V. Krishnamurthy, who had made a great reputation in public sector corporate management. I had first met him more than thirty years earlier, when I was private secretary to the minister of industrial development when, under the ministry, he was running the boiler plant of BHEL in Tiruchirappalli. I had been impressed with his abilities. When he came to Delhi to ask me to persuade my minister to split BHEL into four separate entities so that he could become CMD of the boiler plant unit, I gently reprimanded him for not setting his sights higher to become CMD of the corporation itself.

My prediction turned out to be correct. He went on to become Secretary, heavy industry, before taking over as CMD of Steel Authority of India Limited (SAIL), which he turned around during Rajiv Gandhi's premiership from a corporation losing Rs 1 crore per day into a corporation earning profits of Rs 1 crore per day (which, in the 1980s, was impressive). When George Fernandes targeted him, I stood up for him in Parliament.

I explained to Krishnamurthy what I had in mind. I asked him to chair an independent advisory committee on 'Synergy in Energy' that could report on the feasibility of merging the oil and gas sector PSEs into one giant corporation. I suggested a few members, whom Krishnamurthy happily accepted, and he asked whether his friend G.V. Ramakrishna could also be included. They then got down to work and I strictly kept myself away to ensure their independence.

I made the cardinal error of leaving it to the ministry officials, oil PSU top honchos and the chairman to work out their terms of reference. The advisory committee skewed these to satiate the bees in their bonnet instead of answering the key question I had put to them of merging our oil sector PSUs into a single giant conglomerate.

A few months after the committee had been established, Krishnamurthy called on me, asking confidentially what it was that I hoped would be the committee's principal recommendation since he saw no point in presenting a report that would be rejected. I told him that I had left them completely autonomous in order that they may objectively evaluate my proposition while taking into account possible objections, even fundamental ones, to the proposal.

As for what I sought in terms of recommendations, I had already made it clear to him when I approached him, and subsequently in well-publicized public statements, that I hoped we could have a single petroleum giant. He went away sagely nodding his head. It was not I but he, as chairman, who had sought the meeting with me, and that rendered me somewhat complacent about the outcome.

When, six months later, they presented their report, I found I had been conned. As for the central issue of financially strengthening our capacity to compete successfully for exploration projects abroad, particularly against the two Chinese mega giants Sinopec and CNPC, the only relevant sentence in the entire report on E&P abroad was the injunction:

> Overseas E&P should be pursued aggressively by targeting at least 15 per cent of crude oil imports through (the) equity oil route within the next 2–3 years.

Yes, but how?

The advisory committee made two recommendations: one, that the managing director of ONGC Videsh Limited, a subsidiary of ONGC, be made vice chairman of ONGC; two, just as ONGC had been given its very own overseas subsidiary in OVL, so also should OIL be given its very own poodle, to be called OIVL (OIL INDIA Videsh Limited)!

Nothing about Chinese (and other) competition; nothing about Fortune 500 listings; nothing about the number of bids lost to the Chinese and other MNCs; nothing about actually reaching the target of 15 per cent. For the rest, the status quo to be maintained, with minor changes and some homilies doled out.

The committee's report contained one other passing reference to my proposal: 'Any mega entity dominating the energy market has ambiguous implications.'

Vijay Kelkar explained this gobbledygook, giving the example of Petroleos de Venezuela S.A. (better known by its initialism PDVSA) disproportionately influencing politics and policy in Venezuela owing to its huge financial clout. Taking into account that Hugo Chavez was the president of the country and had been invited to India as a state guest in March 2005, the advisory committee had shied away from naming him or Venezuela and opted for the ambiguous expression 'ambiguous'!

The committee then considered the possibility of establishing a single corporation but rejected this: 'While this could work well in a centrally controlled single-party political system, it may not be feasible in a democratic society which requires a consensus-based approach.' They proposed that rather than integrate our oil and gas companies into one giant conglomerate, we might follow the example of Singapore's TEMASEK. What they forgot, or chose to ignore, was that there are no oil companies under the TEMASEK umbrella.

They backed up this argument with the example of Coal India Limited, a public sector holding company, which they held to have 'failed'. The analogy was completely irrelevant to what I was proposing. Coalfields in India had been developed by a number of private enterprises, largely in colonial times, and had been taken under the government's wing during the rash of nationalizations in the wake of Indira Gandhi's electoral triumph in 1971.

There was a world of difference between bundling nationalized private sector companies immediately after nationalization into one public sector holding company and merging navratna PSEs of long standing into a single entity, principally to give the new mega-entity the financial clout to win competitive bids in international markets.

The committee did not even look at this angle. Instead, they held that replicating the example of Sinopec and CNPC, which arose out of merging earlier Chinese entities and dividing the responsibilities of the two giants on a geographical basis, was not politically feasible in a democratic, multi-party system. This was yet another red herring irrelevant to the purpose for which the committee had been formed.

The advisory committee's tame recommendation was for the setting up of a National Shareholding Trust (NST), which would hold all government shares in oil and gas PSUs. This, of course, would fulfil the honchos' dream of insulating them from the government but would do nothing to improve our competitiveness vis-à-vis our main competitors for oil/gas assets abroad, the Chinese mega giants CNPC and Sinopec.

Ultimately, the committee's pedestrian recommendations amounted to no more than marginal tinkering with the existing system. They did not advocate bold, innovative, systemic change. The only merger they were ready to recommend was of 'existing stand-alone subsidiaries with parent companies'; then they recommended establishment of a downstream regulatory authority and 'strengthening' of the DGH – without saying how!

The report was a major setback for me. I stalked out of the conference room in a foul mood and, eluding the media packing the corridor, shut myself in my office. Mohanty offered to present a critique of the report, which he did do with great panache. But I decided to quietly bury the report – exactly as Krishnamurthy apprehended I might. No one else took any action on it. I never again spoke to Krishnamurthy.

Worst of all, at least from my point of view, was that Natwar was out of the ministry the following month (November 2005) over the Volker report on Saddam's oil-for-food scam.[14] I am persuaded by Natwar's account that he was framed. I was dropped from the ministry a few months later. The oil diplomacy group was disbanded. Talmiz Ahmad was repatriated to the MEA. Oil diplomacy went into a limbo.

Tsunami hits my constituency

On 26 December 2004, Boxing Day, a new word of Japanese origin entered our everyday vocabulary: 'tsunami'. I got a call from S. Rajakumar in the constituency to say that something awful had happened on the coast and he was rushing there to see what it was all about. When he called me back, I found that the tsunami had had its landfall in Nagapattinam district, including the northern half of the district which fell in my constituency.

I was given the prime minister's Air Force plane to fly to Chennai and went to inspect the damage there. Next day, I took one of the oil company helicopters and, after a brief inspection of Cuddalore, where the Sikh district collector Gagandeep Singh Bedi was making quite a name for himself with tsunami relief, I landed in Mayiladuturai and drove straight to the coast.

It was a horrific spectacle. Boats had been carried by the waves thousands of yards inland and dumped in awkward positions in the fields. Huts had been blown away as if they were toy houses. At every doorstep people were nursing their injuries. The dead were uncounted, but the smell of death was everywhere. It was devastation on a scale I had not ever encountered.

The survivors stood around listlessly, traumatized. We decided to drive south to Nagapattinam city to alert the district collector to the disaster that had overtaken the northern part of the district, which no one was talking about, their attention being focused on the devastation caused in the southern Nagapattinam port area.

I prevailed upon the collector to see for himself the destruction further north. He came later, accompanied by a very competent IAS officer, Dr Radhakrishnan, a former Nagapattinam collector, specially deputed to assist in tsunami work.

We also learned that Sonia Gandhi was arriving next day with the *raksha mantri*, Pranab Mukherjee. We returned to Nagapattinam city to receive them, and I prevailed on the pilot to bring them to my constituency without undertaking the required test landing. I argued that as I had already landed in my oil sector helicopter on the playing field of a school in the vicinity of Poompuhar, that might be taken as the trial landing.

The pilot sportingly agreed and flew the *raksha mantri*, the Congress president and me, along with the rest of the entourage, to Poompuhar, where there was no formal reception. But the party were able to see for themselves the horrors of the tsunami. I declined to fly back to Delhi with them saying my duty lay here.

Having visited many of the hard-hit locations, I decided that I could help more if I assigned N. Venkataraman of my private office to handle the consequences of the tragedy at the constituency end. He and Rajakumar did a splendid job. I left for the capital where a lawyer friend of mine, Kavi Tulsi, had arranged with the local Sikh community for truckloads of relief supplies to be sent to our coastal area and to set up a 'langar' (free food camp) in Poompuhar.

After he had spent several weeks in the constituency supervising the emergency relief work, and after my own frequent visits to the area whenever I got a break from my ministerial obligations, I felt able to call Venkat back to Delhi once the state government got its act together and the global NGO community moved in. This turned out to be a political mistake, for the tsunami victims soon forgot our emergency relief work when others were gearing up and remembered only the more permanent measures of relief and rehabilitation undertaken by others in our wake. I gained no electoral kudos for having been first on the scene.

The Eternal Flame (Swatantra Jyot) at the Port Blair Cellular Jail

My predecessor, Ram Naik, a pleasant person who was an ardent RSS man, asked me whether he could be invited to the inauguration in August 2004 of the 'Eternal Flame' (Swatantra Jyot) at the Port Blair Cellular Jail. I replied that he was most welcome.

On making further inquiries, I learned to my horror that the Eternal Flame was not really designed to commemorate the freedom fighters who had been martyred as 'lifers' in the jail, but to raise Naik's hero, V.D. Savarkar, to the level of the real heroes of our freedom movement and to the shocking exclusion of the biggest hero of them all, Mahatma Gandhi. So, I had the Savarkar plaque replaced by a plaque commemorating Gandhi-ji. This was, of course, anathema not only to Naik but the entire Sangh Parivar, who were, in any case, mourning their loss of power to a resurgent Congress led by their *bête noire*, the Italian-born Sonia Gandhi. Naik, in particular, was incensed by my action. So, L.K. Advani took up cudgels for him in the Lok Sabha.

Repeatedly forcing adjournments of the Lok Sabha for the best part of a fortnight, they stalled proceedings demanding I apologize. When the Leader of the House accepted their demand for a statement, I drafted it and showed it in advance to the Speaker, in accordance with the rules. He approved the draft, subject only to my dropping the sentence contrasting the Quit India movement's slogan, '*Karenge ya Marenge*' (Do or die) to my concocted BJP slogan '*Karenge ya Maarenge*' (Do or kill). That statement was never made, as the BJP members would not stop heckling when I rose to read it. While Sonia, Pranab and the Congress/UPA generally supported my stand as vigorously as the BJP and its cohort opposed it, I was stunned by Prime Minister Dr Manmohan Singh's answer to a question at a press conference about the rumpus: 'I do not believe in talking ill of the dead.' My silent reaction was, 'In that case, Heil Hitler!'

Prevented from explaining the rationale of my action, I gave an interview to Vir Sanghvi of the *Hindustan Times* in which I pointed out that I had lit the flame on 9 August, the anniversary of 'Quit India' day, sacred to the memory of the freedom movement (which Savarkar had described as 'Split India Day'). Bizarrely, there was no mention at the Eternal Flame monument of Gandhi-ji. The only way we could have rectified this insult to his memory was by removing one of the existing plaques.

The remaining plaques commemorated freedom fighters like Bhagat Singh and Madan Lal Dhingra, who had actually sacrificed their young lives. I said it would diminish the memory of the martyrs if it also included people who had not been martyred even though they might have been incarcerated in the Cellular Jail. Savarkar, I noted, died peacefully in bed twenty years after Independence at the ripe old age of eighty-three. Moreover, while there was no doubt that Savarkar was a patriot, he insisted his country was a Hindu nation. He also insisted that Muslims constituted a different nation. My patriotism embraced equally all the communities of India. Asked specifically whether this was not an insult to Maharashtra, the state to which Savarkar belonged and where he was revered, I replied in the negative, saying the only insult was to the Father of the Nation in not naming him at the Swatantra Jyot.

That, I hoped, would quell matters. But when I visited Mumbai a few months later for a function organized by a parastatal oil company's trade union to celebrate their golden jubilee, goons wrecked the venue. The police stopped me as we were on our way there and took me to the local police station for my safety. When I was next invited to Mumbai for an *India Today* function, I was astonished to find all side roads blocked to give me smooth passage to the Taj, but violent louts, who had clandestinely taken a room in the hotel to attack me on arrival, were thwarted because I had taken a later flight than the one announced. They avenged themselves by smashing everything they could in the reception area. This led to my being escorted out of the hotel to a guest house deep inside the airport. Then, when I attended a family wedding reception a few weeks later, I found myself protected by a veritable army of police (someone told me numbering 400). And when I rushed to Mumbai to see ONGC crewmen who had been rescued from a burning rig at Bombay High, I was advised at my hotel not to personally accept grievance petitions, as was my wont, because the unionized hotel employees had been instructed to physically assault me if I got anywhere near them!

Additional Secretary Talmiz Ahmad

My stepping beyond my bounds on the IPI and MBI pipelines, as the MEA saw it, was compounded by my asking for the deputation of Talmiz Ahmad as my additional secretary for oil diplomacy. He is an old and much valued friend, whom I had leaned on when he served as my second secretary (commercial) in Baghdad (1977–78). The foreign office offered one of their surplus joint secretaries. This was unacceptable to me. I needed an officer who would be senior enough and self-confident enough to hold his own vis-à-vis his senior IAS counterparts in the ministry and the oil honchos, as well as the interfering busybodies from the MEA and the displeased foreign secretary, and would get on well with the retired ambassadors in the oil diplomacy group. Most important of all, I wanted someone senior enough to act as my advance man in negotiations I would be undertaking with my counterpart ministers in other countries. I trusted Talmiz. I had confidence in his diplomatic skills. And I found his friendly and open manner reassuring. He reciprocated in full measure and continues to remain among my closest friends. Indeed, he was so enthused by his assignment to P&NG that he has grown into one of our most renowned experts on international petroleum issues and is a regular on global think tank circuits on energy security and climate change.

What I had in mind were not tasks to be entrusted to a run-of-the-mill surplus MEA joint secretary whose loyalties and self-interest would primarily lie with his ministry of origin. I knew Talmiz would pledge himself to me first, foremost and last. So, I went straight up to his minister, K. Natwar Singh, and secured his approval to the MEA seconding Talmiz to a new post as additional secretary in my ministry. All this greatly riled the MEA. In choosing between massaging their egos and getting on with my job, I preferred the latter. This has not earned me many friends in my own peer group, but, in Edith Piaf's immortal words, '*Je ne regrette rien*' (I regret nothing).

Oil diplomacy group

Another source of tension was my setting up an oil diplomacy group, under the chairmanship of M. Hamid Ansari, a veteran of our diplomacy in *registan* (the desert) whom destiny kissed to become vice president of India for a full decade (2007–17). The group included my IFS contemporaries who had achieved rare distinction in economic diplomacy or had served with kudos in countries of hydrocarbon importance.

The MEA was, again, not amused. Nor were the IAS officers manning P&NG. They felt transgressed upon. So, the minute I was out, the group was dissolved, without even a letter of thanks to the members. I had to intervene with my ministerial successor, Murli Deora, to get even this common courtesy extended to them. It was done, but grudgingly. Pipeline diplomacy was abandoned.

Directorships in 'navratnas'

There were a number of independent directorships to be filled in various navratna oil PSUs. I had been keeping my hands off this hot potato under the legal cover of these entities being 'autonomous'. I had, however, received a call from the Congress president's political secretary that I should await a list he was sending me before making any decisions.

The list, when it was received months later, was so blatantly nepotistic that I merely sent it to the minister of heavy industries, who was required to vet the list before bringing it to the attention of the PSUs concerned. The list was, of course, leaked to the media in early September, and I found myself besieged at my home by cameramen, anchors and reporters.

I rang Pulok Chatterjee in the PMO. He was coordinating with the Congress president, and he said he would consult her and come back to me with her final order. I was eventually allowed to withdraw the list. That saved me politically but stained my reputation indelibly.

Relations with ONGC

A very public spat arose between the chairman of ONGC, Subir Raha, and me over the poor record of new discoveries by ONGC, compared with the record of extraordinary discoveries bruited about by Reliance and GSPC (which later proved exaggerated).

I was also over-influenced by my petroleum secretary not being able to get convincing arguments out of Raha for ONGC's less-than-impressive performance. Raha's argument was that unlike manufacturing units, targets could not be fixed for oil and gas discoveries. Oil and gas exploration was essentially an informed gamble. Every well drilled was a considered risk. It sometimes worked and sometimes did not. That was inherent in the process. Moreover, the DGH existed to check whether discoveries allegedly made had actually been made or were being announced without due verification and certification. This, he claimed, was what was happening with regard to the much-hailed 'discoveries' by Reliance and GSPC in the KG basin offshore Andhra Pradesh. Of course, the firms themselves were careful not to make any such boasts before DGH verification, but the stock markets had been tipped off, leading to killings on the Bombay Stock Exchange (BSE). The international oil community also appeared to have accepted these unverified claims as genuine.

Raha believed the petroleum secretary was over-impressed with unproven claims while he himself was anchored in reality. ONGC was indeed as anchored in the KG basin as Reliance/GSPC, as it was in exploring elsewhere in the Bay of Bengal, such as in the Mahanadi basin in Odisha and offshore the Sundarbans in West Bengal. But PSEs could not do what private entities were adept at: leaking insider information to stock exchanges to exponentially raise their market cap and rake in profits engendered by such volatility.

I felt bound to back my secretary. I had a nagging feeling that Raha was covering up for a lack of 'animal spirits' in his giant parastatal. Finding me siding with my secretary, Raha overwhelmed me with documents and data,[15] much of it quite irrelevant, but I had to plough through them to try to separate the wheat from the chaff. Before I could quite do so, the prime minister summoned a meeting at which I did my best to explain that it was increasingly disturbing to see the contrast between the gung-ho private sector and the lassitude in our public sector. I repeated the aphorism about oil discoveries beginning not at the drill site but in the mind. I also talked about our failure to acknowledge and vigorously follow-up worldwide networking of R&D centres, which were better placed than perhaps we were to overcome the horrendous technological issues that beset our search for recoverable domestic hydrocarbon reserves.

I survived that interrogation and Raha's public outbursts were muted, but I could hear the knives being sharpened.

Actually, Raha was right. The Reliance 'discoveries' have since been shown to be largely empty boasts, and GSPC has gone so belly-up that under the auspices of the Gujarat CM-turned-PM, ONGC has been obliged to take over GSPC, despite GSPC being loaded with a debt burden of some Rs 20,000 crore. Unfortunately, Raha is no more, but I would like to publicly tender this apology to him for the many harsh things I said about him and ONGC, and for my not having supported the renewal of his chairmanship. *Mea culpa*.

China visit

The Krishnamurthy advisory committee having let me down on strengthening our financial muscle to compete with China's oil giants, I decided to visit China to see if I could work out a modus vivendi with them. To this end, I sent a strong team of officials to Beijing in August 2005 to prepare the ground. They did a splendid job of drafting the MoUs that would be signed on my visit. In Delhi, I engaged with both the Chinese ambassador to New Delhi and the Indian ambassador to Beijing to establish the parameters of Sino-Indian cooperation in the oil/gas sector.

In January 2006, I set out for China accompanied by a large delegation of public sector heads including the CMDs of GAIL, IOC, OIL, HPCL, and Engineers India Limited (EIL), the MD of OVL, the director of BPCL, DGH, the ED of the Petroleum Conservation and Research Association, our ambassador to Beijing, the Joint Secretary from the MEA, and Additional Secretary Talmiz Ahmad. There was much scepticism about my visiting China to secure the cooperation of our principal competitor in the oil and gas exploration sector, but, against all expectations, the talks went so satisfactorily that the *Financial Times*, Hong Kong edition, ran a lead story on the front page with a large photograph of me and the banner headline, 'China and India forge alliance on oil supplies'.

The MoU I signed with my counterpart, Ma Kai, chairman of the National Development and Reforms Commission and just about the senior-most authority on energy in the Communist Party of the People's Republic of China, provided for us to consult with each other before making bids for overseas oil and gas assets to forestall competitive bidding, which in the end only benefited the seller and lost the ultimate victor billions of dollars. To this end, we agreed that GAIL would take the lead in establishing an office of all our hydrocarbon PSUs in Beijing to enable a measure of coordination with Chinese companies when both countries were competing for assets abroad.

The MoU also provided for 'cooperation across the hydrocarbon value chain' including 'exploration and production; downstream projects; strategic storage and stockpiling; research and development; conservation, promotion of environment-friendly fuels; and the promotion of unconventional fuels, such as coalbed methane, coal gasification and hydrates'.

There could have been no more comprehensive an MoU, especially as the ministerial MoU was backed up with five inter-corporate MoUs between GAIL on our side, and CNOPC, Sinopec and Beijing Gas on theirs, and between our OVL and CNPC, as also between the DGH and its Chinese counterpart, the Research Institute of Petroleum Exploration and Development (RIPED). Nevertheless, my successor, Murli Deora, was persuaded to return to Beijing in under a year to seek an alternative MoU. Ma Kai must have laughed up his sleeve at this absurdity!

The Chinese government kindly accepted my request to deliver a public lecture. Of course, the audience was carefully selected and about 200 English-knowing persons were packed into the auditorium. I was given free rein to express my views.

The speech highlighted many of my deepest convictions. I started with the assertion that India and China needed to attain high rates of growth over at least two decades to eradicate poverty. This in turn meant high energy demand. With both India and China significantly dependent on imports to meet their rising consumption, energy security was a major policy goal we shared. Hence the high priority being given in both countries to both the domestic and external dimensions to ensure energy security.

China's energy security, I said, called for supplementing the domestic effort with engaging the globe. So did India's. It was, therefore, hardly surprising that 'almost everywhere in the world that an Indian goes in quest of energy, chances are that he will run into a Chinese engaged in the same hunt'. Aggressive bidding by both parties only pushes up the price of the asset. So, the real winner is always the seller, who receives a substantially higher remuneration because of the intense competition between China and India. Could this change if we looked upon each other not as strategic competitors but as strategic partners? Could we replace, or at any rate moderate, bidding against each other through prior consultation?

It was, I explained, in search of such cooperation to the mutual benefit of our two countries that I had come to Beijing. I elaborated that the principles which could inform such cooperation were the same as the Panchsheel's Five Principles: 'peaceful coexistence'; 'equal cooperation'; 'mutual benefit'; 'mutual respect'; 'enhanced understanding'. I dubbed this the Panchsheel that should inform the approach of both countries to 'Asia's quest for energy security'.

Citing an important article by a Chinese scholar, Shi Yadong of the Development Research Centre of China's State Council, I drew attention to his perceptive observation that 'Asia as a whole is a giant buyer in the world energy market but not a strong one'. I went on to commend his call to rectify this by 'Asian countries speed[ing] up establishing the Asian Energy Community'. I reinforced this by quoting from the Indian and Chinese prime ministers and the Chinese president, and detailed the steps taken in the direction of evolving an Asian identity in the global energy market through the two round tables of Asian energy ministers held in New Delhi. China had participated in both.

To this end, I said, my Chinese counterpart Ma Kai and I had entered into an MoU on 12 January that laid 'a historic foundation for the all-round development of energy cooperation among our two great countries'.[16]

The speech received a standing ovation that lasted several minutes, but I never did discover whether this was in appreciation of my remarks or standard courteous Chinese Communist Party procedure!

Termination of my term

The speech in Beijing turned out to be my swansong. A fortnight after my China visit, towards the end of January I was on a visit to my constituency when I received a call from the PMO. The PM came on the line and almost apologetically told me that he was obliged to change my petroleum portfolio. He quickly added that he was keen on retaining me in the same portfolio because I was doing such an excellent job of it, but was not sure he would succeed as he was under pressure.

I finished the village assembly meeting as quickly as I decently could and rushed to Mayiladuturai to see the news on television. My last hopes were shredded as I saw confirmation of my being the only minister whose portfolio was changed. It was also announced that Murli Deora, a close family friend of the Ambanis, would succeed me. The circle was squared.

After an agonizing night, I rushed back to the comfort of my family. Suneet was calm as usual, playing her balancing Libra role of pulling me up from the depths when things were going wrong and pulling me down from the heights when things were going right. My eldest daughter, Suranya, was indignant. She thundered that my party had no respect for 'talent' and wanted only 'sycophancy'. She felt I was being 'wasted' and was extremely upset at this 'blatant injustice'.

My second daughter, Yamini, was away in Bangkok on official work, and when she heard the news she was so disturbed that she went for a long ruminative walk in the crowded streets of the city.

Sana, my youngest, out at Harvard, comforted me with a covering note that read:

> It's taken 26 years for me to understand what it is that you, as a father, have given to Suranya, Yamini and me. More than the election victories, fame and political achievements, it is the example you have set for us by living your life being true to yourself and your principles. I think this poem sums it up better than I ever could.
>
> Love, Sana

And she reproduced Rudyard Kipling's *If*, with the haunting lines:

> If you can meet with Triumph and Disaster
> And treat those two Impostors just the same . . .
> Yours is the world and everything that's in it,
> And – which is more – you'll be a Man, my Son.

I think it was worth getting unceremoniously dropped to receive that compliment!

I sought an appointment with Sonia Gandhi. Where I had expected her to be like the prime minister in congratulating me on the work done but regretting that I had to be reshuffled, I was taken aback to be attacked with the words, 'Why are you saying in private conversations that you were removed for refusing to collect money for the party?' In fact, the only persons I had spoken to were members of my family. I wondered how she was aware of my 'private conversations'. Was every room in my home bugged?

Sonia Gandhi reminded me that I had been told at the very start that my petroleum portfolio was 'temporary', and now that she had found a replacement, it was time for me to move on. That sounded fair enough. But when she sought to sweeten the pill by telling me that I was to be put in charge of the ministry of sports and youth affairs, I could almost see my world falling apart.

She, of course, thought I would be thrilled to be virtually in the same position as her husband, who started his political and administrative career by supervising the Asian Games in 1982. What she did not know – and I could not have expected her to know – is that I had a personal horror of sports ever since I discovered in childhood that I was all thumbs and toes, besides being flat-footed, when it came to games of any description. I was perhaps the only sports minister in world history to have never teed off on a golf course. I also greatly resented the privileging of brawn over brain at school. I recalled the irony of my predecessor, Sunil Dutt, having invited me once to his ministry and my thanking destiny for having spared me that portfolio.

My sister Tara, who had accompanied me to 10, Janpath, was shocked at the expression on my face as I emerged from Sonia Gandhi's office. We went home in a daze to learn that my successor, Murli Deora, had been calling. I called him back. He said he had decided not to take over office until I went along with him to Shastri Bhavan. We agreed to go together the following morning. Although I had rather hoped that he would want me to brief him, he made no inquiries but instead unrolled an email from Rajeev Chandrasekhar and read out the draft of his introductory remarks to the press. I discovered, somewhat to my dismay, that an ex-minister has as much news value as a dead fish on a fishmonger's slab.

Press comment was kinder. Siddharth Varadarajan wrote in *The Hindu* that I had been 'unceremoniously' removed 'to the sound of popping champagne corks at the US Embassy in Delhi and Reliance Petroleum headquarters in Mumbai, no doubt'.

While almost all the papers wrote of my being reshuffled in a similar vein, *The Indian Express* lead editorial on 30 January 2006 lashed out at me:

Replacing Mani Shankar Aiyar with Murli Deora shows a welcome

> recognition of realpolitik. Aiyar was a shade too enthusiastic about the problem-fraught Iran pipeline and a bit too keen to wrap a quasi-foreign policy around it. It also rewards a Congressman (Deora) who's an instinctive economic liberal, a sadly rare breed in the party.

Meanwhile, Venkat from my personal staff had quietly transferred my personal papers to my new office and escorted me there when the press conference ended. I walked out with a heavy heart. It was injury enough to be the only cabinet minister to be reshuffled and insult enough to be given a portfolio I did not want.

As I stepped over the threshold of C Wing on the other side of Shastri Bhavan, where my new ministry was located, I pause to take up my principal portfolio in which I remained unchallenged for all five years of the UPA government, the ministry of Panchayati Raj.

9

Ministry of Panchayati Raj

(2004–2009)

I have described my learning experience with Panchayati Raj in my description of 'The Rajiv Years'. Just as I had found myself a place in my house football team by teaching myself to kick with my left foot, so also had I secured my cabinet niche by specializing in an area of little or no interest to anybody else. Indeed, Vir Sanghvi told me that whenever he raised the subject of Panchayati Raj with any PMO officer, they would all shrug their shoulders at what they perceived as an eccentric hobbyhorse of the PM's, brought on by my 'undue influence' over him.

In fact, it was the other way round. Finding no one else in the PMO who shared his passion for local self-government, Rajiv had come to rely on my enthusiasm for the subject. Recognizing this, Sonia Gandhi had insisted on not only creating, for the first time in India's history, a ministry dedicated to Panchayati Raj, but had also overruled objections from most of her close advisers (except Natwar Singh) to induct me into the cabinet at a rank higher than minister of state with independent charge.

The problem with holding charge of a new ministry was, precisely, that it did not exist. There was me and no one else, except a joint secretary from the ministry of rural development who made it clear that she had personal reasons to revert to her state cadre. I nosed around and rediscovered Sudha Pillai, inducting her as my first recruit to the position of additional secretary in the new ministry. She was not only knowledgeable but also very enthusiastic about local self-government in rural India and had considerable administrative skill.

Instead of leaving her to intellectually engage with Panchayati Raj, I had to first inflict on her the boring but necessary task of finding physical space for the new ministry and discussing with the Cabinet Secretariat ways in which the required complement of staff for the ministry could be located.

The only assistance I could offer was that of my private secretary in the ministry of Panchayati Raj, Ashutosh Dikshit, whom I had first met when he was servicing the JPC on the Ketan Parekh scam. Within weeks however, Sudha Pillai was compelled to take indefinite long leave to look after her son who had fallen seriously ill while studying in California.

I was extraordinarily lucky in then finding Wajahat Habibullah, who had preceded me to the PMO in handling rural development under both Indira Gandhi and Rajiv Gandhi. He was enthusiastic and willing to leave the glamour of being secretary, ministry of textiles, to take over as secretary, Panchayati Raj, a considerably lower-profile job.

With Wajahat in charge, we soon had our complement of officers, and the UNDP provided us with an adequate number of research consultants to get on with the job. Alas for me, but not for the country, Wajahat was selected a year later to be the first chief information commissioner to look after implementation of the Right to Information Act. It took a while to find an interested adviser in the Planning Commission to replace Wajahat – Meenakshi Dutta Ghosh, IAS.

The work of the ministry of Panchayati Raj got under way with a conference of chief ministers called early in the government of Dr Manmohan Singh, on 29 June 2004, to discuss rural development. I requested the PM to add the subject of Panchayati Raj to the conference, and he readily agreed. With the able assistance of his joint secretary, R. Gopalakrishnan, we were able to put together a draft speech for the PM which, in retrospect, gave us all the ammunition we needed.

This included institutionalizing panchayats, focusing on devolution of funds and functionaries in harmony with the devolution of functions, and ultimately making rural India the site of the country's growth ambitions.

'State subject'

The principal conundrum I faced was the same as the one faced by Jawaharlal Nehru and Rajiv Gandhi, as prime ministers, and by technical experts like Balvantray Mehta and Ashok Mehta: how to reconcile Central government activism on a strictly state subject, the Constitution having placed Panchayati Raj squarely in the state list. Happily, in all states which fell within the ambit of the 73rd Amendment, except Bihar (which was holding out on some aspects of reservations for women), such conformity state legislation had gone through during the decade that preceded the launch of my new ministry.

My problem, therefore, was to get a national consensus, such that the states/UTs would agree to take the steps required for effective devolution of power, effective empowerment and efficient, honest grassroots development through a transparent democratic ethos in our villages. The conclusions hammered out at the seven round table conferences on the different key aspects of Panchayati Raj, which we held in seven different regions of the country, provided a comprehensive national basis on which to move forward. I was most reassured by the ease with which the consensus was achieved, resolving with no great difficulty the different views expressed by different state ministers. I underestimated the gap between the applause the reading of the consensus fetched and the commitment to actually implement what had been agreed upon. I soon discovered this gap but, nevertheless, soldiered on.

My next task, as I saw it, was to tour the states and UTs to discuss and forge consensus on the state-specific actions to be taken to further the consensus hammered out at the round tables.

I drew up a schedule of state/UT visits. I principally used the services of an extraordinarily bright and keen officer of the Karnataka cadre, T.R. Raghunandan (Raghu), who I had picked as joint secretary in the ministry of Panchayati Raj. The procedure I worked out was to send Raghu in advance to the state capitals to work out with his state counterparts state-specific draft MoUs.

After touring panchayats at all three levels – village, taluka/block, and district[1] – in different parts of a state with the state Panchayati Raj minister, I would finalize detailed MoUs and sign them, along with the chief minister. The MoUs were signed by the chief ministers, and I indicated the way forward and gave us the legitimacy to inquire at the state level about the progress made. Different officers of the ministry were tasked with the follow-up work.

Many of these tours were very fruitful, particularly those to Karnataka, Kerala, Andhra Pradesh, Goa, Maharashtra, Haryana, Punjab, Himachal Pradesh, Uttarakhand, Chhattisgarh, Jharkhand, Odisha, West Bengal, Sikkim, Assam and Arunachal Pradesh. Some visits to the UTs also worked out well, such as those to Lakshadweep, the Andaman and Nicobar Islands, and Diu–Daman–Nagar Haveli.

It required some heavy leaning from Delhi to get the MoUs signed in some states and UTs, including Puducherry, Chandigarh and CPI(M)-ruled Tripura. Madhya Pradesh and Rajasthan, both under BJP governments, also proved tough eggs to crack. A few crucial visits, including to large states like Uttar Pradesh, Bihar and Gujarat, could not take place at all owing to the non-cooperative attitude of the chief ministers concerned.

Tamil Nadu was an especially unfortunate experience for me, as my attempts to rope in the minister concerned were repeatedly rebuffed, greatly damaging my political standing with our alliance partner, the DMK. The DMK is the party most keen on undiluted state rights. Therefore, they considered my taking any interest in a state subject as going against the fundamental principles of federalism. Indeed, my TN colleague, P. Chidambaram, had attempted early on to warn me about this. To my eternal regret, I was insufficiently sensitive to this as I thought nothing was being imposed on states. Only suggestions were made to them, which would be acted on only if the states agreed. Moreover, it would be entirely up to the state concerned to act on the suggestions, MoU or no MoU. By the time I fully realized how touchy the TN state government was on issues on the state list, it was too late to

Orating into the microphone, with Suneet backing me, May-June 1991

Addressing a street audience in Kumbakonam, August-September 1999

Launching, with Prime Minister Narasimha Rao, my Panchayati Raj Yatra

On stage, before Sonia Gandhi unveils Rajiv Gandhi's statue at Porayar, in my Tamil Nadu constituency, 22 September 1995

With Kalaingar Karunanidhi and 'Dalapati' Mu. Ka. Stalin, Chennai, 2006

As the AICC in-charge of the Northeast hill states, addressing a public rally in Agartala, Tripura, 2001

Being sworn in by President A.P.J. Abdul Kalam as Cabinet Minister, May 2004

With Yasser Arafat at Rashtrapati Bhawan, January 1994

With Lakshman Kadirgamar, foreign minister of Sri Lanka, in New Delhi, 2005. He was assassinated in August that year.

With my counterparts from Myanmar and Bangladesh on the A3 Rig of Myanmar where GAIL discovered gas, January 2005

With Iranian President H.E. Mohammad Khatami, Tehran, June 2005

With Saudi Oil Minister Al-Naimi flying in his private plane to the oil-rich Empty Quarter, Saudi Arabia, March 2005. Suneet is seated in the rear.

Exiting with Suneet from the Iranian National Museum. Ambassador K.C. Singh is in the rear, Tehran, 2005

Greeting Norway's Minister of Petroleum and Energy, Thorhild Widvey, at Oslo, August 2006. Allegedly, this is the only photograph in which she has ever been seen smiling and laughing.

Cartoonist Ajit Ninan's take on my quest for gas pipeline from all over our proximate Asian neighbourhood.

Strolling garlanded (centre) through a village in Rajasthan to a Gram Sabha meeting, 2005

Being welcomed by a lady Panchayat President at her village in Jabua district, Madhya Pradesh, 2006

With Panchayat leaders in Kinnaur, Himachal Pradesh

At a Gram panchayat in Karnataka, March 2005

Gram Sabha meeting in Paschim Tajpur (south) in Shaikal Gram Panchayat, Assam

Dancing with Bodo girls in Assam on a visit as Minister for the DoNER

At Tawang, Arunachal Pradesh with Chief Minister Dorji Khandu looking on, January 2007

With an Arunachali fan in Itanagar, 2008

Grand release by Prime Minister Dr Manmohan Singh of NER Vision Document 2020 in the presence of Governors and Chief Ministers of the Northeastern states, New Delhi, 2 July 2007.

My life-long inspiration: working in my MP's office with portraits of Mahatma Gandhi, Pandit Jawaharlal Nehru and Gurudev Rabindranath Tagore, hanging at my back, 2001-04

In the presence of Prime Minister Dr Manmohan Singh, Vice President Hamid Ansari and Hon'ble Speaker Somnath Chatterjee, being honoured by the President of India, Pratibha Patil, with the 'Outstanding Parliamentarian Award 2006' presented at the Central Hall, Parliament House, September 2008.

Rahul Gandhi, MP, releasing the Hindi translation of my book Remembering Rajiv, *Teen Murti Auditorium, New Delhi, 2011*

Family photograph at our Golden Jubilee Wedding Anniversary, 14 January 2023

Leela, our youngest granddaughter, delightedly discovering a copy of her grandfather's memoirs in a bookstore in New Delhi, December 2023

Suneet and I celebrating the wedding of one of our daughters with a lifelong friend, Raj Bhasin, looking on.

Suneet and me at Halong Bay and Hanoi, Vietnam, October 2024

persuade the minister, Thiru Mu. Ka. Stalin. My error became a significant contributory cause to the distinct lack of enthusiasm on the part of the DMK cadres in my campaign for re-election in 2009. So, I lost that election. Subsequently, I made it up with Stalin, but my electoral defeat was my political Waterloo.

Most of these visits were completed between July 2004 and April 2006, but continued in fits and starts in the more recalcitrant states in a somewhat abbreviated manner right up to 2009. I visited over 100 village panchayats, scores of intermediate panchayats and several district panchayats in dozens of regions in most of the states/UTs of India.

Promise of Grassroots Development

To follow up on the MoUs, I allocated different regions to different officers so they could tour them, supplementing my visits. To forestall their journeys from deteriorating into mere 'rural development tourism', as Robert Chambers once described it, the idea was that the officers would be sent to pursue implementation of the MoUs with their state counterparts. But I was unable to enthuse them to carry out these tasks systematically and scientifically. Patient negotiation with their state counterparts was not their forte.

Most, though not all, of the officers seemed to think that functioning as think tanks was not their job. What they avidly wanted to do was to 'administer' – principally clear, or question, or reject 'utilization certificates' (UCs). UCs are documents issued by Block Development Officers (BDOs) to certify that moneys have been spent on approved projects and programmes, in accordance with the prescribed guidelines for the schemes. They are the chief instrument for supervising and monitoring progress in implementation of projects and ensuring there is no misuse of funds. The problem is that the UC certifies the efficiency and integrity of the very state functionary who writes it out! Our attempt was to get UCs approved and endorsed by village gram sabhas before issue. State governments generally preferred to avoid getting entangled at the grassroots, leaving it to their BDOs to figure out how to satisfy the bosses in Delhi.

Hence, when the PM decided in 2007 to allot implementation of the Backward Regions Grant Fund (BRGF) to the ministry of Panchayati Raj, our administrators' interest was sparked far more by this 'scheme' than by the larger, systemic issues, which called for intellectual grappling. That, however, did not bother me too much, because the prime minister had ensured that a development plan prepared at the grassroots level by the elected representatives had to be filed with the ministry before seeking release of the BRGF grant. I thought this a good way of bringing into operation a crucial component of the scheme, namely, grassroots development planning, as the very foundation of the system.

Indeed, I was so intrigued to be informed by my officers that the best district plan had come from Hailakandi, a remote district of the Barak Valley in Assam wedged between Tripura and Mizoram, that I decided to visit it myself to meet the elected district president of the panchayat, the genius who had produced the plan. She turned out to be a young woman in her early thirties, educated and well turned out, but looking a little bewildered at the praise I was showering on the district development plan.

The truth then came tumbling out. Neither she nor any of her district panchayat members knew anything about the district plan filed in their name; it was the local development officers, under the watch of the collector and BDOs, who had prepared the plan without consulting any panchayat representatives – and had secured the grant!

This was just another of the many examples of 'monitoring' by joint secretaries sitting in the remote Bhavans of New Delhi. When it came to intellectual engagement with concepts, as distinct from accepting or rejecting UCs, the average civil servant did not quite know what he/she should be doing. Thus, the focus of the ministry of Panchayati Raj (MoPR) started getting diffused. The ministry was not concentrating on the larger picture but getting diverted all the time by minor details. I felt I was losing control of the narrative.

'Where is the revenue stream?'

I then deluded myself into imagining that I had recaptured the narrative going by the outcome of a one-day visit I made to Washington, DC, in

November 2006 to address a retreat of World Bank officers on Panchayati Raj in India and its more general lessons on local self-government as the motor of democracy and development. The invitation was extended by one of the local self-government enthusiasts of the Bank, Junaid Ahmed of Bangladesh, who was sector manager for social development in South Asia.

As my daughter Yamini was getting married later that month, it took some persuasion for my wife to let me go to the US on a visit of under twenty-four hours. But the visit turned out to be potentially very fruitful for Panchayati Raj. At the lunch that followed the lecture, one of the World Bank vice presidents, Praful Patel, a Ugandan of Indian origin, was so enthused by my suggestion of a fund to incentivize states to devolve effective power to the panchayats and for individual panchayats to be transparent and accountable in their dealings that at the lunch itself he rang the World Bank president, Paul Wolfowitz, and asked him to make space in his diary to immediately meet the minister of Panchayati Raj from India.

Intrigued, Wolfowitz set aside a few minutes for me immediately after lunch. We trooped up to his splendid office, and in a few succinct words I explained to him my proposal. He first inquired about the numbers involved, and then remarked that in dealing with India, the numbers were always huge. He then cocked an eyebrow and asked if a billion dollars would do for starters!

I was quite taken aback, but even more pleased to find that he was offering the money through the International Finance Corporation (IFC) window, which meant there would be no interest charged on the loan, only service charges of 1 per cent annually and a forty-year repayment period. Clutching this bonanza in my hand, I returned to Delhi in high spirits and asked to meet the finance minister.

Perhaps because finance ministers are used to billions of dollars being thrown around, the FM poured cold water on my enthusiasm and asked, 'Where is the revenue stream?' As I struggled to respond, he closed the meeting abruptly saying my joint secretary could meet his joint secretary so we could understand the meaning and implications of the 'revenue stream'.

That left me gasping for room to explain that a revenue stream could be expected from a project like a dam but had to be conceived otherwise with respect to a systemic programme aimed at better governance and, therefore, greater efficiency of costs and returns. The ultimate purpose of Panchayati Raj being to deliver public goods and services – more efficiently and at lower costs – at the doorstep of the rural poor through their own elected representatives, whom they could hold accountable, the 'revenue stream' would result from higher efficiency and lower administrative costs but could not be estimated as income with which to pay off the debt, as could perhaps be calculated for, say, a toll highway or a power plant. In any case, the loan was going to come through the soft window of the World Bank – that is, without interest – and with a repayment period of four decades. So, what was the problem?

As T.R. Raghunandan, my joint secretary, wrestled with his counterpart in the finance ministry over the required 'revenue stream', he asked Indira Rajaraman of the National Institute of Public Finance and Policy (NIPFP) to help out. I went to the prime minister who, in contrast to the finance minister's brusque manner, gave me a patient hearing and the space to put my argument before him. At the end of the discussion, he said he agreed with me and thought the finance ministry should initiate the formalities to secure the soft loan of $1 billion (approximately forty times my ministry's annual budget!)

When Indira Rajaraman's paper was received, Raghu and I repaired again to the finance minister's chamber and were delighted to find his mood totally altered. He was ready to accept our proposal to formally approach the World Bank. However, he cautioned that he was yet to read Indira Rajaraman's paper but added that he had high respect for her.

When I returned triumphant to my office and was engaged in getting through to Junaid Ahmed and Praful Patel in Washington, I received a call from the finance minister saying he had read through Indira Rajaraman's paper but could not find any evidence of a 'revenue stream' that he or his successors could use to repay the loan.

At this point, I should have prepared a note for the cabinet, even if might have been rejected at the level of the empowered committee of secretaries, as I already had the PM's approval in principle in my pocket. But my inexperience in handling domestic administration, combined with my officers not recommending such a course of action, meant that I allowed myself to be defeated at the starting post. I have ever since regretted this.

Perhaps an extenuating cause was my preoccupation with arrangements for my daughter's wedding, as well as a new responsibility thrust on my shoulders. I had been asked to take charge of the ministry for DoNER in addition to youth affairs and sports.

State of the Panchayats report

The decision taken at the Srinagar ministerial round table to prepare annual reports on the state of the panchayats appealed to the officers, largely because it enabled them to order the submission of state reports, which would then be collated into an annual report and fed into the Devolution Index, which was commissioned from the National Council of Applied Economic Research (NCAER), and later from the Indian Institute of Public Administration (IIPA).

This report gave a fair idea of the positive and negative trends in the implementation of Panchayati Raj, although we could never disentangle what was mandated by the state law from what was actually implemented. We also could not question how far the statistics supplied were fact or fantasy. Nevertheless, all said and done, and whatever the limitations, we produced the first annual report without any serious complaint from any state or damage to our reputations.

Prime Minister Dr Manmohan Singh was so enthused with this plan of producing annual state-of-the-panchayats reports that he pressed us to present the following year a mid-term appraisal of the state of the panchayats, which he instructed be tabled in the House and a discussion scheduled.

I was very pleased at the all-party welcome given to the report in the House. About twenty-five to thirty members, representing all the principal parties, participated. I was careful to mention their names and the points they had made in my reply to the debate. Opposition speakers in the debate did not play politics around Panchayati Raj but almost unanimously praised the initiative. They also made many useful suggestions. My officers in the gallery and I took extensive notes of what was being spoken, and I collated many of them for a four-hour reply in the Lok Sabha spread over two days.

In so far as the successes were concerned, I said I believed the single biggest success was our institutionalization of Panchayati Raj, which we could sum up in three words: we had made Panchayati Raj 'ineluctable', 'irremovable' and 'irreversible'. We would never go back to the bad old days of no Panchayati Raj. Moreover, we had ensured that there would be regular elections. The Supreme Court, I reminded the House, had recently endorsed this view.

I then referred to the state election commissioners having formed a common platform to share their experiences and inform us of their conclusions. They had been to the election commissioner of India to argue their case for a common electoral roll for all elections and the right to use electronic voting machines (EVMs) in local body elections.

In consequence of this kind of institutionalization, we now had close to 2.5 lakh elected local body institutions in rural and urban India, comprising 2,33,251 village panchayats, 6,105 intermediate panchayats and 519 district panchayats; plus, of course, the urban local bodies (which did not fall in my jurisdiction).

In these elected institutions, we had close to 32 lakh representatives in all the local bodies and approximately 28.3 lakh representatives in our panchayats. Of these 28.3 lakh panchayat representatives, there were 14 lakh women in the local bodies as a whole, and marginally over 10 lakh women in our village panchayats.

This had been described by an Opposition MP as 'momentous'. While the share of women in the Lok Sabha was only 8 per cent, in the village panchayats, in sharp contrast, there was a willing acceptance of something over 1 million elected women among the poorest and most oppressed villagers of all castes and communities. Moreover, there were more women contesting and winning than they were entitled to only by reservations.

Further, representation in the reserved SC seats was 46 per cent as against 33 per cent reservation. Together, the SCs and STs constituted 31 per cent of our elected representatives, which was much higher than their share in the population. SC and ST women were doing so outstandingly well in panchayat elections that the prime minister himself had noted that 'there are now more women in India in positions of elected authority than in the rest of the world put together'!

I next referred to Prime Minister Rajiv Gandhi having often said that we may be the world's largest democracy, but we were also the world's least representative democracy. Now, with well over 30 lakh elected representatives in the panchayats and urban local bodies, India had been transformed into the world's most representative democracy. This, I submitted, was an achievement without parallel in the world and without precedent in history.

I then turned to the vexed question of the Constitutional position of the ministry of Panchayati Raj. Faced with the Constitutional conundrum that Panchayati Raj was on the Constitution's state list, but that very same Constitution obliged me to ensure a measure of similarity in the implementation of Panchayati Raj across the country, I decided that all the Panchayati Raj ministers of India could get together and discuss how to move forward. I also knew that Panchayati Raj was too complicated a subject to deal with in a meeting of a day or two. So, I made an appeal to my colleagues, who immediately accepted it, that within a space of 150 days between July 2004 and December 2004, we should meet seven times in seven different parts of India and discuss the eighteen identified dimensions of Panchayati Raj to arrive at points for action. We succeeded, I informed the House, in producing a compendium with respect to these eighteen dimensions of Panchayati Raj, which extended to approximately 150 agreed steps to be taken.

Having prepared this document, which was unanimously accepted by all participating state ministers, I said I had sent the compendium to every chief minister of India and none had raised any objection to it. So I set out on tours to the state capitals to sign with chief ministers agreed state plans to move towards genuine and effective devolution of the panchayats.

They signed readily enough, but implementation on the ground was slow and piecemeal.

I then identified for the House the four basic reasons, in my view, for the inadequate implementation of what had been agreed by the chief ministers and me, the union minister concerned.

The first was the devolution of functions through Activity Mapping, that is, listing illustratively which activities relating to a particular devolved subject were to be undertaken, respectively, by the village panchayat, the intermediate panchayat and the district panchayat. Preparation of Activity Maps for each subject or scheme of devolution, on the principle of subsidiarity, I emphasized, was the essential precondition for successful devolution.

Only once such an Activity Map was ready could you have the second priority – devolution of finances, patterned on the same Activity Map.

The third would follow. By matching the devolution of functions and finances, you could ensure the devolution of functionaries. So, the Activity Map was the beginning not only of devolution of functions but also of devolution of finances, and, therefore, devolution of functionaries.

The fourth priority, I held, was district-level planning, in conformity with the relevant Constitutional provisions. Guidelines for district planning had been circulated. The Planning Commission, I continued, was undertaking a major exercise in the context of the Eleventh Plan to rationalize our Centrally Sponsored Schemes (CSS). In the process of rationalizing CSSs, I hoped we would also be enabled to clarify the role of the Panchayati Raj Institutions (PRIs) in implementing the CSSs. (Unfortunately, that never happened and the loss of interest at the higher levels of the Planning Commission proved the principal roadblock in our moving forward.)

I then moved to another aspect of Panchayati Raj – training and capacity building, especially of newly elected women representatives, which appeared to be of general interest. We had incorporated in the annual report tabled in Parliament the expert committee report on the capability building framework and training. The head of the UNDP division that dealt with local self-government had told me that he had never before read a more thorough report on how to conduct training and capacity building for our Panchayati Raj representatives. Therefore, I hoped we would get considerable UNDP financial support, provided, of course, the Government of India itself was happy with this scheme and asked for the money. (It didn't!)

I turned to 'district planning', the fourth priority. Drawing attention to the very detailed provisions in the Constitution on district planning, I explained that the district planning committee (DPC) was required to 'consolidate' the district plan. Consolidation required that there should be a village plan, an intermediate panchayat plan, a district plan and a municipal plan by the *nagarpalikas* and the town panchayats. The consolidated 'draft' district plan was then to be submitted to state governments for technical fine-tuning before being sent on to the Planning Commission. Thus, what was eventually approved would combine grassroots priorities with the overall perspectives of development, making inclusive governance the key to inclusive growth.

I then got my teeth into the importance of 'incentivization' to induce states to move on 'effective devolution' and of PRIs to be more 'transparent and accountable' in their transactions. To do this, we had asked the NCAER to prepare for us a Devolution Index, completely objective and completely scientific. I said I had approached the World Bank to get us a substantial amount of money to be able to genuinely incentivize the states to empower their panchayats. (This initiative was stymied by the finance minister.)

I also referred in some detail to the Gram Swaraj Yojana my ministry had initiated, under which the infrastructure requirements of the panchayats – including panchayat premises, staff and cyber connectivity – might be assured.

I summed up with the PM's observation:

> This Report highlights the lack of basic resources, facilities, connectivity and staff in many panchayats . . . The Ministry of Panchayati Raj has prepared a Gram Swaraj Yojana which aims to supplement State efforts

> in this regard . . . but the primary responsibility remains that of the States and, I hope, they give high priority to ensuring this.

I followed this with drawing the attention of the House to a key issue of national security, Naxalism. I explained that there were nine states which had Fifth Schedule areas, that is, areas of tribal concentration incorporated within the boundaries of the state, and it was in these areas that Naxalism was most serious. Happily, the Constitution had mandated Parliament to enact legislation to bring Panchayati Raj to these areas. Accordingly, The Provisions of the Panchayats (Extension to Scheduled Areas) Act, [PESA] had been passed in 1996.

It was perhaps the most effective conformity legislation for Panchayati Raj, as it provided for panchayats to be established for each habitation and not for a conglomeration of villages, as was the practice elsewhere.

I was deeply convinced, I added, that it was only by implementing this Act that we would be able to roll back the wave of Naxalism, for it was only by empowering the people through their panchayats to build their own destiny that we would be able to effectively and definitively end the Naxal problem.

Why? Because PESA, I argued, provided mandatorily for the Gram Sabha to identify beneficiaries; approve plans, programmes or projects prepared by the Panchayat; and, most importantly, authorize the issue of utilization certificates (UCs). Hence, it would be fair to say that the best Panchayati Raj Act anywhere in the country was PESA. Which was why the PM had said:

> PESA is the single most important instrument in our armoury for dealing with the economic and emotional alienation of our tribal brethren, which lies at the root of the growing menace of Naxalism. Its effective implementation would, I believe, generate a deep sense of effective participation among our tribal people in the conduct of their own affairs . . .

I pleaded with the House to take this seriously. It was not by guns or police forces or by intelligence alone that we would be able to combat the internal threat of Naxalism. It was only by grassroots democracy that we could empower the tribal people living in Naxal-affected areas to disavow the Naxal and get on with building their own destiny by their own effort. (As readers will discover for themselves at a later stage of this book, I have had to pay a heavy political price, personally, for advocating this view, which was not shared by the home minister, P. Chidambaram.)

I made several other points in the hour or so that I continued speaking, but I refrain from summarizing them because this short version is already too long.[2] I think it was this one speech that was responsible for members from virtually every party recommending to the Hon'ble Speaker that I be selected for the Outstanding Parliamentarian Award for 2006.

But, notwithstanding the flowery compliments I received after my Parliamentary speech of December 2006, I lost momentum and could feel the tyres being deflated as we moved into the second half of my term.

Losing momentum

Other setbacks followed, such as the law minister's refusal to endorse a proposal I had made, based on Rajiv Gandhi's conception of alternative, cheap dispute resolution through elected Nyaya Panchayats (justice panchayats), which would complement grassroots development through the elected panchayats. Also, ideas like computerization of panchayat proceedings, the role of the Gram Sabha in social audit, and removal of parallel bodies from matters devolved under state legislation to the panchayats, stagnated rather than grew apace.

I was also very disturbed that despite much goading, neither the Planning Commission nor the home ministry was taking seriously the Bandyopadhyay Committee report, which highlighted full-throttle implementation of PESA as the key to ending insurgency by Naxal terrorists in the troubled forest regions of central India. Here too, perhaps, I should have pressed ahead with a note for the cabinet.

I also found it tough going to get the role of panchayats emphasized in the single most important programme launched by UPA-I, the Mahatma Gandhi National Rural Employment Guarantee Act (MNREGA). So, when I pointed this out to the cabinet, an almost last-minute decision was taken to get the law minister briefed by my secretary, Wajahat Habibullah, to include an appropriate reference to PRIs. It is only thus that panchayats gained a toehold in the scheme, which has proved to be the most enduring of the post-Rajiv Gandhi rights-based UPA schemes – saved, as it were, by the bell. I only wish the prime minister had entrusted implementation of MNREGA, instead of the BRGF, to the ministry of Panchayati Raj.

Fortunately, Forest Minister P.R. Kyndiah was much more accommodating of PRIs in his legislation for protecting the rights of tribal and other forest dwellers. But that Act too has been more honoured in the breach than in practice.

Perhaps the principal setback was regarding our adapting the Chinese model of 'Town and Country Planning' to our conception of rural business hubs with the participation of panchayats. I called this the P4 initiative: Public–Private–Panchayat Partnership initiative. In Sunil Munjal, chairman of the CII, I found an enthusiastic partner. Between us, we set up a number of major and minor meetings of CII members with panchayat representatives. Although a number of MoUs were signed, very few plans really took off.

The one question I could not answer to the satisfaction of the private and public sector representatives was what 'additional value' panchayats would bring to the project. Also, what financial incentives would be on offer from the government or commercial banks if they were to enter into such novel ventures?

Our businessmen regarded the Chinese experience as irrelevant. My total inexperience of, and ideological alienation from, the ethos of the corporate world combined to make the proposal of little interest to hard-headed businessmen, despite the encouragement of the CII chairman.

Moreover, I was deeply disappointed with the course of discussions in the Empowered Group of Ministers (EGoM) set up under Pranab Mukherjee to process the very positive recommendations on Panchayati

Raj of Veerappa Moily's second Administrative Reforms Commission. We had only one meeting where the two other ministers of the empowered group, Ram Vilas Paswan, handling social justice, and Renuka Chowdhury, handling women's affairs, made it clear that they would not devolve their powers to the panchayats. Clearly, other Central ministers too would also decline to devolve to unknown panchayats the powers they were wielding.

At the heart of the panchayati raj implementation problem lay the troubled Centre–state fiscal relationship. While under a third of net national revenues were allotted to the states, well over two-thirds of economic development and social welfare responsibilities were the domain of the states.

Over time, the states, unable to finance their responsibilities, had surrendered a sizeable share of these Constitutional responsibilities to the Centre. The Centre then exercised its expanded jurisdiction by establishing, with the craven cooperation of the states, the so-called CSSs, of which there were nearly 150 when Dr Manmohan Singh's government took office.

Moreover, centralized planning had also taken its toll, the relationship between the grant-giving Planning Commission and the state chief ministers being the principal determinant of state government performance in poverty elimination, education, health, sustainable development, irrigation and drainage, rural housing, drinking water and sanitation, women and child welfare, affirmative action for the historically disadvantaged, and other myriad matters impinging on daily life for India's rural millions.

As there were no apparent signs of the Central government drastically revising the existing pattern of Centre–state fiscal relations, the principal source of panchayat revenues would remain CSS funds.

If, therefore, Activity Maps could be incorporated in the CSS guidelines, an avenue for channelling sectoral development funds to the panchayats was the obvious course. The Activity Map could be conceived at a broad level, dividing administrative duties for any given devolved subject between the state administration and the panchayats or could be taken to a high level of sophistication and put through a strainer to nuance where the Centre had an indispensable role, the state its role and the panchayats at district, intermediate and village levels their roles.

Thus, for example, the 2013 expert group I chaired (known colloquially as the 'Aiyar committee') identified some 300 activities that came under the Sarva Shiksha Abhiyan (Education for All) programme. These were then meticulously shared out in theory between the Centre, the states and the units of local self-government. Most of the Central ministries/ departments found it more difficult to deal with the sophisticated model than with the broader schema.

The prime minister's review of the Common Minimum Programme undertaken some six months into his tenure found that no CSS guidelines were incorporating Activity Mapping as an essential component. So, the cabinet secretary was instructed to issue a circular to his fellow-secretaries ordering them to ensure that Activity Mapping was done to enable earmarking of panchayat shares for transmission to panchayat accounts.

I was somewhat complacent in imagining that this circular from the Cabinet Secretary would suffice to whip everyone into shape. But when I found that the orders of the Cabinet Secretary were being observed only in the breach, I leaned on him to set up a team comprising Panchayati Raj Secretary Meenakshi Datta Ghosh and Renuka Vishwanathan, his additional secretary, to go to the fifteen principal secretaries who accounted for some 60 per cent of all CSS funds, to work up Activity Maps for their respective CSS.

But by the time they submitted their report – and I must add that it was a very comprehensive report that had the concurrence of the secretaries concerned – there was a change of guard in the office of the Cabinet Secretary, and the preparatory work done by Meenakshi and Renuka was never taken to its logical conclusion. For me, it was yet another flop show.

Planning Commission woes

I had vested high hopes in the Planning Commission. Immediately on taking over, the new deputy chairman of the commission, Montek Singh

Ahluwalia, a college friend of mine and a former PMO colleague, had, after meeting me to chat about Panchayati Raj, appointed V. Ramachandran, former Kerala Chief Secretary and long-serving vice chairman of the State Planning Board and a knowledgeable authority on Panchayati Raj, to prepare a paper on district planning.

V. Ramachandran produced a masterpiece. An officer of the Planning Commission, A.S. Sahota, who had been earmarked for the ministry of Panchayati Raj, adamantly held on to his Planning Commission post to ensure that guidelines based on the recommendations of the Ramachandran Committee were issued before he left the commission.

But, having issued the guidelines, the Planning Commission lost all interest in following up on them. In introducing the initial Constitution amendment bill in 1989, Prime Minister Rajiv Gandhi had insisted that no state plan would be validated by the Planning Commission unless it was based on district plans submitted by district planning committees established under the Constitution. So, that avenue too was blocked.

My last throw of the dice was organizing, at Sonia Gandhi's instance and with the PM's blessings and encouragement, the Burari conference on the outskirts of Delhi, of panchayat representatives from all the states and UTs to mark the fifteenth anniversary of the gazetting of the Panchayati Raj Constitution amendment, hereafter to be designated National Panchayati Raj Day, 24 April.

This huge logistical exercise was made possible by the dedication and hard work of my director (administration) Avtar Singh Sahota and his team, to whom I shall remain ever grateful. The conference was personally attended and addressed by both the PM and the Congress president (an unprecedented joint appearance by them at a government-sponsored event).

But while most of the participants were generous in their praise of the opportunity given them to express their views, and of the assurance of creature comforts for their stay, the eventual outcome was simply not commensurate with the effort that went into organizing the conference.

The Planning Commission was particularly reluctant to give Panchayati Raj the headroom it deserved. This was largely because of the deputy chairman, Montek Singh Ahluwalia, having become a law unto himself.

I went to see him (although, hierarchically speaking, it was he who should have been answering my summons). Instead of listening to me, he harangued me, as was his wont, for half an hour, and then impatiently signalled that the meeting was over without caring to find out why I had come visiting.

So, I went to him again on behalf of the 3.2 million elected Panchayati Raj representatives. Our personal friendship dated back to our days together in St Stephen's. While he always had a rather haughty manner, it had become worse with the praise heaped on him by corporate honchos and their cheerleaders in the media for the contribution he had made to creating, through economic reforms, millionaires by the thousands and billionaires by the hundreds.

The Planning Commission had allegedly ensured that the largest number of those below the poverty line were pulled above it, albeit only in terms of the Planning Commission's definition of the 'poverty line'. Other estimates, such as those made by my other eminent economist friend, Arjun Sengupta, showed that the so-called 'poverty line' was actually a 'destitution line' and that Montek's millions had been pulled out of destitution, but left in poverty.

However that might be, his knowledge of, and interest in, Panchayati Raj was revealed in his celebrated autobiography, *Backstage*, which contains precisely two passing references to Panchayati Raj. He later sent an email message to me, copied to several others, saying I had a somewhat 'romantic' view of village life. I retorted by saying that the only Village Montek knew was the one located in Lower Manhattan.

When, therefore, I went a second time to meet him to plead the cause of my millions, I began by sternly warning him that, in view of the harangue he had inflicted on me, I had not come to listen to him but for him to listen to me. I then subjected him to a tirade for the same half-hour to which he had subjected me. At our next encounter, he greeted me with the words, 'What a marvellous cataract of words!' But he did nothing about anything.

I had to mournfully agree when Raghu called on me in early 2009 to say, 'I am sorry, Sir, but you seem to have lost the plot.' There was as little true achievement in the years 2007 and 2008 as there had been genuine achievement between 2004 and 2006.

I hoped that I would be able to regenerate the required momentum after the coming Lok Sabha elections. Raghu himself took voluntary retirement from the IAS to devote himself to teaching local self-government at educational and training institutions, and emerged as one of the most well-known Panchayati Raj activists in the country.

Why have we not succeeded in pushing through genuine Panchayati Raj?

The basic problem has its roots in the Constitution, as adopted in 1950, not incorporating local self-government in the scheme of governance. In all older democracies, democracy had begun centuries ago at the local level – the parish, the county council, the elected sheriff, the elected mayor, etc. – long before evolving into a Parliamentary system at higher levels. We in India too had an ancient system of panchayats, but this had been disrupted by monarchical, imperial feudalism, followed by colonial systems of top-down administration. What we needed was the restoration and modernization of Panchayati Raj to serve, through the Constitution, as the foundation of a democratic Parliamentary order, integral to a system of Centre–state–local self-government institutions. As Sonia Gandhi once remarked, 'We need a strong Centre, strong States and strong panchayats.' The superstructure of Centre-state relations was erected by the Constituent Assembly, but not the foundational base of grassroots democracy in our villages and urban slums.

When Rajiv Gandhi sought to graft Constitutional local government on to extant institutions of administration and democracy that had existed at the Centre and states for nearly half a century since the promulgation of the Constitution, the existing institutions at both the state and Central levels pushed back as hard as they could. Overcoming institutional inertia and resistance became the principal task of the new order ushered in by the 73rd and 74th Amendments. That was the key challenge I faced upon becoming the first-ever minister of Panchayati Raj. I made a beginning, but the task was less than half-finished when I lost the elections of 2009, and the ministry passed into other hands. In the last three decades since the Constitution was amended as never before or since with the introduction of two new Parts, Part IX 'The Panchayats' (73rd Amendment) and Part IXA 'The Municipalities" (74th Amendment), my assessment is that while all states have made some progress towards genuine devolution, the Centre has not pushed them as hard as the situation demands. So, we have the shell of devolution but not enough of its substance.

Gandhi vs Ambedkar

Local self-government through the Constitution did not happen at the very beginning, principally because Dr Ambedkar pitted himself against Mahatma Gandhi's conception of elected village panchayats as the very foundation of an authentic, indigenous system of Indian democracy. The Mahatma had set out his framework for India's new republic in a 1946 publication, *A Gandhian Constitution for Independent India*,[3] written by his close associate, Sriman Narayan Agarwal. In his foreword for the book, Gandhi-ji said he had not had the time to write the book himself, but it accurately reflected his own views. In the book, village panchayats were projected as the foundation of democracy in free India. It recommended direct elections only at the village level and indirect elections to all higher levels to minimize what we today call 'money power' and 'muscle power'.

Ambedkar, who regarded villages as 'the ruination of India' and 'a sink of localism, a den of ignorance . . . leaving the Scheduled Castes in a state of eternal perdition . . . living a life of degradation, dishonour and ignominy', angrily refused to even mention the words 'Panchayati Raj' in his draft Constitution, published in December 1947. Gandhi-ji wrote a pained rejoinder to what Ambedkar had to say, but before the argument could really be joined, the Mahatma was assassinated on 30 January 1948. With Gandhi-ji martyred and Nehru sitting it out on the sidelines and leaning towards a largely Westminister type of democracy, it was with the greatest difficulty that the Gandhians, led by a Madras member, K. Santhanam, and a future Speaker, Ananthasayanam Ayyangar, succeeded in persuading the law minister and the Constituent Assembly to pass an anodyne reference to 'village panchayats' as 'units of self-government' in Article 40 of the non-justiciable, non-enforceable Directive Principles of State Policy.

By the time Nehru awoke to the realization that panchayats were the only available instrument for reliable 'last-mile delivery' of public goods and services, and undertook in 1959 a 'revolutionary' step in reorganizing the paternalistic system of feudal and colonial administration, the Constitution had been long passed and promulgated. Thus, a fierce wall of resistance to further devolution of power to the panchayats had been built into the Constitution. Rajiv Gandhi recognized that for this reason the Constitution had to be amended to bring in Panchayati Raj – but without removing the Constitutional provision that local self-government was an exclusively state subject. While, therefore, the mandatory provisions of his amendments, which institutionalized Panchayati Raj and made it ineluctable, were put in place, they constituted but the shell. The substance of devolution lay in the recommendatory provisions that were in the domain of state governments – who had the most to lose if devolution of power were made genuine. This is the continuing conundrum.[4]

The former Rajya Sabha MP and well-known Marathi journalist, Kumar Ketkar, has fed me the intriguing argument that Panchayati Raj was doomed from the start because it was the outcome of Rajiv Gandhi's Congress centenary speech in which he had called for driving out 'the brokers of power' in the party. After that call was given, the 'brokers of power', who were the active members of the Congress party at the grassroots, decided that if they were to remain in their remunerative positions in the lower rungs of the party, it was Rajiv Gandhi who had to be driven out. They were encouraged to do so by V.P. Singh and his cohort, who formed the National Front as an alternative to the Congress. That is how Rajiv dropped from well over 400 seats in the Lok Sabha to under 200 – the biggest electoral fall in our history.

I am not entirely persuaded of Ketkar's point, because V.P. Singh kept the Constitution amendment bills alive through his tenure, making but a few (and mostly constructive) amendments on the margins. Subsequently, under P.V. Narasimha Rao's premiership, all parties (other than the Dravidian parties) voted in favour of the bills after they had been scrutinized by the joint select committees. Rajiv Gandhi was in fact addressing a felt need to fill the lacuna of little or no local self-government in our Constitutional order.

More to the point, after the Constitutional amendments were enacted, we were confronted with a lack of enthusiasm for effective devolution of power on the part of most state governments, for if true devolution took place they would be robbed of substantial powers of discretion and patronage. While, therefore, state governments were ready to meet their Constitutional obligation to pass conformity legislation to bring the state statute books in sync with the 73rd and 74th Amendments, they were not sincere about taking the steps required for effective devolution to ensure that units of local self-government functioned not as agents of the state government but were empowered to be truly autonomous in addressing local issues. Devolution was, therefore, deliberately kept pro forma. There were some exceptions, of course – Kerala, Karnataka and Maharashtra (and Madhya Pradesh under Congress CM Digvijaya Singh) being among them. And all states did progressively move – albeit at snail's pace – towards the larger objective, but they were most unwilling to deprive themselves of the leverage they enjoyed in being seen as the principal instruments of development in the villages and slums of rural and urban India where the bulk of the votes lay.

As for the government at the Centre, almost all the ministers were loath to see the powers they wielded through programme-specific agencies pass on to elected local authorities over whom they had no control. Of course, both the prime minister and the Congress president held a deep conviction that Panchayati Raj was the singular road forward for inclusive governance to lead to inclusive growth, but were, understandably, not willing to rock the boat by overruling the reluctant ministers. Rajiv Gandhi might have done so, but Rajiv was no more. His passion had died with him. And I was too frail at political craft to make the radical systemic revolution that Panchayati Raj entailed. After all, Mahatma Gandhi had tried and failed; Jawaharlal Nehru had desperately tried – and got virtually nowhere; Morarji Desai wanted Panchayati Raj to be his principal legacy, but his government fell even before Ashok Mehta was able to present his report;

and Rajiv Gandhi was tripped at the starting point. Rao washed his hands of the whole project once the amendments were passed; Dr Manmohan Singh's sound words went floating on air. And, following them, I was left stranded with my Walter Mitty dreams.

10

Ministry of Youth Affairs and Sports

(2006–2008)

I had hardly crossed the threshold of my new office in the ministry of youth affairs and sports when two senior officials from our sports federations launched themselves into a tirade against Suresh Kalmadi. He was the chairman of the Indian Olympics Association (IOA) and, in that capacity, had been put in charge of the Organizing Committee (OC) of the forthcoming 2010 Commonwealth Games. Besides, he had been a Parliamentary colleague and we had been quite good friends on the social circuit.

I was absorbing their complaints when my secretary, S.Y. Quraishi, came in to brief me and highlighted the problems the ministry was having with the Commonwealth Games boss, particularly the vexed question of his inordinate delays in furnishing the UCs that the government's general financial rules (GFRs) obliged us to examine and pass before releasing additional instalments of funds to the OC headed by Kalmadi. For further clarification on this serious pending issue, I tried to reach out to my immediate predecessors, Prithviraj Chavan and Oscar Fernandes, who had held temporary charge of the ministry on the unexpected death in May 2005 of the first UPA minister of youth affairs and sports, the well-regarded Sunil Dutt, to seek their advice.

I never succeeded in tracking down Oscar. But as soon as Parliament convened a few weeks after I took over this responsibility, Prithviraj

Chavan came up to me in the Central Hall. I was relieved to see him but most disturbed when he said that unless I got 'regularized' the hundreds of crores of rupees being advanced to Kalmadi's OC, I would find myself in 'great trouble'. I asked the obvious question: Why had he not done anything during his tenure to 'regularize' what was going wrong?

He answered elliptically. He first explained that the heart of the problem lay in Kalmadi seeking more and more instalments of government funds without providing, as required under the rules, UCs that would establish that previous instalments had been spent with due probity and propriety on the purposes for which the money had been released. I knew that already. Prithviraj then came to the real reason for his not having pressed Kalmadi to provide the required UCs: 'I am from Karad,' he said, 'and Kalmadi is from Pune. So, this involves Maharashtra politics. Since you are from Tamil Nadu, you will not have the problems I had.'

Intimations of impropriety

After checking with Secretary Quraishi, I called Suresh Kalmadi and his senior colleagues in the OC for the Commonwealth Games for a meeting about a month after taking office. Finding Kalmadi repeatedly brushing aside the question of UCs, I remarked, 'Suresh, I have no desire to share a cell with you in Tihar Jail, nor do I wish to bring you chocolate cake in prison.'[1] That put the lid on our relationship, and he complained about my remark to the Congress president. She only sounded amused.

I was also hamstrung by Kalmadi's inclusion in the EGoM on the Commonwealth Games despite his not being a minister. I went to see the chairman of the EGoM, Arjun Singh, minister of human resource development, and sought a meeting of the EGoM without Kalmadi's presence. While this was being set up, Kalmadi, understandably, went to the prime minister to complain of his exclusion from the meeting. The PM, in turn, instructed me to relent, and we had another unfruitful EGoM meeting.

Frankly, I was bewildered at Kalmadi's refusal to furnish UCs. Was it because he thought this bureaucratic nonsense, or was it because there was something to hide? My bewilderment was shared not only by Secretary Quraishi but also by Rita Menon, the additional secretary in the revenue department in the finance ministry. In these circumstances, I declined to join Kalmadi's delegation to Melbourne to formally take over the baton from Australia, the previous host, to organize the next Commonwealth Games. This, of course, became another bone of contention.

On reflection, I think the adamant stand I took was not only on account of the lack of financial propriety and the warning by my predecessor, Prithviraj Chavan; it was also because I felt deeply humiliated, even insulted, at being removed without explanation from the petroleum ministry and dumped into a job in which I had never had any interest.

Other members of my staff would be greatly excited about famous names in sports coming to visit me; I was only embarrassed to have never heard of them. I wanted to get out of the job as soon as I could and, therefore, took every opportunity to make my dissatisfaction apparent to the prime minister and others.

I particularly remember one occasion when, in the prime minister's presence, I was presenting the CNN-IBN TV18 Greatest Sportsman of the Year award to the chess maestro Vishwanathan Anand (who, incidentally, was born in Mayiladuturai). Anand himself was not present, but his parents came on stage to receive the award. As I handed it over, I announced into the microphone, 'To the greatest sportsman of India from the worst sports minister India ever had.' I could hear the audience gasp.

I thought Kalmadi and I might lower the temperature by jointly visiting London, where the Commonwealth Games Secretariat is located. We were briefed by Sebastian Coe, the famed athlete who had grown into the United Kingdom's most renowned sports administrator. I was particularly taken by Coe's justification for the huge spending on the Commonwealth Games, not only with respect to transport and sports infrastructure but, much more importantly, in bringing welfare benefits to members of communities who were otherwise not much into sports.

For me, this was dramatically illustrated when we visited Manchester, which had recently hosted the European Games. At the site of the swimming pools, I was taken to a pool located below the main pools. This had initially been used for training and practice before the swimmers went upstairs for competitions.

As I was aware that Manchester was a major centre for Muslim immigration, largely from Pakistan but also from India, I mischievously asked whether the swimming pool facility was extended to Muslim women who would not wish to be seen swimming in the company of males.

The very serious reply I received impressed me deeply. The Manchester city authorities had, in fact, set aside Thursday afternoons for veiled women to visit the premises and be taught swimming by women instructors. I also learnt that the facility had been built near the university, far from the main venue for the European Games, specifically to cater to the sports requirements of the thousands of students at Manchester University.

Moreover, the main Games stadium had been located in the rundown docklands area of Manchester, which had once been a major port importing raw cotton and exporting cotton textiles. My guide told us that as a result of redevelopment for the Commonwealth Games, families that had been unemployed for two generations had found work, and that a well-known food store chain which had been opened for the Games continued to be in operation, with all the staff securing full-time employment. I also learnt that the information technology network for the Games had been put up by Microsoft, which, after the Games, decided to make the venue the headquarters of its European operations.

Also, by slightly adapting the athletics stadiums to suit football requirements, the Manchester City Club had found a place to challenge its more renowned rival, Manchester United. Manchester City has since gone from glory to glory. All this truly amounted to 'leaving behind a legacy' of the Games for the local community, including the poorest and most deprived.

This was in sharp contrast to what was happening in India. Although Kalmadi had won our bid against Hamilton, Canada, by a whisker, principally by claiming that we would be building new sports venues for the Commonwealth Games in Bawana, a slum with mainly SC residents on the outskirts of Delhi, we had gone back on our word and were renovating, at a huge cost, the Jawaharlal Nehru Stadium in the centre of posh New Delhi. All Bawana got was an incinerator to burn the capital's rubbish.

We had also pledged that hostel accommodation for the visiting athletes would be in and around Delhi University so that students could then use the facilities after the Commonwealth Games. But the Kalmadi OC had pulled back on that too and were engaged in building, again at an enormous cost, a brand-new Commonwealth Games village and, at further cost, connecting roads and flyovers. There was no social spin-off or 'legacy' to justify the enormous costs we were incurring. This made me even more inimical to the way we were preparing to host the Commonwealth Games.

Matter of the UCs

On returning to London from Manchester, Kalmadi and I went to the Commonwealth Games Secretariat and met the senior sports administrators charged with monitoring the progress of work. Much to Kalmadi's embarrassment, they made evident their deep dissatisfaction and continuing concerns over the way things were going for the 2010 Games in India.

Then came the report of the Commonwealth Games committee on the state of preparation for the 2010 Games. This report was discussed in Kuala Lumpur but was not shared with the ministry. Kalmadi's OC claimed that the report was strictly the property of the IOA and could not, and would not, be shared with the Government of India. From news reports and other sources, my ministry picked up bits and pieces of the damaging criticisms in it.

The final crunch came when I sought a meeting of Arjun Singh's EGoM to find a settlement to the irksome question of UCs. My secretary had a discussion with Rita Menon, additional secretary, revenue. When the EGoM convened, the finance minister was yet to arrive. As we waited, Rita Menon was asked to make her comments, and she was categorical that UCs must be cleared before fresh instalments of funds were released.

However, when the finance minister joined the meeting, he brushed aside his additional secretary's insistence on UCs and said I should release the next instalment while awaiting submission of UCs. Going by past experience, I knew this would not be a smooth exercise, but was overruled by the finance minister and the deputy chairman of the Planning Commission. The EGoM chairman went along with that view.

Furious, I wrote in confidence to the finance minister that I saw no reason why I should be in breach of the GFRs issued by his ministry, and would, therefore, like the finance ministry to itself release the required instalment to Kalmadi without making my ministry the channel.

As anticipated, I received a stern reply saying the procedure was for the finance ministry to release the budget grants and for individual ministries, in turn, to release the required instalments to the implementing authorities of approved schemes.

I hardly needed instruction. My question related to the impropriety of releasing the next instalment without receiving or clearing the required UCs for the earlier ones, thus exposing me to criticism from the Comptroller and Auditor General (CAG). I also wrote a letter marked 'Secret' to the prime minister, explaining my reservations, but did not receive a response. Meanwhile, my secretary succeeded in wangling some kind of UC out of the OC, and, availing of this fig leaf, I agreed to the release of the next instalment of funds.

I found it utterly shocking that a relatively poor country like India should be spending such enormous sums – estimated by at least one knowledgeable source at Rs 70,000 crore[2] – on a showy and transient event when a fraction of the money spent could easily go into building India as a 'sporting nation'.

At the time I left the ministry in 2008, the total expenditure on the Commonwealth Games (CWG) by all departments and the Delhi government had been kept at under Rs 10,000 crore – way too high, in my view. But over the next two years, the outlay shot up over seven times to the staggering and almost unbelievable figure of Rs 70,000 crore.

The organization of the Games – as distinct from construction and infrastructure for them – was budgeted at just under Rs 900 crore when

I joined the ministry at the end of January 2006 and was brought *down* by a little over Rs 200 crore over the two-year period of my helming the ministry. But eventual releases to Kalmadi's OC from the sports ministry nearly doubled after my exit – to Rs 1,628 crore.

Yet, and notwithstanding larger and larger sums of money being appropriated for infrastructure and other construction, as well as releases to Kalmadi's OC for ever more meretricious spending, the Commonwealth Games became an object of ridicule in the international press and the domestic media. In view of my own controversial stand and adversarial attitude to Kalmadi, I pleaded with the PM and others concerned for a minister of state to be attached to the ministry exclusively to look after the Games independent of me (the role Buta Singh, as minister of state, had played when Rajiv Gandhi had organized the Asian Games in 1982), but that was never accepted.

Asian Games, 2014/Olympics, 2024

While my conflict with Kalmadi over the Commonwealth Games kept mounting, another related issue came to the fore. Kalmadi's ambitions were not limited to the Commonwealth Games 2010 but extended well beyond, to hosting the Asian Games in 2014 and then the Olympics in 2020 or 2024. Cabinet approval to bid for the Asian Games had been given before I took charge as minister, and I had quietly registered my disapproval by not joining Kalmadi on any visit to any of the Asian countries that would be gathering in Kuwait in April 2007 to canvass votes for India to host the next Asian Games.

When it came to approaching the cabinet to sanction sums of money for the bidding process and subsequent preliminary arrangements, I found it impossible to reconcile the proposal with my conscience, despite the cabinet having earlier approved the bid in principle. My sports secretary, Madhukar Gupta, was horrified when I insisted on drafting the Note for Cabinet myself, recommending that we reject the proposal – so much so that he refused to sign it.

I then thought I would sign the note myself, since it expressed my personal view, but the Cabinet Secretariat cautioned me that the procedure was for an officer in the ministry to sign it.[3] Madhukar Gupta then deputed the joint secretary in the international sports division, Rahul Bhatnagar, to bring me to my senses. Bhatnagar's quiet, reasoned and persuasive argument was that with cabinet having sanctioned our bid, how could the sports ministry now argue against funds to pursue the bid?

I, therefore, offered to redraft the note, not as an expression of the sports minister's personal opposition, but, after laying out the background and setting forth possible objections, leaving the matter for decision by the cabinet. After I redrafted the note on the basis of this compromise, Bhatnagar kindly signed the note and I was able to take the battle to the next level.

At this point, the PM had a private word with me. He said that when the note came up for discussion in the cabinet, he would give me all the time I needed to express my objections to hosting these international games successively and would only then invite comments from other cabinet members. He was as good as his word. Although the atmosphere was electric with disapproval of my stand as we assembled in the cabinet room, I was afforded all the time I needed to place my 'ideological' objections before my ministerial colleagues.

I had also received a chart from the MEA carrying the responses of our diplomatic missions in Asian countries relating to our prospects for winning the Asian Games bid. The chart clearly established that the rival bid for Busan, South Korea, was receiving a far more favourable response. There were many reasons, including the obvious one that Games are awarded to cities, not countries, and New Delhi had already hosted the first and tenth Asian Games, in 1951 and 1982. My own view was that if we had selected Imphal in our Northeastern state of Manipur, which, as a sporting state, had a good sports stadium and a sports-crazy youth population, rather than Delhi, our bid might have received more favourable attention from our Asian neighbours, and from me as sports minister!

While the MEA chart came as something of a damper for those ministers who had decided to line themselves up behind Kalmadi, they were fairly vociferous in supporting the need to press our bid for the Asian Games. The two ministers I had lined up to endorse my line failed to attract the attention of the prime minister, although they weakly signalled their desire to speak. The cabinet meeting was wound up with the decision that we would go ahead to bid for the Asian Games.

Given my personal objection to this decision, I decided not to join the delegation to Kuwait city and asked my new secretary, S.K. Arora, to take my place. I was secretly thrilled with the news that Kalmadi's bid had been resoundingly rejected by a large majority of the Asian delegates. Of course, Kalmadi attributed this loss to my personal objections being known in the Asian capitals. Even if he were right, I have no regret at taking the stand I did. I am equally opposed to the attempt of the Modi government to host the 2036 Olympics – appositely enough on the centenary of Hitler hosting the games in Berlin in 1936!

Vision for a 'sporting nation'

Our pathetic haul of medals, placing us, the most populous nation in the world, at the derisory seventieth position of participating nations and teams in the Paris Olympics 2024, has only further proved how right I am in wanting India to become a sporting nation before it takes to being a sports-hosting nation.

Having seen a stop being put to wild imaginings of making India, at an obscene cost, a host of dazzling international sports events, I concentrated my energies on what I regarded as a far more important national goal – that of making India a 'sporting nation'. I decided on drawing in the other department of my ministry, the Department of Youth Affairs, as also my other portfolio, the ministry of Panchayati Raj. Between them, they had the required grassroots instruments and infrastructure to help make India a sporting nation.

I launched a new initiative, called the Panchayat Yuva Khel aur Krida Abhiyan [PYKKA] (in English, Panchayat Youth Sports and Games Movement). The Panchayati Raj ministry was to work with state governments to persuade village panchayats to set aside a portion of village land for building modest to elaborate sports complexes to which the village poor would have easy access. The youth affairs department, for its part, was to arrange expert sports training through its nation-wide Nehru Yuva Kendra (NYK) branches. I wanted panchayats rather than schools to be involved, for school coverage was limited and most rural schools just did not have the land for sports grounds. I was confident the NYK director, Dr Shakeel Ahmed Khan, had in him the dynamism and organizational ability to undertake this onerous task. There was an extant Indian model for organizing regular programmes for sports practice at the panchayat level, which had been in operation for years in Tamil Nadu. On a single acre of land, it provided access to seven different sports disciplines. I used that model to describe how PYKKA might work. The scheme also envisaged competitive sporting events organized by the panchayats, in association with sports federations, at the local village, block and district levels to actively hunt out emerging sports talent while giving ample exposure to our hitherto largely deprived youth for sports activities. We managed to get the Planning Commission to set aside Rs 1,500 crore for PYKKA in the next Eleventh Plan period.[4]

My confidence in the youth affairs department to rise to these new tasks was based principally on the excellence with which the NYK Director General, Shakeel Ahmed Khan, had organized in 2007 the 150th anniversary celebrations of the uprising of 1857, the 'First War of Indian Independence'. The celebration was begun at Meerut, where the sepoys had revolted against their British officers, before marching to the Red Fort in Delhi to get the Mughal emperor Bahadur Shah Zafar to lead them as the symbol of India's liberation from the British East India Company. Bahadur Shah was a reluctant participant, but eventually agreed to play his role. We, therefore, ended the youth procession from Meerut (in which I walked several miles with the youngsters) at the Red Fort. I had roped in Rajeev Sethi, my very creative friend from Apna Utsav 1986, to stage a multicultural show in the clearing before the Red Fort ramparts to highlight different facets of the First War of Independence.

Work on the events had been initiated under the overall guidance of Human Resource Development Minister Arjun Singh, who was eagerly looking forward to addressing the nation from the ramparts of the Fort – as the prime minister did every Independence Day. I did not comprehend the importance Arjun Singh attached to playing an ersatz PM – a post he spent all his political life hankering after. Therefore, in my naive, blundering way, I had separately met the Congress president, Sonia Gandhi, to invite her to the event. She readily agreed to attend and not to speak, in keeping with her husband Rajiv Gandhi's injunction that speeches should be eschewed at cultural performances. It was only on seeing Arjun Singh's face fall when I told him of this that I realized how keen he was to speak from the ramparts of the Red Fort, which he would never have been able to do otherwise. In the event, a compromise was effected: Sonia would attend the function but not speak, while Arjun Singh would deliver himself of a short address. Notwithstanding Shakeel's repeated entreaties, I stuck to the Rajiv line that speeches and culture did not go together and did not exercise my right to deliver an address from the fort ramparts. I don't think Arjun Singh ever forgave me my trespasses, but life went on. Rajeev Sethi's show was, as expected, spectacular and a thundering success. This persuaded me that the NYK and its hundreds of branches all over the country could be relied on to execute their responsibilities in the plan I was drawing up in my mind to harness panchayats and the NYKs, along with the sports federations, in a massive countrywide endeavour to transform India into a 'sporting nation'.

I was also impressed with the organizational abilities of Sailesh, the Joint Secretary who headed the youth affairs department, as demonstrated in his handling of camps of scouts and guides, and in sending large youth delegations to China, Saudi Arabia and the Republic of Korea, in addition to receiving youth delegations in India. I also readied a team in the panchayat ministry. Between them, I trusted Shakeel and Sailesh, in coordination with Injeti Srinivas, joint secretary in the Sports Department and the Panchayati Raj ministry team, to launch PYKKA.

I complemented PYKKA with the drafting of a new 'National Sports Policy', in which I sought to draw on the experience of others. I had been much impressed on a visit to Cuba, where dedicated sports facilities and training for the ordinary poor had converted Cuba within a handful of years into one of the world's greatest sporting nations. I had also learned on visits to Azerbaijan, Saudi Arabia and China how they were extending facilities to ensure 'Sports for All'. Joint Secretary Injeti Srinivas returned from France with a detailed manual of the French law governing provision of sports facilities to the young and the way the law was implemented.

Drawing on these inputs, I wrote the draft of the policy myself and then submitted it to my officers – a reversal of traditional practice. They made useful suggestions, which I incorporated. My draft contained a critique of how the sports federations misspent their resources. They picked up talent they had done nothing to create, discover or nurture, and squandered their resources on participating in sports events abroad or, worse, in organizing glitzy mega events in India instead of discovering and nurturing sports talent at the grassroots.

I also pointed out that in consequence, in terms of medals won, our performance was dismal, and just about the world's lowest in per capita demographic terms. I believed the root cause for this was that instead of concentrating on making India a 'sporting nation' by widening the base to include all young boys and girls in rural and urban India, the sports federations were more attracted to the false glitter of domestic and international competitive events.

They should, I felt, recognize that most schools did not have the grounds to make sports facilities available to students. But we could leverage the PRIs and the countrywide network of NYKs to work towards the agreed but unattained national goal of 'Sports for All'.

I then recommended that, as in Cuba, special sports training should be provided to promising young sportspersons of proven talent (alongside regular schooling), so that they were given every opportunity to hone their sports skills, bearing in mind that a gymnast might be no more than twelve when her abilities might become worldclass whereas, say, a footballer would not be at his peak till late adolescence or early adulthood. It was also necessary, I felt, to widen the net of public support from our cricket obsession to other sports disciplines. I also emphasized the importance of cultivating indigenous games like kho-kho and kabaddi.

Finally, I underlined the need for the new 'Sports Policy' to afford opportunities for youngsters with disabilities, girls and women, and socially disadvantaged sections of our society to take to sports and games without discrimination.

I predicted that if such a policy to make India a sporting nation were adopted, institutionalized and adequately funded, we would soon see glory in international sports arenas. If we continued with what we had, our sports performance would continue in the same rut to which it had been reduced.

Most of the heads of our score or so sports federations were pot-bellied politicians with long-abandoned connections to the sport concerned. When I circulated the draft of the new 'Sports Policy' to them, I was sceptical of how they would react, especially as all the sports federations were affiliated to the IOA. They were leaned upon by Kalmadi to not cooperate with me. In the event, I received only one set of comments from my old friend and political associate, K.P. Singh Deo, a trim and athletic brigadier in the territorial reserves, but his comments were too negative for my purposes. He basically argued for the status quo to be maintained and the sports federations to be left to their own devices. The others simply did not reply.

I was not too surprised.

Eventually, I persuaded Vijay Malhotra of the BJP, who was the long-serving and much-respected vice president of the IOA, to meet me with a representative delegation of the federations. Before that could happen, I was relieved in April 2008, while abroad, of my ministerial responsibility for sports. My draft 'Sports Policy' remained on the anvil and was never submitted to the cabinet.

Thus ended my association with a ministry that should never have been entrusted to me. But that is not the end of the story. For, a few weeks before CWG 2010 was to be kicked off, I was caught in the middle of a media exposure of how ill-prepared we were for the Games.

Row over CWG

Should I have been more discreet, even restrained, in publicly criticizing, particularly on television, the way Kalmadi's OC was going around organizing the Commonwealth Games at ever-increasing and enormous expense? Perhaps yes – if only to save my skin. Certainly no – if I were to be true to myself.

It all started – at least in public – long after I ceased to be minister of sports. As minister, I had confined my serious reservations to inner government circles. My going public about it was accidental. In 2010, the year of the Games, I was nominated to the Rajya Sabha. A few months later, in July 2010, I stepped out of the chamber into a dreadful monsoon downpour. A passing TV journalist asked me whether I thought the rains would ruin the Games. I laughed and said that while the monsoon rains would do a great deal of good to our farmers, I hoped, using a well-known Punjabi folk phrase ('*beda garak*'), the monsoon rains would drown out the Games. On reaching home, my daughter informed me that the TV channels were going berserk at this remark. I could hardly have withdrawn it.

By sheer coincidence, the channels, especially Times Now, which had Arnab Goswami at the time, and expert sports commentators like Nalin Mehta and Boria Majumdar, had by then discovered all that was going wrong with the Games. This was also picked up, as it inevitably would be, by the international media, and I was pestered for interviews and panel discussions. All my pent-up frustration poured forth as my worst apprehensions had been proved true. Several immediate incidents – the discovery by a CWG inspection team of dogs lying in beds for athletes at the filthy and incomplete Games Village, ill-laid tiles causing foot injuries to competitors practising in the swimming pools, and an under-construction bridge collapsing and killing a labourer – led to a media furore. My oft-repeated warning that Kalmadi's OC was not up to the mark and possibly neck deep in dubious deals was being echoed and was reverberating as if we were yodelling in a Swiss valley. Sonia Gandhi sent Ahmed Patel to ask me to desist. I limited my comments, but the media were in relentless pursuit of me. In any case, my adverse remarks were part of the public record.

At this point, an alarmed PM stepped in. Sidelining Kalmadi's OC and my successor sports minister, M.S. Gill, he put the Cabinet Secretary,

K.M. Chandrasekhar, in charge of retrieving the situation. The Cabinet Secretary did his best, and kudos to him.[5] If only the government had listened to my pleadings and those of my predecessor, Sunil Dutt, and put a minister of state in charge of CWG instead of Kalmadi's Organizing Committee, as had happened with the Asian Games 1982, our reputation as a nation might have been saved. But the damage had been done, and it would be decades before any Indian bid to host a major sports event would be taken seriously. As it was, Kalmadi spent ten months in Tihar Jail. I did not have to share a cell with him, nor did I bring him chocolate cake.

But, of course, there were, and always will be, serious consequences to expressing opinions contrary to those of one's party and government. This was also true when it came to me.

Two years after I had lost the 2009 election, Prime Minister Manmohan Singh, during an interaction in 2011 with media editors, replied to a question from a leading proprietor-editor asking whether, in addition, I had 'ideological' objections to the CWG, I had not raised any 'financial' objections. The PM replied in the negative. The fact was that I had raised my concerns in a secret letter to the PM about financial improprieties relating to my being pressured to release additional instalments of funds to Kalmadi's OC without his supplying UCs for the previous instalments he had received. What was the difficulty in meeting this routine, bureaucratic requirement unless the OC had something to hide? So, when I found a well-known TV maven waving a copy of my secret letter to the PM on which my signature could be clearly seen, I admitted that I had raised questions of financial impropriety in organizing the Games. This, it was felt in higher political circles, amounted to my letting the side down.

So, the new sports minister, Ajay Maken, was instructed to release a press statement quoting my assurances in Parliament that arrangements for the Commonwealth Games were well in hand. (Did Maken really expect me to launch an expose on the floor of the House about what I was complaining about in secret and confidential communications to the EGoM and the prime minister? That would have been really letting the side down!)

I was particularly irked by Maken's use of the word 'dichotomous', for it seemed to me that it showed he had been coached to denounce me thus.

So, in a TV interview with Bhupendra Chaubey, I asked how a mere B.Sc. pass from Hans Raj College came to use such a big, big word. Of course, this was academic snobbery at its worst, but I felt justified in trading insult for insult because of what I perceived as the injustice of his press release. TV commentators, particularly Rajdeep Sardesai, were not of this view, and I became for weeks the butt of their sarcasm and whipped-up indignation.

Meanwhile, at the Rajya Sabha

Although such controversies resulted in my rarely being asked to represent my party in debates in the Rajya Sabha, in stark contrast to my repeatedly being so tasked in my first term under P.V. Narasimha Rao and in my second term under Sonia Gandhi – and, more generally, being alienated from the mainstream and leadership of the party, my niche expertise in technical and administrative matters was recognized. So, while being kept out of political issues, I was consistently nominated by the Parliamentary party to represent the Congress in several important select committees, including the key select committee on the proposed Good and Services Tax (GST). I was also asked to chair three important committees set up, respectively, by the PM and the finance minister, Pranab Mukherjee, on nuclear disarmament, the zonal cultural centres (ZCCs) and Panchayati Raj. I was also fielded as the Congress candidate for my TN constituency in the 2014 elections.

There was nothing new in my taking an independent line on public issues. I am far from convinced that MPs should act like good little boys and meekly follow the leader. If we don't speak our minds, as Congress MPs were encouraged to do by Nehru, how will the leader ever learn what his or her followers really think? I had, after all, expressed my dissidence in the past on the dilution of secularism, on the government's failure to protect the Babri Masjid, the grant of diplomatic status to our relations with Israel and many other public issues under Narasimha Rao, Congress President Sitaram Kesri (1996–98), and even Sonia Gandhi herself. This had not come in the way of my rising from the back benches to the cabinet.

Therefore, while the roots of my current and total alienation from the party might be traced to my public comments on the Commonwealth Games, its proximate causes were related to events post my retirement in 2016 from the Rajya Sabha, to which I will come in the final chapter of this book.

I return to my earlier question: Should I have been more discreet and restrained in the matter of the Games? Possibly – but then, that would not have been me. I was and am keener on making my point than on climbing the greasy pole. Particularly in my first two terms in the Lok Sabha (1991–96 and 1999–2004), I had frequently spoken against government policy. In doing this, I believed I was representing a long democratic tradition that included Nye Bevan, Michael Foot and Tony Wedgewood-Benn in the UK, and numerous Democrats and Republicans in the US, let alone dissidents in European parties and our own Young Turks (Chandra Shekhar, Mohan Dharia, et al.), besides Mahavir Tyagi, Feroze Gandhi and others in carrying forward the tradition of 'dissidence within the party', which, during the freedom struggle, had given us the likes of Jawaharlal Nehru, Subhas Chandra Bose and Jayaprakash Narayan. Without fierce internal disputation on policies and people, political parties in democracies become personality cults, which ultimately dooms the party. Perhaps this is why I am 'A Maverick in Politics'.

11

Ministry for the Development of the North Eastern Region (DoNER) (2006–2009)

Soon after he was sworn in as PM, Dr Manmohan Singh tasked the DoNER ministry in 2004 with preparing a detailed vision document setting out the road towards development goals in the North Eastern Region (NER) over a fifteen-year period, that is, by 2020. Not satisfied with the considerable research somewhat haphazardly thrown together by my predecessor, P.R. Kyndiah, Doctor Sahib appointed me as minister in October 2006 to undertake this gruelling but vital national task.

There was no ministry I enjoyed more than DoNER. It reintroduced me to a part of India that had always fascinated me. Rajiv Gandhi shared my affection for the region and its people, and together we had extensively toured all the NER states several times (except, curiously, Sikkim), often by road, going into remote villages in thick forests, landslide-prone hillsides and soaring mountaintops, getting acquainted with a most friendly people and their rich and diverse cultural heritage.

Later, in the early noughties, the Congress president appointed me the Congress observer in charge of the Northeastern hill states. This gave me wide scope to travel extensively in the region, particularly in Nagaland, Manipur and Tripura, which were going to the polls and, to a somewhat lesser extent in Meghalaya, which was also going to the polls in early

2002. This laid the ground for my being appointed minister of DoNER in October 2006, a post I retained for the best part of three years. DoNER was a satisfying exercise, both professionally and personally. I used it to set up a series of intensive visits to the individual states of the Northeast and made some extraordinary trips to some of the most beautiful, untouched parts of India. I usually undertook these trips on behalf of the ministry of DoNER, but I combined them with my other responsibilities in the ministry of Panchayati Raj and the ministry of youth affairs and sports. During election campaigns, I also sometimes had to wear a fourth hat – on behalf of my political party.

New thinking on the Northeast

I began my term by gathering together in a meeting of the North Eastern Council (NEC) the chief ministers/governors of the eight states that comprised the NER. The two day-long interaction gave me a wide perspective of their concerns, and it was then decided, at my initiative, to deepen this perspective by holding sectoral meetings in each of the NER states (Manipur opted out, saying they lacked adequate suitable accommodation) on the identified sectors of priority to the state governments.

These repeated get-togethers, where discussions on sectoral issues lasted for a full day or even two, with inputs from domain experts and not just ministers or administrators, provided the opening to associate the DoNER ministry in a meaningful manner with the inputs being put together at the NIPFP (the ministry of finance's think tank) for the Vision document commissioned by the prime minister.

I also brought in a team of area specialists to generally supervise the technical work being assiduously undertaken at the NIPFP. The area specialists were led by the veteran journalist B.G. Verghese, who had for years passionately advocated development of the NER, and L.C. Jain, a Gandhian activist with long-standing interest in the region. From the start, I knew the most searing objections to the vision document would come from Sanjoy Hazarika, a very well-informed Assamese commentator heading a well-known NGO, unless we co-opted him. So, I did.

I also felt it necessary to propagate the draft documents at public meetings in academic institutions in all the states of the Northeast to promote public acceptance or propose modifications of the proposals. Accordingly, as many as twelve public hearings were held in the NER before we finalized the document. I then took it to Agartala in May 2007 for endorsement by the chief ministers and governors of the region. Also, of course, we were able to feed the conclusions of our sectoral meetings into the technical, almost econometric, exercise undertaken at the NIPFP.

I think I would be correct in stating that we inspired a very participative approach to an otherwise dull and statistics-ridden work. All went well till virtually the last moment, when a pamphlet was prepared showing Darjeeling district as part of the NER. This aroused the ire of the chief minister of Sikkim, Pawan Chamling, and I had to promise him that all copies of the pamphlet would be destroyed and a fresh map prepared, correctly showing the contours of the NER, before I could persuade him to not boycott the proceedings. I also had quite a difficult time making changes in the text to meet the ideological objections of the CPI-M chief minister of Tripura, Manik Sarkar.

The vision documents, in two volumes, began with a joint vision statement signed by the governors and chief ministers, plus me as the union minister for DoNER and the three other members of the NEC. It set out our priorities in seventeen key paragraphs, which ranged from high rhetoric to minute technical detail.

Vision 2020

The vision statement began by recalling that 'at Independence, the North Eastern Region was among the most prosperous regions of India' but over the next sixty years had slipped 'in most important parameters of growth'. It went on to proclaim that 'the purpose of this Vision document' was to return the NER to 'the position of national economic eminence it held a few decades ago', and to 'so fashion the development process that growth springs from and spreads out to the grassroots', in order that the region may play 'the arrow-head role it must play in the vanguard of the country's Look East Policy'. It was stressed that with the NER economy growing at half the GDP growth rate of the rest of the country, if we doubled growth rates in the NER – an entirely feasible objective if the report's recommendations were accepted and acted upon – we would attain the PM's much-cherished goal of the country as a whole scoring and sustaining double-digit growth.

Pointing to the India–Pakistan war of 1965, which resulted in all transit facilities through East Pakistan to our Northeast being terminated, thus reducing the geographical link between the NER (barring Sikkim) and the rest of India to a mere '29 kilometres' (the width of what is called the Siliguri Corridor, the so-called 'chicken's neck'), the document stressed the need 'to end the region's geo-political isolation' if we were to 'put it on the path to accelerated and inclusive growth'. This made Bangladesh a critical partner in the exercise, as we would have to transit through that nation's sovereign space to effectively link the Northeast with the rest of India.

It also underlined the perception that 'inclusive growth calls for inclusive governance', founded on the 'long-established traditions of community-based economic and social organization' of the NER. Accordingly, the vision document called for 'involving . . . the various institutions of democratic, representative, participatory institutions for popular development'.

The vision statement then turned to summarizing the sectoral requirements, the highest propriety being accorded to agriculture and allied activities 'which comprise over 80 per cent of the Region's gross domestic product'. As many as sixteen different key steps were specified to promote a 'Green Revolution' by rapidly replacing 'traditional cropping patterns (with) short duration, high yielding varieties of paddy in the *kharif* season, and in the *rabi* season by wheat, maize, mustard or vegetables (like potatoes, onions and garlic), along with soil nutrients like lime and the judicious use of pesticides' in order to 'genetically augment agricultural productivity'. In addition to, as well as to facilitate, this switch-over from single cropping to multi-cropping, the vision statement outlined several complementary steps to be taken, including land reforms, cold storages and cold chain links, and better rural credit and banking.

Although I am deliberately eschewing the technical details in the statement, which may overburden the general reader, in the context of the pivotal role of agriculture in the economic future of the NER, I will allow myself to draw attention to later specialized chapters of the vision document, which supplement this broad assertion of the priority to be accorded to agriculture by noting that 'over 86 per cent of population in the Region resides in villages', with 'about 40 lakh hectares under cultivation, 97 per cent (of which is) under food grains production'. The key problem was the very low land productivity, estimated at 1,520 kg per hectare, with only 20 per cent of the sown area being under irrigation, despite the abundant rainfall in the region and the mighty Brahmaputra flowing through Assam.

The Vision 2020 document suggested an increase in agricultural growth rates from 2 per cent between 2007 and 2010 to 3 per cent between 2010 and 2015, further raising it to 4 per cent between 2015 and 2020, in order to take production of food grains from 75 lakh metric ton (MT) to 110 lakh MT by increasing land productivity from the current 1,520 kg/ha to 1,650 kg/ha, realistically putting the accent on increasing crop intensity through double cropping, high-yielding varieties, and by bringing additional acreage under cultivation through wasteland and command area development.

Emphasis was also placed on horticulture, recommending for this extension services, marketing links, cold storages and processing facilities as well as creation of 'non-farm employment opportunities' through small-scale agro-processing units for oil extraction, and processing of ginger and turmeric as well as a host of fruits like pineapple, strawberry, passion fruit, apple, orange and banana.

Floriculture (particularly cultivation of exotic anthurium, roses, leather leaf fern, lilium, bird of paradise, etc.), as well as cultivation of a wide range of medicinal and aromatic plants, forest products, sericulture, rubber and tea potential, were highlighted, and emphasis placed on bamboo as a local resource, as 60 per cent of the country's bamboo resources and as much as 20 per cent of the world's bamboo resources, comprising 136 species, including eleven exotic species, are found in the Northeast.

The bamboo products market for Northeast output already amounted to $5 billion, and could be vastly expanded by 'scientific methods for production and cultivation, post-harvest treatment technology, product development and adequately trained manpower'. The crying need was for adequate infrastructure to undertake large-scale harvesting of 'gregarious flowering' of bamboo, bearing in mind that this was the root cause of twenty years of insurgency in Mizoram in the period 1966–1986.

Noting that the NER was importing 50 per cent of its milk consumption, 87 per cent of its consumption of eggs and almost 55 per cent of its fish consumption, the vision document emphasized the 'vast potential' for expanding poultry, animal husbandry and pisciculture in the region.

The vision statement went on to call for 'massive investment' in irrigation, flood control and drainage systems to prevent waterlogging. Measures for water harvesting, moisture conservation and prevention of soil erosion, especially in the hill areas, 'was considered of crucial importance for the realization of the agricultural potential of the region'. The importance of power to modernize agriculture in Assam's two major valleys and the quite separate issues of power in the hill states were highlighted. These requirements were dealt with in great technical detail in the later chapters of the document.

Equal priority was given to the aching need for 'connectivity' by road, rail and inland waterways to far-flung towns and villages, and air connections to and within the region, besides connectivity through cyber and telecom.

The vision statement emphasized that human resource development in the region required the setting up of centres of excellence like IITs and IIMs, investing in border infrastructure (most of the Northeast's borders were international, and it was a gateway to Southeast Asia), and activating tourism in the region.[1]

Happily, in the end we had a triumphant launch of NER Vision 2020 by the prime minister at Vigyan Bhavan on 2 July 2007. He was bountiful in his praise of the report. My private secretary, Vanlalvawna, a

Mizo officer, did an outstanding job of gathering nearly 2,000 members of the NER community in Delhi to attend the release ceremony, perhaps the largest-ever gathering of people from the Northeast the capital had ever seen. Not only was the main auditorium jam-packed, we had to take two additional conference rooms with video facilities to accommodate the overflow.

Following the release of the document, I got down with ministry officials to setting up seventeen sectoral groups that would, on a permanent and ongoing basis, bring together the ministry of DoNER and the NEC Secretariat with representatives of the Planning Commission and the Union ministries/departments/agencies concerned, to oversee and ensure progress with respect to the sectors involved.

After putting this follow-up action in motion, I went off to fight my Lok Sabha election. I lost. And my successors were not very interested in implementing Vision 2020. Strangely, the prime minister, who was the main dynamo driving the exercise, also seemed to have lost interest when he lost me. So, the ministry of DoNER took far too long to set up these groups and was less than successful in provoking them to action. Unsurprisingly, therefore, instead of becoming a 'permanent and ongoing' set of bodies to oversee the economic development of the Northeast the groups were dissolved very quickly after they had presented a single report each.

Consequently, Vision 2020 withered on the vine. A subsequent evaluation I prepared about a decade later for a private initiative demonstrated how everything was where it was in 2004, let alone in 2007 or later.[2] The Northeast continues to be neglected, despite grandiose announcements to the contrary and occasional spurts of growth. Its huge potential, both as a region and as a bridge to fast-growing South-East Asia, remains more in the realm of dreams than in the realm of reality.

12

Elections 2009

As 2009 dawned, the Lok Sabha elections loomed. My electoral assets consisted principally of the alliance with the DMK continuing to hold, and my majority of nearly 2,00,000. That had been clearly whittled down, but, I thought, not entirely eliminated.

I could also point to the tsunami relief work that my colleagues and I had undertaken at the worst of times, the numerous small buildings I had constructed and the welfare projects I had undertaken, including an air-conditioned burns ward at the Kumbakonam general hospital after a devastating fire in a primary school that drew nationwide attention, and eventually a similar ward in Mayiladuturai. Also, over ninety community halls were constructed in villages around the constituency. Many schools were given benches, laboratory equipment and computers, and a few were given laboratory and library buildings and compound walls as well. Drinking water facilities were also provided to schools that needed them. Another significant contribution was the desilting of the Thiruvali tank, for which I had gone to make a representation to Jayalalithaa in Nagapattinam when she set her goons on me.

Under the Sports Authority of India, we started the Rajiv Gandhi Sports Centre at Mayiladuturai. We also established the Rajiv Gandhi Centre for Aquaculture on the outskirts of Sirkazhi under the aegis of the Marine Products Export Development Authority (MPEDA). While these projects met urgent public requirements, the work an MP does, as

Gujral Sahib had told my wife before the 1996 elections, garners him much grateful praise from the public but very few votes. That is the strange paradox of electoral politics.

I placed my hopes for re-election mainly on my successful campaign to retain the very existence of the Mayiladuturai constituency after the Delimitation Commission's first draft had deleted it. I allowed myself to believe that pulling off this feat would win me a unique kind of distinction among my electors. So, I appeared before the Delimitation Commission at their public hearing in Tiruchirappalli.

Section 3 of the Delimitation Commission Act specified three criteria to determine the contours of any given election constituency: geographic contiguity; economic integrity; and public opinion. I argued before the Delimitation Commission that the geographical contiguity of my constituency had been disrupted by the proposal to merge that half of the constituency which fell in Nagapattinam district with assembly constituencies that fell in another district north of the Kollidam river, the river with the widest drainage in Tamil Nadu. Therefore, I stressed, only fish and not the general public could swim across the breadth of the river. This transgressed the criterion of 'geographical contiguity' in the matter of my constituency.

As for 'economic integrity', while farming and fishing were the predominant – indeed the only activities that characterized the economy south of the Kollidam – it was industry and mining that were the drivers of economic development in the constituency of Chidambaram to the north. Thus, the proposed reorganization of the constituency violated the criterion of 'economic integrity'.

And as for the third criterion of 'public opinion', I turned dramatically to the crowd that had been brought in from the constituency. Speaking in Tamil, I asked those among the gathering who were in favour of retaining Mayiladuturai as a Parliamentary constituency to raise their hands. A forest of hands went up – in the end I became one of the few in Indian Parliamentary history to have succeeded in overturning a draft decision of the Delimitation Commission.

Anti-incumbency and Stalin's displeasure

While counting my blessings in estimating my election prospects, I was only too aware that this was less than half the story. For I could sense a strong anti-incumbency sentiment that demanded a change, reinforced by a tailwind of the key DMK minister M.K. Stalin's disenchantment with me.

He was my main concern. M.K. 'Dalapati' Stalin was my counterpart Panchayati Raj minister in the state, and although we had a very cordial meeting in Gandhigram to discuss a possible joint tour of the panchayats in Tamil Nadu, as I had been undertaking in other states, there was no follow-up invitation from him.

Meanwhile, my senior TN colleague, P. Chidambaram, had cautioned me that the DMK government in the state was dead against my Panchayati Raj activism at the Centre as Panchayati Raj was an exclusively state subject under the Constitution, and the DMK in particular was zealous in protecting state rights. I was, of course, well aware of this, as I have explained in my chapter on the Ministry of Panchayati Raj, but while most other state governments were willing to discuss matters with me and show me what they were doing, the DMK ministry was adamant on not even entertaining my request. However, given the amiable way in which my fellow DMK MPs and ministers were treating me, and the always cordial reception I received from the chief minister, 'Kalaignar' Karunanidhi, I thought 'Dalapati' Stalin had simply forgotten our Gandhigram consensus decision. So, I kept reminding him whenever I chanced to meet him. This, I learned, had greatly annoyed him. I tried making amends, but it was not enough for him to be persuaded to visit my constituency to campaign for me. That signalled to the DMK cadres that my possible defeat would not carry any reprimand for them. While, therefore, the DMK formally did its duty by me, the enthusiasm that had characterized my victorious 2004 campaign was conspicuously absent in 2009.

Moreover, once Rajakumar had become an MLA, he lost almost all interest in taking me on village visits. He seemed to think his new political and social status required him to stand on platforms, not squat on the ground with poor villagers. That virtually ended our extensive touring of the previous eighteen years – win or lose – which had so signally contributed to public approbation of my endeavours on behalf of my constituents as an MP, and even when I was an ex-MP.

So, while villagers turned up in their scores, even sometimes hundreds, for the foundation stone-laying and inaugural functions that Rajakumar organized, they rarely saw me as a minister sitting with the poorest of the poor in the midst of their hovels. The intimacy was missing, the personal interaction was absent; the distance between the podium and the audience was not the same thing as sharing a common space with them.

It was also clear that Rajakumar was upset with his jurisdiction being cut in half when I decided to open a party sub-office in Kumbakonam under T.R. Loganathan. Principally owing to Rajakumar's hostility towards Loganathan and his sense of deprivation, Loganathan slowly slipped out of Rajakumar's supervision and control to run a separate and independent fiefdom in that half of the constituency which fell in Thanjavur district. As Loganathan had an excellent rapport with the local DMK leaders, I was content to leave it at that.

Moreover, in saving Mayiladuturai as a Parliamentary constituency, I had lost Kodavasal block to the neighbouring Nannilam constituency. It was in Kodavasal block that I had repeatedly received my largest majority. In place of Kodavasal, two other blocks of Thanjavur district – Papanasam and Ammapetai – had been added to the Mayiladuturai Parliamentary constituency. This meant I had to devote a disproportionate amount of time touring the two new blocks.

Final blow: Sri Lanka's merciless assault on Tamil civilians

I could sense that the winds of change were blowing, but I hoped against hope that I would squeeze through. My pollster friend rang me in considerable alarm in the middle phase of the campaign to say my rating was running a mere 1 per cent above my AIADMK rival's and that I must do something about it. I did not know what I could do and prayed instead that the pollster might be wrong.

The final blow came on the very eve of polling. In Sri Lanka, President Mahinda Rajapaksa moved into the strongholds of the LTTE to finally finish them off. The LTTE leadership had deliberately and cruelly constructed a human shield to protect their armed cadres. For the Rajapaksa government, the massed cohort of innocent Tamils counted for little, given the prospect of dealing a final, crushing blow to the LTTE. The horde of unarmed civilians was massacred in targeted artillery fire.

This was the lead story in every newspaper and on every TV screen, even as voters walked to the voting booths. The AIADMK had obtained a morphed photograph of me welcoming Rajapaksa at my daughter's wedding reception. The photo was widely distributed along with voters' slips by my opponent's team. I crashed to defeat by a margin of 36,000 votes.

13

Decline . . . Fade Out . . . Fall: 2016–24

On returning to Delhi, I discovered I was the only member of the cabinet to have lost in a general election where the Congress seats soared from 140 to 206. I was traumatized. Apart from attending the last meeting of the previous cabinet and visiting Rashtrapati Bhavan for the President's banquet in honour of the outgoing government, I took to hiding out in my eldest daughter's Gurgaon apartment, occupying myself with my first grandchild, Uma, born while I was in the middle of the campaign (on 12 April). To distract myself, I found myself obsessively searching through brochures to buy a car for myself and the family. I simply did not know what I was going to do.

In the midst of this angst, I received a very sympathetic telephone call from the Congress president, who was delighted that I was going to the United States for a seminar on comparative local government convened by Nobel Laureate Joseph Stiglitz of Columbia University.[1] She asked me to meet her when I came back to India. When I did, I found her most concerned about my future but was still a little surprised when she said I was not to quit my official residence. She did not explain why.

Decline (2009–2016)

A few days later, I found myself appointed to the largely sinecure post of honorary adviser to the Bureau of Parliamentary Studies and Training, the upside of the appointment being the right to government residential accommodation at 12, Safdarjung Lane. It provided me with an office in the Parliament House annexe to store some of the books from my overflowing library, but for the rest it seemed like a dead end, albeit a comfortable dead end. I compensated for this by accepting every invitation I wangled to go out on lecture tours, flogging, too, my latest collection of columns from *The Indian Express*: *A Time of Transition: From Rajiv Gandhi to the 21st Century* (Penguin Random House, New Delhi, 2009).

My peregrinations took me to Columbia University, Cambridge, Oxford, Berlin, Brown University, Stanford, Washington, DC, Los Angeles, London, Prague, Dhaka, Singapore, Melbourne, Aix-en-Provence, Venice and Bangkok; and very frequently to Islamabad, Lahore and Karachi. While in itself quite enjoyable, I was distressed at the pointlessness of such an existence.

Nomination to the Rajya Sabha

On one of my trips abroad, to Ditchley Park in the UK in March 2010, a young Youth Congress worker rang me from Mumbai to congratulate me on my elevation to the Rajya Sabha. I was astonished but very, very pleased at this wholly unexpected and unanticipated reinstatement in Parliament – and that too for six years. The only fly in the ointment was that I was to be a President's nominee, the downside of which was that I could not be restored to the cabinet.

Nemesis, however, was waiting around the corner ('with lead piping in her stocking', as P.G. Wodehouse might have said). It came down on me in a most unexpected manner. I had long been campaigning for the conscientious implementation of The Provisions of the Panchayats (Extension to Scheduled Areas) Act (PESA) as the most effective and humane way of containing Naxalism. In the second week of April, the Naxal guerrillas in the forests of central India struck at a detachment of our security forces, killing as many as seventy-six of them.

I was most disturbed. So, I rang Digvijaya Singh, a former chief minister of Madhya Pradesh, when what is now Naxal-troubled Chhattisgarh was part of his domain. I poured my heart out to him and found in him a most sympathetic listener who believed, on the basis of his vast experience in tackling Naxalism, that the approach I was laying out was the optimum one.

He added that he thought both Sonia Gandhi and Rahul Gandhi were inclined to my view, and I should, therefore, seek a meeting with them to explain alternative ways to the bullet to deal with the problem. I was pleased but a little surprised that Digvijaya had taken so much time off to discuss this with me as our conversation had lasted more than half an hour. It was only later that I learnt that he was at the bedside of his wife, Asha, a terminal cancer patient, in a hospital in faraway Houston and, therefore, not pressed for time.

A day later, early in the morning, a reporter from NDTV turned up at my residence. He slapped on my table a copy of the *Economic Times*, which contained an interview given to a reporter by Digvijaya. Without naming me and taking the burden of the argument entirely on his shoulders, Digvijaya in the interview entirely endorsed my approach to tackling Naxalism. Towards the end, Digvijaya was asked whether he had brought his views to the attention of the home minister, P. Chidambaram. Digvijaya had replied by describing Chidambaram as 'arrogant' and unwilling to listen to advice.

The camera was then set up for the NDTV reporter to seek my reaction to the Digvijaya interview. I replied that I did not agree with Digvijaya a hundred per cent or even a thousand per cent, but 'one lakh per cent'! Towards the end of the interview, the reporter asked whether I shared Digvijaya's opinion of the Union home minister, P. Chidambaram. I cautiously replied that as PC was a senior colleague of mine from the same state of Tamil Nadu, I would not like to comment on him. Typical of television news broadcasts, when the interview was telecast, the 'one lakh per cent' comment was highlighted and the 'no comment' on Chidambaram was deleted.

A day after the telecast, *The Indian Express* front-paged the interview with a headline that burnished my 'one lakh per cent' remark. But the report attributed my remark to Digvijaya's assessment of PC and not, as was my intention, his assessment of the Naxal problem.

This snafu seemed unimportant while I prepared for my swearing-in the following day, 15 April 2010, as a newly nominated member of the Rajya Sabha. About an hour before I was to leave for Parliament, the Congress president came on the line and gave me a furious tongue-lashing. I suspect (but do not know) that the home minister had got in touch with her to protest Digvijaya's public criticism of him, apparently endorsed by me. I tried to get a word in edgewise, but she was in such a fury that I deemed it unwise to try to explain matters to her till she had calmed down. That moment never came – and marks my 'Decline ... Fade Out ... Fall'.

Where I thought another opportunity would soon arise to clear the air, it never did. Instead, it signalled the end of a personal relationship with her that had its origins in my working with her husband from the mid-eighties.

The other obvious proximate cause was my ferocious and adverse commenting on the Commonwealth Games. My further guess is that Congressmen who resented my being helicoptered into high places without putting in the grassroots efforts that had won them their spurs availed themselves of the opportunity to avenge themselves on me, especially given that I had lost my election at a time when Congress fortunes were spiralling upwards. That is my guess. I really do not know. But I recalled that Rajiv had warned me on my seeking voluntary retirement from the IFS that 'the system would never accept' me.

Do I regret having spoken out on the Games? In hindsight, I see that that was the beginning of my political decline and fall. So, of course, I am unhappy about the consequences, but I would be false to my maverick self if I were to regret having spoken out. Having seen what was going horribly wrong and having been warned against it, should I, as the minister responsible for it, have just ducked when everything I had apprehended was happening as I had feared, right on the eve of the Games, and ignored the damage this was doing to India and to our government in the eyes of our people and the world at large? Perhaps a clever politician would have done just that. I am not – and never was, nor aspired to be – a clever politician. But given that the Commonwealth Games springs to commentators' tongues to explain the electoral disaster that was to overtake the Congress in 2014, perhaps it was just as well that I was not a clever politician. It is hard to be good.

'Unparliamentary' maiden speech

Meanwhile, soldiering on as a newcomer to the Rajya Sabha, if not to Parliament, I thought the chair (my old friend and foreign service colleague, M. Hamid Ansari) would ensure that the usual conventions observed for 'maiden speeches' – no interruptions and no time limit – would prevail in my case. My opening line related to the leader of the Opposition having referred to Left-wing socialists like me as 'half a Maoist'. I said it was, indeed, an honour to be called 'half a Maoist' by 'a full-fledged fascist'! This led to such a row that the House remained disrupted for three whole days.

I tried to get order restored by offering to table my speech instead of delivering it. The chairman – putting aside our decades-long personal friendship to do his duty as the presiding officer of the Rajya Sabha – said this was not the practice in the Upper House, adding that 'the Opposition laid a trap, and you walked into it'. The impasse continued.

Then, Pranab Mukherjee asked me to meet him. He patiently explained to me that while the Lok Sabha had its own compilation of 'unparliamentary' expressions, which allowed for use of the expression 'fascist', he had himself been pulled up by the chair in the Rajya Sabha for having used the word 'fascist' as that word had been banned as 'unparliamentary' in the Houses of Parliament in Westminister, which was the standard to which speeches in the Rajya Sabha were held. He persuaded me to apologize.

So, I found a form of words to apologize without apologizing to allow proceedings in the House to be resumed. I sought to make my maiden speech, in effect, an attempt to explain to my indignant Congress president why I had reacted as I had to the killing of over seventy security personnel by Maoist Naxals in the forests of Bastar, the proximate cause of her disenchantment with me.

Anyhow, since I regard that 'maiden speech' as among the most important I delivered in my twenty-five years in parliamentary politics, I offer here a summary of my argument:

> The prime minister had publicly stated that 'the single gravest challenge to internal security' lay in the Naxal-affected districts that comprised a third of the districts of India ranging from the hard core where armed Naxalite cadres had effectively displaced the local administration to districts that were 'most-affected', 'less affected' and 'on the periphery'. The root cause for the rise of Naxalism in the tribal areas of central India lay in 'the patent failure of the States concerned to meet the real development requirements of the tribal folk' through 'participative development' as provided for in the PESA, a law passed all of 13 years ago by Parliament, as required under the 73rd amendment. PESA had been drafted on the basis of the Dilip Bhuria report of 1995 and been reviewed in the 2008 report of the Bandyopadhyay committee on 'Development Challenges in Extremist Affected Areas'. The latter, in particular, had emphasized that both the Union and State governments 'have in practice treated unrest as a law-and-order problem' while their own 'official documents' are fully cognizant of the cause-and-consequence effect of 'extremism and poverty', of the ineffectiveness of 'all development schemes', in which the 'deep relationship between tribals and forests' is disrupted, and 'tribals suffer unduly from displacement'.
>
> We had discussed this, I informed the House, at a Workshop convened by the ministry of Panchayati Raj in December 2008, attended by an authorised representative of the Home ministry. The conclusions drawn, with the concurrence of the Home representative, recognized that 'an important cause of disenchantment in these districts was the sense of injustice'; thus, 'extremism was frequently the response to perceived exploitation'. Moreover, 'lower-level functionaries' were 'perceived as antagonistic to the common people, the poor and specially the tribal'. Also, 'the judicial process' was found to 'not solve the problems of the disadvantaged' and 'in many cases was used to

deprive the tribals of their rights'. The Bandyopadhyay committee report ended on a signal note of wisdom and compassion: 'There will be peace, harmony and social progress only if here is equity, justice and dignity for everyone.'

Having set out the background, I proceeded to outline my three-pronged solution: PESA; the Central budgetary outlay for tribal areas development; and the recommendations of the Thirteenth Finance Commission for direct support to the panchayats.

I explained that PESA contained all the ingredients needed to persuade the tribal people that development could be based on their own perceived priorities and would be undertaken not by imperious bureaucrats but by themselves through their elected representatives. I quoted chapter and verse from the text of PESA to show that elected panchayats had to obtain the informed agreement of Gram Sabhas to secure their 'approval of all plans, projects and programmes proposed by the panchayats', as also Gram Sabha approval of all utilization certificates before these were issued. The Gram Sabhas also had the 'statutory right' to be consulted on any issue affecting 'forest produce', 'prospecting or mining', or 'relating to alienation of land'. These safeguards had been reinforced by legislation on the 'rights of forest dwellers' and the 'rights to resettlement and rehabilitation' in the event of displacement. The conscientious implementation of all three laws would do more, I urged, than 'AK-47s and unmanned drones to combat the alarming spread of Naxalism in these areas'.

This, however, would not be enough. It had to be backed by assured funds. The Central budgetary outlay for rural development stood at Rs 1,30,000 crore (then!) augmented to Rs 1,60,000 crore annually by the 13th FC grant to the panchayats. If even a third of this overall amount were to reach the panchayats directly in the one-third Naxal-affected districts, the humongous sum of Rs 40,000 crore could immediately be earmarked for tribal panchayats, or deposited where possible in their treasury or bank accounts, for them to spend on their priorities and on plans, projects and programmes approved by them tribal village-by-village.[2]

I concluded by reminding Members that we could thus give the tribal communities 'a clear choice between state-sponsored participative development in which the tribals themselves are the key decision-makers, on the one hand, and certain death at the hands of the Maoists, on the other'. I described this as 'draining the swamp as the best way of ridding it of alligators'. That, I urged, is the way forward: 'drain the swamp by empowering the people, not empowering contractors and multinationals, and, above all, not empowering the bureaucracy and technocracy in these areas which have been only oppressive of the tribal people for the last six decades'.[3]

I never learned whether Sonia Gandhi read the speech – or extracts from it – or not. I had hoped these arguments would reach the higher echelons of the party. I don't think they did. And I was too much of a coward, too overawed by Madam Gandhi, too dependent on her patronage, to risk the cutting edge of her tongue to give her the speech and seek her understanding – which would have been the correct 'maverick' thing to do. In the end, I blame no one more than my own pusillanimity for the decline in my relationship with our party's First Family. So, my isolation from the party mainstream continued. Saifuddin Soz, leading the party in Jammu and Kashmir, told me he had suggested my name for general secretary as I was considered the most sympathetic Congressman in the Valley, but a horrified Congress president had asked how so sensitive a post could be given to a 'loose cannon'!

'Politically Incorrect'

Since ceasing in 2009 to be a minister, I continued my ceaseless flow of columns, articles and book reviews, and found myself appearing increasingly on television shows.

NDTV proposed a daily show titled 'Politically Incorrect', very ably anchored by Ankita Mukherjee and featuring the BJP/RSS-inclined columnist Swapan Dasgupta (now a Rajya Sabha MP) and me (then also a Rajya Sabha MP) embattled every evening on a topical issue. Since we were ideological opposites, Swapan took a 'saffron' line and I a Nehruvian stand, thus making the debate a reasoned polemic between a member of the BJP and a member of the Congress, although both of us were careful to identify ourselves as expressing 'personal' and not 'party' views.

While this proved popular, when the show was converted into a weekly performance in front of student audiences filmed on the campuses of different educational institutions of the national capital, it became something of a hit (among English-speaking audiences). In about a year's time, however, 'Politically Incorrect' was taken off air because NDTV found the campus sequences too expensive to film. Or so they said!

The fallout of these debates was that Swapan and I became favourites on a range of TV shows. He was later rewarded, deservedly, with a seat in the Rajya Sabha (but has been surprisingly restrained in the House while remaining vocal on TV). I expressed myself vigorously on my 'magnificent obsessions' – secularism, Pakistan, Palestine, nuclear disarmament, Panchayati Raj, etc. Although I might have been somewhat more ahead of the curve than the party on some of these issues, I was never reprimanded or restrained.

The explosion of interest in these TV appearances doubtless had much to do with my having compared our hosting the Commonwealth Games to an owl dressing itself in peacock feathers.

A few days ago, my wife overheard a passer-by outside my daughter's house inquiring who stayed there. On being told, he remarked, '*Accha, woh imaandaar aadmi ki beti!* (Oh, that honest man's daughter!)' Was such a public reputation not worth the wrath of the party that I had brought upon my head?

My party and I

Notwithstanding my seniority in the party, I was kept out of its Parliamentary executive. And although in my fifteen years over three terms in the Lok Sabha, I had frequently been among the principal spokespersons of the party, especially on politically controversial matters, in my six years in the Rajya Sabha, I was deliberately ignored by my party whips and rarely included in the list of Congress speakers submitted to the chair. I suspected this was on orders from above.

Nevertheless, I was, of course, an automatic choice when technical issues were to be discussed in Rajya Sabha select committees (such as on the Mines and Minerals Bill and the GST) but was excluded from most political issues and downgraded even on foreign policy matters. The only exception was when Pranab Mukherjee ordered that I lead the Treasury benches in the debate on the budget he had presented.

Outside Parliament, I was extremely busy. I found myself nominated as chair of three important committees/expert groups: the first on updating the Rajiv Gandhi nuclear disarmament Action Plan; the second, to review the performance on the ground of the ZCCs in relation to the objectives set out by Rajiv Gandhi; and the third to examine how PRIs might be better leveraged for the last-mile delivery of public goods and services to the intended beneficiaries. While I was and am grateful to both Dr Manmohan Singh and Sonia Gandhi for having recognized my contribution to these three niche initiatives, I also wryly noted that these schemes were not connected to the current regime but to the Rajiv legacy. I was a holdover from the past, not a player in the present.

Nuclear disarmament

I was sent as a Parliamentary delegate to the United Nations General Assembly (UNGA) session in October 2010, assigned to the First Committee that deals with disarmament issues. I drafted my own speech and sent it in advance to the Permanent Mission of India at New York, which was deeply distressed since the draft called for immediate time-bound universal disarmament, in keeping with the Action Plan for nuclear disarmament that Rajiv Gandhi had presented some twenty-two years earlier. The officers concerned arrived at Newark airport to receive me and gave me an alternative draft, to be read out without question.

Realizing that my statement had to be in conformity with government policy and that our policy had altered since we became a de facto nuclear weapons power in 1998, I understood that the time was not ripe to make a radical departure without due authorization.

Very annoyed, I read out a somewhat amended version of the draft that had been imposed on me and bided my time to lobby with other delegates for a First Committee resolution that would at least set out the first principles of the Rajiv Gandhi's Action Plan (RGAP).

Deeply disappointed, I returned to Delhi to find an astonishing letter from Shivshankar Menon, the national security adviser, relaying the prime minister's request that I serve as chairman of an expert group constituted to examine the continuing relevance of Rajiv Gandhi's 1988 Action Plan for a Nuclear-Weapons-Free World Order, and updating it.

Seven members were requested to join the group. These were: Professor Amitabh Mattoo, a disarmament expert at JNU and now dean, School of International Studies, JNU; Dr Arvind Gupta IFS (retd), who held the Lal Bahadur Shastri chair at the Institute of Defence Studies and Analyses; Commander (Retd) C. Uday Bhaskar of the National Maritime Foundation, later replaced at the commander's request by Admiral L. Ramdas, former chief of naval staff; Dr Manpreet Sethi, senior fellow at the Centre for Air Power Studies; Ambassador Satish Chandra IFS (Retd), distinguished fellow at the Vivekananda International Institute; Ambassador Saurabh Kumar of the IFS (Retd), former permanent representative of India to the International Atomic Energy Agency, Vienna; and Siddharth Varadarajan, editor of *The Hindu*.

The group received evidence from Ambassador Muchkund Dubey, who had drafted the Rajiv Gandhi Action Plan (RGAP 88); Ambassador C.R. Gharekhan, who had headed the Permanent Mission of India at the UN at the time; and Ambassador Ronen Sen, the IFS officer who was joint secretary in Rajiv's PMO at the time of the preparation of RGAP 88. The group also heard evidence from four international experts on disarmament issues.

The group submitted its unanimous report within ten months. It started by setting out the background, which included highlighting the Indian Working Paper (WP 06), formally submitted by Pranab Mukherjee (as minister of external affairs) to the UN General Assembly in 2006. This was an updating and summation of RGAP 88.

The evidence that emerged during our hearings was that soon after presenting his Action Plan to the UN, Rajiv Gandhi had ordered the preparation of a nuclear weapons test. This apparent contradiction (which first struck me as 'hypocrisy') had a rationale that lay at the heart of Rajiv's presentation in New York, namely, that the world was not divided between Nuclear Weapon States (NWSs) and non-nuclear weapon states (NNWSs) as the Nuclear Non-Proliferation Treaty (NPT) had assumed but now included a third category, the Threshold Nuclear Weapon States (TNWSs). If even now, the NWS showed the least inclination to cap, reverse and eliminate their nuclear weapons, there was an even chance the TWNSs would also restrain themselves at the threshold; otherwise, the TWNSs would soon be claiming NWS status by indubitably demonstrating their nuclear weapons capacity. To this end, he ordered preparations for tests to begin, knowing full well that Pakistan already had the Bomb or would soon be acquiring it. He thus expected to show the NWSs that his prediction of TNWSs like India (and several others) going overtly nuclear was no empty threat but a real and present danger.

Therefore, argued our report, given President Obama's speech at Prague which won him the Nobel Peace Prize (for intention more than achievement!) and the UN Secretary General's plea for a 'Nuclear Weapons Convention' to attain a world without nuclear weapons, and 'the growing international convergence, at least in civil society the world over' around the 'basic tenets' of the Indian argument which 'linked non-proliferation and arms control to the goal of disarmament', it was time India resumed its role in the vanguard of the global movement for nuclear disarmament which would make us the 'first of the States armed with nuclear weapons to argue for their time-bound elimination'. We should urge 'not unilateral but universal disarmament'. The report also drew pointed attention to a study by an Indian scientist at MIT on the likely consequences of a nuclear bomb being dropped on Mumbai. The casualty figures were horrifying.

The report went on to suggest that India should

> . . . assume a high profile role in advocating the basic ideas and goals set out in RGAP 1988, as adapted by WP 06 [by bringing] issues of nuclear disarmament prominently on the agenda of India's bilateral strategic dialogue with the two principal NWS . . . [initiating] bilateral dialogues on nuclear disarmament issues with all other NWS and SNW/near-SNW, including Pakistan [as well as promoting] in concert with NAM and the New Agenda Coalition . . . the proposal for a treaty incorporating binding negative security assurances.

When we presented the report to the prime minister, we were overwhelmed by the praise he heaped on us (for a report he had not yet read!) But unsurprisingly, our recommendations were never pursued. The national security adviser leaned on the ministry of external affairs to assist us in organizing a very good university debate at Vigyan Bhavan, but in his inaugural remarks, the national security adviser took such a hard line as to negate the substance of all our observations and recommendations.

Then, in response to a question about the threat from Pakistan, Ambassador Arundhati Ghose stirred the latent paranoia in students' minds to such an extent that my pathetic attempts to distinguish between 'unilateral' and 'universal' disarmament were blown away. The House resoundingly voted against the motion 'This House believes in nuclear disarmament'. When Rakesh Sood, who had no empathy or association with RGAP 88, was appointed as the PM's special envoy for disarmament, it became clear to me that the appointment of our informal group was an eyewash.

Zonal Cultural Centres

I was delighted to find that I had then been tasked to chair a review committee on the working of the ZCCs. To assist me, my members included Sitakant Mahapatra, a former secretary in the ministry of culture and a well-known Odiya poet, and the Mumbai-based film and theatre genius, Amol Palekar, who had organized in Mumbai in January 1989 the second *Apna Utsav* (a national cultural festival, focused on folk and tribal performing arts). Our committee succeeded in collating a vast amount of information, set out in charts and tables as well as described in prose, highlighting the achievements and drawing attention to the drawbacks of the ZCCs, severally and together, in the decade and a half that had passed since the Mumbai *Apna Utsav*.[4]

Some of these drawbacks and derogations are summarized below:

Whereas the 'primary function' of the ZCCs had been envisaged as undertaking 'the work of cultural propagation and dissemination in rural and mofussil areas, including urban slums', the review committee discovered that, 'to a large extent', the ZCCs have 'not conformed to the initial vision'. It was found statistically that whereas some of the ZCCs had, till the mid-1990s, conducted their programmes in the designated areas to the extent of 35–38 per cent, and some even up to 61–76 per cent, the conduct of programmes had now plummeted to between 2 per cent and 10 per cent in most ZCCs, resulting in 'the increasing trend of programme expenditure in urban areas, much of it in venues frequented more by the prospering middle classes than the deprived sections of the urban population'.

Pari passu, where headquarters' expenditure had initially been strictly restricted in order to concentrate on outreach programmes, the review committee found that there had been 'a spate of infrastructure creation at the headquarters of ZCCs and the *shilpgrams*', and 'in consequence, a disproportionate share of the ZCCs' budgets (were) being earmarked for new infrastructure and/or maintenance of existing infrastructure'.

The report described '*yatras* and chain programmes' as 'the backbone of outreach programmes' and made references to past chain programmes such as the Parvatiya Parv, the Seemanchal Yatra and the Ganga Yatra. It pointed out that *yatras* and chain programmes, like the West Zone Cultural Centre (WZCC's) Paschimala, had been held in 290 blocks of the west zone in 1988 but had since declined regrettably to a miserable 29 blocks in 2009/10.'

The review committee also underlined the need for the ZCCs to go back to the past practice of participating in melas and traditional festivals.

To this end, the committee recommended revival of the biennial *yatras* climaxing in an Apna Utsav and suggested that the silver jubilee Apna Utsav take place in a major metropolis. (Instead, the silver jubilee Apna Utsav was held as a one-off event in Mohali in the minister's home state.)

On the other hand, the review committee hailed the new '*guru–shishya parampara*' scheme and suggested that '*kendras* or mini-cultural centres' be set up in the homes of retired gurus 'or in buildings nearby' so as to make the *guru–shishya parampara* an outreach training programme. The Committee suggested the reconceiving of the *guru-shishya parampara* scheme 'as a cradle-to-funeral-pyre scheme' for 'discovering and nurturing young talent till it comes to full blossom and, when the artiste's performing years are on the wane, offering continuing career and livelihood opportunities by promoting the artiste, who was once a talented young *shishya* to the status of an experienced and valued *Guru* to carry the tradition forward'.

Other recommendations included raising the remuneration paid to folk and tribal artistes; documentation, 'especially of dying or threatened art forms', to be 'undertaken by experts and expert bodies', not ZCCs themselves; encouraging innovation, 'especially in relatively new domains of culture such as photography, cinematography, the graphic arts, hybrid arts'; and putting in place systematic 'talent searches in rural and mofussil areas and among the deprived populations in urban slums', as well as training youngsters, encouraging new and upcoming artistes and providing them public exposure through the electronic media. It was also proposed that 'legacy industries' – that is, creative and cultural industries – should be included in the work programme of the ZCCs, besides promoting collaboration with Akademis and other cultural bodies.

After this review, the report suggested two major institutional changes. First, 'mobilizing and assiduously promoting a close and symbiotic relationship between the ZCCs and local self-government institutions (PRIs) so that cultural efflorescence at the grassroots' is accompanied by 'inclusive governance, also at the grassroots'.

The second major institutional innovation recommended was the setting up of an Indian Council of Zonal Cultural Centres (ICZCC), in view of the manifest need to continuously and conscientiously supervise and monitor the activities of the ZCCs. The proposed ICZCC would monitor the range and quality of programming and put in place a functional system of continuous cultural audit to undertake an independent assessment of the extent to which ZCC programmes were matching or deviating from the objectives.

In September 2013, about a year after the report had been submitted, I was surprised but pleased to receive a communication from the ministry of culture appointing me the chairman of the ICZCCs with cabinet rank. This was perhaps because the other members of the proposed council were the seven governors charged with guiding the seven ZCCs. I am certain this was the Congress president's doing. Unfortunately, I could hold only one meeting of the ICZCC before the government bowed out in May 2014.

Panchayati Raj

I had tried to persuade the prime minister to allow me to chair an expert committee to look into Panchayati Raj to assess the progress made in fulfilling the objectives of the 73rd Amendment (Part IX) of the Constitution. Although Montek Singh Ahluwalia agreed to be my emissary and Jairam Ramesh promised to press the case for such a committee, they did little or nothing – or were, perhaps, dissuaded from persisting.

It was only at the instance of Finance Minister Pranab Mukherjee that the expert committee was established, on 27 August 2012. Its mandate was summed up in its cumbersome title: 'Expert Committee to Leverage Panchayati Raj Institutions for the More Effective Delivery of Public Goods and Services'. I was designated the chairman. The six other members included Thomas Isaac, the world-renowned founder of the People's Movement for Decentralized Planning; Nirmala Buch, IAS (retd), a well-recognized champion of women and ST in Panchayati Raj; M.N. Roy, IAS (retd) who had served with high distinction as Secretary/ Principal Secretary, West Bengal Department of Panchayati Raj and Rural Development, had led the 'largest literacy movement of the country' and pioneered the 'people's movement for public health and sanitation';

and Joe Madiath, founder-director of Gram Vikas in Odisha and other NGOs working in Odisha at the grassroots. The committee also included the director, National Institute of Rural Development, Hyderabad, who, however, took little interest in the proceedings. The committee received invaluable assistance from its principal consultant, T.R. Raghunathan, especially in preparing the Activity Maps.[5]

Heavily referenced and backed by detailed statistical data, and a comprehensive bibliography, the five-volume report amounted to an *Encyclopaedia Panchayatica*. It is impossible to summarize in a few paragraphs a five-volume report running to 1,823 pages but let me attempt the impossible.

The report began by noting that even in the state list in the Seventh Schedule of the Constitution, as initially promulgated, the local authorities were labelled as 'units of self-government', not as units of self-governance. This was the litmus test of the issues before the committee. Were PRIs being treated as implementing agencies of the state and Central governments, or as 'institutions of self-government'? If PRIs were falling short of this Constitutional requirement, what steps might be taken to rectify this?

'Effective Devolution' and 'Activity Mapping'

The principal finding of the committee was that the last-mile delivery of public goods and services was woefully inadequate because 'the devolution of the three Fs – Functions, Finances, Functionaries – (to the panchayats) has been far from in accord with the letter and spirit of the Constitution amendments'. To achieve such 'effective devolution' – the term used in the amended Constitution (Article 243G) – it had to be understood that there could be no devolution of 'subjects' but only devolution of 'activities' since every subject listed in the Eleventh Schedule of the amended Constitution required some activities to be performed by the Centre; others by the state; and only the rest at the appropriate tier (district, intermediate, village) of our three-tier system of Panchayati Raj. So, scientific devolution had to begin by identifying the activities to be performed for each subject and then mapping these activities to the most suitable level of governance on the principle of subsidiarity, which holds that anything that can be done at a lower level should be devolved to that level. It is only through such 'Activity Mapping' that the first of the three Fs – Functions – could be effectively devolved to PRIs. And thereafter the devolution of the next two Fs – Finances and Functionaries – should be undertaken to conform to the activities set out in the 'Activity Map' relating to any given Function.

The report went on to argue that as the bulk of funds for rural development and welfare was being routed through CSS, the Centre should set the example for the states by attaching a model 'Activity Map' according to the guidelines of every CSS. How this could be done was illustratively set out in Volume 4 with respect to eight CSSs that accounted for nearly two-thirds of all CSS expenditure.[6] That would enable each of India's 2,50,000 panchayats to not only know what they were supposed to do for economic and human development, social justice and people's welfare, but also to have readily at hand the financial resources and the required administrative and technical functionaries to undertake these duties under the general direction and supervision of the elected panchayat members. Such a pattern of devolution would apply *pari passu* to the panchayats at the intermediate and district levels. Thus, could best be fulfilled the Constitutional obligation that the panchayats at all three levels work not as agencies of the state/Central government but as 'units of self-government', to quote the very words of the amended Constitution (Article 243G).

Involving the public through gram sabhas

In addition, it was essential to involve the people through their elected panchayats at all three levels, and in consultation with gram sabhas (village assemblies), in determining the priorities for development, social justice and welfare for each village, block/taluka and district. These priorities should be set out in annual and long-term plans prepared by village panchayats in consultation with Gram Sabhas, and by intermediate and district panchayats in respect of their jurisdiction, as set out in the Activity Map. The amended Constitution provided that these village, intermediate and district plans (Article 243ZD) should be 'consolidated' by the District Planning Committee as a 'draft' district plan to be further refined at higher levels by incorporating the expressed priorities of the people themselves. To facilitate the preparation of such people-oriented plans, the Planning Commission had commissioned Guidelines for District Planning from V. Ramachandran, vice chair of the Kerala Planning Board, who did an outstanding job of covering all aspects of district planning step by step. Yet, noted the Aiyar Committee, there had been 'little progress except in a very few states'. The Planning Commission guidelines on district planning 'appear(ed) to have been largely observed in the breach'. The report noted:

> . . . devolution is the essential condition for Human Development Indices (HDI) to improve . . . the greater the measure of devolution, the more significant the outcomes . . . PRIs have to be given a central role in CSS and state programmes to secure a much higher score on HDI values . . .

It was also noted that the alleviation of poverty and growing inequality remain largely unaffected 'by the mere existence . . . of elected local government principally because the establishment of these institutions . . . has not been followed by . . . processes of devolution'.

The committee strongly recommended that a beginning be made by the Central government setting the example by incorporating relevant directions in the advisories in CSS guidelines for accountability towards Gram Sabhas. These guidelines should advise statutory rights for the Gram Sabhas and the specific points on which elected representatives and officials of the PRIs would be answerable to Gram Sabhas.

The committee further recommended that the Centre draft a model Gram Sabha Law with a view to urging that appropriate state legislation be undertaken in this regard since 'the more effective the process of devolution, the more meaningful is Panchayati Raj; the more involved are the members, the more lively is the Gram Sabha; and less nefarious the nexus between the lower bureaucracy and the panchayat members, the better it is for sound Panchayati Raj.'

The committee stressed, particularly, that 'incentivizing' Panchayati Raj would give better results than 'didactically' seeking better outcomes. To this end, it recommended that Finance Commission grants should be separately given for 'incentivizing states to devolve' and to PRIs to be 'transparent and accountable in their transactions'.[7]

In essence, the committees found that effective devolution is the key to securing better outcomes for the more effective delivery of public goods and services.

Women in panchayats

The report extensively dealt with the status and empowerment of women in the panchayats, noting that at 14 lakh elected women representatives in our rural and urban local self-government institutions, around one lakh of whom held office as president or vice-president, India had more elected women than 'the rest of the world put together'. But this achievement was marred by inadequate devolution to the panchayats, leaving men and women representatives similarly unempowered.

SC/ST and panchayats

The report also gave detailed consideration to the status and empowerment of SCs and STs and found that, by and large, social acceptance had been secured for the unique reservation system for PRIs that reflected, in reservations in the panchayats at each level, the degree of concentration in each village, block/taluka and district, of these historically disadvantaged sections of the population, aimed at ensuring that their representation and leadership would correspond to their share of the population at each level and that the SCs/STs would not be hampered by millennia of discrimination. For STs in Fifth Schedule areas, the report made a strong pitch for the full-throttle implementation of PESA.[8]

Corruption and the panchayats

All these issues were tackled from the angle of ensuring a genuine democratic process at the grassroots. The report noted the inverse relationship between corruption and effective Panchayati Raj: the better the functioning of the panchayats, the less the corruption; the worse the functioning of the panchayats, the more the corruption and resort to money and muscle power in elections.

This summary in a few paragraphs of a report running to nearly 2,000 pages is, of course, not comprehensive but it is hoped that the points outlined would give the reader at least an inkling of the thrust of the Aiyar Committee's recommendations.

Formal release of the report

I had set the tight deadline of 24 April 2013, the fifteenth anniversary of the entry into force of the 73rd Amendment on its notification in the Gazette of India. We readied the report on time after studying the vast literature on the subject, and after examining 160 witnesses comprising Union and state government officials, interested MPs and MLAs, panchayat representatives, a selection of those involved with organizing panchayat elections and auditing panchayat accounts, some of those who had served on State Finance Commissions, technology experts, including the founder of Aadhar and pioneer in direct benefit schemes, Nandan Nilekani, NGOs with field experience of panchayats, academics and activists.

Follow-up: Discovering the discontents

I decided to personally follow up our report's main recommendations with the Planning Commission and cabinet secretary and ministers/secretaries of the principal ministries involved. My first and most heartening meeting was with Montek Singh Ahluwalia, then deputy chairman, Planning Commission, who, I thought, had stood in the way when I was a minister, but gave me both his time and attention when I went to present him our final five-volume report.

Looking at the length of the report, Montek asked me to orally summarize my expectations of the Planning Commission. I did so and was highly pleased when he instructed one of his most able members, Arun Maira, to put up a note to him containing the proposed action points.

My satisfaction was short-lived. A few weeks later, I went back to the Planning Commission to call on Arun Maira. He said he was going to be meeting the deputy chairman within the next few minutes with his note on action to be taken. I quickly glanced through his note, expressed my satisfaction and said I would wait till he returned. When he returned, his face had fallen.

Apparently, Montek had waved away the note as an irrelevancy and spoken about something else. Thus ended the involvement of the Planning Commission. I was, of course, doubly upset at my treatment as a minister being compounded by this mistreatment of me as the chairman of the expert committee.

I found a more ready welcome with the Cabinet Secretary (my former financial adviser in P&NG and Panchayati Raj, P.K. Sinha) but no action was taken, especially as Dr Manmohan Singh's government had entered its lame-duck stage. I got the same result from some of the other secretaries and ministers I called on, including Jairam Ramesh: initial enthusiasm followed by apathetic disdain. Within a few months, Dr Manmohan Singh's government had become history, and the expert committee report sank with them. The Modi government that followed has assiduously ignored the report. The only action they have taken is to remove the five volumes from the ministry of Panchayati Raj website![9]

Panchayati Raj in the party

After I had organized forty nation-wide seminars on Panchayati Raj in almost all the states and UTs, Sonia Gandhi, as president of the party, decided to set up the AICC's Rajiv Gandhi Panchayati Raj Sangathan (RGPRS) in mid-2004. As by then I had been named India's first-ever cabinet minister for Panchayati Raj, she appointed a good friend and colleague of mine, B.K. Chandrashekhar of Bangalore (Bengaluru), who had shown some interest in local government, as the national convenor. However, as he was preoccupied with Karnataka politics, he could neither find the time nor did he have the inclination for this party responsibility at the AICC. So, on being elected to preside over the Karnataka Legislative Council, he resigned, and the Congress president entrusted me with the double charge of Panchayati Raj in the party in addition to Panchayati Raj in the government. The party post outlasted my ministerial assignment.

My effort was to get state-level units established so that we might mobilize Congress panchayat representatives and Congress-inclined representatives, past and present, and even losing candidates, to constitute a supplementary party cadre for party work at the grassroots and to act as what I dubbed a '*vanar sena*'[10] of the Congress at election time. It had some resonance but not enough, principally because of the ambiguity of the standing of the RGPRS, which was neither a frontal organization nor headed by a designated AICC general secretary. This left the RGPRS as neither fish, flesh nor herring when it came to integrating it into the established structure of the party. However, our higher authorities did not agree to do this, with the result that outcomes were patchy.

Rahul Gandhi becomes party VP

At this stage, Rahul Gandhi was elected vice president of the party in January 2013. He had expressed great interest in his father's most important legacy, to the extent that he categorically told me in March on the podium of a women panchayat members' rally in Talkatora Stadium that, whereas he had earlier agreed with me 75 per cent on Panchayati Raj, he was now 100 per cent convinced that I was right!

I had barely stopped preening myself when I was summoned by the party president in August, just five months later, and peremptorily told that Rahul wanted me to relinquish my post of national convenor in favour of Meenakshi Natarajan. I, of course, readily agreed – for what is Caesar's must be rendered unto Caesar.

That ended Rahul's 100 per cent agreement with me and any relevance I might have had to party policy on Panchayati Raj (or, indeed, any other matter). Only weeks earlier, I had submitted my expert group's five-volume report on 'Leveraging Panchayats for the More Effective Delivery of Public Goods and Services', my magnum opus on the subject based on over a quarter of a century steeped in the subject. Yet, neither Rahul nor Sonia was to ever again interact with me on the subject. I not only felt very let down but also wondered how they could so casually cast to one side a key aide to Rajiv Gandhi on his impassioned advocacy of deepening democracy through effective local self-government, and who, as they knew, had single-handedly pursued that goal after Rajiv Gandhi had passed away. I was following up our recommendations with the ministries concerned, but the sudden removal of my party prop greatly weakened my efforts.

In any case, we had only a few months of office left. Our defeat in the elections the following year (2014) had been rendered inevitable by the paralysis of governance that overtook UPA-II in its last two years, 2012 to 2014.

Stasis in governance

In 2012, the prime minister underwent operations for multiple coronary bypasses. He never quite recovered physically. It slowed him down and this showed up in governance.

As for the party, there was no official announcement about the Congress president's health when she took ill at about the same time as the PM. As no one knew even where she was being treated, every rumour had its day. When the media learned she was at the Sloan Kettering in New York, which specializes in cancer treatment, it was not long before 'knowledgeable' people who claimed to be 'in the know' were shaking their heads and solemnly saying it was 'pancreatic cancer', which meant she only had a few months to live. Given the tumultuous twelve years that have passed since then and her remaining cheerfully among us, it is obvious that the secrecy shrouding the matter only led to idle and sometimes vicious speculation.

It soon became clear that in both the offices – the PM's and the party president's – there was stasis, a distinct absence of governance, while several crises, particularly Anna Hazare's 'India Against Corruption' movement, were either not handled effectively or not handled at all.

The choice of Rashtrapati: Manmohan Singh or Pranab Mukherjee

Personally, I was of the view that Pranab Mukherjee should have been given the reins of the government and Dr Manmohan Singh elevated to President of India when the office of Rashtrapati presented an opening in 2012. This was principally because we needed a very active PM in good health and with the energy to lead the government (Pranab*da)* and a person of high distinction who had served his country exceptionally well (Dr Singh) to preside over the nation. Pranab's memoirs indicate that this was in fact contemplated. He says that while Sonia Gandhi was 'on holiday in the Kausambi hills', she had given the 'vague impression' that she was considering making Dr Singh the 'presidential nominee'. This led Pranab to wonder 'if she selected Singh for the presidential office, she may choose me as the prime minister'.[11]

For reasons to which neither I, nor it seems anyone else, was made privy, the decision was taken to retain Dr Manmohan Singh as PM and shift Pranab Mukherjee upstairs as Rashtrapati. That, in my view, doomed any prospects the Congress might have had to form UPA-III. While the Indian media slammed the government, *Time* magazine ran a very damaging cover story that described Dr Singh as a 'Do Nothing' Prime Minister. True, Pranab's left-wing reputation would have disturbed the business community (and the Americans) if he were made PM, but there was no one more experienced than him. I hazard the view that if this obvious step had been taken, we would not have gone into a paralysis of governance and thus opened the door to the worst excesses of Hindutva in the general elections of 2014.

Let me explain this in greater detail. The second UPA government had got off to a bad start. A report from an obviously biased comptroller and auditor general (CAG) speculatively alleged that the first UPA government had robbed the nation of the mind-boggling sum of Rs 12 lakh crore, that is, 12 followed by 11 zeroes, in terms of spectrum charges foregone by handing over licenses for 2G spectrum in 2007 to favoured firms at the much cheaper prices charged for 1G spectrum in 2002. The telecom minister at the time was A. Raja of the DMK, a brilliant upcoming Dalit lawyer with a very pleasant manner and a great political future.

The CAG had, in fact, posted a range of possible losses where Rs 12 lakh crore was a highly suspect upper limit, but it caught the fevered imagination of the media and people at large and became a by-word for unchecked allegations of corruption against the second Manmohan Singh government. The defamation of the Singh government gained wide currency even as Raja and Kanimozhi ('Kalaignar' Karunanidhi's daughter) were sent for more than a year to Tihar jail in judicial custody. The defence mounted for them by the government was half-hearted and unconvincing. This gravely distanced the DMK from the Congress, resulting in our mutually very beneficial alliance in Tamil Nadu breaking down, to the advantage only of Jayalalithaa's AIADMK.

The courts eventually cleared both A. Raja and Kanimozhi of all charges, but the government failed to rise adequately to the minister's defence, preferring to play off the back foot rather than mount a bold, aggressive defence against baseless allegations.

There was a series of other allegations relating to Law Minister Ashwini Kumar and Railway Minister Pawan Bansal. The government and the party were unable to carry credibility in answering the charges to an obviously sensation-hungry media and thought the issues could be quashed by getting the ministers concerned to resign. That resolved nothing, and only aggravated the harm the unproven allegations caused to the government's reputation.

The Commonwealth Games scandal, described earlier, also contributed to blackening the government's face in the eyes of the general public. But what, perhaps, put the lid on the UPA government's election prospects was the mishandled Anna Hazare-led agitation, 'India Against Corruption'.

India Against Corruption

The minister of home affairs, PC who initially refused Anna Hazare permission to conduct his fast in the Ram Lila grounds, eventually caved in and the Ram Lila grounds became 'ground zero' for a much-publicized agitation.

I think the lowest point in UPA-II's reign was when three Union ministers went to Delhi airport to receive the private aircraft of Baba

Ramdev, the highly controversial 'godman' who was supporting Anna Hazare. They took Baba Ramdev to Claridges Hotel to persuade him to abandon Hazare. He insincerely signed an agreement with them, only to escape their clutches and find his way back to his agitating colleagues.

As the agitation gained unprecedented popularity and support, the home ministry ordered a midnight raid on the sleeping protesters, which led to a public outcry.

Initially, there were sniggers when Baba Ramdev was caught attempting to sneak away from the camp hidden in a burkha in the dead of the night, but the joke was on the home ministry for its total mishandling of the agitation. Indeed, the government's panic and overreaction stood nakedly revealed when Anna Hazare attempted to take his agitation to Mumbai where it was a total flop. No part of India other than Delhi wasted any time on Hazare and his antics. His much-publicized fast (*anshan*) could have been better handled. The impression made on the general public was that government panicked.

While Hazare himself refrained from entering the political fray, one of his principal lieutenants, Arvind Kejriwal, opposed him and formed the Aam Aadmi Party (AAP).[12] Few rated this new entrant seriously, but the Congress was routed in the state elections in the National Capital Region of Delhi of January 2013, securing only eight seats in comparison to the twenty-eight won by the 'dark horse', the AAP. To stop the BJP, which had won the largest number of seats – thirty-two – from forming the government, the Congress, though worsted at the hustings, extended its 'outside support' to the AAP. The arrangement lasted only forty-nine days but brought the AAP leader centre-stage in national politics. In the Delhi state elections that followed in 2015, AAP secured sixty-seven out of seventy-two seats. The Congress party's biggest loss was the defeat of the outstanding Delhi CM, Sheila Dikshit, who had built a formidable reputation over her fifteen-year tenure as CM. But, where she thought her crowning achievement would be the CWG, the shenanigans around the Games signally contributed to her undoing.

My own most telling memory of the meltdown of UPA II was of returning home one evening to find my wife, Suneet, sitting before the TV set with a shattered look on her face. When I inquired what the matter was, she raised her stricken face and exclaimed, 'No scams today!'

We, therefore, went into the 2014 general elections very much a runner-up. In the event, the election exposed the Indian National Congress as a broken reed that fell from 404 seats in 1984 to 44 seats in 2014.

My 'chaiwallah' comment

For me, personally, the 2014 elections began on a wrong note. The AICC convened in a pre-election plenary session on 17 January 2014 in New Delhi. I was interviewed in the convention hall of Talkatora Stadium by the TV news agency ANI. Narendra Modi, the presumptive BJP PM candidate, was being bruited about as the obvious winner of the coming general election.

I was utterly horrified that a man stained, I thought irretrievably, by the 2002 carnage of Muslims in Gujarat, could aspire to lead the India of Mahatma Gandhi and Jawaharlal Nehru. So, in the interview I stressed that it was outrageous for a man who did not know that Alexander had never come to Pataliputra or that Taxila (Takshashila) was in present-day Pakistan to seek to step into Jawaharlal Nehru's shoes. The people of India would never accept this, I said, adding, 'Never! Never! Never!' in thundering tones. I then quipped that if, after he lost the election, Modi still wanted to serve tea, we could make some arrangements for him here.

This was touted then – and ever since – as my having said that Modi could not become PM because he was a 'chaiwallah'. I never called Modi a 'chaiwallah' and never advanced his having been a 'chaiwallah' as the reason for my believing he would never make it to the post of PM. Indeed, the person who said he was a 'chaiwallah' was Modi himself – to stress his somewhat doubtful claim to humble beginnings. The video of my remarks is still available on YouTube for anyone who cares to look.[13] I have often invited my media critics, and even my party colleagues, to check this out – but they just do not want to because they are committed to their totally false premise that I had indeed described Modi as a 'chaiwallah', who, therefore, could not be the PM. The irony of Modi himself having claimed to be a 'chaiwallah' is lost on them.

Not knowing that this would become the main media story a few hours later, poor Rahul Gandhi singled me out from my obscure corner in the audience to publicly affirm that my championing of Panchayati Raj made me the kind of role model of what the party aimed at ensuring. He also added Sam Pitroda to make us twin role models for party workers.[14]

The media and Modi played out my alleged (but wholly untrue) remark about Modi being unfit to rule as PM because (as he claimed) he had begun life as a 'chaiwallah'. This was no more than a hollow election gimmick that the election pundit, Prashant Kishor, who was given much of the credit for Modi's stunning electoral victory, told me he had exploited to the full through the '*chai pe charcha*' events that he stage managed with a hologram (then unknown and unprecedented) of Modi joining the teadrinkers. It gave the handle to elements in the Congress party to divert attention from the real causes of the party's humiliating collapse at the hustings to shift the blame on this one remark put out in sarcastic, if sneering, jest.[15]

Elections 2014

Unfazed by the media assault, for I had faced several such attacks before, I left for Mayiladuturai soon after the Talkatora Stadium convention to start my campaign even though I had not been named the candidate. The TNCC president, Gnanadesikan, was very upset at this as he was devoted to his patron, G.K. Vasan (the son of G.K. Moopanar), who he expected would be running as the Congress candidate in Mayiladuturai. My instinct and experience of both father and son made me believe that G.K. Vasan would never in these adverse circumstances take the risk of running in a losing election. Some weeks into my individual campaign, Vasan fulfilled my expectation that he would not run, and I was officially confirmed as the Congress candidate.

Once the official campaign started, my earlier principal political aide, Ramachidambaram, who had alienated himself from me to protest the rise of S. Rajakumar, solemnly told me that if I ran as an independent, I would get 1 lakh votes, but if I ran as a Congress candidate my votes would tumble to 50,000. He proved prescient, as the total number of votes I received was a mere 58,000 – a good 15,000 behind what I had polled as an independent back in 1998.

The whole campaign was mismanaged, particularly in the Mayiladuturai segment, but I did much better in the Kumbakonam segment. Still, defeat is defeat. Yet, it did not affect me too adversely as I was already a sitting member of the Rajya Sabha and would continue to be in the House for another two years.

But it was a grave underestimation of the political consequences of this set-back for me, although all Congress candidates (and many from the DMK, who fought independently of us) lost, and lost badly, when we fought the 2014 elections separately without an alliance. Happily, the lesson seems to have been learned and the Congress-DMK alliance in Tamil Nadu was revived and is strong and tested. It is the very foundation on which the Congress might yet bounce back to office, as proved once again in Elections 2024.

Spending MPLADS funds in the constituency

What I was able to do for the constituency in my six years as a Rajya Sabha member was to continue my practice of spending crores of my MPLADS funds on the welfare of the poorest of the poor, almost all of whom belonged to the SC communities, and the needs of rural infrastructure. Although as a nominated member, I was entitled to spend my MPLADS funds anywhere in the country, I decided at the outset that I would continue to treat Mayiladuturai as my constituency.

Besides the infrastructure projects of various kinds and the community halls for which I had gained a name, at Rajakumar's suggestion I started giving out Swaraj tractors with attached trailers for garbage disposal. As my name was emblazoned all over the tractors and trailers, this gave me enormous publicity as the tractor-trailers went around the village panchayats every morning carrying out garbage collection, a badly needed community requirement. And although I was no longer petroleum minister, the oil companies were generous in granting corporate social responsibility (CSR) funds for my constituency as a special gesture of gratitude for my unblemished stewardship of the ministry.

In addition, I took full advantage of a scheme floated by Jayalalithaa, where any pledge of CSR funds was matched by a 66 per cent further grant from the state government that could be availed of for major projects on a far larger scale than possible under MPLADS. Two such projects of note were the repair and renovation of two major hospitals in Kumbakonam – the Coronation Hospital (commemorating King Edward VII's ascension to the imperial throne in 1901, which shows how old and badly in need of renovation and modernization the hospital was) and a maternity hospital for very poor people in a Dalit and minority-dominated quarter of the city, Melacauvery.

I knew none of these initiatives, while immensely popular, would give me any electoral advantage, as Prime Minister Gujral had warned me. My satisfaction lay in the benefits I was reaching to the people without expectation of any political returns. My loss in the election came as no surprise to me. I had fought the good fight and shown my attachment to Mayiladuturai in good times and bad.

Consequences of defeat in the party

The 2014 results were, of course, not just of concern to me at a personal level, but most alarming at the party level. How, after all, could a national party like the Indian National Congress, the 'natural party of governance', be reduced to 44 seats, too few to even claim the right to be legally recognized as leader of the Opposition? There was, of course, much frantic heart-searching in the higher echelons of the party and much despair in the lower ranks. What rankled most was that we had been reduced to this state by a man who had callously presided over a pogrom in his state and filled his campaign rhetoric with not only sly innuendoes about the country's largest minority community but also with bogus promises, such as returning Indian black (unaccounted) money to the country from Swiss bank vaults to fill each Indian's bank account with Rs 15 lakh from the ill-gotten wealth of businessmen, who, he claimed, had profited from

Congress's corruption. '*Achche din*' ('Good days'), he proclaimed, lay ahead – and the Indian public – and worse, the bulk of the media – actually believed him.

The horrendous defeat inevitably lowered morale in the party and led to much soul-searching, as also to a spate of desertions towards the ruling party, which, in a vicious cycle, further lowered morale.

Resuming life in the Rajya Sabha

I resumed my desultory attendance of the Rajya Sabha. When we switched from the Treasury benches to the Opposition in the Rajya Sabha after massively losing the 2014 elections, we could have constructively used our blocking majority in the Rajya Sabha to responsibly carry out our role in Parliament. Instead, almost every morning began with our gathering at Mahatma Gandhi's statue outside the main entrance to Parliament and holding a shouting match till our lungs gave out. A success was chalked up when we managed to get the House adjourned. Indeed, we once succeeded in stopping the House from transacting any business for an entire session. Several of our members loved it and, of course, our leadership was behind this, but I despaired. This was emphatically not why I had striven to be in Parliamentary politics. We had fallen victim to what I had presciently warned against when Priya Ranjan Dasmunsi became disrupter-in-chief back in our days in the Opposition in 1999–2004. We preferred demonstration to debate, and so lost many an opportunity to present our case forcefully, cogently, and logically to the commentariat and the general public.

Sri Lanka and Pakistan

With little going on in the Rajya Sabha, I resumed my frequent TV appearances, and writing columns and articles for the press (and the Internet), and moving around on the lecture circuit in India and abroad.

I particularly enjoyed a long tour of Sri Lanka in January 2015 to produce a multi-part TV serial for NewsX, including an extended stay in

Tamil-speaking Jaffna and the north and east provinces in the company of a very well-informed and highly intelligent Jaffna commentator and activist, Ahilan Kadirgamar. I interviewed a host of Sri Lankan Tamils from across the spectrum about their memories of the conflict: unrepentant LTTE 'freedom fighters'/'terrorists' (take your pick); political activists with other political affiliations; academics and journalists; ordinary fisherfolk; members of the Muslim minority in Sri Lanka who had suffered terrible atrocities and displacement at the hands of the Tigers; Christian priests who had been displaced with their flock and coped heroically with this vicious disruption of their placid lives; those who had witnessed and been traumatized by the loss of loved ones, especially during the brutal liquidation by the Sri Lankan army of the LTTE at the end in and around Mullaitivu, with no regard for the massive civilian casualties; and anyone else ready to talk to the camera.

We went everywhere connected with the war between the Indian Peace Keeping Force and the LTTE, and the ghastly Götterdämmerung of the final days of the war between the Sri Lankan army and the LTTE. We also interviewed in Colombo a number of political leaders and highly knowledgeable political commentators. We had a particularly long and detailed session with Chandrika Bandaranaike Kumaratunga, a friend of mine of long standing and, more importantly, a former prime minister and president of the country, much trusted by the Tamil community, but, ironically, less so by the Sinhala, especially the extremist Buddhist clergy.

We completed our mission by talking in Chennai to a number of committed, knowledgeable and sincere Tamilians, both Tamil Indians and Sri Lankan Tamil exiles. I then joined the NewsX team in editing the transcripts, fitting images to the spoken word, doing voice-overs and generally getting acquainted with the medium. Unfortunately, after having made a good start with screening the first couple of episodes, those in charge of scheduling just broke-off screening the remaining episodes. By the time they resumed the screening, viewer continuity was broken, leaving little impact. But it was a great learning experience for me.

It was also around this time that my interactions with Ahmed Bilal Mehboob and Aasiya Raza of the Pakistan Institute of Legislative

Development and Transparency (PILDAT), begun several years earlier, intensified. Instead of sticking only to politics and Parliamentarians, we roamed far beyond, to exploring shared experiences and the scope for cooperation between India and Pakistan in local self-government, agriculture, rural development, small industry, and other governance issues. We also had one excellent session on the media. We thus brought within our ambit well-informed Pakistanis and Indians who would not perhaps otherwise have ever met.

Our original intention had been to alternate our sessions between venues in Pakistan and India, but visa problems arose soon after Narendra Modi became prime minister and we were compelled to meet in Dubai – which was convenient and comfortable enough, but was not in the sub-continent and, therefore, only emphasized the unreality of the human bonds we were attempting to build across a frontier of hostility. The PILDAT exercise supplemented other efforts, by former foreign minister Khurshid Kasuri, Professor Pervez Hoodbhoy and others, to keep Track–II humming.

This afforded me numerous opportunities to wander all over Pakistan and speak at various venues on our mutual relationship, warts and all, to generally appreciative audiences, reinforcing my conviction, born in Karachi decades earlier, that our foreign policy fails to mine the abundant goodwill that exists in every section of public and government opinion in Pakistan, including the Pakistan armed forces. I am convinced we can find a meaningful via media through dialogue and expand the bandwidth of the dialogue to cover not only key political issues but also other matters of common human and development interest.

When I counted, I found I had made as many forty visits to that country in the forty years that had passed since I had been transferred out from Karachi in January 1982. I rather suspect no other Indian has been as frequent a visitor to Pakistan. For this, I have been pilloried in sections of the media, particularly right-leaning ones, and by sections of my own party. This has greatly damaged my public image, but I have the satisfaction of having stood by my unconventional (maverick) views on an important issue of national interest.

Travels in our neighbourhood

Besides trips to different parts of the globe and visits to my daughter, Sana, in the wider Boston area, I also availed of opportunities that arose to deepen my personal links with friends in South Asia – Bangladesh, Bhutan, the Maldives and Nepal.

Relations with Nepal: Modi's Nepal Policy

With politics and Parliament drifting away from me, I spent more time on these miscellaneous activities than on Parliamentary issues. The only notable exception was my speech in the Rajya Sabha in December 2015[16] on India's relations with a key neighbour, Nepal, the guardian of the central sector of the Himalayan chain that separates both countries from China.

Modi had succeeded in alienating 'Hindu' Nepal almost as much as he had Islamist Pakistan, largely because he treated Nepal as a subordinate state even as the proud Nepalese were asserting their independence and sovereignty, and their right to a secular Constitution in the wake of their having extinguished the previous Hinduism-oriented monarchy.

In the autumn of 2015, the Nepal Constituent Assembly, which had been deadlocked for seven years in drafting its Constitution, suddenly, and quite unexpectedly, broke the deadlock with the three principal Nepalese parties – the Nepali Congress, the United Marxist Leninists and the Maoists – coming together and being joined by an important faction of the Terai plains political establishment, the Madhesi Forum Loktantrik. They signed among themselves a 16-point pact, which held the promise of cutting the Gordian knot that had held up a Constitution for the new republic for seven long years. With the plains and the hill areas of Nepal largely united, the country could now embark on the road to securing the required two-thirds majority that would at last set Nepal on the road to becoming a stable, Constitutional republic.

Instead of welcoming this major development, the Modi government was furious. This was principally because instead of announcing that Nepal remained a 'Hindu state', the Nepalese Constitution proclaimed Nepal a secular democracy. Even the 'Explanation' to Article 4, which defined 'secularism' to mean 'religious and cultural freedoms, including protection of religion, culture handed down from time immemorial (*sanatana dharma*)' did not appease Modi and his cohort. Whereas Modi had wanted a single Madhesi province to be constituted in the plains of the Terai (where most of the inhabitants were of the same ethnic stock as the neighbouring Indians, unlike in the hills), the Constitution provided for two provinces in the east and the west of the Terai, with five districts merged into the adjoining hill provinces. 'The Indian leadership took this as a grave "affront".'[17]

Foreign Secretary (now Foreign Minister) S. Jaishankar was rushed to Kathmandu on 18–19 November 2015 where, with all the diplomatic charm at his command, he sternly reminded Maoist party chairman and deputy prime minister-elect, Prachanda, 'Had we not supported you, had we not given you shelter, you would still be in the jungles . . . Now you are doing this?' Demanding suspension of the promulgation of the Constitution for at least fifteen days, Jaishankar threatened other coalition leaders – Sher Bahadur Deuba and K.P. Oli Sharma, and even Prime Minister Sushil Koirala – in similar terms while delivering 'a blunt message' 'about the manner in which they have gone about adopting the country's new Constitution'.[18]

Was India a member of the Nepal Constituent Assembly to demand a stay on the vote? Was Nepal a sovereign, independent state or a vassal of India's? No wonder the day after Jaishankar disgraced his parent service, the Nepalese president snubbed him and Modi by proclaiming the Constitution.

In contrast to India's boorish behaviour,[19] Ambassador Wu Chuntai of China said the following: 'As a friendly neighbour, the Chinese side notes with pleasure the Nepal Constituent Assembly endorsed the new Constitution.' And US Ambassador Alaina Teplitz commented, 'The Constitution, looking at this in a historical context, is a huge milestone for Nepal.'[20]

In that winning way he has, Jaishankar had warned the Nepalese that 'India would not support the new Constitution and added that support from the rest of the world would have no meaning'.[21] Meanwhile, a blockade was 'unofficially' imposed by India on Nepal, with the farcical claim that it was the Madhesis, not India, who were not permitting essential supplies from reaching landlocked, earthquake-ridden Nepal.

It was against this background that I rose to speak in the Rajya Sabha on 7 December 2005 as the last speaker from the Opposition benches. I said the statement (on Nepal) by the minister of external affairs repeatedly used the word 'advice'. But by converting 'advice' into 'orders', we had ruined our relationship with our most important strategic neighbour, for you cannot force your advice on a sovereign, independent nation and its Constituent Assembly.

I pointed out that 105 of the 116 representatives elected from the Terai had voted for the Constitution. Only eleven elected members of the Terai had voted against it.

Then I used sarcasm and the device of the rhetorical question, or rather, a series of rhetorical questions, to pointedly criticize the BJP government's Nepal policy. I asked, given the voting, what the representative view of Terai voters was. Should we interfere in Nepal's affairs to the extent where we tell the voters of the Terai whom to vote for?

I then turned to the PM's special envoy Dr Jaishankar's 'mission' and, quoting from a newspaper comment, said that the Nepalis were comparing the special envoy of the Indian government to Lord Curzon, the former Viceroy of British India. 'To my personal knowledge,' I said, 'this Foreign Service officer is a very well-behaved, well-spoken young man. So, when he struts and hectors as if he were Lord Curzon, was it under instructions from the PMO?'

I then asked the House a loaded question: Would we have stood for a foreigner arriving uninvited in 1949–50 to tell us to not adopt or promulgate our Constitution, and not to proclaim it on the announced date? Yet, that is exactly what we had done in Nepal. Nepal had arrived at a national consensus. Why were we trying to undermine that national consensus? If we could amend our Constitution 122 times, why could we not trust the Nepalese to make any required amendments after promulgating their new Constitution? The Nepal cabinet had openly stated there were outstanding issues and pledged that they would sort these out through amendments to their Constitution.

India had sent not a word of felicitation, no congratulations, on Nepal changing a Hindu kingdom into a secular republic. Is this the manner in which we treat a sovereign neighbour of ours?

Naturally, the Chinese had stepped in. We gave the Chinese a golden opportunity of going one up on us.

The perception of us in Nepal, I went on, was seriously damaging to Indian interests. One commentator had written in the *Nepali Times* that all the goodwill from Modi's initial visit the previous year 'has now been squandered by the decision-makers in New Delhi who have callously turned an entire generation of Nepalese against India'. Another Nepali commentator, Krishna Sanjali, had said, '[T]he standoff between the two neighbours is not really about the recently adopted Constitution or the rights of the excluded plains community, it is about bruised egos in the New Delhi establishment.'

In Nepal, I continued, children are being told they cannot go to school because India is stopping them. Women are being told they cannot have food, fuel, medicines and vaccines, because India is stopping them.

We had always considered Nepal our *paasbaan* (frontier guard), and we were now humiliating this *paasbaan*. I asserted that we had, in effect, imposed an undeclared blockade on Nepal. This had alienated an entire generation and an entire people. Was this our strategic objective?

The UNICEF had estimated that 3 million Nepali children under the age of five were at risk of death or disease if the blockade continued. This was a human tragedy. As Dr Karan Singh had suggested, we ought to have airlifted vital medical supplies and should have found a way to meet Nepal's fuel needs, for if we did not, Nepal had an alternative. It could open up the route to Tibet – and China would be delighted.

There was suspicion everywhere that we were siding with the agitators. If true, this was bullying. I appealed to the House to avoid a situation in which clashes were provoked. Let us, I underlined, turn to the Nepalese as a friend; or else we would forfeit the goodwill of the Nepalese people – and lose to the Chinese. (That is exactly what has happened.)

Reactions to the speech

My speech had unexpected traction in Nepal. There was general relief there that, at long last, here was an Indian MP willing to speak up for them. Not only was the Nepalese media lauding me, even in distant Boston, a Nepalese migrant ran up to me at a bus station to thank me profusely with tears in his eyes. An Indian friend visiting Bangkok recounted a Nepalese beseeching him to convey Nepal's eternal gratitude to me. The Nepalese ambassador sent me an invitation from his government for me to visit the country. Successive Nepal PMs asked to meet me when visiting Delhi. It was a fitting climax to my twenty-one years in Parliament.

End of term

On 22 March 2016, my term in the Rajya Sabha ended. Suneet and my daughters organized a farewell tea party, which was attended by Sonia Gandhi, among others. While she was her graceful self, there was no indication of what, if anything, she had in mind for me.

I rushed back to the House from the party to make my farewell remarks – and thus ended my quarter-century roller-coaster ride in politics – both in and out of Parliament.

I began my brief farewell speech by reminding the House that in 1991, twenty-five years earlier, I had first entered the sacred precincts of the Parliament as a Lok Sabha member from Tamil Nadu. I had had the good fortune of being twice re-elected to the Lok Sabha from my home state. In 2010, I was nominated to the Rajya Sabha. I was now completing a quarter-century of my association with Parliament.

I said I had known Parliament earlier as an official in the MEA and later in the PMO. Indeed, my first visit had been as a student undergraduate in 1960 – about fifty-six years ago – when I heard Comrade S.A. Dange lash out at Pandit Jawaharlal Nehru for having dismissed the democratically elected Communist government in Kerala. The memory, I said, that abides with me is the complete silence and decorum in which Dange was heard out and the dignity with which the prime minister rose to reply.

I went on to underline that the working of democracy in the House was such that a thirty-six-year-old leader of a small opposition party, one Atal Bihari Vajpayee, could call on Prime Minister Nehru, who was twice his age, in the middle of the India–China war and demand that Parliament be convened to debate the war – and the PM immediately granted the request. That was democracy at its best.

In contrast, these last six years in the Rajya Sabha had been a somewhat disillusioning experience. The scale and length of disruptions had been without precedent. And, what a pity this was, what a tragedy, because the debating talent here matched any in the world.

I went on to point out that when I was conferred the Outstanding Parliamentarian Award for 2006, I had pledged that I would henceforth refrain from slogan-shouting or entering the Well of the House. I was proud to have kept my word for all of the last decade.

I added that, of course, I had rarely made a speech, either in the Lok Sabha or in the Rajya Sabha, from which the chairman had not felt obliged to expunge at least half a dozen words. I often thought this was because strong words spoken in irony are, sometimes, taken as unparliamentary and that was, in many ways, my misfortune for speaking far too often in English.

I said I knew the chair had been attempting to convene a meeting of party leaders to work out a methodology that would replace disruption and demonstration with reasoned debate. I wished him all the best. I hoped his relentless efforts would be crowned with success.

The time had now come to say farewell. I was doing so with a heavy heart because so much remained undone or half done.

I concluded that I had had the opportunity of viewing Parliament in every possible dimension – from the official gallery as a civil servant to serving as an MP on the back benches, both on the Treasury side and in the Opposition, and both in the Lok Sabha and the Rajya Sabha. For five brief years, I had also had the opportunity of participating in both Houses as a cabinet minister. Each of these experiences had its own reward. Therefore, while thanking my colleagues in both Houses, I wished to particularly thank those responsible for nominating me to this House. I was taking my leave with gratitude and with many warm memories. May our democracy flourish. May this Parliament flourish.

Jai Hind!

And with those last words spoken, I stepped out of Parliament – my workplace for a quarter-century, and only been back once! The end of my term in the Rajya Sabha marked my decline in public life (2009–16).

Fade out (2016–2017)

During a social conversation with Sonia Gandhi in late 2014, I mentioned that I had been asked to write my autobiography, and I was taken aback by the unexpected alacrity with which Madam Gandhi responded to say that it would be a good idea. That was when I realized that she had no plans for me to continue in active politics.

I had grave doubts about telling the story of my life as I felt I had achieved nothing noteworthy to warrant writing an autobiography. In any case, I was hoping Sonia Gandhi would find me a suitable party position.

As Sonia Gandhi had shied away from meeting me one on one since I had reacted as I did to the horrific killing of 76 security personnel in Bastar in April 2010, I pinned my hopes on Rahul, who was crowned vice president of the Congress at the Jaipur AICC in January 2013. I could not, however, decipher the implications of his acceptance speech, it being little more than a lamentation at having been offered a crown of thorns.

I have recounted how, soon after being named vice president, Rahul had told me he agreed with me 100 per cent and then went on to remove me from the only party post I held. I have also recounted how my meeting with the Congress president in 2013, when she informed me of my losing my only party post (RGPRS), turned out to be the last bilateral I had with Sonia over the next ten years, despite trying frequently to get through to her. This was also the case with Rahul and with Priyanka, after she entered politics. This is often put down to the 'feudal' atmosphere of the party and its 'authoritarian' ways.

I am not so sure. Leaders like them are pressed for time. So, they ration the time available to them to get on with their priorities and the advisers they trust instead of wasting precious minutes listening to grievances of people they do not prioritize. I was once favoured; this changed 180 degrees from 2010 onwards. I do regret that, but I can see why the roulette wheel of good fortune circled away from me. Once I was driven to the outer penumbra, I experienced what I think many party people and superannuated Congress leaders experience. I also think this is true of all parties. Ask Jaswant Singh or L.K. Advani or Murli Manohar Joshi or even Atal Bihari Vajpayee. If time is on your side, as it is when you are younger, you can work on options to struggle upwards again; but once time starts running out, options too start running out. In politics, as in perhaps other vocations and professions, veterans who fall don't have the time left to recover their earlier standing. That was certainly the case with me. Hence my 'fadeout'.

Fall (2017–2024)

I can date my fall precisely to 7 December 2017.

On 7 December 2017, I received repeated phone and text requests from ANI, a TV news agency, for an urgent 'byte'. I asked them to meet me in the lobby of the very fancy five-star hotel at which I was meeting a friend, the distinguished ex-foreign minister of Pakistan but, quite properly, the guards refused admittance to a scruffy TV crew. Eventually, in view of their persistent hounding of me, I allowed myself to meet ANI on the outskirts of the hotel.

They principally wanted me to comment on the wholly baseless charges in vulgar language made against Nehru and the Congress by Prime Minister Modi at the opening the previous day of the splendid new Ambedkar Bhavan. I replied that it was Gandhi-ji who, far from denigrating Dr Ambedkar, and notwithstanding their well-known differences, had insisted on Ambedkar's inclusion in the first cabinet of independent India, and it was Nehru who had given him charge of the law ministry and nominated him as chairman of the drafting committee that was preparing the Constitution.

It was true, I continued, that Dr Ambedkar had resigned when Nehru did not take up for immediate legislation the 'Hindu Code Bill', which Babasaheb had framed in his earlier incarnation as a member of the Viceroy's Executive Council, but Nehru preferred postponing discussion on what he knew would be a highly contested legislation, even within the Congress, till after he had received a national, democratic mandate in the first-ever general elections based on universal adult suffrage, scheduled a few months hence.

True to his word, Nehru had done just that, and despite President Rajendra Prasad's refusal to sign the bills after they had been passed by Parliament, had overcome that impediment to realize Babasaheb's dream of radical Hindu reform. That showed how committed Nehru was to Dr Ambedkar's goals.

In so casually twisting recorded history to pursue narrow electoral, partisan ends, Modi, I said, was revealing his true 'uncultured' nature. And when he came to the present and mocked Rahul Gandhi, asking what Rahul knew of Babasaheb Ambedkar when he was obsessively visiting temples to discover Baba Bhole Nath, Modi's rhetoric sank to such depths, I could only say that he was a '*neech kisam ka aadmi*'[22](a low kind of person).

Minutes after my comment was telecast, Modi, who was campaigning in Gujarat (at Limbayat in Surat district), twisted my words to claim I had described him as a 'low-caste' man, that I had said, 'This Modi belongs to a *neech* caste, this Modi is a *neech*.' This was completely untrue. I had made no reference to Modi's caste; I had not called anyone 'low caste'. Yet Modi, it was reported, had referred to me or my remark some twenty times in his fifty-minute speech – that is, an average of once every two and a half minutes.[23] Modi knew what he was doing: laying a trap into which the Congress would be caught. The desperately anxious Congress leaders swallowed Modi's lie hook, line and sinker.

As the Congress panicked, Rahul Gandhi tweeted in response to Modi: 'I do not appreciate the tone and language used by Mani Shankar Aiyar to address the PM. Both the Congress and I expect him to apologize for what he said.'[24]

The Congress campaign in Gujarat was running on the wholly misconceived notion that Rahul Gandhi was going to win the state in his very first election outing after being elected party president. So, the party and the leadership persuaded themselves that I had upset the applecart. No one cared to ask me or check the video. No one paused to ask themselves whether, given my personal background and my long record of diplomatic and political service, I could ever have thrown out a casteist slur. No one even checked out Modi's long record of twisting words in no-holds-barred election contests, where facts and truth are the first casualty. (The BJP calls this '*jumla*' politics: the politics of spicy slogans – and damn the truth!)

What the Gujarat Congress quickly grasped was that I had unwittingly offered myself as the sacrificial goat for the Congress losing the election (which it did by a convincing and unarguable margin, 99 to 77, with a vote difference of 49.05 per cent to 41.44 per cent).

To hold me personally responsible for such a definitive defeat was to laughably accord to my one phrase – which Modi had deliberately perverted – an influence that it could never have had without explicit high-level Congress endorsement. Yet, that was the inevitable outcome of Rahul listening to erroneous counsel and ordering me (on Twitter!) to apologize.

After spending the afternoon hounded by TV cameras, particularly inveterate media enemies such as Arnab Goswami's 'Republic' channel, I learned in the evening that Ahmed Patel, political secretary to the Congress president, had been trying urgently to get through to me. When he eventually did, he remarked that he was seeking to contact me only to ask me to publicly apologize for my remark as that would be politically expedient, but, as he had already heard me doing so on TV, that was that.

Imagine, therefore, my astonishment on returning home to find on my cell phone a vicious text message from an anonymous source informing me that I had been suspended from the party.[25] I slept on it, only to learn from *The Indian Express* next morning that Arun Jaitley had tweeted that the sequence the Congress had adopted was a 'deliberately casteist statement, a convenient apology, a strategic suspension'.

Ravi Shankar Prasad had claimed that the Congress 'could not digest the fact that the son of a poor tea seller had become the Prime Minister'. Amit Shah had weighed in with a list of all that Modi had been called by Congress leaders from Sonia Gandhi down: 'Yamaraj; *Maut ka Saudagar* (Merchant of Death)*;* Ravan; *Gandi naali ka keeda* (a dirty drain insect); Monkey; Rabies victim; virus; Bhasmasur; *Gangu teli*; goon.'

So, on the evening of 8 December, when a 'show cause notice' was delivered to me, signed by three senior Congress leaders – A.K. Antony, Motilal Vohra and Sushilkumar Shinde of the Congress Central Disciplinary Committee – my first reaction was: Why me alone? Why not every Congress man and woman who has vented his or her spleen with the words listed by Amit Shah?

I also regarded it (and still do) as extremely unjust and unfair that disciplinary action against me was being initiated without any party leader taking the trouble to call me and ask me to explain myself.

Instead, unilaterally and without due process, they accepted Modi's word for it that I had described him as a 'low-caste' person. They had clearly not plumbed the depths of the man who was PM but preferred to give a dog a bad name and hang it. I was deeply upset, swinging on my emotional pendulum from fury to wonderment that I was being abandoned without explanation.

The Kasuri dinner

It was to get worse.

Khurshid Kasuri, my Pakistani friend from our Cambridge days and the most constructive foreign minister India has ever had in Pakistan, had sent me a message saying he was visiting Delhi for a marriage in his family and his only free evening was on the day of his arrival, 6 December. The strength of the impression he had made on leading Indians was illustrated by my invitation to meet Kasuri at my home being accepted by our former prime minister, Dr Manmohan Singh; former Vice-President, M. Hamid Ansari; former external affairs minister, K. Natwar Singh; former chief of army staff, Gen. Deepak Kapoor; a clutch of former ambassadors/high commissioners to Islamabad; the serving high commissioner of Pakistan; a sprinkling of journalists who had studied India–Pakistan relations; and others with expertise or experience in diplomacy with Pakistan. All spoke briefly, and Kasuri replied to the discussion before we adjourned for dinner.

To my astonishment, Modi twisted this informal courtesy event into a 'conspiracy' involving the highest in our land – aimed, he claimed, at foisting a Muslim as the chief minister of Gujarat (hinting at Ahmed Patel)! With heavy insinuation, he said: 'Pakistan's high commissioner, former foreign minister, India's former vice-president and India's former PM Manmohan Singh all met at Aiyar's house for three hours and then, the next day, Mani Shankar calls Modi *neech* . . . what is the reason for such a secret meeting amidst Gujarat elections?'[26]

Modi went on to accuse me of having gone to Pakistan to take out a contract ('*supari*', in gangster language) to get him eliminated.[27] He was referring to a 2014 trip I had made, where I had been asked on a Pakistani TV channel what steps needed to be taken to restart the Indo-Pak dialogue. I had said:

> First, you need to remove Modi . . . otherwise the talks will not move forward.
>
> Interviewer, laughing: But (to) whom are you saying this . . . are you saying this to ISI to remove Modi?
>
> Mani Shankar Aiyar: No . . . no . . . we have to wait for four years for this. These people (the other Indian panelists) are very optimistic about Modi, they think that talks will move forward with Modi's presence, but I don't think so.[28]

So, I called each of the signatories to my 'show cause notice' in turn. Sushilkumar Shinde asked me to meet him, under cover of the winter darkness, not at his AICC office but at Jawahar Bhavan, where the Rajiv Gandhi Foundation Trust, of which he was a member, kept its office. Shinde arrived, jumped out of his car, pulled a set of keys out of his pocket and wordlessly signalled to me to follow him into the office. When we were safely settled, out of sight and hearing of any passing Congressman, he requested me to not answer the show cause notice until they had had time to consult Rahul Gandhi to ascertain what I should say.

I then went to see the second senior member of the disciplinary committee, Motilal Vora, who too wanted me to meet him not publicly in the AICC office but privately at his residence. He repeated Shinde's request to me to not respond to the show cause notice until the disciplinary committee had consulted with the incoming president (Rahul Gandhi) and advised me on what to say. And when I met the chairman of the disciplinary committee, A.K. Antony, next morning, he too repeated the formula. All three encouraged, almost pleaded with me, to proceed on the family vacation we had planned in Goa over the New Year, and suggested I meet them on my return. I was partly appalled and partly reassured and went on to Goa on a vacation overshadowed by the Sword of Damocles hanging over my head.

The climax to the whole sorry episode came about with mutually negotiated statements made in the Rajya Sabha on 27 December 2017 by the leader of the House, Arun Jaitley, and the leader of the Opposition, Ghulam Nabi Azad, to end a week of disruption:

> THE LEADER OF THE HOUSE (SHRI ARUN JAITLEY): . . .
>
> Let me categorically state that the Hon. Prime Minister in his statements or speeches did not question nor did he mean to question the commitment to this nation of either Dr Manmohan Singh, the former Prime Minister, or Shri Hamid Ansari, the former Vice-President. Any such perception is completely erroneous. We hold these leaders in high esteem. Thank you.
>
> LEADER OF THE OPPOSITION (translated by the author from the Urdu original):
>
> Sir, on behalf of my party, I too would like to give the assurance that we too do not wish to cast aspersions on any leader, or, from our side, on the person of the respected Prime Minister, who should not be spoken

of in such terms. If, during the elections, some members of our party have given any such statement which has detracted from the Prime Minister's standing, we would wish to disassociate ourselves from such remarks and not want in future to expect any such expression to be used as would detract from the Prime Minister's dignity.

And thus was I cast to the wolves!

After I returned from Goa in early January 2018, I waited for the members of the AICC Central Disciplinary Committee to get back to me. None did. So, I called them. The Three Musketeers said they were yet to meet the newly sworn-in Congress president, Rahul Gandhi, while earnestly reiterating their plea to me to not reply to the show cause notice until they had met Rahul and got back to me. They never did.

Meanwhile, Rahul Gandhi kept me away as if I were a political leper. There was no word of explanation, no opportunity afforded to me to state my case. Yet, to third parties like Shashi Tharoor and Kapil Sibal, who dared raise the issue with him, Rahul would protest his great affection and regard for me. Bizarrely, he told N. Ram of *The Hindu* that he 'loved' me! Yet, no occasion was afforded to me to meet him or to talk to him. It was ostracism at its worst. As for the very senior members of the disciplinary committee, they just went possum, warning me not to meet them and not to send my reply to the show cause notice until they had informed me of what to write. Bizarre!

An attempt to reach out to Rahul

This farce went on for the better part of six months. Then, on the eve of my wife and I leaving for Boston to spend a few weeks with our daughter, who was teaching at MIT, I called Priyanka and requested her to convey my birthday greetings to Rahul on 19 June while I was away. She asked why I could not send him my good wishes myself and seemed quite taken aback to learn that I was not allowed to communicate with him till my suspension from the party was revoked.

She started asking how, in that case, I was in touch with her, and quickly corrected herself to say, 'Ah! I see – because I am not in the party!' She then suggested I send her my greetings and she would pass them on to her brother.

As there were still a few weeks to go for the birthday, I thought this a window of opportunity to press my case for re-induction into the party. Accordingly, on the Delhi–Doha sector of our flight to Boston, I drafted my plea for revocation of my suspension, thinly disguised as a letter of birthday greetings. When we landed at Doha, I handed over my draft to Suneet. She was scathing. 'Don't you have any self-respect?' she asked me. 'Why are you cringing like this?'

I honestly did not know. That was the standard mode in which Congressmen begged and pleaded with their president for their rights. Here I was, Suneet replied, begging on bended knees before a man thirty years younger than me. For what? After three decades of serving the party and standing up for his father?

So, on the next sector, Doha–Boston, I rewrote the letter. Suneet took the draft from me and quickly glanced through it. She chastised me once again: Did I not have, she repeated, any self-respect? Did I have to crawl to demand my right to a hearing, to seek justice and fairness, to make my case before the person responsible for my arbitrary suspension? What was I after? A small corner in the Congress sun after having proved my worth over the past quarter of a century? Did I not realize that I was being made a scapegoat by people who wanted to save themselves? Could I not see that as they had no further use for me, I was being discarded like soiled tissue paper? Why not just walk away with my honour intact? Don't run after them, she admonished me, especially after the abominable way in which I had been treated.

I withdrew my second draft and embarked on a third. That she refused to even see. The rest was up to me. I sent off the third draft and waited weeks for a reply. When it did come, it was just a routine letter of thanks for the birthday greetings that Rahul must have sent to hundreds of people. Of my personal issues, not a word.

Then, all of a sudden, K. Raju, IAS (retd), at the time one of Rahul's closest aides, dropped in to confidentially inform me that I was being re-inducted into the party on Rajiv Gandhi's birthday, 20 August, and I would have a meeting with Rahul on that day. I was, of course, pleased, but was flabbergasted to see Rajdeep Sardesai, two days before Rajiv's birthday, waving an AICC letterhead on the small screen, saying it was a handout from the party announcing the end of my period of suspension. I never received a copy!

But a further surprise was in store for me. When I reached Vir Bhumi, the memorial built around Rajiv Gandhi's samadhi, where his mortal remains had been consigned to the flames, rumour was rife that Rahul would be leaving immediately after the event for Hamburg via London. So, what of my promised meeting with him? It did not happen, not then nor later. Period.

Elections 2019

With my term over in the Rajya Sabha in March 2016, I found myself wondering how to get myself reassociated with the Congress party and politics. The party was out of the question as the leadership seemed determined to have nothing to do with me. The only window I could perceive was the Lok Sabha election in 2019, nearly three years later. So, I visited the constituency as often as I could to keep my links with the people alive. The reaction I received was most encouraging, simply because of the people's disenchantment with the AIADMK MP who had defeated me in the previous election in 2014, which the Congress had fought desperately without a DMK alliance. I also tried to assiduously cultivate the DMK leadership in the constituency; they readily accepted me as the obvious candidate for 2019. My work for the constituency as a Rajya Sabha MP received much appreciation.

The only fly in the ointment – and it was a very large fly – was that the DMK general secretary, 'Dalapati' M.K. Stalin, who had succeeded 'Kalaignar' Karunanidhi[29] when he died on 7 August 2018, continued to be disenchanted with me. This was aggravated by a self-inflicted wound when I went to Chennai about a month later, principally to convey my condolences in person to the new DMK leader.

What had happened in the interim between Kalaignar passing away and my proceeding to Chennai was that I had been reinstated in the Congress on 18 August. To celebrate the removal of my suspension, the district president of Thanjavur North told me that our District Youth Congress president was organizing a big rally in Raya's auditorium in Kumbakonam to welcome me along with the new Youth Congress members he had recruited. I remained for three days in Chennai, fruitlessly waiting for an appointment with the new DMK leader, but I did get to see his sister, Kanimozhi, MP, and conveyed my condolences to her and asked her to pass them on to her brother.

At about 10 p.m. on the very night of my departure an hour later for Kumbakonam, Rajakumar rushed to my guest house to say he had persuaded 'Dalapati' Stalin to receive me the following morning. Caught between cancelling my train ticket and cancelling the celebratory youth rally, I made the gravest mistake of deciding to go on to Kumbakonam. I knew I would have to pay a heavy price for this lack of propriety, but after nine months of exile from the party, I was seduced by the prospects of a huge welcome. In the event, the Kumbakonam Youth rally turned out to be a modest affair in the much smaller of the two Raya auditoriums. I thus lost out on both counts.

The horror at the disrespect I had shown towards their leader spread through the ranks of the DMK in my constituency, and I realized that I had quite unnecessarily blotted my copybook.

There then arose a serious health issue. My excellent cardiologist at the Apollo Hospital in New Delhi, Colonel Dr Hariharan, was intrigued that for five years running my annual thorium tests at the Apollo facilities had shown no change in my heart condition. So, Dr Hariharan decided that I should undertake another test at Mahajan Imaging, which had sophisticated equipment to revolve 360 degrees around what he suspected might be the damaged area. Sure enough, the test at Mahajan Imaging revealed considerable blockage at the rear of a vital artery. I was, therefore, advised to undertake a bypass surgery as soon as possible. News spread rapidly that I was disabled and might perhaps not be in a position to contest the coming elections in April–May 2019.

However, before undergoing the procedure I did inquire from Colonel Hariharan and the surgeon, Dr B.N. Das, whether I would recover in time to be able to campaign as a candidate in the coming elections. On their assuring me that I would have fully recovered by the first fortnight of March, I went under the scalpel on my wedding anniversary, 14 January.

The skill of the surgeon was legendary, and the operation went through smoothly. Thereafter, I let it be known to our leadership that I was fit and healthy to be their candidate. On finding that my request was not carrying adequate resonance at the highest level, I had my first-ever meeting on party/political matters with Priyanka Gandhi on 17 February 2019. We spoke mostly of her father and my association with him, but, towards the end of our cordial conversation, I requested her to put in a word for me with her brother. After some persuasion, she kindly agreed to do so and called me later in the evening to confirm this. I, therefore, started gearing myself up for the elections. At first, things seemed to be going extremely well, but from the middle of March, I began finding that the Congress negotiators were not pushing hard enough for Mayiladuturai to be included among the Congress constituencies in their seat-sharing conversations with the DMK. This caused me considerable concern, but I did what I could to canvass my candidacy and strengthen my preparations.

At the end of March, I was in Mumbai when I received a call from Rahul Gandhi's closest aide, K.C. Venugopal, general secretary (organization), saying that Stalin had pressed for including Mayiladuturai in the DMK quota and Rahul Gandhi had eventually agreed to surrender the constituency to our alliance partner. However, said Venugopal, it had been confidentially agreed that a Rajya Sabha seat would be made available to the Congress, to which, by way of compensation for the surrender of my Lok Sabha constituency, I would be nominated. As Venugopal speaks with a thick accent and my hearing was growing very weak, I called Mukul Wasnik, the general secretary in charge of Tamil Nadu who was accompanying Rahul and Venugopal. Mukul confirmed all the points conveyed to me on Rahul's behalf by Venugopal. I was left deeply disappointed at having been deprived of a constituency I had assiduously cultivated over three decades, but I was somewhat relieved that my

Parliamentary career, halted since 2016, would after all, be resumed. Half a loaf, I reckoned, was better than none.

'Fate, as ever, was waiting at the corner with its lead piping close at hand,' as P.G. Wodehouse would have said. Rahul won his Wayanad seat (while losing badly to Smriti Irani in the family borough of Amethi in UP), but the Congress as a whole crashed to its second successive humiliation at the polls. Rebuffed at the hustings, Rahul resigned from the post of president and went into virtual political exile. This put the future of the party and its leadership in serious jeopardy.

The collateral damage for me, with Rahul walking out, was that no one remembered his pledge to me when by-elections to the Rajya Sabha took place, and so he was not around for me to remind him of his pledge. When I went to see Venugopal who had conveyed Rahul's promise to me, I was treated so rudely and boorishly that I decided never to have anything to do with the man again. In consequence, with Rahul abandoning ship, the promises made to bring me into the Rajya Sabha from my home state, Tamil Nadu, went by the board.

Rahul resigns and orders exploration of other options

We drifted along aimlessly despite the unexpected opening to the leadership of the party that had arisen with Rahul's exit, leading to much speculation within the party. I attended a dinner thrown by Shashi Tharoor, at which I was taken aback to see even P. Chidambaram present. His son Kartik and Kapil Sibal were amongst the most vocal in seeking free, fair and democratic elections to the party presidency as the key to rejuvenating the party. But nothing further came out of this dinner and the initiative passed to a group of twenty-three prominent Congressmen selected by Ghulam Nabi Azad, who was both chairman and spokesman of the group. I was deliberately excluded because Azad suspected I might be a fifth columnist for the Gandhi family! I realized that I was unwanted by both the party leadership and the most prominent dissidents. This revealed to me, as never before, the extent of my failure to integrate or ingratiate myself with any section of the party, starkly revealing to me the extent of my isolation. It was then that I fully understood what Rajiv Gandhi had meant when he cautioned me as I transitioned from the civil service to politics: 'The system will never accept you.'

My TV appearances also dried up, especially when anchors like Rajdeep Sardesai discovered me adamant in describing the Gandhi family as the 'bonding adhesive' of the party, without whom the party would disintegrate into several factions. Knowing that I was being pushed to the margins, I think Rajdeep was disillusioned to find me still playing the 'loyalist'. He did not see that I was actually playing the 'realist', because even in its darkest days, which was the period 2019–2022, the party workers and leaders instinctively saw that without the Gandhi family holding the party together, it was not revival but anarchy in our own ranks that stared us in the future. This, plus my absence from the list of Congress official spokespersons, led to my fading out from TV screens and even from much of the print media. Of course, the exciting new media was 'social media', but I was really too old a dog to learn new tricks and, therefore, was not even on Twitter or WhatsApp, let alone Facebook or other such platforms. My daughters are now threatening to teach me the ropes and put me on social media.

Covid and its fallout

The onset of the Covid-19 pandemic in March 2020 made it even easier for me to isolate myself from the media – and the media from me. I quickly became a distant memory and found myself being stared at long and hard in public places, with people thinking they recognized me but not quite remembering from when and where.

In October–November 2020, Suneet and I found ourselves in hospital for three long weeks, down with relatively severe attacks of the pandemic. Fortunately, excellent (but very expensive) medical attention pulled us out of the crisis. We were left both physically weaker and considerably lighter in our pockets, but, unlike so many others, still alive and recovering. Our brilliant doctor, Dr Suranjit Chatterjee, took me by surprise when we went to him for our first post-hospitalization check-up, saying that I was, far and away, the more seriously infected. It had seemed to me when we were in hospital that Suneet's condition was more serious. We both recovered slowly, and within a month or so of our being discharged were both back in fine fettle.

The Covid lockdown opened an unforeseen window to actually begin writing these memoirs. Once I had put my finger to the computer, I astonished myself by the flow of words on which were carried the vessel of my remembrances of events from birth and infancy over the next eight decades and well into the present. Having finally finished my long manuscript and sent it off to the publisher, I sat back complacently thinking the job was over. This was far from the case. The inordinate length of the memoirs resulted in the publisher throwing up her hands, remarking, 'I had asked for your memoirs, not this *War and Peace*!' My manuscript was returned not sheared but slaughtered. I had to reconceive, reorder, rewrite and re-edit large parts of it, and secure mutual agreement to its being divided into two volumes of memoirs and a third companion volume on my years with Rajiv Gandhi.

All this took much of my time and attention, but my heart still lay in politics and public life. My column in *The Week*, and articles and book reviews in newspapers and magazines continued, and I had time to read and research, but there was little sign of my rehabilitation in the party. Indeed, the only political events to which I found myself invited were those organized in the Malabar region of Kerala by our long-standing ally, the Indian Union Muslim League (IUML). But the IUML-affiliated organizations through which I was invited belonged to civil society rather than the political space in which I had spent the past three decades and more.

While my isolation from the political mainstream and the Congress party grew more and more acute, needless difficulties were arising regarding my visiting my constituency which, since the 2019 elections, had been represented by our ally and partner, the DMK. The only aperture to a political future that I could perceive was the Lok Sabha election of 2024.

The Congress believed, quite correctly as it turned out, that a Bharat Jodo Yatra by Rahul Gandhi, who would walk over 4,000 kilometres from Kanyakumari to Kashmir between September 2022 and January 2023, would revive the party's fortunes. I was at the start in Kanyakumari; then at Malappuram in Kerala; Indore in Madhya Pradesh; Alwar in Rajasthan; Faridabad in Haryana; Delhi; Pathankot in Punjab; Kathua to Samba in Jammu; and, finally, in Srinagar for the final climax. Whenever he spotted me, Rahul was most friendly and welcoming, but I felt disturbed at his concern that I was not physically up to the mark as, after a few minutes of walking together, he would entrust me to one of his aides to put me into one of the vehicles following the marchers. That was when I began to realize that in contrast to my view of myself, he considered me an 'old man', ready to be put out to grass. That view of me as an aged has-been, out of touch with the present, has proved to be my political nemesis.

I also felt that Rahul found my personal atheism and my secular fundamentalism sat ill with his own deep interest in Hindu philosophy and mythology, on which he had shared his views with me at a two-hour long one-on-one meeting eventually set up at his initiative in March 2022. He had carefully steered the conversation away from any discussion about my role in the party or my future in politics to a discourse on matters spiritual. I was later told by a close aide of Rahul's that while the party was prepared to go along with my views on Panchayati Raj and even Palestine, they could not accept my line on secularism and Pakistan.

'Memoirs of a Maverick'

In August 2023, the first volume of my memoirs, titled 'Memoirs of a Maverick', dealing with the first fifty years of my life, was published. There was a special thrill, which I suppose all authors experience, on holding the first copy of their book in their hands. The publisher booked the Kamaladevi multi-purpose hall at the India International Centre for the launch on 23 August 2023, and Vir Sanghvi sportingly agreed to be in conversation with me.

I then sought a meeting with Sonia Gandhi to present her with a copy of the book and, if I felt encouraged, invite her to the launch. She kindly agreed, for the first time in a decade, to receive me at her residence-cum-office at 10, Janpath. When I entered, I began by saying it had been ten years since I was last in the office attached to her home. She knew that and nodded in agreement. I then gave her a copy of the book and invited her to the launch. I was pleasantly surprised when she replied that as she expected to be in Delhi on that date, she would like to attend. There was a last-minute hitch when her staff asked mine not to seat her in the middle of the front row, as we had planned, but at the edge of the first row, so that she could rise with the least disturbance and leave in the middle of the event. As it was, she thoroughly enjoyed Vir's conversation with me and laughed and smiled at my reminiscences, particularly of the time I served with her husband. She stayed right to the end, and I was both pleased and relieved as the media would have gone to town if she had left early, alleging she was angered or upset by something I had said!

Elections 2024

This generous gesture led perhaps to my being suddenly and quite unexpectedly invited to a tête-à-tête with Sonia Gandhi on 5 February 2024 on the eve of the Lok Sabha elections. She very courteously asked me to begin. I said that notwithstanding my age (82, going on 83), I had the good fortune of being in good health and sound mental condition. I should, therefore, be afforded the opportunity of completing the Parliamentary work entrusted to me by Rajiv Gandhi when he agreed in October 1989 to my taking voluntary retirement from government service to join him for a life in politics. Accordingly, I would like to be named the Congress candidate to the Lok Sabha in the 2024 elections from the constituency I had assiduously cultivated over the past three decades and from which I could confidently predict I would be elected by a huge majority. Pointing to the constituency having been surrendered to the DMK in the previous election, I said that if 'Dalapati' Stalin were insistent on keeping the constituency, perhaps, as a second preference, I could be found a place in the Rajya Sabha from Tamil Nadu or elsewhere.

She noted my requests and ended the meeting on an exceptionally encouraging note, saying she would do her best to try to bring me into the Lok Sabha. After nearly fifteen years of frustration, I emerged from her office floating on a cloud of hope and expectation. I realized, of course, that the single biggest hurdle would be to get the DMK to relinquish Mayiladuturai, which they had acquired only five years earlier after a hiatus of nearly half a century. So, I was both intrigued and relieved to find that in the TNCC there was a quite lively expectation of the constituency being returned to us.

What it took me a little while to learn and absorb was that Mayiladuturai was not being retrieved for me but for a close aide of Rahul Gandhi's, Praveen Chakravarty. A young man of very considerable talent, he was, however, tainted in the eyes of the DMK by a rumour associating him with a chain of events that had led to the defamation of the DMK leadership and, in consequence, the DMK's very able and highly regarded finance minister, P. Thiyaga Rajan, losing his finance portfolio. An infuriated DMK seemed set to prevent Chakravarty from being named as the candidate for Mayiladuturai. As against the advantages to the Congress of having Praveen in Parliament, the fact is that he had no particular family or ancestral connection to the constituency and could, therefore, be accommodated somewhere else while I was given the opportunity of completing my innings in Mayiladuturai with dignity, respect and courteous consideration. Hoping for some such conclusion, I allowed myself to entertain hopes of a satisfactory outcome. By the middle of March, it had become clear that Praveen Chakravarty's candidature was completely unacceptable to the DMK leadership; yet there remained every prospect of Mayiladuturai being restituted to the Congress. This encouraged me to entertain the prospect of ending my political career in Parliament, in harness and with my boots on.

A radical young poet, equally talented in Tamil and English, Meera Kandasamy, whom I met at the Goa Literature Festival, kept feeding me on the telephone with inside information on how things were shaping up in my favour. I was inclined to believe her because although she was only retailing political gossip, she did know all the main players in the TN Congress and the DMK, and, therefore, at least some of what she was saying was connected to reality or her informed perception of the ground situation. Her main aim seemed to be to ensure justice for the former TN finance minister by ensuring that Praveen Chakravarty did not get the ticket. At the same time, she genuinely seemed to believe that my work as an MP was exemplary and that the values I cherished were precisely what the nation needed at that juncture. However, while she appeared to me to be on fairly intimate talking terms with the second rung of power in the DMK, she did not appear to have any real access to the very top.

On the other hand, the proprietor-editor of *The Hindu*, N. Ram, had enjoyed the greatest possible access to 'Kalaignar' Karunanidhi, and this had persisted into the regime of 'Dalapati' Stalin. When Ram called me from Chennai early on the morning of Holi, 25 March 2024, he began by saying he had excellent news to convey. He had just returned from a morning walk in the spacious, forested grounds of the Adayar Theosophical Society, where he had run into 'Dalapati' Stalin taking his morning constitutional. Stalin, he said, had sent him as his personal envoy to Mumbai to speak to Rahul Gandhi about the DMK's reservations regarding the suitability of Praveen Chakravarty as the candidate of the DMK–Congress alliance in Mayiladuturai. Ram said that for the first time ever, his conversation with Rahul about Rajan/Chakravarty was rough at the edges, but Stalin's views had been unmistakably conveyed to Rahul, who, after further persuasion, had agreed not to field Praveen. Stalin had concluded the conversation, said Ram, by saying the way now stood clear for Mani Shankar Aiyar or his daughter (in case I felt I was too old) to contest the elections. To say the news sent my spirits soaring to seventh heaven would be to understate my reaction. Here was Stalin himself canvassing my candidature. All hurdles had been cleared and I could look forward to a majority of 3,00,000 votes or even 50,000 more! It felt as if I had been retrieved from death row just before my execution.

I was also amused at the irony of being invited by the Dravidian leader to establish a political dynasty on the banks of the Cauvery from where his ideological forebears in the Dravidian movement had made it impossible for my father to have a career in his home state. This had driven my father to distant Lahore!

My euphoria was reinforced by a long call from ex-finance minister P.T. Rajan to my daughter, Yamini, with whom he was very friendly. He told her how glad he was that all had ended well, and he was confident that I would be elected with perhaps the biggest margin of all Congress candidates in the fray.

Time was running out. The last date for nominations to be filed was 27 March, and here we were with less than forty-eight hours to go and no word from the Congress high command as to who was to be the candidate. To reach the constituency in time to file my nomination papers, I just had to leave next morning on the day-long air journey from Delhi to my constituency via Chennai and Tiruchirappalli, followed by a three-hour car ride to Kumbakonam. I landed in Tiruchirappalli in high spirits and set out for my constituency with high hopes.

The blow came when I was just a few kilometres short of my destination. I put through a call on my mobile phone to Rajakumar, who had been deliberately avoiding me through all these dramatic developments. I was surprised to learn he was still in Chennai, deeply distressed at what he called a series of calls to him from P. Chidambaram in Delhi. Chidambaram told him Chakravarty's candidature was off and Rahul Gandhi was looking for a Vanniyar candidate to be fielded by the Congress in Mayiladuturai. Rajakumar said there was no such candidate locally available, and, in any case, it would take most of the campaign time to introduce a fresh face to the electorate.[30] He also added that my being a Brahmin had never been an electoral disadvantage because the electorate accepted that I was completely free of any caste or religious prejudice. It would be best, he had said, if the high command were to nominate me. Chidambaram had replied that my name was not even under consideration because Rahul Gandhi had ruled me out at the very start (without telling me or conveying this to me) as being far too old, at 82 going on 83, to contest an election. He was looking for someone near his age, and preferably from an extremely backward caste (EBC), like the Vanniyar. While it was uncertain who would be the candidate, the only certainty was that Rahul Gandhi would not agree to my being the candidate. He could have told me – but didn't.

I was crushed. My hopes had been raised high and I could not agree with such discriminatory 'ageism'. I had specifically raised the question of my being an octogenarian in my conversation with Sonia Gandhi on 5

February. And she had agreed that my physical and mental fitness made my age irrelevant. But I had been warned by Sonia Gandhi's closest aide that in the event of Rahul thinking differently, his mother would defer to him. That is what had happened. I was now a 'Maverick Out of Politics'!

I must add that the Vanniyar candidate selected, Advocate R. Sudha, president of the TN Mahila Congress, won the election handsomely with a majority of 2,70,000 votes. I find her much more deeply steeped in TN politics and the ethos of the Congress party in the state than I ever was. I hope she works assiduously with the SCs and the minorities, as I did. I have told her so. It is my warm relationship with the SC community and the religious minorities, Christian and Muslim – that I leave as my main political legacy to my constituency of three decades.

14

Musings and Reflections on a Long Life

I should perhaps have realized earlier than I did that the party found me a liability and so I should have either changed track or just put 'finis' in my mind to any further return to active politics. Because I did neither, I underwent some of the worst years of my life, hoping desperately for rehabilitation while it dawned on me slowly but insistently that I was no longer wanted or valued by my party.

Given that I had had such an unsatisfactory time in the Rajya Sabha and the party, my wife and my very supportive daughters – and my closest friends – all wondered why I was not content to rest on my laurels. I replied I did not know, but it seemed to me that politics was an addiction: once you took to it, it infected you for life. Also – perhaps 'Alas'! – I was neither temperamentally inclined to hang up my boots nor inclined to walk out of the Congress.

My daughters, adult women with strong opinions, joined forces with their equally strong-willed mother in wanting to know why I was not ready to accept that the Congress wished to have nothing to do with me – and, in any case, was not the party in terminal decline? Was it, therefore, not time to call it quits? And did I not realize how much harm I was doing to family happiness by moping around instead of sensibly closing the door on a dead and irretrievable past?

Others said this was not a setback but an opportunity for me to strike out on my own, to form my own party and challenge both the government and the principal party of the Opposition. Most of my friends, particularly Shekhar Dasgupta, whose advice I had valued ever since I joined college at the age of seventeen, urged me to get the hell out and do whatever else I wanted. I did not need the party. Indeed, the party label was, like Shylock's gaberdine, a 'badge of shame'. I thought long and hard about this but was unable to agree.

I tried explaining – to little avail – that in twenty-five years I had failed to establish a political base of my own. My electoral victories – and defeats – had been determined by the alliances the Congress had struck, or failed to strike, in Tamil Nadu.

Moreover, no one who had left the Nehru–Gandhi mainstream of the Congress party had survived, except very temporarily: not JP, not Ashoka Mehta, not Acharya Narendra Dev, not Kamaraj, not Morarji, not Chandrashekhar, not Charan Singh, not Jagjivan Ram, not G.K. Moopanar, not Sharad Pawar, nor any number of lesser beings.

Others pointed out that the Congress had long drifted from its ideological moorings. That, I retorted, was reason enough to pull the Congress back to basics from within rather than bark from outside. To that the obvious counter was that there was no platform within the party that provided a forum for debate.

Moreover, on TV and through my columns, I had been relentlessly urging Opposition unity to take on the BJP, and it would be ridiculous to add to Opposition disunity by increasing the number of groupuscules contesting the already overcrowded political space.

Whatever the deficiencies of the Congress and the Gandhi family – and they were legion – the Congress could only survive with the Gandhis, for the Gandhis were written into the party's DNA, and the survival of the Congress was the only hope of saving the country from the sinkhole of the Sangh Parivar's Hindutva.

The Congress was unanimously agreed on one point: the top leadership had to vest in the Gandhis. This was not because the party was 'dynastic' or 'feudal' but because party workers had repeatedly, over decades, demonstrated that whatever the challenges faced by the Congress, and whether in victory or in defeat, the binding adhesive of the party, the glue that held it together, was the Gandhi family.

When Rahul surrendered his presidency in 2019 after a second humiliating defeat and ordered the party to choose another leader – anybody, he said, but the Gandhis – the CWC, after day-long confabulations among themselves, requested senior leader Mallikarjun Kharge to inform the Gandhis that the party would accept no one but a Gandhi. Sonia was persuaded to act as interim president till an election could be held. In a contested election later, Mallikarjun Kharge was elected president. The Gandhi family had signalled earlier that he was their choice. The party cast a majority vote for Kharge but continued to regard Sonia and Rahul as their legitimate leaders.[1]

Freed of the onerous and tiresome tasks of party president, Rahul undertook two cross-country yatras, south to north, 4,000 km, and east to west, around 3,000 km, and then led the party, as part of the INDIA alliance, to a stunning revival in the 2024 election. He is now the leader of the Opposition in the Lok Sabha and in fighting form. The Congress is beaming. Its adherence to the family has been vindicated.

It astonishes neutral observers and angers the Opposition that the Congress persists with the Gandhis through thick and thin. Why? Only because the ordinary Congressman knows that the Gandhi family constitutes the still centre of the whirlpool that sucks down other aspirants. So, Congress persons instinctively recognize that the family is the party's greatest political asset, and in egging us on to rid ourselves of the Gandhis, our opponents (and their friends in the media) are indirectly confirming that the Gandhis are indeed the party's biggest asset.

As for myself, I have no expectations of a resumption of my political life. But as that is not the end of my natural life, I now have the time and opportunity to pause and reflect, to count my blessings.

Counting my blessings

Amma

Perhaps I should begin with my feisty mother. She was the single most powerful influence on my personality and thinking. Mothers have their children in thrall at a vulnerable time when they are at their most impressionable. So, for better or for worse, their minds get moulded by the almost sole power in their lives till they grow older. At that point, many things change, but the maternal foundation and scaffolding remain. You spend the rest of your life conforming to what you have seen and been taught, or rebel. But even your rebellion is a reaction to what has been thrust on your mind and value system as you grew up.

In my case, that was even stronger because I was the eldest and most favoured of four siblings, and because my father, when he was alive, was rarely around and died when I was not yet in my teens. All this led to a strong bonding with my mother, with all the positivity and negativity that comes with such bonding.

Had Amma been a less dominant personality, my reactions to conforming and rebellion might have been gentler. She was very strong-willed, and I saw that leading her into *cul-de-sac*. I also saw that it was that strong will which brought her the patronage of those better off than her – for not her benefit but the benefit of us, her children. Thus, she would storm into the homes of relatives, near and distant, or of friends, near and distant, and plant herself there till we had long overstayed our welcome.

She would also barge into ministerial homes and even Rashtrapati Bhavan to secure our interests. But her very determination and strength of will also landed us in many embarrassing situations. I would cringe and seek an exit – and she would come down on me with her favourite expletive for me: 'Neville Chamberlain', uttered with the utmost contempt. The charge was true. I always preferred reconciliation to confrontation. I never shied away from confrontation, but if compromise was feasible I always preferred that to confrontation. I think both characteristics owe a great deal to conforming to, and also rebelling against, her methods.

Perhaps her two greatest gifts to us, her children, were austerity and education. Given the uncertain financial situation in the family after my father's sudden and wholly unanticipated death, she prioritized education for us, however expensive, and herself lived a simple, ascetic life and taught us to live with prudence (all travel in third class and no 'home clothes' till Uncle Mirza stepped in).

The fruit of such temperance was that we continued, after my father was no more, to receive the most expensive education the country could provide (whether it was also the best is a question I struggle with even in my eighty-third year). I am afraid The Doon School made *Macaulay ki aulad* of all three brothers, but my sister, Tara, who went to the less expensive and less invasive St Thomas' School, remains the traditionalist. Both Jam and I, and Mukund, drifted in the direction of scepticism about religion and even outright rejection despite, or perhaps because of, Amma's overbearing religiosity.

But while she was strong-willed and highly opinionated, she was also very democratic. We were allowed, even encouraged, to express and hold a contrary view. There was no restriction on debate and argument, but if she took a stand, however unreasonable, she would stick to it even if it made her and us miserable.

This was revealed at its worst when we chose our partners. The first to demand his right to marry whom he wished was my brother, Jam. Although he postponed his wedding by six months in deference to Amma, she behaved atrociously at the ceremonies, needlessly insulting his in-laws and relatives by marriage who dared cross her path. The tension she generated eventually resulted in his marriage breaking down in a little over a decade.

Having witnessed that, I was most circumspect when it was my turn to marry against her wishes. Although it caused a certain amount of anxiety in my fiancée's family, I refused to get married until I had in hand my transfer orders to a distant foreign posting. So, it was only when a return to Brussels – this time as First Secretary in our Mission to the European Economic Community – was finally confirmed that I fixed a date, so that we could escape Amma's baleful interference.

She did attempt to make a nuisance of herself at the pre-wedding ceremonies, but eventually took the defiance with good grace and moved on to the Sivananda Ashram for the next seventeen years, even if it meant living alone, when she had three well-off sons and a daughter to live with. It was only cancer that brought her to my home for the last few months of her life and gave me the opportunity of bonding with her till she passed away.

The leitmotif of her life was her quest for spirituality. She spent much of her days in temples and ashrams – dragging her children behind her, and in consequence turning off all her sons from what passed for religion, but not from the philosophy that underlay her religious quest. We were, I think, subliminally influenced to understand the basic philosophical insights that informed the religion into which we were born.

In keeping with her spiritual beliefs, my mother, despite (or, more probably, because) of her intense religiosity was completely secular, believing all religions to be fundamentally true and stretching towards the same goal. So, she herself went reverentially to any place of worship and treated equally those of different faiths.

In what remains for me an unexplained contradiction, she was fiercely critical of fellow Hindus of slightly different persuasions and contemptuous of their rites and rituals. While these contradictions doubtless influenced our minds – somewhat positively, but even more negatively – I summed up what I owed to her in my dedication to her of my 2004 book, *Confessions of a Secular Fundamentalist* (published sixteen years after she had passed away) with my cryptic description of her as both 'religious *and* secular'. For better or for worse, it is only through her that I can interpret to myself my life and the choices I made.

Suneet

The wisest thing I ever did was to overcome my inhibitions and hesitations and ask Suneet, beside a garbage dump, to marry me! Through her, I have found balance. She encourages me to lead my life according to my impulses but is restrained when things go well and pulls me up from the depths when things go wrong.

Astrologers might say that her being a Libran to my Aries, having been born exactly six months apart – me on 10 April and she on 10 October – we have made the perfect match. My verdict after more than fifty years together is that I would not have made it this far but for her always-sound advice and guidance, her solidarity and loyalty, her enveloping love and care.

Our daughters

A further blessing are my three wonderful and gifted daughters: Suranya, born in Brussels, 1974; Yamini, born in Baghdad, 1976; and Sana, born in Karachi, 1979. I have been enwrapped in their abiding affection from their childhood and enabled to find my way by their wise counsel as they grew into adults.

Suranya, my eldest, is an impassioned fighter-activist for the rights of the dispossessed. She was created a Laureate by the Nordic Human Rights Council for her relentless struggle to retrieve children unjustly taken from their parents by child protection services. As a lawyer with degrees from both Oxford and New York, she has extended her jurisprudential knowledge to Indian victims of insensitive child protection services in Norway, Germany, the United Kingdom and the United States, as also to a miscellany of others – Lithuanian, Rumanian, Czech and Scandinavian – entirely pro bono. She is a persuasive freelance writer and illustrator, an accomplished intellectual and aesthete whose interests range from law and justice through mathematics and science and medicine to books and painting, Hindustani music, the cultural/religious traditions of our composite heritage, and our hallowed indigenous values. She is truly a Renaissance figure, loyal to me to a fault. I know she'll always be there for me. (She once reprimanded me when she was a young woman in the throes of a personal crisis, 'You're never there when we need you.' I still cringe at that lapse!)

She is married to Uday Walia, a brilliant lawyer, who appears, on the surface, to be of a reserved and retiring disposition until one chances on something that interests him – and then he blossoms. They have two children: Uma, 15 in 2024, an astonishingly precocious and athletic teenager, shy but deeply affectionate, passionately interested in photography, and her younger brother, Kabir, now 13 in 2024, obsessed with football and other sports but also academically accomplished, playful and deeply affectionate.

On 22 January 2024, Suranya undertook a fast for three days to express her opposition to 'what is happening in Ayodhya (as) a lie, a celebration of wickedness, a desecration of Hinduism, and an affront to our civilizational heritage. I am fasting as an act of protest and sorrow'. She said she was fasting 'first and foremost as an expression of my love and sorrow to my Muslim fellow citizens' and also as 'an expression of my love for my Mughal heritage . . . that was not imposed (but) grew here, from this soil and is unique to this land'. Denying the Hindutvawadi insistence on 'one religion, one culture, one language', she said, 'You can equally develop a cosmopolitan and porous identity' just as she has 'no difficulty in embracing diverse ideas and practices while all the time thinking of myself as a Hindu'. The Ayodhya agitation, she argued, was 'never about devotion to Lord Ram. It was always only about Hindu chauvinism and insulting Muslims.'[2] She was mercilessly and relentlessly trolled but remained strong and standing. I received a notice from the politically ambitious president of my residents' welfare association to remove myself and my daughter from the habitat of my co-residents as we had 'hurt their religious sentiments', and numerous unsolicited invitations to 'Go to Pakistan' thus proving Suranya's point about the aim of the agitation having been to 'insult Muslims' for not being Hindu!

Yamini, our second daughter, has shone as president of one of India's most respected think tanks, the Centre for Policy Research (CPR), elected to that position when she was not quite 38, a widely hailed columnist for the *Hindustan Times* and other papers and journals, including *Foreign Affairs* and *The Economist*, on current political and economic issues, a fixture on the seminars circuit, and my best-informed adviser on anything political, economic or personal. Yet, it is for these very qualities of head and heart that she has been targeted by a vicious government. It has been an attack without a goal, unless providing a platform for all ideologies to find expression while retaining her own opinion is illegitimate. She has stood up to all this needling from government agencies for the better part of two years with no compromise of her rights or principles, but, after suffering her institution's assets frozen and her right to foreign funds aborted, and domestic financers fleeing like lemmings, and government funding cut off, leading to a reduction in her staff and associates from over 200 to under twenty, she has decided to resign from her position at CPR to take up a year's assignment in the US as a visiting fellow at Brown University,

Providence, Rhode Island, while she works out her future plans. She has not accepted defeat and is determined to return to India in ten months to resume her courageous professional life in her own land and on her own terms. I applaud her resolve. We are immensely lucky that she and her gifted husband, Adarsh Kumar, an adviser to the World Bank in Delhi, have consented to live on the floor below us when in Delhi, so we get to see a lot of them and their children, Rukmini (12 in 2024), an intelligent, twinkling, fun person, and Raghu, 9 in 2024, a bundle of sheer joy, bright as a pin and eternally wielding an imaginary cricket bat. He tells me that I am 'the best grandfather in the world'!

The youngest of our daughters is Sana, an outstanding historian with tenure as a professor of South Asian and global modern history at the Massachusetts Institute of Technology (MIT). After having earned her doctorate from Harvard with a highly regarded doctoral thesis published as *Indians in Kenya* (Harvard University Press, 2015), she has just completed her second book on Burma's relationship with India and Indians during the period of Burma's integration with British India until its separation in 1935 and is, thus, on the edge of being named a full professor. She is married to a fellow academic, Vipin Narang, holding a chair in political science at MIT, specializing on issues of nuclear conflict and their avoidance. He has just completed a most satisfactory two-year stint at the Pentagon and looks set for a very promising future. They too have a boy, Ishaan, eleven in 2024, who is already demonstrating a promising talent as a violinist, and a girl, Leela, aged seven in 2024, a cuddly, mischievous prankster with a very quick temper but brimming with *joie de vivre*.

Sana too, like her sisters, is among my closest advisers and top guide to mediaeval and modern South Asian history and contemporary politics. 'The Child' indeed is 'Father to the Man'!

Continuing to count my blessings

Having been born in the early years of the Second World War, I reflect on the horrors of the world wars, Partition, hundreds of proxy wars and armed revolutions. I am deeply grateful that I have never (except tangentially) been caught up in any of these brutal events. I have lived my life in peace.

That is a great blessing; could there be any blessing greater? More to the point, I have never been personally embroiled in communal riots, or in any of the incidents of mass violence that have stained our contemporary life in India. I have only read of them in the papers. What a miraculous existence!

I have also – touch wood! – never been involved in any physical accident that caused serious injury. There were a couple of incidents in my early years in Brussels where I made serious mistakes in following the traffic rule of '*priorité à la droite*' (priority to the right), which caused an ugly smash-up of the cars, but, fortunately, without injury to me and my co-passengers, or to those in the other vehicles.

As for personal tragedies, I did lose my father at twelve in an air crash; my eldest nephew, Varadhu, on his opening day at school when he accidentally tumbled down an iron staircase; and my much-loved youngest brother, Mukund, who took his own life at thirty-two. But compared with the horrific experiences of many others, I realize I have been spared the worst.

The other blessing I must mention are the houses my wife Suneet has built for us. For a small-town hick like me, I never imagined I would be living in the aesthetic beauty of a home in Sainik Farms built at little cost in a traditional style using materials hunted down by Suneet in junk yards and warehouses in Puducherry, Tamil Nadu, Gujarat and Old Delhi, and lovingly restored by her. We also have a town house, which she conceived and built in the burning sun with technical assistance from a group of brilliant architects, Ambrish Arora and Siddharth. So innovative was the result that in a global competition for professional architects, the house was shortlisted among the final six.

I have also had honours bestowed on me, such as the Outstanding Parliamentarian Award, 2006, and an Honorary DSc. I particularly cherish my Cambridge college, Trinity Hall, having bestowed on me the very rare distinction of being elected an Honorary Fellow in 2010. The only other South Asian alumnus to be so recognized was half a century earlier – Sir Khwaja Nazimuddin, the second governor general of Pakistan and also second prime minister.

As I wheel into my ninth decade, I can also be grateful for being in robust good health for a person of my age and sedentary way of life. I have, of course, had my health problems, including an operation in 2019 for bypassing blocked arteries and a bad attack of Covid in October–November 2020. But, by and large, I have been free of all but minor ailments and some impairment of hearing. Above all, I have been free of life-threatening illnesses that have cut short the lives of several contemporaries.

I have also been privileged in education and lived in material comfort almost all my days. I have found a measure of success in both my careers, as a diplomat and a politician, as well as in the media and as the author of ten books:[3] Of course, there have been setbacks and hurdles to cross, some insurmountable. But, much of the time, I have been able to negotiate my way past them or overcome them. And I am proud to say, 'I did it my way!'

'Character Is Destiny'

Until the final obliteration of my political life on 26 March 2024, the pendulum of my destiny swung between high hope and deep despair. Now that it has definitively ended in exclusion from my own party, I think I should search within myself for the reasons why my political life has been the roller-coaster ride it has been, for, as Socrates said, 'the unexamined life is not worth living'.

So, where do I search? Clearly, within myself, for, as another great Greek philosopher, Heraclitus of Epheseus, famously remarked, 'Character is Destiny'. So, what is there in my character that accounts for my successes and that accounts for my equally frequent failures and, particularly, my final exile from my party despite having all my faculties still with me?

The conclusion I have come to is that it is the same personality traits which bore me to the summit that are also responsible for my ending as an outlier.

The principal of these personality traits is my way with words: 'the gift of the gab'. It is this felicity with words that won me essay prizes and debating competitions at school and college; that propelled me to the top of the university in my BA Economics (Hons) final exams; that ensured my rise in a very short time to the higher echelons of the Cambridge Union; that accounted for my high position in the civil service examination; that was the fundamental reason for Foreign Secretary Ram Sathe selecting me as the ministry's spokesman and my later being named the conference spokesmen for the 7th Nonaligned Summit in New Delhi; that swiftly raised me to the role of principal speech writer for Prime Minister Rajiv Gandhi in succession to the legendary H.Y. Sharada Prasad; that gave me a high-profile role in my very first term in Parliament; that made me something of a media star as the highest-paid columnist in the country and a much-sought-after TV participant; and, finally, in the four ministries I headed as a cabinet minister.

It is also this felicity with words that has undermined me. Even in my PMO days, a prominent journalist had labelled me as 'the Brahmin with a peculiar sense of humour'. The consequence, over the years, has often been that it is I who have created the quip that killed me. Had I less felicity with words, I would not have achieved the unusual successes that have come my way, nor the ultimate failure that, particularly over the last eight years, has doomed me. That is one cause of the paradoxes governing my life.

The other advantage/disadvantage lies in my opinionated convictions, which I have never been able to keep to myself. I have always delighted in being a 'maverick', wading into controversy, unconventional, unorthodox, and yet articulate about my non-conformist views. While this personality trait has made me stand out among the crowd, it has also brought upon me the frowns and disapproval of those who tread accepted ground, and even enmity from those who cannot stomach my line. This, of course, extends to political opponents such as the BJP but also includes those in my party who regarded me as a loose cannon damaging the party with my outrageous views. This, along with my verbal felicity, has resulted in my perceived faults overriding my perceived 'virtues'. In the evening of my life, I reflect that I might have been wiser to follow the French diplomat Talleyrand's dictum, '*pas trop de zèle*' (not too much zeal). But, alas, that would not have been me.

Additionally, there is the genetic arrogance that escapes me when my disapproval turns to sneers. The cutting edge to my tongue gains me a few laughs, but eventually more disdain. My quick repartee traps me in bitter polarization. My individualistic views soon transform into eccentricity. I am at my best when I am the team leader; and at my worst when I am part of a team. What I consider principled difference is considered by others as crass indiscipline. I tend to add layer upon layer on my arguments when a simple statement of my position might more effectively explain my stand. Above all, for all my political ambitions, I lack charisma to rise in public esteem. I thought I could impress my footprints on the sands of time. Instead, the sands have swept away my footprints. I have to acknowledge that in politics my reach has always exceeded my grasp.

A college friend of mine told me the other day that I had a remarkable ability to 'make enemies'. My extrovert ways, my 'hail fellow well met' manner, have also made my circle of friends and well-wishers wide and varied. So, I suppose my enemies and my friends are two sides of the same coin.

In sum, I agree with the words Shakespeare put into the mouth of Cassius, 'The fault, dear Brutus, lies not in our stars but in ourselves that we are underlings.' The reasons for my successes and failures are to be found rooted in the deepest recesses of my psyche. Hence, I have little to show by way of lasting achievement. My principal passions have remained unaccomplished:

- Pluralism/Secularism as the running theme of nation-building, without which we would be building not a modern nation but a castle of sand bereft of our civilizational inheritance and the values of our freedom movement
- Panchayati Raj: securing inclusive development through inclusive governance
- Peace with Pakistan as a foreign policy and national security imperative
- Peaceful coexistence with China
- Kashmir: Integration with India, not just territorially but more importantly by emotionally integrating alienated sections of J&K, particularly in the Valley, into the Indian ethos by assuring them of

democratic self-government with full fundamental rights, and identity, dignity and personal security for each Kashmiri individually
- Ending genocide in Gaza and oppression in the West Bank, ensuring an independent state for Palestinians in their homeland, and justice for the dispossessed and displaced
- Universal nuclear disarmament along the lines of the Rajiv Gandhi Action Plan 1988: The Bulletin of the Atomic Scientists reports that on 23 January 2024, its Science and Security Board in consultation with its Board of Sponsors, which includes nine Nobel Laureates, has set the Doomsday Clock at 90 seconds to midnight in 2024 – 'the closest to global catastrophe it has ever been'.[4]

I would like to briefly highlight some of the elements of my unfinished agenda, my 'unfinished journey'. Many aspects of these issues have been substantively described in the two earlier volumes of these Memoirs, leaving just a few points on the following three subjects that might require clarifying.

Pluralism/Secularism:

In 2004, I published my *Confessions of a Secular Fundamentalist*, in which I defined my understanding of the much-debated concept of secularism:

> Secularism is not about giving primacy to my beliefs. It is about respecting the right of others to hold beliefs I do not hold.

The late eminent jurist, Fali Nariman, rang me to say he thought that line best summed up what we as a nation should regard as the running theme of our nationhood.

Till 2014, there was little doubt that secularism was embedded in the pluralistic values permeating our national life, whichever the party in power, notwithstanding many injustices inflicted on our minorities, including the 'egregious violation' of judicial injunctions and barbaric violence that accompanied the 1992 dismantling of the Babri Masjid. As I write these three volumes, political power has passed to a faction of the saffron right that repudiates kindness and concern for non-Hindus as '*tushtikaran*' (appeasement).

This is a rejection of the innate humanism of the all-encompassing traditions of the freedom movement in which the forces that have now emerged as politically dominant played a wholly negative role. Why 80 per cent of our people should quiver at the prospect of 14 per cent Muslims being assisted to overcome their insecurities and their social, educational, economic and political disabilities, as clearly and objectively laid out in the Justice Rajinder Sachar report, is as inexplicable as it is pervasive.

This provides political cover for the vicious majoritarianism now overcoming the structures of governance. What is most distressing is that the 'secular forces' appear to be cowering behind protective walls to show themselves to be 'good Hindus' instead of confronting, directly and head on, the forces of communal evil.

Fundamentally, this is a struggle between two alternative ideas of India. I deal with this key issue in considerable detail in the next and last chapter, 'Curtain Call'. Here I just wish to contrast, without comment, the words of the principal protagonists:

Jawaharlal Nehru:

> Hindu nationalism was a natural growth from the soil of India but inevitably it comes in the way of the larger nationalism which rises above differences of religion or creed.

Vinayak Damodar Savarkar, originator of the concept of Hindutva:

> Every person is a Hindu who regards and owns this Bharat Bhoomi – this land from the Indus to the seas – as his Fatherland (*pitrabhu*) and Holy Land (*punyabhu*) – the land of origin of his religion and the cradle of his faith . . . We are Indians because we are Hindus and vice versa. India must be a Hindu land, reserved for the Hindus . . . Hinduize all politics and militarize Hindudom!! – and the resurrection of our Hindu Nation is bound to follow

Guruji Golwalkar, the long-serving sarsanghchalak (general secretary) of the RSS (1940–1973) and admirer of the race theories of the Nazis:

> We Hindus are at war with the Muslims, on the one hand, and with the British, on the other . . . There are only two courses open to the foreign elements, either to merge themselves in the national race and adopt its culture, or to live at its mercy so long as the National Race may allow them to do so, or quit the country at the sweet will of the National Race. The foreign races in Hindustan must either adopt the Hindu culture and language, must entertain no ideas but those of (the) Hindu race and culture, that is, the Hindu nation, and must lose their separate existence to merge in the Hindu race; or may stay only subordinated to the Hindu nation, claiming nothing, deserving no privileges.

Deendayal Upadhyaya, the ideologue who completed the political agenda of 'Hindutva' with his coda on 'Integral Humanism':

> There are no separate cultures here for Muslims and Christians . . . Today their (Indian Muslims') centre of loyalty is outside Bharat. The Muslims must completely change their sentiments and views . . . There is no minority in this nation

Rajiv Gandhi speaking in the Lok Sabha on 3 May 1989 affirmed:

> A secular India alone is an India that can survive. Perhaps an India that is not secular does not deserve to survive

That alone is reason enough for me to want to continue in public life. The time for cerebral secularism is over. The time for secular activism is now.

Panchayati Raj

Panchayati Raj is the Constitutional injunction for empowering, at the ground level, women, OBCs, SCs, STs and the generality of our population who have not been able to scramble on to the 'growth' wagon. Although 'socialism' stands discredited in the contemporary national vocabulary, there is a need for institutionalized systemic ways of narrowing inequality, instead of treating inequality as collateral damage in the growth story.

Panchayats offer an institutionalized, nation-wide mechanism for doing so. In practice, however, the political influence of elected panchayat representatives is marginal, even non-existent. This is because the forms of administrative and economic empowerment envisaged in Parts IX and IXA of the Constitution (the 73rd and 74th amendments), as well as the PESA law, have not been acted on, except to some extent, in a few states.

Most distressingly, though these deficiencies are well-recognized in the Congress, little is done by the party to prioritize the rectification of these deficiencies.

The Congress does not have a cadre like the RSS. Even if it gets its message right, it does not have the ground forces at the grassroots to be able to effectively deliver the message. Now, the need for an army of footsloggers becomes imperative. But to conjure up such an army out of thin air is an impossible task, given the Congress culture, its ethos, its organization and even its constitution.

However, a readymade body of workers with political interest and local political influence has been potentially available. I do not believe there is any road to Congress rejuvenation other than the Panchayati Raj route.

There is no doubt that we cannot imitate the RSS. But we don't need to and would rapidly become a quasi-fascist party if we did. The panchayats offer a readymade route to discover who are the popular leaders, young or older, men or women, who are the most trusted and most followed at the booth level. This is most true of village panchayats where, in most states, elections are held without recognized party symbols. While national and state political parties do in fact back so-called 'independent candidates', even if 20 per cent of the winning candidates (reflecting the Congress vote share at the national level) are truly mobilized by the Congress, they would constitute a formidable '*vanar sena*', as I have described it, to enable the party to build a grassroots support base at booth level to take on our principal rival, the communal forces.

The total number of elected panchayat representatives is over three million. On the assumption that a third of them are Congress or Congress-inclined, we can recruit from the panchayats some ten lakh foot soldiers. This would be in addition to whatever numbers we are able to mobilize otherwise. Importantly, about 50 per cent of this cohort would be women and it would include numberless SCs and STs, electable minorities and a grand haul of OBCs.

The poor, who ought to be the natural constituency of the party, would necessarily be more than adequately represented. They would provide the grassroots voice that has been lacking in the party. It would make for a revolutionary change in the profile of the Congress in every village and mohalla. And it would change the current shape of the party, perhaps knocking some 'caged parrots' off their perches. This approach to change has to be reformist rather than root-and-branch revolutionary. Change also has to be undertaken persistently, step by step. It has to be led from the top and made pervasive by a leadership committed to change.

There would, of course, be internal party opposition to bringing in a new source of leadership at the grassroots that would disturb the current order, but firmness of purpose on the part of the party leadership might yet win us the day.

The institutions are there for the asking; the ground-level leadership is waiting to be tapped; the messengers are in place to carry the message. All that remains is for the top leadership to endorse a message summed up by Rajiv Gandhi in two phrases – 'Maximum Devolution' and 'Power to the People'. I hope the party listens.

Pakistan

Pakistan is my 'magnificent obsession'.

With Pakistan, our relations, especially since 2014, remain stuck in a rut. Of course, Pakistan has made its contribution to this impasse by resorting to cross-border terrorism and undiplomatic hate speech. But the impasse is also the consequence of the demonization of Pakistan in India with the ulterior purpose of demonizing our Muslim minority, especially those who stand up for their rights.

I have tried to highlight in these memoirs the enormous reservoir of goodwill for India that exists among the people of Pakistan at large. I have sought to emphasize that such sentiments are to be found in all sections that formulate policy in Pakistan: society at large; officialdom, including the Foreign Office; wide swathes of the media; even the armed forces and the intelligence community.

Instead of attempting to leverage these favourable elements, our Pakistan policy has allowed itself to revert to acute hostility and closing channels of communication when elements in Pakistan who are opposed to reconciliation and rapprochement resort to cross-border violence and terrorism. Our understandably infuriated reaction serves only to disrupt dialogue and instigate Pakistani hate speech in international forums, and the two countries are thus locked into a vicious cycle of mutual hostility.

Instead of insulating the dialogue from the speech and actions of those who frown on dialogue, dialogue is thus held hostage to these disruptions. Of course, such disruptive practices will impact public opinion and the political articulation of such negative trends, as we have seen time and again; hence the imperative of fostering continuous dialogue by making it 'uninterrupted and uninterruptible'. Alas, this view has had no resonance in India and little in Pakistan.

Why do I persist with this apparently hopeless mission? Principally because I do not think we can preserve the integrity of our nationhood until we seamlessly absorb 200 million Indian Muslims into the fabric of our nation That requires our working out a *via media* with Pakistan. That can only be achieved by engaging with them, however dim the prospects might appear at the start

Often when I say this, I am portrayed as pro-Pakistan. But I am actually pro-India for, in advocating good relations with Pakistan, I strongly believe this will contribute to the much-needed emotional integration of our own nation. India without its astonishing diversity is unthinkable. Hence, we need to own and proclaim our religious minorities, especially Muslims, as our own people; to enable them to live in peace, dignity and physical security so as to pursue progress with their identity intact. True, reforms are needed to many aspects of the Muslim way of life in India. But reform is possible only if the community does not feel itself under siege, as it does. It is only when they feel free that they will follow the path of several Islamic republics – and even monarchies – that have set the precedent for reform, especially with regard to gender justice.

This is increasingly hampered by conflating 'Pakistani' with 'Muslim' in our everyday political vocabulary. Till a few years ago, whether it was the Congress or Vajpayee or others in office, it was considered bad form to taint our largest minority with the 'Pakistan' label, but over the last ten–eleven years, such communal prejudice has received official blessings and patronage.

In this perspective, the dogged pursuit of a viable relationship with Pakistan becomes more a matter of domestic policy than of external affairs, muting the 'othering' of the Muslim minority by embarking determinedly (not intermittently) on a path to the progressive normalization of India–Pakistan relations. Instead, the present policy appears to aim at aggravating relations with Pakistan to consolidate a domestic anti-Muslim vote bank.

Perhaps Bollywood more than any other segment of national life represents the immutable values of humanity, compassion and the celebration of diversity. I find it of great symbolic significance that where before Partition, a hugely talented Pathan actor, Yusuf Khan, was advised to change his name to Dilip Kumar, our most influential music director A.R. Rahman changed his given name at birth, Dilip Kumar to Rahman when he converted to Islam, and yet made it big in post-Partition India.

There is also an obvious message in Muslim Bollywood icons of an earlier era changing their screen names to the demurely Hindu 'Madhubala' and 'Meena Kumari', whereas the current crop of rock stars have humongous public followings under their unabashedly non-Hindu names of Shah Rukh Khan, Salman Khan, Saif Ali Khan, Aamir Khan and Katrina Kaif. And perhaps it is for this very reason that Bollywood has been used for target practice, the nation ricocheting with extremist slogans to 'Go to Pakistan' – never, note, to Saudi Arabia or Indonesia, always, 'Pakistan'.

This kind of minority bashing always goes up when the India-Pakistan dialogue is put on the back burner and it is muted when the two governments engage with each other. Ceasefire violations, cross-border firing, and incidents of terrorism also tend to decline when attempts are made to talk, and, conversely, to rise when there is an intergovernmental stand-off.

That too is part of the rationale for urging an 'uninterrupted and uninterruptible' dialogue. We need measures other than breaking off the dialogue process and hitting each other's people with visa denial to demonstrate our anger and resentment at acts or suspected acts of perfidy.

From the Indian perspective – and perhaps also the perspective of a majority of Pakistanis – the overwhelming role of the military in Pakistan's India policy is held (in both countries) to be a principal roadblock to reconciliation. The argument goes thus: What Ayesha Siddiqa calls Pakistan's Military Inc. will never permit hostility between the two countries to be reduced for that would cut off the branch on which the Pakistani defence forces are perched.

But many Pakistanis claim that revanchist sentiment in the Indian establishment, including the Indian military, is so strong and persistent that the dismemberment of Pakistan in 1971 was only the prelude to the destruction of rump Pakistan; hence Pakistan's need for eternal vigilance.

Both these views are a case of the wish fathering the thought. I don't believe that the actual course of India–Pakistan relations validates the view that India cannot deal with the Pakistani military; or that India is still hankering after a restoration of Akhand Bharat. Let us take first the Indian view of the Pakistan military. It is rooted, I think, in Gen Ayub Khan's coup of 1958. Please remember that in 1958, nearly three-quarters of a century ago, almost all top officers of the Indian military were either Ayub Khan's contemporaries, or even his seniors in the British Indian army. India did not want Bonapartism. Gen Thimayya's resignation (later withdrawn) at about the same time as the Ayub coup was considered, perhaps erroneously, as an ominous straw in the wind.

But it was the Ayub regime that suggested a 'Trieste' solution to Kashmir – that is, let the status quo lie, and postpone resolution to a future generation – if I am to credit the story recounted to me by India's high commissioner to the Ayub government, Rajeshwar Dayal. And it was indubitably during the Ayub regime that the Indus Waters Treaty was signed, a treaty that has weathered three major wars and other armed conflicts and continues to offer a forum for the resolution of water disputes. Moreover, it was during that regime that Sheikh Abdullah, Jayaprakash Narayan and others were, by all accounts, pursuing a promising peace mission to Pakistan in May 1964 when Nehru died and our envoys returned to India without completing their mission.

Yes, the battle in the Rann of Kutch in April 1965, and Operation Gibraltar in August that year, followed by the September War, also took place during the Ayub dispensation. Yet, all the evidence points to the civilian, Zulfiqar Ali Bhutto, being the hawk who pushed for war claiming that once Pakistan attacked India, Zhou Enlai had assured him China would initiate a pincer movement that would trap the Indian army on two fronts. It was, therefore, not surprising that it was Field Marshal President Ayub Khan who signed the Tashkent agreement, while disagreement with it was registered principally by his civilian colleague, Bhutto.

It was during the regime of Zia-ul-Haq that there was a new impetus given to people-to-people relations, including the opening of the Indian Consulate General in Karachi. In the winter of 1986–87, when the temperature started building up over Operation Brasstacks, Zia-ul-Haq and Rajiv Gandhi were effective partners in defusing the threat of war.

Although Gen Pervez Musharraf's coup was universally looked at with deep disapproval and suspicion, coming as it did in the wake of Kargil 1999, it was under his aegis that the composite dialogue (that is, the dialogue initiated in 1997 on the eight priority subjects mutually agreed by the two countries) made progress and the Tariq-Lambah backchannel on Kashmir was fruitfully promoted.

Of course, one can also point to the Nehru–Liaquat Pact of 1950, the Simla agreement of 1972 and the Lahore Declaration which was signed by Vajpayee in 1999, as the handiwork of civilian Pakistani governments.

In fact, I do not think the objective record suggests any insuperable difficulty for India dealing directly with the Pakistan military, or dealing with a civilian government that has the military breathing down its neck. In any case, if Pakistan cannot emerge out of the military shadow, what can

India do about it? We have to deal with whoever is in power and while we sympathize with the widespread Pakistani desire to become a full-fledged democracy, we have to make do with whatever is on offer, just as they have to deal with whatever government is in Delhi.

I do not think we in India should postpone any amelioration in our relations with Pakistan till some nebulous future when Pakistan will have a democratically elected political authority that keeps its military in check. Peace is an imperative now, not a consummation to be postponed indefinitely.

The widespread view in Indian circles that Pakistan is a 'failed' state or a 'failing' one is also delusional. Pakistan is firmly anchored in history, civilization, ideology and spiritual belief. It has one of the largest populations in the world (even if it's small relative to India), with a high degree of political and philosophical sophistication, a resilient economy and a globalized elite, a strong bureaucracy and a stronger military, and an extremely lively and informed media. Of course, it is currently experiencing great difficulties, particularly in its economy. But so have all of us in South Asia faced economic crises and, like Pakistan, emerged from under the shadow of crisis to register impressive rates of recovery.

Pakistan is no war-torn Afghanistan swirling in chaos and sucked inexorably into the vortex of religious extremism. Any Indian strategy built on the assumption that Pakistan cannot hold is misconceived, misplaced and dangerously misleading. Equally unrealistic are doomsday prophecies of Pakistan falling into the maw of fanatical terrorists or disintegrating irretrievably into a congeries of nations.

Pakistan is here to stay, and it would be best to deal with it on those terms. While it is the duty of the intelligence community to conjure up far-fetched scenarios and prepare for them, statesmen are required to handle the here and now. That calls for engagement with a Pakistan that will last, not an assumption that Pakistan is on its last legs.

The endemic issues between Pakistan and India are, from a Pakistani perspective, Kashmir and water; from an Indian perspective, it is cross-border terrorism. I have no readymade answers. I doubt anyone has. But is that cause to despair of any solution ever being found?

The historical record would appear to disprove any military solution to Jammu & Kashmir. Pakistan's attempt to annex the maharajah's state when he and Sheikh Abdullah were readying to throw their lot in with India failed; so did Operation Gibraltar in 1965; so did the attack on Akhnur that followed; as did the hostilities on the Western Front in 1971; as did the Kargil misadventure; as did the proxy wars of the nineties; and as did the numerous dramatic but doomed terrorist assaults from Mumbai (2008) to Pulwama (2019) and the many in-between.

On the other hand, while India's 'surgical strikes' into limited territory on the 'other side', or the air attack on Balakot, might have served a domestic electoral purpose, no military action has provided a lasting political or diplomatic solution. There is no military solution, and subversion will not work. Indeed, such military alarums only disrupt any dialogue or prospects of dialogue.

In such a stand-off, is jaw-jaw impossible? The United Nations has in effect washed its hands of the issue; the question of Jammu and Kashmir remains on the UN agenda but lies dormant ever since India and Pakistan agreed at Simla in July 1972 to discuss bilaterally all issues related to J&K. Notwithstanding the naysayers – and there is no dearth of them in either country – progress has indeed been made. These issues are an integral part of the Composite Dialogue initiated in 1997. And, to go by available records, a framework for a resolution of the tangled Kashmir issue reached an advanced stage under the aegis of President Musharraf and Dr Manmohan Singh through the Lambah–Tariq back channel.

Even if that progress is not acknowledged now, it does seem feasible to hope that the resumption of back-channel contacts might move matters further forward. The two countries have demonstrated that, when the waters are not muddied, they can talk to each other even on Jammu & Kashmir and inch towards an agreed settlement. Neither military action nor encouragement to cross-border terrorism can do that.

Water is a most serious issue and upper and lower riparians, whether within our respective countries – such as Punjab and Sind in Pakistan, and Karnataka and Tamil Nadu in India, for example – or between our respective countries, will have to find answers in twenty-first century technology, not in twentieth century polemics.

The total availability of water has run low. India and Pakistan started in the 1950s with a per capita availability per annum of about 5,000 cubic metres, but water availability in both countries has since declined to under 2,000, in Pakistan more sharply than in India, down to about 1,200 against India's 1,800.

Water shortage is common to both of us and is, indeed, a global problem common to virtually every country. Some would call it the most important universal challenge of our times. Israel has shown the way to the conservation of water through drip and sprinkler irrigation, and I imagine that it is in such technology that the answer lies.

But while technology may hold the secret, there is no denying the fact of water deprivation or the politics flowing from it. That is where the Indus Waters Treaty has proved its immense worth. The numerous mechanisms it has for finding acceptable ways of resolving agonizing issues, as was demonstrated, for example, over Baglihar and Kishanganga, are solid examples of India and Pakistan being able to discover forums of settlement in preference to the aggravation of real problems and real issues.

I now turn to the Indian priority – terrorism. Till 9/11, cross-border terrorism was one of several subjects under discussion in our bilateral composite dialogue notwithstanding the proxy war in Kashmir and the jehadi strategy of bleeding India with a thousand cuts. The attack on our Parliament on 13 December 2001 led to the armed confrontation of Operation Parikrama but did not stall either the Agra Summit, or the Islamabad Declaration of January 2004, or the dramatic progress between May 2004 and March 2007, when the going was never better.

The Al-Qaeda attack on the Twin Towers brought American retaliation to the borders of Pakistan. Ever since, terrorism has become a global issue, perhaps the most important issue before the international community. In the war against terrorism, Pakistan, willy-nilly, has become a front-line state, with horrific consequences for itself. No state has suffered as much from terrorism as Pakistan itself.

I think there needs to be much wider appreciation in India than at present, of how terrible is the daily threat of terrorism in Pakistan and, therefore, how steely is the will of the Pakistani people to not let their country be taken over by suicide bombers and pathological killers.

I do believe that while segments of considerable strength and influence in the Pakistan establishment have been, and are complicit in terrorism directed against India, there are sensible countervailing forces within the establishment who recognize that terrorism is no way of securing Pakistani national objectives, and that being in league with fanatical terrorists gives the country an odious reputation in international circles and serves only to strengthen international support for India.

The Indian establishment, on the other hand, and almost all Indians remain unconvinced that India-directed terrorism is seen in Pakistan as an unmitigated evil that must be stamped out. But while that hurdle looms large on the road to the resumption of normalcy in our dialogue, I do believe that as Musharraf and Manmohan agreed in 2007 at Havana, only a joint strategy to counter terrorism will enable India and Pakistan to overcome what is a joint threat to both our peoples.

We either hang together or hang separately. The challenge is to set the stage to being together on this issue instead of languishing in confrontation. There is little sign of this happening, but I remain persuaded that the threat to both of us is so great from what is in practice, a single undifferentiated source of extreme danger to both countries, that sooner rather than later a joint process will have to be set in motion.

Palestine

I was first exposed to the horrors of Palestine when I prepared for a speech at the Cambridge University Union Society on the motion, 'Israel is a dream at the Arabs' expense'. The only times I have been to Palestine was to Gaza in 1998 at the invitation of Yasser Arafat, and to Ramallah on the West Bank in 2017 for a Palestine solidarity conference. And I have become something of a regular on the Palestine conference circuit that has taken me frequently to Beirut, Johannesburg and Istanbul.

Everything I have learned about Palestine – 'the twice promised land', as a wit remarked, referencing the 1917 Balfour Declaration that promised it to both communities – has only strengthened my view that the miseries inflicted on the blameless Palestinians cannot be exorcized by imposing a Jewish state in Arab lands, for, as the Mahatma remarked, 'Palestine belongs to the Arabs as France belongs to the French and England to the English.'

I believe the narrow, religion-based nationalism of Israel is the role model for Hindutva ('Hindudom', as Savarkar described it) in our country. That is not the India we set out to build in 1947, the year when India and Palestine were both partitioned, with equally disastrous consequences for human values in both regions and the coterminal unfolding of conflict.

I hope, but do not expect, the Indo-Israeli relationship would be reviewed if and when there is a regime change in India. But, irrespective of what our governments decide now, or in the future, I will continue my impassioned espousal of the Palestinian cause.

I deeply regret the Indian abstention on the UN resolution on the verdict of genocide returned against Israel by The Hague International Court of Justice in the context of Israel's revenge attack in Gaza, in the guise of winkling out Hamas, that has taken nearly 40,000 civilian lives, mostly women and children, and the repeated displacement of nearly all of Gaza's population. The root cause of India's abstention is Modi's disavowal of Nehru's advocacy of a one-state federal solution to bind Arabs and Jews in a common nationhood and its replacement by 'total solidarity' with Netanyahu's Israel.

Nuclear disarmament

I was so shell-shocked when I learned in May 1998 that India had become an overt nuclear-weapons power that my mother-in-law inquired if there had been a death in the family.

Unlike the vast majority of my compatriots, I felt no pride in the achievement, only aching sorrow at our having joined the race instead of opposing it as we had done for half a century, when we had been the world's foremost advocate of nuclear disarmament – the goal of the UN's first-ever resolution [UNGA resolution (I)].

India had consistently advocated nuclear disarmament right from August 1945 when Hiroshima and Nagasaki were devastated.

My mind went back to all I had heard:

> *Mahatma Gandhi:* I did not move a muscle when I first heard the atom bomb had wiped out Hiroshima. . .I said to myself 'Unless the world now adopts non-violence, it will spell certain suicide for mankind. . .In

> the age of the atom bomb, unadulterated non-violence is the only force that can confound the tricks of violence put together.'
>
> *Jawaharlal Nehru*: . . . such weapons appear to me so evil in every way that their use can only result in greater evil. . .[W]e believe that complete disarmament of all nation-states should be aimed at, and is in fact an urgent necessity if the world is not to be reduced to barbarism . . . these weapons, and the magnitude in which they will be employed, have erased the differences between the capacity to inflict punishment and of receiving the same, for the side that employs them is not immune from the lethal effects of their own offence. It is a dangerous delusion to believe that nuclear weapons have brought us peace;
>
> *Indira Gandhi*: Each day, each hour the size and lethality of nuclear weapons increases. The hood of the cobra is spread. Humankind watches in frozen fear.
>
> *Rajiv Gandhi*: Humanity is at a cross-roads. One road will take us like lemmings to our own destruction. That is the path indicated by doctrines of nuclear deterrence. The other road will give us another chance. That is the path signposted by the doctrine of peaceful co-existence. Nuclear deterrence is the ultimate expression of the philosophy of terrorism: holding humanity hostage to the presumed security needs of a few.

But all this was blown away with the proclamation of India as a *de facto* nuclear-armed state on that dreadful day in May 1998. Even so, Prime Minister Vajpayee declared, 'These tests do not signal a dilution of India's commitment to nuclear disarmament.'

Prime Minister Dr Manmohan Singh's subsequent message to the London meeting of Global Zero (22–23 June 2011) was unambiguous. This was thirteen years after India had become a declared Nuclear Weapon Power:

> India has been steadfast in its support for global, non-discriminatory, verifiable nuclear disarmament. . .There is need for meaningful dialogue among all states possessing nuclear weapons to build trust and confidence.

An international consensus has now emerged at the UN, including several nations enjoying the protection of the US nuclear umbrella, in the years since Dr Manmohan Singh spoke. Where Jawaharlal Nehru's voice was a lone one in the early years, and Rajiv Gandhi's was not much less lonely, nor Manmohan Singh's, there is now a clear majority of the UN General Assembly in favour of disarmament. As many as 122 member-States voted to adopt the TPNW, with 94 signatories and 70 State-Parties, as on 24 September 2024. So, the advocacy of universal nuclear disarmament in verifiable stages leading to time-bound elimination is no longer a lonely task as it perhaps was when India was in the forefront of the movement. Another member-State, the Solomon islands, has also announced its adhesion as we go to press.

The advocates of the TPNW include some NATO nations that have been squirming under the US nuclear umbrella. The 71st State-Party to announce its adhesion on 25 September 2024 (Indian Standard Time) has been Indonesia despite its relationship with AUKUS, the alliance of nuclear weapon states in the Asia-Pacific region of nuclear weapons. So, the advocacy of universal nuclear disarmament in verifiable stages leading to time-bound elimination is no longer as lonely a task as it perhaps was when India was in the forefront of the movement.

The arguments we made against the threat or use of nuclear weapons then are as valid today as they were then. Of course, we were not before 1998 an NWS. But why after becoming an NWS are we slavishly adopting the same deterrence doctrines we used to denounce before we got the Bomb ourselves? Which is precisely why I think we should be the first NWS to join those urging the abjuring of weapons of mass destruction that cannot bring peace, only wreak humongous destruction. Unfortunately, we have no Nehru with the guts to lead us on a mission of '*Ekla chalo re*'.

15

Curtain Call

I was six when Jawaharlal Nehru became our prime minister. I was twenty-three when he died. So, my entire childhood, adolescence, higher education and early youth was dominated by this 'Gentle Colossus'. He was not only a great man; he was also an exceptionally good man. But, of course, he was human. He made mistakes, the consequences of some of which continue to be with us. But it was he who gave us a coherent and cogent 'Idea of India' as I found in my mid-teens when I first read Nehru's *An Autobiography* and was in my early twenties when I discovered his *The Discovery of India*.

When I take a broad-spectrum view of his life and his written works, I see that the fountainhead of the values by which I have tried to live my life (and the missions – largely unfinished – that I have made my own) owe almost everything to my understanding of Nehru. The learning I had from these two books was supplemented by early readings of the Mahatma, Swami Vivekananda, A.L. Basham's *The Wonder That Was India* and others, including Dr S. Radhakrishnan's *The Hindu Way of Life* and Kshiti Mohan Sen's *Hinduism*.

Lessons learnt

The first and most fundamental lesson I absorbed, from which everything else has flowed, is that the evolution of our civilization took place through five millennia of successive eras of political turbulence and economic disruption caused by repeated military invasions. Whatever the immediate reactions might have been to such attacks from the outside, which were often cruel and destructive, over time India's ancient civilization displayed the resilience and flexibility to absorb, assimilate and synthesize the best that came from the outside while preserving the essence of what was our own, instead of surrendering to outright subjection or resorting to outright rejection, as had been the case with most other nations and civilizations. There were also periods when those who came from outside – such as the Sakas, the Hunas and, to some extent, the Bactrians – merged into our religious identity and civilizational values. Under the Kushanas, particularly King Kanishka, Buddhism, born in India, flourished, as did Jainism, which also has its roots in India. The ancient tree of our civilization sprouted many branches which even challenged the roots and led to new flowering. Every spiritual or aesthetic innovation was accommodated and made part of our own heritage. This was the key takeaway from Nehru's *The Discovery of India*.

Unity in diversity: The lesson that follows

It followed that while we were neither the most ancient of all civilizations – at least Egypt, Mesopotamia and China were older – nor the only one to have demonstrated continuity over five thousand years, ours is the only civilization to have flourished in heterogeneity rather than homogenization. This made for diversity on a scale unmatched anywhere else in the world or at any time, past or present. We flourished because we had found 'unity in diversity'.

Thus, the preservation of diversity to ensure our unity requires not just the acceptance but also the celebration of diversity in all its many hues: diversity of race and skin colour; diversity of ethnicities; proliferation of languages and dialects; harmonious coexistence of different cultures and subcultures; and, above all, plurality of spiritual belief and religious faith, combined with such intense interaction between them as has never been witnessed anywhere else.

In this manner, the pursuit and celebration of diversity becomes the most consequential requirement of national unity.

The influence of the Buddha and Emperor Asoka on Nehru's mind

In pursing the doctrine of 'unity in diversity', *The Discovery of India* underlines the influence of Buddhism on Nehru's mind. He was deeply inclined towards the Buddha's doctrine of non-violence. He was perhaps even more moved by the Buddha's stress on compassion towards the weak. These twin doctrines – Non-violence and Compassion – found expression in Emperor Asoka's statecraft which Nehru lauded in his *The Discovery of India*.[1] Therefore, not vengeance on those who had split the nation but compassion and concern for the forty million Muslims left behind in independent India became the drumbeat of the Constitution. The Hindutva forces characterize such compassion as '*tushtikaran*' or 'appeasement' of the minorities.

Religion and nation-building

In the circumstances of Nehru's time, when religion was being used by both Muslim and Hindu communalists to divide, not unite, the single most important application of the principle of 'unity in diversity' was to relations between religious communities. While Muslims led by Jinnah insisted, particularly in the seven years run-up to Independence and Partition, that Muslims and Hindus were not two religious communities but two completely separate nations, Hindu communalists held a parallel view that Hindus and Muslims were indeed separate nations and could not be artificially conjoined in one nation. Only Hindus, they held, could be true Indians as they regarded India as not only the land of their birth but also as their Holy Land, whereas Muslims looked west beyond India to Arabia to find spiritual succour. Nehru regarded this view as nonsense since Hindus and Muslims, for the better part of a millennium, had occupied a common territorial space and interacted so closely with each other that to attribute different nationalities to them flew in the face of his discovery of India. In Nehru's 'Idea of India', as explained in the sections that follow, Hindus and Muslims had much more in common than differences of faith, especially as our civilizational characteristic of 'unity in diversity' had most strikingly stood the test of time in inter-faith relations. Gandhi-ji, for his part, totally and unreservedly endorsed this view precisely because he was a model Hindu and yet had showed in political action during the Khilafat movement and dramatically during the partition massacres, that Hindu–Muslim unity was for him an article of faith. The Mahatma remained rock solid in his conviction that whatever the circumstances that had forced partition upon us as the price to be paid for independence, our first duty was to treat the Muslims who remained in India as equal citizens, eschew religious discrimination and all forms majoritarianism. This was not a country for Hindus alone but for all its citizens, whatever their religion. He supplemented this belief with working for the best of relations with Pakistan – and paid with his life at the hands of Hindutva for his humanity and compassion.

Secularism as the principal building block of nationhood

That is the origin of Nehru's insistence, backed by the entire membership of the Constituent Assembly, in making 'secularism' the principal building block of our Constitution. To help the nation get over the trauma of Partition, 'secularism' was the imperative to harness all the communities of the country to a common national endeavour, as opposed to the goal of an exclusively Hindu Rashtra (nation-state) advocated by the Hindu right.

'Secularism', as expounded times without number by Prime Minister Nehru through the entire period of my growing to adulthood, seemed to me the core and leitmotif of Nehru's 'Idea of India'. To abandon or dilute 'secularism' amounted, in my mind, to denying the greatest gift of our ancient heritage: the ardent desire to see all religions (and no religion) coexist in peaceful interaction, to continue our millennial tradition of living together with all our many religions and their diverse beliefs, rites and rituals and consecrated festivals. A key ingredient of 'secularism' in our Constitutional democracy has been that the State has no religion to better enable it to treat followers of all religions equally, with a special emphasis on protecting the fundamental rights made available in the Constitution to the minorities as citizens of the nation. This is a key provision of our Constitution that has been blatantly transgressed since Modi and his cohort came to office ten years ago.

The 'scientific temper'

Nehru stressed the need to cultivate in ourselves and our people what he called the 'scientific temper'. The scientific temper included, of course, elevating science to a national priority expressed in state-funded science and technology institutions that have earned international fame and provided the manpower and womanpower that, besides taking Indian science and technology to new horizons, is also enabling the global science and technology community to rise to new innovative heights, as evidenced by the number of Non-Resident Indians (NRIs) and Indian origin citizens helming information technology firms in Silicon Valley and elsewhere. Even as Nehru established the three Akademies to promote the fine arts, the performing arts and literature in all languages, bringing about a post-Independence Renaissance in our millennia-long quest for artistic excellence, he was almost single-handedly responsible for the Indian Institutes of Technology, the National Laboratories for Physics and Chemistry, the All India Institute of Medical Sciences and the high priority accorded to the growth and development of the national network of research institutions under the Council of Scientific and Industrial Research. The annual Indian Science Congress, which Nehru assiduously attended, afforded a platform for not only interdisciplinary exchanges but also for interaction between scientists and government authorities to determine areas of policy that would encourage greater scientific and technological exploration.

But, I would argue, the 'scientific temper' meant most of all weaning our people away from superstition and outmoded social practices, especially those that were cruel or discriminatory, inhibiting the rise of women and historically disadvantaged and oppressed sections of society. Moreover, it meant that while we needed to recognize and respect the importance of mythology in the making of the national memory, it was essential to distinguish between mythology and history. Mythology arose from imagination, rumination and musings where fantastic superhuman and supranatural achievements were endowed with credibility by skilled poets and dramatists. Such mythology manifested itself in profound spiritual writings, millennial epics, immortal poetry, great literature and sophisticated art, but was not to be mistaken for sober history.

History and historiography require the rigorous collating of facts, placing them in chronological order and then interpreting what had happened and why in a scientific manner that proceeds from hypothesis to theory to considered conclusions that could and should be challenged, even replaced, by the application of the same rigorous method to new or additional facts and alternative logic.

Scepticism's origins in the Rig Veda

This, in turn, meant that nothing may gain everlasting acceptance, everything could be challenged. Nehru traced this intellectual tradition of scepticism, as opposed to rigid dogma, to the seventh verse in the *Rig Veda*, the first of the four Vedas that constitute the storehouse of ancient Indian thought and knowledge.[2] The verse speculated over the question that lies at the root of all religious thought: Who created this universe and everything wonderful that is in it?

The verse begins by saying no one knows. It then suggests that 'only He knows'. And the next line speculates, 'And perhaps even He knows not'! This punchline typifies the open-mindedness of Indian thought, its refusal to accept answers set in stone, even respecting schools of thought, such as the Charvakas, who denied the existence of a Supreme Being. I know not of any other religious tradition that shows such tolerance and accommodation to even diametrically opposite beliefs. It has led to there being no concept of 'blasphemy' in our ancient belief systems. It also facilitated the Buddha's rejection of prayer to an Almighty in preference to an eight-fold path of living an ethical life. Nobel Prize winner Amartya Sen has more recently and resoundingly discovered the essential thread of Indian thought in our having always found our true selves as *The Argumentative Indian*.

India encounters Islam

Nehru argues that this long tradition of questioning and listening to perceptions other than our own prepared us, as it prepared no other people, for meeting the spiritual and ethical challenge of Islam. When I reflect on the India of the Modi era in the light of Nehru's perception of Islam and India, I note that while every other country and region either gave itself over to a complete conquest of mind, spirit and faith to the Message of the Prophet Muhammad, or totally rejected its innovative, creative and provocative ideas, in our subcontinent alone, Islam coexisted with existing spiritual beliefs, as Nehru's *The Discovery of India* showed. In consequence, after a millennium of interaction and 666 years of Muslim sovereigns ruling over much of our land (1192–1858), the Muslim population of India, according to the census of 1872, was limited to a quarter of the inhabitants. Three-quarters of all Indians continued to belong principally to the majority religion that went by the catch-all name of 'Hinduism'. A somewhat inefficient way of imposing 'slavery' on Hindus for 'a thousand years', don't you think?

India's unique reaction to Islam: Neither victory nor defeat – only co-existence

The explanation lies in the contrast between the Indian encounter with Islam and Islam in the rest of the world. Elsewhere, Islam was either totally accepted or totally rejected. In India alone, Islam coexisted with other religions. To the west of India, all through Afghanistan, Iran, the Arab nations and Türkiye, and right across North Africa from Egypt to Mauritania on the Atlantic coast, Islam was triumphant. So was it to the north of our subcontinent in Central Asia. The triumph even extended for nearly seven centuries (from 711 to 1492) to Andalusia, that is, Iberia (today's Spain and Portugal) in Europe. It was also totally triumphant to the east of India from Bangladesh to Malaysia to Indonesia (the world's largest Muslim nation) to the southern Philippines. At the same time, when the Muslim forces were defeated at the Battle of Tours (732 CE) in France and later at the gates of Vienna, the defeat was as total as victory elsewhere. In India alone, Islam co-existed with other religions from its early beginnings in the seventh century down to the present.

Of course, all wars, all invasions, all expansions of empire and feudal tyranny entail crimes against humanity, barbaric destruction, pillage, rapine and rape on a horrific scale. This was certainly evident when the Islamic sword came to and ruled over India. But this was also true of Hindu rulers conquering other Hindu rulers through all of our history.[3] It is evident in Savarkar's glorification of violence.[4] What, in many ways, is unique to India is how the Hindu religion flourished through a millennium of interaction with politically authoritarian Islam.

Bhakti: Five facets

The dominant school of spirituality among Hindus from about the twelfth century (that marked the beginning of Muslim rule) was Bhakti Yoga or devotion to the Divine. Fascinatingly, the Bhakti movement evolved and spread not when there were Hindu emperors on the throne but when Muslim sovereigns ruled over much of India. There were five facets to the Bhakti movement that merit particular attention in the context of religion and the principle of 'unity in diversity'. Nehru touches on all five facets but as he ruled when the saffron forces had been worsted in elections, he did not go into detail on these issues. I have built upon his insights to flesh out my thesis.

Facet one: Bhakti saint-poets and Muslim rulers

The first is that this Hindu spiritual movement stretched over five centuries of Muslim rule from about the twelfth to thirteenth centuries to the end of Aurangzeb's reign in the early eighteenth century, five hundred years later. This was the half-millennium of the Delhi Sultanate, the Lodhi kings and the Mughals, before the latter started disintegrating over the next century and a half. Over these five hundred years, while Muslims sat on their imperial thrones, the hearts of the majority were being captured by a host of Hindu saint-poets and philosophers including Ramanujacharya, Swami Ramanand, Sant Tukaram, Krishna Chaitanya, Sankardev, Sant Ravi Das, Sant Surdas, Mast Qalandar/Jhule Lal and, above all, by Mirabai, a Hindu poetess–saint, and Kabir, born a Muslim. They were allowed to preach and persuade without let or hindrance from the powerful Muslim sultans and badshahs, nawabs and nizams, who reigned over much of the land.

Indeed, the *Ramcharitmanas*, the most popular and revered of the many versions of the epic, especially in the Gangetic plain, and the *Hanuman Chalisa,* were composed by Acharya Tulsidas Goswami (circa. 1511–1623[5]) in Ayodhya in the shadow of the very Babri Masjid whose deliberate vandalization has determined the course of events that has led to the last disturbing decade (2014–2024) of majoritarian attempts at political, social, cultural and religious dominance. There is no evidence of Acharya Tulsidas having targeted in his immortal writings the Babri Masjid built within his eyesight when he was seventeen, about a half-century before he began his monumental and deeply influential religious works. There was self-confidence in the Bhakti movement. Hindutva is imbued with an inexplicable inferiority complex.

Facet two: Bhakti and the Sufis

Secondly, the Bhakti movement intertwined itself with the mystical Sufi tradition of the Muslims, both dedicated to immersing the self totally into the Divine. There was much that they took from and gave to each other. The climax of the Bhakti movement was the Sikh faith that so synthesized the main tenets of the *sanatana dharma* (the Hindu 'eternal faith') with the wisdom of Islamic, particularly Sufi, teachings (Baba Farid, Bulle Shah and others), that when Maharaja Ranjit Singh decided to build the Golden Temple in Amritsar, the most important shrine of the Sikhs, he invited a Muslim *pir* to lay the foundation.

Facet three: Amir Khusrau and the evolution of Hindu-Muslim cultural synthesis

Third, parallel to the joint evolution of Bhakti and Sufism, Amir Khusrau (1253–1325) and his spiritual mentor, Nizamuddin Auliya in Delhi, were working on a fusion of the best in the ancient Indian tradition with the best in the new cultures from Persia, Central Asia, Arabia ad Türkiye that entered the land with Islam. Closely associated with Amir Khusrau was Gopal Naik, one of the many Hindu court musicians in the courts of the Delhi Sultanate, who by carrying forward the dhruvapadas and rasas of the Natya Shastra (which Muslim artistes took to with enthusiasm), brought about schools of great Hindustani music, including at least three new ragas contributed by Amir Khusrau himself. This cultural synthesis led to a musical tradition that has produced highly reputed artistes, both Hindu and Muslim, through the centuries down to the present day. It is in classical Hindustani music that the cultural ties which bind together the star artistes of the Hindu and Muslim faith most strikingly manifests themselves. In our own day, the maestro of the oldest Hindu musical instrument, the Rudra Veena, has been Ustad Asad Ali Khan, the dean of music at Delhi University. In the Carnatic tradition, we have had another Muslim, Sheik Chinna Moulana, who so mastered the sacred Hindu *nadaswaram* that in 1998 he was honoured as 'Sangeetha Kalanidhi', the highest award of the Madras Music Academy. Can we think of Ravi Shankar without his brilliant percussionist, Allah Rakha? Or the *jugalbandhi* (duets) of Bismillah Khan (shehnai) and N.G. Jog (violin) without recognizing the Hindu–Muslim synthesis? Or the sarod without Amjad Ali Khan? The list is endless.

Such fusion and synthesis extended to virtually every aspect of life from tailoring to hairdressing (arts which the Muslims brought with them), to cuisine and apparel, to exquisite handicrafts and handloom textiles and jewellery that were the envy of the world.[6] Amir Khusrau gave us the Hindawi language that drew from Brijbhasha mingled with imported languages and has now led to our principal national language, Hindi. Further fusion of Hindi and its variants with Persian birthed the other great subcontinental language of Urdu, whose efflorescence from the mid-eighth century under the later Mughals and their successor feudatories, especially in Awadh, right up to the present began. It is widely acknowledged that it is with the poet-doyen Mir Taqi Mir (1723–1810) that Urdu, the language of the soldiers' camp, emerged as a vehicle of great poetry and prose.[7] The Urdu ghazal had much in common, especially in its structure, with the *doha* (couplets) of Bhakti Yoga as did the qawwali with the popular *bhajan mandali*. Exponents of these arts included Muslims and Hindus. The synthesis led, besides fresh departures in high literature, immortal poetry and classical music, to the introduction of new musical instruments such as the sitar, and innovations in dance forms, of which Kathak is the most notable. During this phase of cultural and civilizational synthesis, painting, sculpture and architecture, indeed the entire range of aesthetics, knew no distinction between Hindu and Muslim but happily synthesized their respective traditions into a specifically Indian mould.

Facet four: Muslim rulers and Hindu subjects – the early beginnings of 'secularism'

Fourth, such prolonged and profound spiritual and cultural interaction was facilitated by Muslim rulers from at least the time of Iltutmish (reigned 1211–1236) and certainly after Ghiyasuddin Tughlaq (reigned 1320–1325) – notwithstanding the ghastly reign of Alauddin Khilji (reigned 1296–1316). They realized that their empires in Hindustan could be stable and lasting only if they respected the ancient, durable and deeply held spiritual beliefs of the vast majority of the local population. Perhaps the most definitive direction in this regard was Babur's letter to his son, Humayun, where he warned that if Humayun wanted to preserve and expand the empire that Babur had founded in 1526, it was imperative to let the Hindus remain Hindus.[8] Humayun had the most constructive and cordial relationship with Hindus, particularly Hindu intellectuals, astrologers and astronomers, which disciplines were for Humayun a passion. Akbar (reigned 1556–1605) then initiated the process of inter-faith dialogue and translating the major Hindu epics and religious texts into Persian, a task that was taken forward by his successors over the better part of a century. His ateliers, which were filled with Hindu and Muslim artistes of the highest calibre, made lasting contributions to painting, especially of miniatures, and sculpture and other arts and crafts integral to the composite Indian heritage.[9]

Above all, this deep interaction of the indigenous with the imported reflected the determination of the Muslim rulers to make Hindustan their homeland, not a colony of a distant homeland, as the British did. After Ghazni's predatory raids from AD 999–1027, and, following Ghori's ascension to the throne of Delhi in AD 1192, the Muslim invaders came not as predators but as settlers.

Please note that 387 years passed between Muhammad ibn al-Qasim's military expedition in Sindh, which lasted a few months, and Ghazni's repeated raids starting in 999 CE, and a further 165 years between Ghazni's last raid and Ghori ascending the throne of Delhi, making a total of 552 years when much of India was ruled by Hindu kings. It was a period when numerous Hindu kingdoms, such as the Rashtrakuta dynasty (sixth to tenth century) in the west and, in the south, Hoysala (1000 to 1346), Chola (300 BCE to 1279 CE), the Pandyas (sixth to tenth centuries CE and later from the thirteenth to the fourteenth centuries), the Chera (200s BCE to 1100s CE), and Vijayanagar (1336–1646), ruled vast territories and large sections of the population. In the east, it was the Hindu Sena dynasty that ruled from 1070 to 1230. I think this set of facts effectively demolishes the saffron myth of a millennium of slavery.

Facet five: Spiritual syncretism continues despite military conflict

Fifth, when Muslim rule was challenged by Sikh and Hindu revolutionaries in the last quarter of the 17th century, it is significant that Aurangzeb's armies were led by Hindu Rajputs, Jaswant and Jai Singh, and Shivaji's personal bodyguard was a Muslim. Equally, the militant rise of the Khalsa under Guru Gobind Singh was against political repression and oppression, the spiritual content of the holy Granth Sahib continuing the syncretic tradition of synthesis. Little wonder that when the *sipahis* (sepoys) rose in mutiny in the First War of Independence (1857–58), they marched to the Red Fort in Delhi to proclaim the Mughal emperor, Bahadur Shah Zafar, not any Hindu aspirant, as their symbolic leader.

Facet six: The flourishing of the Ganga–Jamuni 'tehzib'

It was arguably in the courts of the later Mughal emperors, especially under Bahadur Shah Zafar – himself a poet of considerable talent – and the nawabs of Awadh, of whom Wajid Ali Shah (reigned 1847–1856) deserves special mention for his remarkable artistic sensibility, that the 'Ganga–Jamuni *tehzib*', that is, the evolution of a shared, participatory culture among Hindus and Muslims, reached its apogee without either community compromising on core religious beliefs.[10] It is this *tehzib* that constitutes the essence of 'secularism' in independent India. In English, it is called our 'composite' culture or civilization.

Cultural relations under British imperialism

When the British ruled India for close on two centuries (from around 1757–1947), several Indologists among them made outstanding contributions to discovering and chronicling our past,[11] but, unlike the Mughals and their predecessors, the British remained foreigners, cherishing their homeland across the distant seas and intending to return there when their tours of duty were over (loaded with Indian loot, more often than not). This is what made them colonialists and imperialists, foreigners of a different order to those who had settled in India and made India a home for themselves and their progeny. Nevertheless, millennial India absorbed and synthesized the best of their heritage, weeding out the undesirable. Therefore, although Gandhi and Nehru and a vast army of non-violent freedom fighters fought against the subjugation of the nation, they continued the civilizational tradition of assimilating and synthesizing the best the West had to offer. They also pressed to the cause of Indian freedom the tenets of John Stuart Mill's *On Liberty* (1859), which the British boasted informed their style and system of government at home. The Indian freedom fighters demanded to know why such liberty was being denied to Indians.

The young Jawaharlal championed '*poorna swaraj*' (complete independence) when the veterans, including his father, were content to limit their demand to 'Dominion status' within the British Empire. However, despite his profound patriotism and stirring nationalism, Jawaharlal had no inhibition in immersing himself in Western philosophy, Western literature, Western science, Western history, Western languages and Western culture without losing either his roots in, or his admiration of, all that India had to offer. In consequence, where the forces of Hindutva propagated the insult that Nehru and his ilk were '*Macaulay ki aulad*' (Macaulay's children, implying their illegitimacy), Nehru declared that India 'looked upon the world with clear and friendly eyes'. Such cosmopolitanism, that exalted the Indian tradition while recognizing the cultural worth of others, was much more in accord with our civilizational heritage than Hindutva's narrow-minded focus on only the indigenous as authentic.

Independence, at last

Nehru led the way to our newly independent nation, celebrating this composite way of life to erase the monumental horrors that had followed from Partition, including the unforgivable assassination of the Father of the Nation by a terrorist who regarded himself and his heinous act as the very pinnacle of Hindutva. Nathuram Godse, the assassin, went twice to Savarkar's residence in Shivaji Park, Mumbai, before embarking on his flights to Delhi to seek his mentor's blessings, who readily gave them to Godse.[12]

In striking contrast, the Nehruvian view held that the civility of a state is to be measured by its treatment of its minorities. Accordingly, and particularly because the Muslim elite had departed to Pakistan, abandoning millions of poor, disadvantaged Muslims to the care of India, Nehru went out of his way to underline that his government's duty lay in ensuring the identity, dignity, security and progress of India's Muslim citizens. In particular, he emphasized that their way of life and personal law would be safeguarded along with our other minorities. He also recognized that while some of the minority communities like the Parsis and sections of the Christians were educationally advanced, and therefore socially and economically ahead, the bulk of the Muslim community, apart from the remnants of the aristocratic and upper class *ashrafiya*, was in dire need of special measures for their educational, social and economic progress, and the preservation of their religion and culture. Thus, respecting the right of others to hold beliefs that were not our own became a core principle of 'secularism'.[13]

Diversity and democracy

Nehru recognized, too, that 'diversity' extended most significantly to political ideology and opinions. Where leaders of most emerging nations stamped out diversity from their politics to consolidate their dictatorial rule, Nehru firmly believed in the blooming of a diversity of political views to enrich the process of nation-building. Opposing opinions had to be given freedom of expression and assembly, provided only that hate speech and incitement to violence were eschewed, prohibited and punished. Full-fledged democracy was, therefore, imperative, which included not only holding regular, free and fair elections but also, most importantly, respecting the independence from the executive of institutions sanctified by the Constitution, such as a parliament reflecting the preference of the people; an executive government that lasted only till it enjoyed the confidence of the legislature; a judiciary to render impartial justice and ensure that the executive functions were in full accord with the Constitution, especially its provisions for the fundamental rights of the people; an independent Election Commission that, without fear or favour, would impartially concentrate on its crucial task of ensuring free and fair elections; a comptroller and auditor general to monitor government spending to ensure probity in governance; and ensuring continuing public accountability by encouraging a free and unchained media. When financial scandals surfaced, one of them involving his close associate, V.K. Krishna Menon, India's high commissioner in London (the army jeeps scandal) or the unearthing by his son-in-law, Feroze Gandhi, of the Mundhra scandal, Nehru unhesitatingly ordered enquiries to maintain the probity of government. As for the administrative services, its members might exercise their constitutional right to vote for whom they preferred but, in their official work, were to be inured from political parties. This also applied to the armed forces. It was through these institutions balancing each other that the fundamental rights, which determine the quality of democracy, would be secured, and space created for dissent, however harsh or biting, as well as, most importantly, the peaceful change of regime. While firmly putting down the spread of hatred, especially communal hatred, through the First Amendment to the Constitution, Nehru stood even more firmly against any form of authoritarianism or suppression of the propagation of alternative Ideas of India.

Notwithstanding his huge popularity with the people, he was dead set against the cultivation of a personality cult. Long before he became PM, and in an era dominated by the likes of Hitler, Mussolini, Stalin, Franco,

Salazar and Tojo in Japan, Nehru, in an article in the Calcutta *Modern Review* in 1937 under the pseudonym of 'Chanakya', warned of the danger of adulation of Jawaharlal going to Nehru's head, turning him into a tyrant. He wished to be constrained by the manacles and fetters of democracy.

Although as PM, Nehru was initially little concerned with local self-government as the foundation of true democracy, he progressively discovered that the absence of Panchayati Raj rendered the superstructure of democracy at higher levels weak, unstable and disturbingly distanced from people's participation. Worse, the bureaucratic delivery of public goods and services was grossly inefficient and left the hapless people at the mercy of an indifferent and unresponsive administration. Therefore, having experimented with BDO-based 'Community Development', Nehru concluded by the end of his first decade as PM that it was only through the political, administrative and financial empowerment of popularly elected panchayats at the village, block and district levels that inclusive development could be secured for the welfare and progress of the people. So enthusiastic was his advocacy and pursuit of Panchayati Raj that he told a gathering of State community development ministers that Panchayati Raj would be the 'most revolutionary development' because 'behind it were all the forces which, when released, will change the structure of the country'.[14] He sought this non-violent structural revolution by extending democracy and development through self-government at the grassroots to those most in need, fully cognizant of the inequality inherent in crony capitalism enmeshing high politics and big business into a common web, to which the only countervailing force could be inclusive growth through inclusive governance, especially given that 'Equality' was one of the goals sanctified in the Preamble to the Constitution.

Nehru, Nonviolence and Nonalignment

Finally, Nehru promoted a foreign policy for the new country that reflected in its external dimension the values that had informed the freedom movement under Mahatma Gandhi. Nonviolence was extended into Nonalignment. (The hyphen was removed from both words in Indira Gandhi's time to stress that each was a positive concept on its own and not just a negation of other diametrically opposed concepts.) The first of the precepts of Nonalignment was the affirmation in foreign affairs of our domestic sovereignty, that is, *poorna swaraj* (complete independence) in addressing issues of foreign policy, unfettered by positions taken by dominant powers and their military alliances. While eschewing military alliances, India would, however, be active in international affairs, judging issues on merit refracted through the prism of national interest. Nehru clarified repeatedly that Nonalignment was not 'neutrality'. We would not remain isolated from other nations or refrain from expressing our views on international issues. The earliest manifestation of this was our vote against the partitioning of Palestine in November 1947, a few months after Independence, which the West – led by the United States and Britain – and the East – led by the Soviet Union and its bloc – were championing. We were the only non-Muslim, non-Arab, Asian country to consistently oppose the vivisection of the land 'from the river to the sea'. How right we've proved to be!

Second, we would continue the struggle for liberation from colonial rule and racial prejudice in other countries since, in Nehru's words, even as peace was indivisible, so also was freedom and independence 'in this one world of ours'. Third, that the overarching goal would be to end the 'Quest for Dominance' that had brought misery to so many through all of recorded history.[15]

Fourth, to begin with our own continent of Asia, by transforming the Asian Renaissance sparked by Asian liberation movements into an Asian Resurgence in close partnership with China aimed at restoring Asia to the vanguard of the advancement of human civilization, the position Asia had held till but two centuries earlier. This found expression in the organization in March 1947, even before India had gained Independence, of the Asian Relations Conference that brought the countries of Asia and Asian freedom movements on to a common platform for the first time ever.

Fifth, we would be at the forefront of the movement for universal disarmament, starting with nuclear disarmament, to save humanity and our planet from total destruction.

In so asserting our right to a foreign policy of our own in a world divided into rival warring camps that allied every other country to one or the other side, Nehru assured newly independent India of a role in international affairs quite disproportionate to our political clout, our economic strength or our military capacity. It was a foreign policy as courageous as it was wise. True, the call to '*ekla chalo re*' resonated in free India but drew the ire and contempt of both Cold War camps. Then they found that India was the only peace broker they could find to bring an end to the Korean War. In 1953, the armistice and ceasefire in the Korean Peninsula were brought about by offering Nehru's India the chairmanship of the Neutral Nations Repatriation Commission. A year later, in 1954, it was India that was requested to chair the three International Commissions of Supervision and Control set up for Vietnam, Cambodia and Laos under the Geneva peace accords. Nehru's India also led the peace-keeping force set up for Gaza after the Suez conflict of 1956, and the later hotspots of Cyprus and Congo. So effective was our punching above our weight in international affairs that where initially we had walked alone on the Nonaligned path, by the time the Nonaligned Movement (NAM) convened in New Delhi for the NAM summit of 1983, more than two-thirds of the member-States of the United Nations, representing more than half the world's population, had declared themselves Nonaligned.

Nehru also led the way, in the UN and outside, to decolonization virtually everywhere. After uniting the emerging nations of Africa and Asia at Bandung in 1955, he, along with Marshall Josip Broz Tito and others, launched a wider movement of political resurgence of emerging nations through the Movement of Nonaligned Countries that drew in Latin America, the Pacific islands and Yugoslavia. Meanwhile, the Kashmir imbroglio at the UN resolved itself after initial setbacks by Nehru harnessing the Soviet Union's veto to our cause. Our staunch independence made our voice the most influential of the non-nuclear powers in disarmament matters despite our being among the very few to remain out of the 1968 Nuclear Non-Proliferation Treaty in protest against its discriminatory provisions.

Of course, there were several shoals that Nonalignment ran into and some contradictions that harmed NAM's credentials, particularly the disastrous war with China in October–November 1962. But, by and large, Nehru, combining principle with pragmatism in the philosophy and practice of Nonalignment, gave us (and over a hundred newly independent countries that followed) a moral standing in the world that Mahatma Gandhi's Nonviolence had earned for us as we struggled towards freedom and independence. Nehru was the Man of Peace the world needed and turned to. It made my generation and me, in particular, proud of being Indian.

The advent of Hindutva

For an overwhelming majority of Indians, particularly those who had experienced or witnessed the horrific massacres and displacement of millions during Partition, it was Nehru's 'Idea of India' they embraced much more than its polar opposite, the ideology of 'Hindutva'. Nehru's Congress, and thus his 'Idea of India', reaped victory after victory in repeated elections right through his lifetime and for decades later. This made his 'Idea of India' the theme of nation-building over at least the first seven decades of nation-building regardless of the party or coalition in office. This was true of not only the Congress but also much of the Opposition as well, barring the fringe Hindutva elements. But particularly through the movement to dismantle the Babri Masjid and build a grand Ram temple on what was claimed to be the birthplace of Lord Ram – the Ram Janmabhoomi – the alternative 'Idea of India' gained traction and dramatically overtook the India National Congress in the elections of 2014 to promote 'Hindutva' as the underpinning of what the movement took to describing as the 'New India'.

Is Hindutva a passing aberration?

How did this happen and how lasting will the political dominance of Hindutva be? The general view is that while Gandhi and Nehru might have temporarily drawn a veil over underlying Hindu–Muslim antagonism, what has surfaced under Modi is the true Hindu nation, proud of its heritage, wary of the exclusion of centuries of fruitful interaction with Islam which, they claimed, masked the ghastly atrocities that Hindus underwent during Muslim rule. The proof of this, they say, lies in the two stunning election victories (2014 and 2019) that graced Modi's rise to power, which, in their view, have delegitimized the earlier Nehruvian 'Idea of India'.

Elections and Hindutva

This seems to me a somewhat simplistic assessment of the astonishing majorities that Modi secured, in terms of seats won. For, as a per centage of the popular vote, Modi got only a third of the vote in 2014. That rose four per centage points to 37 per cent in 2019. At least a half of all Hindus did not vote for him nor did over 60 per cent of all Indians. He gamed the system of 'first-past-the-post' to give himself a massive majority of seats (just as his opponents, particularly the Congress, had done in the past but with considerably higher vote shares). How fragile such gaming is, was revealed in 2024 when, despite a decline of a single per centage point in his popular vote, Modi's seat share plunged to a mere 240 from 303, thanks to a higher Index of Opposition Unity. His clay feet were revealed despite his boasting of his non-biological origins and his being an instrument of Divinity.[16]

The transience of Hindutva vs the permanence of 'The Idea of India'

I have explained in a previous chapter how the Congress landed itself in a vacuum of governance in the last two years of its rule (2012–2014) and failed to defend itself against false charges of corruption that were never proved in court. We were also led by an inexperienced and unconvincing leader who could easily be parodied as a '*pappu*' (a useless character). He did not appear to have found his feet in the five years that followed. But after his two cross-country yatras in 2023 and 2024, he seems to have discovered himself and has led his party and, more important, the INDIA alliance, to a splendid show in 2024, ending just a whisper behind Modi and bursting the Modi bubble. Hindus did not become Hindus suddenly in 2014 or start ceasing to believe in 2024. India remains what it has been for millennia – a many-splendoured 'unity in diversity'. All we need to do to win back the hearts of Indians is to show ourselves as secularists of either the Gandhi or the Nehru kind. We need not fall into the trap of first prioritizing the re-establishment of our identity as practising Hindus or follow the BJP into Islamophobia. In short, whatever the nuances of political positions, the essential India is the India conceived by the spiritual beliefs of that great votary of Hindu–Muslim unity, Mahatma Gandhi, and the historico-cultural India 'discovered' by the statesman-historian, Jawaharlal Nehru. In this light, the last ten years (2014–2024) have been an aberration, and the old 'Idea of India' has not been replaced by the current prevalence of the alternative saffron 'Idea of India'.

Moreover, Hinduism does not need an enemy in Islam to sustain itself. For one, Hindu belief long predates Islamic belief. It neither arose in reaction to the semitic religions nor in antagonism to them. Islam was no more than yet another school of belief. For another, there is such a bundle of a myriad gods and godheads worshipped by Hindus, and such multiplicity of Hindu religious thought, religious rites, religious rituals and religious traditions tied into the *santana dharma*, that Hindus have long learned to live with plurality. Hindutva's attempt to pour diverse beliefs and practices into a uniform straitjacket so militates against our Hindu heritage that it makes adherence to such uniformity at most temporary and, in the long run, against the grain of this heritage. I think this is perfectly illustrated by the transformation in 2024 of the mood in Uttar Pradesh, host to the erstwhile Babri Masjid from 1528 to 1992. The wilful mob destruction of the mosque at the instance of the BJP and its cohort did build up over time to popular political support, especially after Modi obtained a favourable verdict from the Supreme Court in 2019. There followed the grand spectacle of the *pran prathishthan* (consecration) at the newly built Ram Temple on 22 January 2024, Modi upstaging the *Shankaracharyas* (pontiffs) and all other priests, to emerge as India's first Chief Priest-cum-PM. It boosted his public image as no PR firm could have conceived. And yet, mere months later, came the BJP's defeat in the parliamentary constituency which includes Ayodhya. The magic of 'Hindutva' lost its sheen in just a few weeks. The defeat in Ayodhya was not an isolated event: all over UP, the BJP suffered reverses. Modi's own majority in Varanasi was slashed from over four lakh to just a lakh and a half. The Samajwadi Party of Akhilesh Yadav emerged the overall winer in a state that till the day before the votes were counted seemed all set to retain its reputation as the impenetrable bastion of Hindutva.

The future of Hindutva

What does this presage for the future of 'Hindutva'? Will Hindutva become the dominant ideology of India, effacing the spiritual and intellectual influence of the Mahatma and Jawaharlal?

The word 'Hindutva' is not a synonym for the religion called Hinduism.[17] Indeed, V.D. Savarkar who originated the political ideology, emphasized that 'Hinduism is only a derivative, a fraction, a part of Hindutva'. Savarkar translated 'Hindutva' into English as 'Hindudom', in the same sense as 'Christendom', that is, 'the rule of the Christian' transposed to India as 'the rule of the Hindu'. For him, the only authentic Indian was he who regarded India as not only his *pitrubhu* (Fatherland) but also his *punyabhu* (holy land). This, of course, ruled out the Muslims and Christians who regarded their holy lands as lying in Arabia and Palestine. This made the Hindu the only authentic Indian.

Savarkar went on to laud the Aryan 'conquest and colonization of lands and tribes' by 'the brutal takeover of territories, in which large armies devastated the landscape by burning it to the ground and massacring the local people' for, in the end, 'the colonizer and the colonized both became Hindu.' Thus, Savarkar urged that since 'Hindus understand themselves as Hindus through acts of violence in the past', the Hindus of the present 'needed to embrace permanent war as part of their future'. Continuing his paean to violence, he emphasized that it must not be forgotten that 'violence was at the centre of the formation of the Hindu as a Hindu' as 'the Hindu became Hindu in the act of violence'. From this assertion it followed that Buddhism was 'the ultimate negation of Hinduism' for Buddhism fostered 'the opiates of universalism and non-violence', making Emperor Asoka's non-violence 'antithetical to being a Hindu'. The longest-serving chief of the RSS, 'Guruji' Golwalkar added to this toxic mix by describing Muslims and Christians as the nation's 'internal enemies'.

Here lies the foundational difference between the Gandhi/Nehru 'Idea of India' and the Hindutvawadis' alternative 'Idea of India' – 'New India' in Modi's formulation. Its most dreadful manifestation was when Savarkar's fanatical followers assassinated the Father of the Nation because the Mahatma wanted to assimilate India's minorities into his concept of the nation. To this end, he also wanted to promote harmony with Pakistan by insisting that Pakistan's share of sterling balances be handed over to them as their legitimate due irrespective of any other consideration. Gandhi's insistence flew in the face of the advice of ministers who were concerned at any addition to Pakistan's fiscal capacity to prosecute war against India. This became the immediate *casus belli* in Hindutva's opposition. Mahatma Gandhi was their prime example of '*tushtikaran*', which, in their eyes, is the gravest sin.

Of course, all this was decades ago. Much has changed in India and the world since Nehru passed away in 1964. It is, therefore, little short of amazing that, despite tattering at the edges, his legacy remained the broad national consensus till half a century of his passing, surviving several changes of government in the 1990s and persisting even during the five-year rule of the Vajpayee government (1999–2004). It is only in the last decade (2014–2024), which brought the Narendra Modi government to office and reduced the Indian National Congress to virtual nothingness, that the Nehruvian legacy has come under serious challenge.

My life under both versions of the 'Idea of India'

I lived nearly 75 years of my life in an India immersed in the Nehruvian ethos. But Nehruvian India now stands largely discredited by the saffron establishment. The alternative 'Idea of India', inherited from Savarkar and Golwalkar, and embodied in Prime Minister Narendra Modi, has taken over since 2014. This book, particularly in its last two chapters, attempts to explain why this changeover from Nehru to Hindutva occurred and why the ideological changeover might yet prove a temporary aberration.

The India of Hindutva ideology rejects, opposes and replaces with its own ideas virtually everything that Jawaharlal Nehru stood for. Its fundamental basis is its loathing of Nehru and its unrelenting efforts to denigrate him. It does not accept 'synthesis' as the intellectual and moral thread running through five millennia of our civilization. It values only what it considers authentically 'Hindu'. Accordingly, it valourizes as 'national' only what it regards as 'Hindu' and dubs those who hold different views on the integration of minorities into the nationhood of India as 'anti-national'. 'Indian' is equated with 'Hindu', thus promoting 'uniformity' at the cost of 'diversity': 'One Nation One Election', 'One Nation One Civil Code', 'One Nation One Flag, One Constitution', 'One Nation One Language', 'One Nation One Religion'. The 'composite' cultural heritage of India is replaced in Hindutva thinking by a 'majoritarian' view that lauds only that which it labels 'Hindu' and discards what it regards as 'foreign'. Cosmopolitanism is frowned upon. The past 1,200 years of Muslim and Christian interaction with India are portrayed as 'dark years of slavery'. Any appreciation of thought or art of Muslim origin is denounced as 'appeasement', and any celebration of anything of European, specifically of British origin, is put down as betraying a 'colonial mindset'. This is the vocabulary of 'New India'.

This is then validated by denying the history and historiography that professional historians have painstakingly stitched together of our Middle Ages. This period extended roughly a thousand years from the eighth century when Muhammad bin Qassim, all of seventeen years of age, arrived at Thatta (near present-day Karachi) at the mouth of the mighty Indus (Sindhu) river till the decline of Mughal power through the eighteenth century. Replacing such objective, well-researched, well-documented and constantly peer-reviewed scientific history, as the saffron set are doing, is an ideologically driven narrative that sees this millennium and the two hundred years of British colonial rule that followed as one long continuum of 'slavery'. 'Good' is found only in what Hindutva regards as 'Hindu' and 'bad' in everything else.

Conveniently blotted out of saffron history is that the Mughal Empire was slowly strangulated over the course of the eightheenth century by none other than Muslims from outside India. The deadly blow came from the sacking of Delhi in 1739 by the Muslim Shia Persian, Nadir Shah and finally, by the Muslim Sunni Afghan, Ahmed Shah Abdali who, having earlier conquered Northwest India from 1756 on, defeated the Marathas at the Third Battle of Panipat in 1761. Abdali then arrived in Delhi with his marauding, pillaging troops to once again mercilessly sack the capital of the Mughal Empire and its core, Shahjahanabad, with rapine that removed every feather from the Golden Bird (*sone ki chidiya*) that was India, leaving it destitute and in ruins. The Mughal emperor and his family were, for the best part of a century, then huddled into corners of the Red Fort under a royal form of 'house arrest'. A poet wittily remarked that the 'Empire of Shah Alam / Extends from Delhi to Palam'. When Shah Alam escaped from his Muslim captors, he became a wandering mendicant, only to return to the Red Fort after his defeat at the hands of the British East India Company at the Battle of Buxar (1764). The British in 1803 under Gen. Gerard Lake completed the ravaging of Shahajahanabad, the heart of Old Delhi. Other parts of the Empire, especially in the north of the country and swathes of the Deccan broke away from Mughal rule, largely, if not entirely, under Muslim usurpers. It was disintegration in the wake of anarchy.[18]

But it is especially under these breakaway Muslim nawabs – particularly in Awadh (Oude or Oudh, as the Brits spelt it) – that the Ganga–Jamuni *tehzib* reached its pinnacle in poetry, literature, music, dance, painting, crafts, textiles and architecture, besides, most lastingly, high cuisine and polite conversation and manners. Nehru knew this. Modi and his cohort apparently don't. So, '1,200 years of slavery'? Really?

Profile of the 'New India'

To this end, the proceedings of the annual Indian History Congress, the pride of Nehruvian India, have been distorted beyond recognition. Respected and renowned historians like Romila Thapar are denigrated. History school textbooks are rewritten to delete whatever does not suit the world view of Hindutva. The thrust of such efforts is to project ideological prejudices and distortions without objective historical basis as 'history'. The Indian Council of Historical Research has been subjected to the same abuse. Scientific method in historiography has been replaced by myth and fiction masquerading as historical fact. Indeed, far from maintaining the distinction between mythology and history, mythology is paraded as history to the detriment of both disciplines.

Similar cavalier treatment is meted out to the 'scientific temper'. The Hindutva-oriented PM solemnly informs the distinguished gathering at the opening of a medical research establishment in Mumbai that ancient Indian science knew 'plastic surgery' as demonstrated by the grafting of an elephant's head on to the god Ganesh (which, in any case, would be 'transplantation' not 'plastic surgery').[19] This assertion is received with politically correct applause. Applause also greets the PM when he says that the 'Pushpak' aircraft of mythology reveals the high technological prowess of our ancients in aerodynamics, avionics and aero-tech.[20] To bewildered air force commanders, he urges them to attack Balakot under heavy cloud cover because he says Pakistani radar cannot penetrate dark clouds.[21] This writer has run out of exclamation marks to punctuate this narrative.

Rational thought and the 'scientific temper' are sought to be substituted at the prestigious annual Indian Science Congress by PM Modi urging the scientists who are gathered to take Indian science into the future, to instead discover the scientific achievements in India's past. These achievements are so well-known and well-documented that the PM's appeal is really designed to secure modern scientific endorsement of flights of imagination in the distant past. Even as mythology is not history, mythology is not science. Both are valuable, but each has its own domain.

Where the Constitution keeps the State above all religions, Hindutva Hindu-izes the State with the PM availing of his exalted office to play chief priest at the inauguration (*pran prathishtan*) of the Ram Temple at Ayodhya.

Hate speech and hate action are fundamentally fuelled by a visceral dislike of anything Muslim. The PM, who loves to be photographed in all kinds of headgear, insults a kindly Muslim cleric by refusing a skullcap presented to him when the cleric calls on him while Modi fasts at Sabarmati Ashram for three days, allegedly to promote communal harmony.[22] The joint celebration of Muslim festivals like Eid is decried as 'appeasement'. Such Islamophobia peaks at election time because the saffron leader believes that nothing gains him electoral support as much as barbed remarks that divide community from community. It is reported that in the 2024 Lok Sabha election, the PM referred directly or indirectly in derogatory terms to the Muslim community in 110 of the 173 election speeches he delivered.[23]

Between elections, hate action is condoned or winked at or even fostered by BJP state governments, most strikingly in the largest Indian state, Uttar Pradesh. But hate speech and action are by no means limited to that state. It is evident in all states where the BJP holds sway such as in Karnataka (before the change of state government in 2023) where a vicious movement was provoked against Muslim girl students wearing their hijab. This toxic atmosphere allows the perpetration of almost daily atrocities against our Muslim minority ranging from targeted assassination of Muslims and their sympathizers, to mob lynching by vigilantes of Muslims over allegations of beef consumption or cow transportation, to calls for genocide of Muslims at a *dharma sansad* (a religious 'parliament'). It extends to police 'encounters' that involve the physical liquidation of principally the so-called 'Muslim mafia', and 'bulldozer' revenge where Muslim homes and shops are razed without due process or any court proceedings. The noble Islamic word 'jihad' is twisted by BJP leaders in responsible positions to qualify not only cross-border terrorist attacks but stretched to 'love jihad' to describe inter-community wooing and marriage – and then further to the BJP chief minister of Assam, in a monsoon downpour leading to inundation in Guwahati city, labelling the cutting of trees by a Muslim-owned private university on the Meghalaya–Assam border as 'flood jihad'![24]

Such hate speech fosters hate action. Atrocities against Muslims have sharply increased, and the community survives in a climate of fear and uncertainty about its future. This is well documented by the Mumbai-based Centre for the Study of Society and Secularism.[25]

Legislation that calls into question the citizenship of Indian Muslims has been rammed through Parliament without consultation or adequate legislative consideration on the back of a brute parliamentary majority (at least till the 2024 elections denied them that majority). What began in Assam, where Muslim immigrants from Bangladesh were described as 'termites' by the union minister of home affairs while overturning the equitable judicial arrangements in place since the 1985 Assam Accord to determine rights to citizenship, was aggravated by passing an amendment to the Citizenship Act, 1955, which, for the first time ever, made religious identity a key criterion for determining citizenship. By excluding Muslims alone from the list of eligible religious categories seeking refuge and citizenship in India from persecution in their countries of birth, this law, combined with the threat of preparing a fresh National Register of Citizens that could well jeopardize the citizenship of large numbers of Indian Muslims, sparked an unprecedented protest.

For months in the bitter winter cold of Delhi, Muslim women peacefully demonstrated in night- and day-long relays at Shaheen Bagh, holding aloft the Preamble to the Constitution (rather than the Holy Quran) to demand that persistent targeting of Muslims be ended. It spawned similar protests all over the country, which were Muslim women-led, Muslim women-organized and Muslim women-promoted to the astonishment of a public that had been led to falsely believe that Muslim women were oppressed, confined to their homes and without any agency of their own. The months-long agitation was ended only because of the onset of the Covid pandemic, but not before vicious communal riots broke out in north-east Delhi. Revealing starkly the saffron prejudice against Muslims, a prominent young leader of the BJP gained notoriety with his repeated slogan, '*Goli maro salon ko*' (Shoot the 'sister-f***ers').

Mocking Muslim personal law and practice as 'barbaric' has become routine in Modi-led India. Banning 'triple talaq' without significant opposition from Muslims or others was easy because it is a practice frowned upon by most Muslim clerics and theologians. Had the prevalence of the practice been data-based, it would have been found that instant triple talaq is a rarity and far from commonplace and has no religious sanction. But it provided a convenient stick with which to beat the Muslim community. It also helped distract attention from Hindu reform, particularly the tax privileges given to 'Hindu Undivided Families' (HUFs) but denied to undivided families of the Muslim and other minority communities.

As a Uniform Civil Code (UCC), in a country as diverse as India where individual identity is, more often than not, tied in with the rites and rituals, customs, usage and practices of the community to which the individual belongs, the Constituent Assembly, after agonized consideration of the controversial issue, deemed UCC to be a desirable objective, but not time-bound for legislation or implementation. It was, therefore, placed in the Constitution's non-justiciable Directive Principles of State Policy rather than included among the Constitution's mandatory provisions. So, the UCC was only one among numerous other constitutional Directives that are acknowledged as governance guidelines but far from being implemented without further consideration. Nehru and his successors, including the Morarji government and the three Vajpayee dispensations, saw that it would be severely disruptive socially to bring diverse usages and customs under a single umbrella. Moreover, several independent Law Commissions have pointed to the non-feasibility of a UCC to replace the personal laws of different communities without first evolving a consensus among them. Far better to underline the need for modernization of outmoded, discriminatory provisions of personal law, especially those that do not meet current standards of gender equality and leave it to the communities themselves to reform their respective personal laws.

This is what had been done for the majority community's personal laws on the basis of Dr Ambedkar's recommendations and Nehru's dedicated leadership that even involved forcing a recalcitrant President to give his assent to the reforms. Moreover, before reforming Hindu personal law, the consent and concurrence of a Parliament, in which Hindus constituted 90 per cent of membership, was obtained when putting the reforms to vote. I have always wondered how a House where Muslim representation has been reduced to a mere 4 per cent and is even more derisory for Christians and other minorities, can legislate consensual reforms to personal law.

Nevertheless, the PM has announced from the ramparts of the Red Fort on our 78th Independence Day the priority his government accords to the UCC, renaming it the 'Secular Civil Code' while denouncing the existing code as 'communal'. The proclamation has spread deep concern among not only the minorities and their sympathizers but even among the coalition partners on whom the third Modi government is dependent for its longevity. The matter stands referred to a Joint Select Committee of Parliament.

A similar attempt to encroach on the administration of Muslim Waqf properties which, before the 2024 Lok Sabha elections, would have been bludgeoned through Parliament, has had to be referred to a Joint Select Committee because the two partners on whom the current Modi government leans like crutches for support have insisted on detailed consideration and reconsideration – standard practice in most democracies, including our own, but largely put in cold storage by the Modi governments in the past decade.

'Hurt sentiment' is frequently invoked but confined to Hindus. 'Hurt sentiment' among Muslims and other minorities is given short shrift. The Places of Worship (Special Provisions) Act, 1991, which decreed that all places of worship will retain their religious character as at Independence, is subverted by Hindutvawadis seeking to build on the Babri Masjid judgement by reopening the question at several sites, including the Gyan Vapi temple and masjid at Varanasi, and the mosque at the claimed site in Mathura of the Krishna Janmabhoomi, with active encouragement from the local judiciary.

The consequence, of course, is that the Hindu citizen is regarded as the true citizen, the non-Hindu a citizen on sufferance. The nationalism of the Hindutvawadi is unquestioned; that of the non-Hindutvawadi is suspect. Hence, the repeated insult: 'Go to Pakistan' aimed primarily at the Muslims of India who have deliberately eschewed that option to proudly proclaim their Indian patriotism.

As against Nehru's strict adherence to open democratic debate in Parliament and a free media (except when freedom of expression is misused to promote communal disharmony and violence), the past decade has seen the PM limit his adherence to democratic norms to grand gestures, such as bowing low to touch his head on the threshold on entering Parliament House, or declaring 26 November as Constitution Day, or prostrating himself before a ceremonial 'sengol', a symbol of monarchy in a Republican Parliament, placed next to the Hon'ble Speaker's chair in the vain hope of garnering votes in Tamil Nadu. He has constructed a (hideous) new building to house the two chambers subtly aimed at obscuring the past history of freedom and democracy and its heroes and heroines. For the rest, the PM has never in ten years answered a Starred Question, rarely turns up to listen to others, and, when he does, indulges in thundering hours-long rabble-rousing befitting an election rally rather than in considered, rational parliamentary debate. Until the 2024 elections forced the Treasury benches to revise their authoritarian ways, they studiously ignored the democratic practice of invariably referring important Bills to department-related parliamentary standing committees where MPs of all parties could question officials and outside experts and suggest amendments or even withdrawal. The failure to do so in regard to three highly controversial Farm Bills has resulted in an electoral backlash that has taken its toll on BJP seats.

This abjuring of Parliament and democratic debate has been accompanied by instances of targeting members whose criticism of the government cuts deep (as in the case of Mahua Moitra[26]) and wholesale suspension of members of the Opposition by the presiding officers of both chambers. The repeated show of bias in favour of their former political party also raises concerns on the encroachment by government on the independence of the presiding officers. This is compounded by political bias in the appointment of members of the Election Commission and the resignation of at least one of them who refused to act on government bidding. Never before has the Election Commission's reputation been as diminished as under the present dispensation. And the same applies to all levels of the judiciary where cases of high public importance are unconscionably delayed (such as the reading down of Article 370 and the consequent division of the state and its downgrading of Jammu and Kashmir to a Union Territory and the collateral detention without trial of hundreds, perhaps thousands, of Kashmiris). When long-delayed judgements do come on issues of high public importance, they appear to be weighted disproportionately in favour of the government. Laws to secure national security are amended to facilitate keeping political and civil society opponents jailed indefinitely in contravention of the standard rule of 'bail not jail' to the point that the Chief Justice of India has confirmed that 'the process itself has become the punishment'. Such leaching of independence and authority of constitutional and mandated institutions has characterized governance over the last decade.

Government agencies, like police and intelligence, investigative agencies, income tax, and the Enforcement Directorate of the finance ministry are weaponized under draconian amendments to existing legislation or new laws passed with little legislative consideration to cow down Opposition politicians (including non-BJP chief ministers), civil society activists (pejoratively put down by the PM as '*andolanjeevis*' – those who live by agitation) and influential independent think tanks like the internationally renowned Centre for Policy Research (CPR). Foreign funding is regarded *ipso facto* as 'subversive' under the new Foreign Contributions (Regulation) Act, 2022, and recipients relentlessly targeted. Under the draconian provisions of the Unlawful Activities (Prevention) Act (UAPA) and the Prevention of Money Laundering Act (PMLA), which were supposed to be used sparingly and only when the *prima facie* evidence is clear and seriously threatens national security or national interest, the accused are incarcerated for years on end, a practice sought to be amended at long last by a Supreme Court judgement that has come after the Modi regime lost its majority in 2024. These strident provisions were routinized to keep critics and opponents of the government in custody for years on end with little deliberate speed demonstrated in bringing cases to court for judicial determination. After years of such persecution replacing prosecution, the Supreme Court is at long last showing signs of taking cognizance of such infractions of basic Constitutional and legal rights.

The freedoms and fundamental rights of the media and mediapersons, that were earlier taken as normal democratic practice, have been suborned by new rules, regulations and government orders, and reinforced by pressure on media owners, under threat of takeover by the oligarchs that the BJP's economic policy has spawned to curtail media criticism of government action and policies. Social media had initially been very effectively deployed by the ruling party as a political weapon against their opponents but now the same social media has turned the tables on the

Modi regime by becoming the last resort of media mavens moving from major TV channels and newly minted small independent media stars. Much more than the regular media, it is social media that more effectively perform the essential democratic duties of the 'fourth estate'. The attempt to curb social media through a new Digital Broadcasting Bill has, for the moment, been shelved owing to adverse public reaction and, more particularly, the reservations of the non-BJP partners on whom Modi 3.0 depends for survival. But the intent to place curbs on media freedom ominously remains.

Thus, the Nehruvian governance doctrine of inclusivity, inuring the civil services and constitutional offices and institutions from party politics, and strengthening grassroots democracy through effective Panchayati Raj, have all been undermined or marginalized. A draconian system of governance – vengeful, authoritarian and centralized – and built around a shameless personality cult, has been the nation's experience of Hindutva government. The promotion of crony capitalism has alarmingly widened income and wealth inequality and led to the business interests of oligarchs prevailing over the interests of the people and the larger national interest.[27] All this has cost the government dear at the polls but seems perversely to have reinforced the BJP leadership's resolve to stick to their divisive domestic agenda.

In foreign policy, denigration of Nehru's Nonalignment takes centre-stage. Nonalignment was a term that had obsolescence built into it. When the Cold War ended, as India had urged it should, 'Nonalignment' in an unaligned world did become obsolete as a word. But as 'Nonalignment' went beyond distancing ourselves from military alliances and involved actively participating in international affairs, India, as we have seen, was able to punch well above its weight as advocates of 'peaceful co-existence'. That is sought to be buried now. There is no achievement in foreign policy in the last ten years comparable to what India under Nehru achieved within a decade of independence in Korea, Indochina, Gaza, Cyprus or Congo. Or the key role Nehru played in persuading the Soviet Union to withdraw its troops from Austria in exchange for a guarantee of neutrality. Or worldwide decolonization, which brough to an epochal end the

Empire-building that had dominated world politics over the previous 300 years. Or the mobilization of three-quarters of the UN's member-States in their refusal to pledge themselves in advance to either side in the Cold War to exercise, as far as possible, their sovereign right to consider issues on merit and national interest. Has any such bold idea been broached for Ukraine? Is there any comparing the current Indian PM's expression of 'total solidarity' with Israel as it prepared to launch its genocide in Gaza, with Nehru's principled opposition to the partition of Palestine, a partition that has brought so much misery to so many for so long?

Instead, the current dispensation has blatantly taken domestic disputes beyond our shores. What we have seen in the last ten years is the repeated misuse of platforms in foreign lands to air in the most derogatory terms our domestic differences of opinion, sometimes in the company of foreign leaders.

The worst foreign policy failure has been the tearing to shreds of what was dubbed the 'Neighbourhood First' policy. China has rejected Modi's early overtures and thrust itself beyond the Line of Actual Control in Ladakh on finding that what is whispered in President Xi's ear is contrary to what is whispered to the US President. In consequence, peace and tranquillity on the border, which prevailed for some thirty-five years after Rajiv Gandhi's visit to China in 1988, has been transformed into grave military tension, now being gradually defused. Relations with Nepal were wrecked by gross and unwarranted intrusion into Nepal's internal constitutional process in 2015, an intrusion from whose adverse consequences we are still to recover. Friendship with Bangladesh lies in smithereens because it was built on shaky partisan foundations now overthrown by the 'Monsoon Revolution' we failed to foresee. Similar partisanship in the internal affairs of the Maldives wrecked relations with the change of government. There is no relationship with Pakistan nor any effort or intention of reviving it. Fortunately, Sri Lanka, despite its internal problems, remains on a relatively even keel because, for once, we are not playing favourites. Bhutan, on the surface, is also keen on asserting its satisfaction with New Delhi, but below the surface there are concerns on India holding them back from settling their border issues with China.

In regard to the SAARC, the Modi establishment has put the only platform of South Asian identity and regional cooperation in deep freeze by holding SAARC hostage to our bilateral problems with Pakistan. It is barely remembered that the fundamental condition on which India acceded to SAARC was that SAARC would not be used as a forum for raising controversies over bilateral political issues. And now we are contradicting ourselves by trashing the only forum at which, besides promoting a modicum of pan-South Asian multilateral and sub-regional cooperation, leaders of SAARC member-States could meet annually on the margins to argue out their bilateral differences and promote bilateral cooperation. Pakistan has not helped by refusing to hold the SAARC summit virtually to get over the impasse.

In matters of war and peace, where Nehru's India was a prime player, our attempts in the last ten years to strut the world stage by being all things to all men has reduced foreign policy to a PR exercise. Events management, showmanship and the projection of a personality cult do not amount to foreign policy. Nor do bear hugs. Substantively, in the last decade, we have had little to contribute to world peace.

Conclusion: The choice before us and our descendants

We are at a cusp in our national life from where we might escape into the sunlit uplands of the Nehru era or revert to the darkness of the first ten years under Modi. What gives me hope is the easy familiarity with ambiguity of the Hindu mind. We have no difficulty in living with unanswered questions. As a people, our civilizational history shows we doubt that any answer is set in stone, especially in the spiritual realm. What Modi has temporarily captured is that section of Hindu opinion that is less concerned with Hinduism than it is with Islamophobia and is focused on hating the Islamic Republic of Pakistan. For them, Modi provides the grisly spectacle of the exhibition on recalling the 'Horrors of Partition', and deliberately choosing Pakistan's Independence Day (14 August) as the day for the nation to reflect on these horrors. It hasn't worked. Because those who experienced the horrors, want to forget them instead of reliving them, and constitute today a rapidly diminishing and minuscule portion of an ageing population. Most Hindus have no problem with their Islamic neighbours, even many who vote for Modi because he is an 'ishtrong' man! Islamophobia is not the Hindu way of life; it is limited to the paranoia of those exposed to a distorted history.

So, Modi's 'Idea of India' is built on fragile foundations and his rule has been an accident of history. That is why great Hindutva thinkers like Savarkar, Golwalkar and Deendayal Upadhyaya never attracted the kind of popular support that Modi received. Without denying that popular support, I neither think his assiduous cultivation of a personality cult can last nor is it transferable. But enough Hindus have been twisted to support the Myth of Modi for his influence to long outlast him.

Hence, my apprehensions about this Modi's India into which my grandchildren have been born and are being nurtured. The contrast to the India in which I and my wife were born and nurtured is stark. It is in striking contrast even to the India in which my daughters were born and nurtured – although by their time Nehru's 'Idea of India' was fraying at the edges. I can only hope that the Lok Sabha elections of 2024 presage a return by the end of the current decade to a freer, kinder and more compassionate India in which all, majority and minority, live together in harmony and genuine democracy, and in a neighbourhood of peace, cordiality and friendship. Otherwise, our grandchildren face a dreadful future. If things don't change for the better, I hope my grandchildren – like their courageous and principled mothers (our daughters) – will demonstrate their determination to stand up for what they believe in without, in the words of Gurudev Rabindranath Tagore, 'bending their knees before insolent might'.

Jai Hind!

Notes

1. A Rookie in Parliament

1. Interested readers might like to see the text of the speech at the book's website: http://www.amaverickinpolitics.com or by scanning the QR code given at the end of this chapter.
2. See *Memoirs of a Maverick: The First Fifty Years (1941–1991)* pp. 349–350 for the full story.
3. *The Insider's View*, Penguin India, New Delhi, 2012.

2. Life as a 'Constituency' MP

1. Reproduced in my book *In Rajiv's Footsteps: One Year in Parliament*, pp. 77–79, Konark Publishers, New Delhi, 1993, reprinted in 1995, and at the book's website: http://www.amaverickinpolitics.com or by scanning the QR code at the end of this chapter.

3. Life as a 'national' MP

1. See *Memoirs of a Maverick*, pp. 305–14 for an account of my personal story and Panchayati Raj and Chapter 5, pp. 203–46 of *The Rajiv I Knew*, Juggernaut Books, New Delhi, 2023, for a more thorough account.
2. The full text is at columns 131–42 of the Lok Sabha proceedings of 11 May 1992. The speech was delivered in Hindi.
3. A somewhat bowdlerized version of this incident has been included by Neerja Chowdhury in her bestseller *How Prime Ministers Decide*, published by Aleph Book Company, New Delhi, 2023, pp. 296–297, in which she suggests that the prime minister 'had reached out to Aiyar to send a message to an agitated Sonia Gandhi'. Neither was Sonia Gandhi in touch with me on this matter nor did P.V. Narasimha Rao even hint at my conveying a message to her.
4. Quotations extracted from pp. 62, 68, 107–115 and 136.
5. See Thomas Picketty, et. al. *Brief History of Equality*, Harvard University Press, Cambridge, 2022.
6. Held at long last by the Supreme Court in 2024 to be unconstitutional.
7. 1973–76, described in *Memoirs of a Maverick*, specifically pp. 158–59 and 160–62.

8. See pp. 157–158 of *The Rajiv I Knew And Why He Was India's Most Misunderstood Prime Minister*, Juggernaut Books, New Delhi, 2024.

5. Round-Tripping

1. Please see my detailed description of, personal reaction to, and critical comments on the pogrom in my *Memoirs of a Maverick*, pp. 248–53, Juggernaut Books, New Delhi, 2023.

6. Life as a Congress Functionary

1. K. Natwar Singh, *One Life is Not Enough*, Rupa Publications, New Delhi, 2014, pp. 318–319.

7. Back to Parliament

1. Recounted by 'Saki' (A.A. Munro) among others.
2. Yatin Oza later joined the BJP, rising to become its official spokesman. Then, disillusioned, he jettisoned the party. That is perhaps the prospective national destiny!
3. Rajiv Gandhi: *Selected Speeches and Writings*, Vol. V, Publications Division, Ministry of Information and Broadcasting, New Delhi, 1991, p. 32.
4 The best short history I know of Tamil Brahmins before, during and after the Dravidian movement ended Brahmin dominance is M.S.S. Pandian, *Brahmin & Non-Brahmin*, Permanent Black, Delhi and Ranikhet, 2007.
5. See S. Narayan, *The Dravidian Years: Politics and Welfare in Tamil Nadu,* Oxford University Press, New Delhi, 2018.
6. See pp. 329–330. Also pp. 318–319, where Natwar says he told Sonia that '"only two people in history had refused the crown, both Italians by birth." "Who is the other?" she asked. "Julius Caesar," I replied.'
7. My Ministerial Assignments: Petroleum and Natural Gas

8. My Ministerial Assignments

1. OPEC Bulletin on the OPEC International Seminar, September 2004, Vol. XXXV, No.7, p. 20.
2. *Ibid.*, pp. 28–31.
3. I was a temporary vegetarian as I had been found by my cardiologist with a block at a crucial junction of two arteries, including the Left Artery Descending (LAD) that carried 75 per cent of my blood.
4. 'New Vistas for Regional Cooperation in Asian Oil Economy', sponsored by IOC and ONGC, 2006.
5. See Rohit Saran, *India Today*, 28 February 2005, from which I have refreshed my memory and used as the basis for this description. My grateful thanks to him.
6. S.K. Lambah, *In Pursuit of Peace*, Penguin Random House/Viking, Gurugram, India, p. 275.
7. *Ibid.*, p. 292.

8. See Khurshid Kasuri, *Neither a Hawk nor a Dove*, OUP, Karachi, 2015, pp. 433–43.
9. *Dawn*, 25 November 2004.
   https://www.dawn.com/news/375153/pakistan-to-go-ahead-with-gas-pipeline-pm. Accessed on 7 June 2024.
   Also, *Arab News*, 25 November 2004. Headline: 'India remains non-committal on Pipeline'.
   https://www.facebook.com/pages/Arab-News/1025087.7124. Accessed on 7 June 2024.
10. VoA News, 27 January 2004.
    https://www.voanews.com/a/a-13-2005-01-27-voa53/308568.html. Accessed on 28 May 2024.
11. See Press Note at https://www.mea.gov.in/bilateral -documents.htm?dtl/6685, VoA News at https://www.voanews/a/a-13-2005-06-07-voa47/294974.html and John Cherian, *Promise of a Pipeline*, *Frontline*, 1 July 2005, at https://frontline.thehindu.com/the-nation/article30205302.ece. Accessed on 28 May 2024.
12. For a brief insider's account of what transpired, see K. Natwar Singh, *One Life is not Enough*, Rupa, 2014, pp. 338–341.
13. *The Hindu*, 3 November 2008. Accessed on 28 May 2024. https://eoi.gov.in/eoisearch/MyPrint.php?2254?000/0017
14. For Natwar's own take on the episode, see his autobiography, *One Life is Not Enough*, pp. 229–241 and pp. 322–323. A fuller account may be seen in Chapter 22, 'The Volcker Conspiracy', pp. 345–370.
15. Very much like Permanent Secretary Humphrey Appleby overwhelming Minister Jin Hacker with mounds of irrelevant documents in *Yes, Minister*.
16. For want of space, the speech has been very briefly summarized. Interested readers are invited to visit the book's website: http://www.amaverickinpolitics.com or scan the QR code at the end of this chapter to access the full text.

9. Ministry of Panchayati Raj

1. In the first half of my ministership, I visited 74 village panchayats, 37 intermediate panchayats and 43 district panchayats in 20 states/union territories of the country. More such visits were scheduled in the second half. Please access the book's website: http://www.amaverickinpolitics.com or scan the QR code at the end of this chapter, to access the full list of panchayats I visited in 2004-06.
2. Any reader interested in perusing the full speech is referred to the book's website: http://www.amaverickinpolitics.com or by scanning the QR code at the end of chapter.
3. Published by Kitab Mahal, Allahabad, 1946.
4. Much as I would like to dilate on the history of Panchayati Raj since Independence, I am constrained to merely refer interested readers to my article 'Inclusive Governance for Inclusive Development: The History, Politics and Economics of Panchayati Raj', in Faguet and Poschl (ed.), *Is Decentralization Good for Development?*, Oxford

University Press, UK, 2015. See also: the opening introductory chapter, paras. 1.1 to 1.8, at pp. 1–6 (and, in greater detail, Annexe 1 to Vol. I) of the 'Twentieth Anniversary Report of the Expert Committee on Leveraging Panchayats for the Efficient Delivery of Public Goods and Services', 2013, chaired by me. Copies of this five-volume report can be made available by emailing me at: 1941msa@gmail.com

10. Ministry of Youth Affairs and Sports

1. This was a glancing reference to a well-known book by Nayantara Sahgal, *Prison and Chocolate Cake*, about visiting her father and her mother's brother, Jawaharlal Nehru, in jail during the Freedom Movement!
2. Boria Majumdar and Nalin Mehta, *Sellotape Legacy: Delhi and the Commonwealth Games*, HarperCollins, Noida, 2010, p. 11 and chart 1.1 on the page opposite, which give the exact figure of ₹70,680 crore.
3. Although I was later to find that PM Jawaharlal Nehru had personally drafted and submitted directly to Cabinet a brilliant note on China and Tibet on 18 November 1950. It was, in effect, a rebuttal of Sardar Patel's letter to him from a few weeks earlier. See Tripurdaman Singh and Adeel Hussain's book *Nehru: The Debates That Defined India*, Fourth Estate, India, 2021.
4. Majumdar and Mehta, op. cit, p. 21 wrote:
   '. . .the then sports minister, Mani Shankar Aiyar, was categorical in his opposition to hosting another event which would do nothing for Indian sport . . . arguing instead for investing money in rural sports. Aiyar was right and, as sports minister, he must also have been privy to the inside story and the escalating costs of the CWG projects: a comprehensive National Sports Policy, one focused on rural development, instead of such events, was what he vehemently argued for. His objections were brushed aside by the union cabinet.'
5. Chandrasekhar, K.M., *As True as My Word*, HarperCollins, Noida, 2020. pp. 193–203, especially p. 200.

11. Ministry for the Development of the North Eastern Region (DoNER)

1. The vision document may be accessed at https://necouncil.gov.in/sites/default/files/about-us/Vision_2020.pdf.
2. My subsequent evaluation about a decade later may be accessed at the book's website: http://www.amaverickinpolitics.com or by scanning the QR code at the end of this chapter.

13. Decline . . . Fade Out . . . Fall: 2016–2024

1. This seminar led to Stiglitz asking Prof. Jean-Paul Faguet of the London School of Economics to put together articles by interested participants in a publication that was titled, *Is Decentralization Good for Development?* (Oxford University Press, 2015). My contribution, '*Inclusive Growth through Inclusive Governance*', has

become a frequently cited article in scholarly publications world-wide on local self-government, as tracked by Academia.edu. They have found nearly a thousand citations of me, many relating to my article in Faguet's publication.

2. Prime Minister Dr Manmohan Singh did in fact approve a modified version of this suggestion and put my former MoPR colleague, Dr Sudha Pillai, in charge of it. I do not know whether Amit Shah abandoned the scheme when he came to the Home Ministry, but this scheme certainly paved the way to the progressive elimination of Naxalism from most affected districts.
3. The speech may be accessed both textually and visually, at: https://rsdebate.nic.in/bitstream/123456789/349356/2/PD_219_06052010_p273_p309_28.pdf.
4. Report of the Committee on Zonal Cultural Centres, Volume I and II, 11 April 2011. As the report has been removed from the website of the Department of Culture, it is being digitized and may soon be seen at my personal website.
5. The contribution of Amit Goel, who was in charge of administration and logistics, needs special mention. As does the loyal contribution of Avtar Singh Sahota of the ministry of Panchayati Raj from behind the scenes. The four interns – Rounaq Ahmed, Vincy Davies, Vijay Srivastava and Ashish Kumar, also deserve sincere thanks for their invaluable help in preparing the eight model Activity Maps.
6. These eight Centrally Sponsored Schemes were the National Rural Livelihoods Mission, the National Agricultural Development Plan, the Accelerated Irrigation Benefits Programme, Command Area Development and Water Management, the Sarva Shiksha Abhiyan (Education for All Movement), the National Rural Health Mission, Integrated Child Development Services (ICDS) and Special Central Assistance to Tribal Sub-Plans. The Activity Map for education, for example, identified some 300 activities relating to the Sarva Shiksha Abhiyan, about 200 of which needed to be performed at higher levels and the rest at the three-tier panchayat level.
7. Please see pp 214–217 of this book regarding the World Bank's and the Finance Ministry's reactions to this proposal to understand its significance or effective devolution.
8. Please see pp. 222–225 and pp. 267–270 of this book and p. 313 of *The Rajiv I Knew* for a full explication of the significance of the PESA legislation.
9. Anyone interested is welcome to contact me at 1941msa@gmail.com and I would be happy to share a hard copy of the report with them. Courtesy of Medha Mujherjee, an Indian scholar at Oxford, who is writing her thesis on drinking water in rural India and has met me to understand better the role of panchayati raj in this vital sector. We are getting the Report digitized and placed on the Internet for anyone who prefers a soft copy.
10. A readily understood reference to the army of helpers put together by Lord Hanuman to help Lord Ram in waging war against Ravana who had kidnapped Ram's wife, Sita.
11. Pranab Mukherjee, *The Coalition Years: 1996–2012*, Rupa Publications, New Delhi, 2017, p. 20.

12. I am afraid I and Ravi Shankar Prasad of the BJP were somewhat responsible for this as we urged Kejriwal on a TV programme to abandon his NGO and take the plunge into politics if he really wanted to make a difference.
13. 'Modi can distribute tea, but never be PM: Mani Shankar Aiyar', ABP News, 17 Jaunary 2014, https://www.youtube.com/watch?v=cXVACYxFyQ4. And can also be accessed at the book's website: www.amaverickinpolitics.com or by scanning the QR code at the end of this chapter.
14. In the 2024 Lok Sabha election, Sam was pilloried, as I had been in 2014, by the BJP and sections of the media for having described Dravidians as descendants from Africa in the course of explaining the diversity of India in race and colour. Astonishingly, for this remark he was dropped from chairmanship of the Indian Overseas Congress. A few months later, he was restored to his old office, but I continue to moulder on the margins!
15. As Karan Thapar has remarked in a recent column, although irony is integral to Western, particularly English speech and practice, it is not much resorted to in our country's indigenous languages, at least in everyday speech.
16. Sansad TV. 'SH. Mani Shankar Aiyar's Comments on the Situation in Nepal and the State of Indo-Nepal Relations.' *YouTube*, 7 December 2015, www.youtube.com/watch?v=rb99bsPrm-E. It can also be accessed at the book's website: http://www.amaverickinpolitics.com or by scanning the QR code at the end of this chapter.
17. Sudheer Sharma, *The Nepal Nexus: An Inside Account of the Maoists, the Durbar and New Delhi*, Viking Press, Gurugram, 2019, p. 422. Sharma is the editor-in-chief of *Kantipur Daily*, Nepal's most widely read English-language newspaper. I have supplemented my reading of Sharma through long conversations with Nepal's leading intellectual, the wise and learned Kanak Mani Dixit. To both, my grateful thanks. An alternative perspective is presented by the serving Indian ambassador at the time, Ranjit Rae, in his *Kathmandu Dilemma* (Penguin/Vintage, Gurugram, 2021), pp. 70-79.
18. *Ibid.*, p. 4
19. Rae, *Kathmandu Dilemma,* pp.78–79 says, 'I slipped out of Parliament as soon as the formal (oath-taking) ceremony was over. . .I did not want to put myself in the awkward position of having to congratulate the leaders of Nepal.'
20. Sharma, p. 412 and p. 4.
21. *Ibid.*, p. 41.
22. https://www.youtube.com/watch?v=HeELTCYNbU
23. *Ibid.*
24. C.G. Manoj, *Indian Express*, 8 December 2017. I have never been on Twitter (now X), so I did not personally see the tweet.
25. Years later, Sonia Gandhi was to tell me that she knew nothing of my suspension. It was apparently a decision taken – in an excess of zeal – by the Central Disciplinary Committee off its own bat and, perhaps, accounted for the long time it took to unravel the decision. On re-reading the 'show cause' notice, I see that it does say it is the Central Disciplinary Committee that has decided to suspend me. I had assumed this was on the instructions or with the approval of the Congress President.

26. *Indian Express*, Liz Mathew, 11 December 2017.
27. Lena Misra, Parimal Dhabi, Aditi Raja, *The Indian Express*, 9 December 2017. PTI reported the same day that Modi had said, '. . . after I became prime minister, this man (Aiyar) went to Pakistan... In that meeting he is seen discussing with Pakistanis that '*jab tak Modi ko rasta se hataya nahi jata*' (until Modi is removed from the way) relations between India and Pakistan cannot improve . . . What is the meaning of '*raste se hatana*'? You had gone to Pakistan to give my *supari*, you wanted to give Modi *supari* (gangster term for "contract to eliminate").' Please note the frequent use of the word 'you' when I, not the audience, is being addressed. This is an idiom often used by Hindi-speakers. I had used the same idiom when responding to the Pakistani TV interviewer.
28. Translation by India Today Web Desk, 17 November 2015. The Web Desk further reported me as telling them: 'How can I ask anybody else to remove my PM? It is a complete distortion of what I said. I did not say somebody else removes Modi. He will be removed by us in the general elections."
29. In Tamil culture, particularly Tamil political culture, politesse demands that an appropriate honorific be placed before the name of any prominent leader. Thus, for example, my constituents invariably added 'Makkal Thondar' (People's Comrade) before pronouncing my name!
30. There was, in fact, a Vanniyar candidate locally available, T.R. Loganathan, my district chief in Kumbakonam, north Thanjavur, but Rajakumar would rather have killed himself than suggest his principal rival for Parliament! But, significantly, P. Chidambaram did not ask me.

14. Musings and Reflections on a Long Life

1. I voted for Shashi Tharoor, fully cognizant that there would be a political price to pay for what would be seen as 'insubordination', but a pledge is a pledge and has to be redeemed, whatever the consequences.
2. It is with pardonable pride as a father that I include the full text of her Statement in this book's website: http://www.amaverickinpolitics.com or by scanning the QR code at the end of this chapter.
3. *Remembering Rajiv*, Rupa Publications (1992); *One Year in Parliament*, Konark (1993); *Pakistan Papers*, UBSPD (1994); (ed.) *Rajiv Gandhi's India* (four volumes), UBSPD (1997); *Confessions of a Secular Fundamentalist*, Viking Press (2004); *A Time of Transition: From Rajiv Gandhi to the 21st Century* (Viking Press, 2009); *Achche Din: Ha! Ha!*, Palimpsest Publisher (2015); and the three volumes of these memoirs, Juggernaut, 2023 and 2024.
4. Mecklin, John. 'A Time of Unprecedented Danger: It Is 90 Seconds to Midnight.' *Bulletin of the Atomic Scientists*, 23 January 2024, thebulletin.org/doomsday-clock/current-time/. Accessed on 25 September 2024.

15. Curtain-Call

1. Nehru, *The Discovery of India*, Penguin Random House, pp. 135–138. In striking contrast, Savarkar loathed Asoka.

2. *The Discovery of India*, p. 80.
3. See Upinder Singh, *Political Violence in Ancient India*, Harvard University Press, London, UK, 2017.
4. See Chaturvedi, *Hindutva and Violence*, State University of New York Press, 2022.
5. Wikipedia Contributors. 'Tulsidas', *Wikipedia*, Wikimedia Foundation, 29 September 2024, en.wikipedia.org/wiki/Tulsidas.
6. See Richard Eaton, *India in the Persianate Age, 1000–1765,* Penguin UK, 2020.
7. Brilliantly captured in Ira Mukhoty, *The Lion and the Lily: The Rise & Fall of Awadh*, Aleph Book Company, New Delhi, 2024
8. 'Timurid-Mughal Archives', *Facebook.com*, 2022, www.facebook.com/TimuridMughalArchives/posts/1004343269691207/. It can also be accessed at the book's website: http://www.amaverickinpolitics.com or by scanning the QR code at the end of this chapter.
9. See Ira Mukhoty, *Akbar: The Great Mughal*, Aleph Book Company, New Delhi, 2020, refracted through Parvati Sharma, 'Akbar of Hindustan', Juggernaut, New Delhi, 2022. The debate continues – in the best traditions of India!
10. Brilliantly captured in Ira Mukhoty, *The Lion & The Lily*, Aleph, New Delhi, 2024.
11. See John Keay, *India Discovered: The Recovery of a Lost Civilization*, HarperCollins, 2001.
12. As confirmed in Justice J.L. Kapoor's investigation report, 1969.
13. May I draw attention to my *Confessions of a Secular Fundamentalis*t, Viking Press, New Delhi, 2004 and 2006, especially chapter 8, 'Why I am a Secular Fundamentalist', pp. 243–253.
14. S. Gopal, *Jawaharlal Nehru: A Biography,* Vol. II, Oxford University Press, 1989, Chapter 45, pp. 398–401. The speech was delivered on 9 December 1960 to a meeting of state ministers of community development.
15. See Vol. III of 'Rajiv Gandhi's India', UBSPD, 1998, titled 'Foreign Policy: Ending the Quest for Dominance'.
16. Narendra Modi. 'PM Modi's Interview to Rubika Liyaquat of News 18 India in Varanasi.' *YouTube*, 14 May 2024, www.youtube.com/watch?v=IfNB1DTKqt0. It can also be accessed at the book's website: http://www.amaverickinpolitics.com or by scanning the QR code at the end of this chapter.
17. A most thorough treatment of Savarkar's thoughts, from which the quotations in this section are taken, is to be found in Vinayak Chaturvedi's *Hindutva and Violence: V.D. Savarkar and The Politics of History*, State University of New York Press, 2022. Easier perhaps to access are two publications by Ram Puniyani; *Reading Savarkar*, Pharos Media & Publishing Pvt Ltd, New Delhi, 2024 and *Indian Nationalism versus Hindu Nationalism*, Pharos, 2016, updated to 2024.
18. Significantly, William Dalrymple's highly readable history of this period is titled *The Anarchy: The East India Company, Corporate Violence, and the Pillage of an Empire*, Bloomsbury Publishing, Great Britain, 2019.
19. Vijayan, Vipin. "Modi @ Reliance Hospital Opening: 'Plastic Surgeon May Have Fixed Elephant's Head on Ganesha.'" *Rediff*, Rediff.com, 25 October 2014, www.rediff.com/news/report/modi--reliance-hospital-opening-plastic-surgeon-may-

have-fixed-elephants-head-on-ganesha/20141025.html; and 'PM Modi's Speech at the Inauguration of Sir H.N. Reliance Foundation Hospital, Mumbai', *YouTube*, 25 October 2014, www.youtube.com/watch?v=HugoRTUkRT0. All these can also be accessed through the book's website: http://www.amaverickinpolitics.com or by scanning the QR code at the end of this chapter.

20. Us Salam, Ziya. 'Age of Unreason', *Frontline*, 20 June 2018, frontline.thehindu.com/cover-story/age-of-unreason/article24200525.ece. Can also be accessed on book's website: http://www.amaverickinpolitics.com or by scanning the QR code at the end of this chapter.
21. Som, Vishnu. 'Row over PM Modi's "Cloud Can Help Us Escape Radar" Comment on Air Strike', *NDTV.com*, edited by Deepshikha Ghosh, 12 May 2019, www.ndtv.com/india-news/controversy-over-pm-narendra-modis-cloud-can-help-us-escape-radar-comment-on-balakot-air-strikes-2036402. It can also be accessed on book's website: http://www.amaverickinpolitics.com or by scanning the QR code at the end of this chapter.
22. Press Trust of India. 'Controversy over Modi's Alleged Refusal to Wear Skull Cap', *NDTV.com*, 19 September 2011, www.ndtv.com/india-news/controversy-over-modis-alleged-refusal-to-wear-skull-cap-468053. Can also be accessed at the book's website: http://www.amaverickinpolitics.com or by scanning the QR code at the end of this chapter.
23. 'India: Hate Speech Fueled Modi's Election Campaign', *Human Rights Watch*, 14 August 2024, www.hrw.org/news/2024/08/14/india-hate-speech-fueled-modis-election-campaign.
24. Jeelani, Gulam. 'Muslim-Owned University Accused of "Flood Jihad" by Himanta Biswa Sarma Shines among Country's Top 200. Details Here', *Mint*, 14 August 2024, www.livemint.com/news/india/muslimowned-university-accused-of-flood-jihad-by-himanta-biswa-sarma-shines-among-countrys-top-200-11723597172440.html. It can also be accessed on this book's website: http://www.amaverickinpolitics.com or scanning the QR code at the end of this chapter.
25. See their 2024 report on '*The Status of Freedom of Religion or Belief in India Since 2014*', Media House, New Delhi, 2024, and the Report of their Citizens Tribunal on *India's Silent Genocide: The Survivors Speak*, 2022, self-published. They can be contacted at csss2work@gmail.com
26. 'Bad Precedent: The Hindu Editorial on the Expulsion of Trinamool Congress Member of Parliament Mahua Moitra', *The Hindu*, 10 December 2023, www.thehindu.com/opinion/editorial/bad-precedent-the-hindu-editorial-on-the-expulsion-of-trinamool-congress-member-of-parliament-mahua-moitra/article67624791.ece. Can also be accessed on this book's website: http://www.amaverickinpolitics.com or by scanning the QR code at the end of this chapter.
27. 'Why family empires dominate business in India', *The Economist*, 12 September 2024, https://www.economist.com/business/2024/09/12/why-family-empires-dominate-business-in-india. It can also be accessed on the book's website: http://www.amaverickinpolitics.com or can be accessed by scanning the QR code at the end of this chapter.

Index

A Note on the Author

Mani Shankar Aiyar was educated at Welham, Doon, St. Stephen's and Cambridge before joining the Indian Foreign Service. He served for twenty-six years in the Foreign Service, including a five-year deputation to Rajiv Gandhi's PMO, from where he took voluntary retirement in 1989 for an alternative career in politics and the media. During his parliamentary career of twenty-one years, he was elected to the Lok Sabha thrice, served as a Cabinet Minister with multiple portfolios in the UPA government (2004–09), and received the Outstanding Parliamentarian Award (2006). He was finally nominated to the Rajya Sabha for a six-year term (2009–2016). Aiyar has also been one of India's most successful political columnists and the author of many acclaimed books.